Created and Directed by Hans Höfer

INSIGHT GUIDES
Mexico

Edited by John Wilcock and Kal Müller
Photographed by Kal Müller and
Marcus Wilson-Smith
Managing Editor Martha Ellen Zenfell

Editorial Director Brian Bell

HOUGHTON MIFFLIN COMPANY

APA PUBLICATIONS

Mexico

Sixth Edition
© 1995 APA PUBLICATIONS (HK) LTD
All Rights Reserved
Printed in Singapore by Höfer Press Pte Ltd

Distributed in the United States by:	Distributed in Canada by:	Distributed in the UK & Ireland by:	Worldwide distribution enquiries:
Houghton Mifflin Company	**Thomas Allen & Son**	**GeoCenter International UK Ltd**	**Höfer Communications Pte Ltd**
222 Berkeley Street	390 Steelcase Road East	The Viables Center, Harrow Way	38 Joo Koon Road
Boston, Massachusetts 02116-3764	Markham, Ontario L3R 1G2	Basingstoke, Hampshire RG22 4BJ	Singapore 2262
ISBN: 0-395-71075-8	ISBN: 0-395-71075-8	ISBN: 9-62421-012-8	ISBN: 9-62421-012-8

ABOUT THIS BOOK

With its fabulous archaeological sites, glorious beaches and a vibrant culture combining Indian, Spanish and contemporary elements, Mexico lends itself especially well to the approach taken by the 186-title *Insight Guides* series. Each book encourages readers to celebrate the essence of a place rather than try to reinvent it to suit their expectations and is edited in the belief that, without insight into a people's character and culture, travel can narrow the mind rather than broaden it.

Insight Guide: Mexico is carefully structured: the first section provides a cultural context by covering the country's history and arts in a series of lively essays. The main Places section provides a comprehensive rundown on the places worth seeing (and *not* worth seeing). Finally, a fact-packed listings section contains all the information a visitor will need on travel, hotels, shops, restaurants and opening times. Complementing the text, remarkable photography sets out to communicate directly and provocatively life as it is lived by the locals.

The Latest Information

The success of this approach helped place early editions of *Insight Guide: Mexico* among the award-winning series' top sellers. But nothing stands still for long, especially in such a fast developing country, and this edition has been thoroughly updated and restructured to take account of the many changes that have taken place in the past few years. In commissioning the new edition, **Martha Ellen Zenfell** and **Dorothy Stannard**, both managing editors based at Insight Guides'

London editorial office, were determined to ensure that this book would remain the most compelling guide to Mexico on the market.

In planning this new edition, they were able to build on the solid foundation provided by **Kal Müller**, the project editor of the original edition. A Hungarian by birth, Müller's affection for Mexico and its culture was aroused in 1957 when he began making frequent trips to Nogales, an Arizona-Mexico border town, and led to his living for two years among the Huichol Indians and marrying a nurse working with the tribes. In this edition, Müller wrote the whole of the history section, as well as the features on people, fiestas, *charros* and bullfighting.

The task of assembling and co-ordinating the team of updaters and new writers for this edition was assigned to **John Wilcock**, an internationally renowned English-born journalist who blazed a career from his native Yorkshire through such publications as the *New York Times* and *Village Voice*. He has also been a regular Insight editor and makes frequent trips to Mexico from his home in Southern California. In between editing the new contributors' work, Wilcock, who was already busy writing *Insight Pocket Guide: Baja*, provided entirely new Places chapters on Baja California, Tabasco and Chiapas, explained the subtleties of tequila drinking for a short feature on the popular Mexican firewater, and tracked the country's latest political developments for a one-page story on Mexican elections.

In addition, Wilcock teamed up with **Margaret King** to produce brand-new chapters on Mexico City and its environs. King, who also wrote the chapter on the Yucatán Peninsula, has lived in Mexico City for 25 years, teaching, translating and studying. She cur-

Zenfell

Stannard

Müller

Wilcock

King

rently works for the University of the Americas, but finds time to undertake freelance assignments, including the writing of *Insight Pocket Guide: Mexico City* and *Insight Pocket Guide: Yucatán Peninsula*.

Another contributor based in Mexico City is **Wendy Luft**, a writer and editor who has worked on numerous books about Mexico. Here she has written the chapters on the Six Central States and Guadalajara.

One of the book's key contributors is **"Mexico" Mike Nelson**, described by *The Washington Post* as "one of the most qualified experts on the subject of motoring in Mexico." Currently based near the Tex/Mex border, Nelson has traveled in Mexico since he was a small child, lived in Oaxaca and logged over half a million miles via car, bus, train and burro – experiences he has turned into print for numerous publications. Here he shares his knowledge of the north of Mexico in the chapters El Norte, Chihuahua and the Northwest.

The remaining Places chapters were written by **Barbara Ann Rosenberg**, a writer who combines her love of travel with her passion for food. She lives in Philadelphia but has studied the culture and food of Europe, the Middle East, India, South America, the Orient and, of course, Mexico. In this guide she has written the Places chapters on the Glamour Coast (including Acapulco), Oaxaca and Veracruz, gives sound advice on "How to Bargain" and brought her culinary knowledge to bear in her piece on chillis.

The features section of this *Insight Guide: Mexico* is largely the work of the original contributors, in particular **José-Antonio Guzmán**, an eminent musicologist who specializes in pre-Columbian musical instruments and here wrote the story on Mexican music and contributed to the People essay; and **Guillermo García-Oropeza**, who wrote about Pre-Columbian Art and the Muralists and laid the foundations for many of the original Places chapters. **Patricia Díaz**, who has long been involved with the *artesanía* of her country, wrote about Mexico's crafts.

The Travel Tips section of the guide was thoroughly revised and updated by **Elaine M. J. Bohen**, a native of Puerto Rico who is currently residing in Mexico City. Bohen, who has traveled the world with her diplomat husband, works primarily as a translator/interpreter, using six languages, but also freelances as a writer.

Stunning Photography

The majority of the stunning photographs in the guide were taken by Kal Müller, though many fresh images have been provided by **Marcus Wilson Smith**, a London-based photographer who has traveled to Mexico on a number of Insight assignments.

Proofreading and indexing were completed by **Tanya Colbourne**.

Nelson   *Rosenberg*   *Guzmán*   *Oropeza*

History

People and Culture

Features

Places

Maps

TRAVEL TIPS

*For detailed information
see page 337*

QUE VIVA MÉXICO!

As neighbors tend to do, the United States and Mexico have loved, hated, tolerated and collaborated with each other for at least 150 years. But a relationship that began with war (the US won) culminated in the signing of the North American Free Trade Agreement (NAFTA), and, as the 21st century draws near, the air is filled with hopeful harmony.

An amazing two-thirds of Mexico's 82 million people – a figure that grows by almost 3 percent each year – is aged 30 or under and, while this provides a large labor force eager to work for wages that might be as low as one-fifth of those common north of the border, it also makes the country unusually susceptible to social influence from its bigger northern neighbor.

Mexico has long been a favorite destination for North American travelers, and not just because of its proximity. Almost one-quarter of the 31 million US tourists who travel abroad each year head south of the border, as do 10 percent of the 7 million business travelers. With NAFTA, the latter group is certain to increase as trade links expand and strengthen, providing opportunities for businesses of all sizes and types.

Contrasts in Mexico are startling. In Monterrey, Pittsburgh-style factories rise out of the desert; in Tabasco and along the Chiapas coast oil rigs look like black exclamation points. Yet oblivious to this frenetic activity, on the Pacific and Gulf beaches some 4 million visitors a year bask under tropical suns and *cha-cha* balmy nights away within sight and sound of Mayan and Aztec pyramids.

Fiery murals blanket Mexico City's public walls, but thick smog blankets the sky, all too often obscuring the volcano Popocatépetl, 75 km (46 miles) to the southeast. No longer is Mexico City a place *Where the Air is Clear,* as Mexican novelist Carlos Fuentes titled his most popular novel. The population of the capital is already 16 million, a figure that may have doubled by the end of the 1990s, making it the biggest megalopolis on earth. Yet outside of the rapidly expanding Distrito Federal, the air is wonderfully clear.

Some 60 native languages are still spoken here by more than 50 indigenous Indian tribes, and there are more than 241,000 km (120,000 miles) of road. It's the most extensive travel network in Latin America.

So, how to explain it all – this fantastic, fabulous, frenetic country? "One does not explain Mexico," says the philosopher Manuel Zamacona in *Where the Air is Clear.* "One believes in Mexico, with fury, with passion, and in alienation."

Preceding pages: raising the flag on the Zócalo; festive parade; Mexican machismo exemplified by the *charros*; taking it easy on Xacel beach. Left, patron saint, the Virgin of Guadalupe.

SMOKING MOUNTAINS AND BLOOMING DESERTS

As is often said, there are many Mexicos. The physical features of the land make for marked divisions. Two great mountain ranges, the Sierra Madre Occidental and the Sierra Madre Oriental, run down from the US border, paralleling the Pacific and Gulf coasts. The mountains give way to the central highlands, the historic heart of Mexico, an area of abut 640 km (400 miles) from east to west and less than 320 km (200 miles) from north to south. This represents just one-tenth of Mexico, but it contains almost half the population.

Looking at a map of Mexico, you'll note a vast, mountainous area in the 160-km (100-mile) belt of land between the bulging Corrientes in Jalisco on the west coast and Veracruz on the Gulf. This area – known as the New Volcanic Axis – is roughly the boundary between North America and Central America. South of that line, lesser mountains form the Sierra Madre del Sur, narrowing down at the Isthmus of Tehuantepec, Mexico's narrowest section, to not much more than 160 km (100 miles) wide. The mountains rise up again east of the Isthmus and continue into Guatemala, while to the north the Yucatán Peninsula, ironed flat by nature, consists of a limestone sheet covered by thin soil.

Varying rainfall: Mountains and highlands characterize much of Mexico, but deserts dominate in the north. In Baja California and in the northern states of Sonora, Chihuahua, Coahuila and Durango, crops can be grown only with the help of irrigation. On the Gulf coast, too much rain – as much as 6 meters (236 inches) each year – washes the land and farmers have to hack away unwanted growth. Perversely, many areas of the north get as little as 10 cm (4 inches) of rain a year. In the central highlands where most of the corn and beans are grown, rainfall is erratic: sometimes a trickle, sometimes a flood.

Many Mexican forests are denuded because indiscriminate cutting of timber, begun in colonial times, still goes on. Of course,

Preceding pages: flamingos over the Yucatán. **Left,** bandillero flowers and maguey cactus.

farmers had to clear land for planting, and in places where large-scale mining went on, the area was stripped of trees. Zacatecas, the silver mining region, was changed from woodland to savannah by tree-cutters. The water table has fallen and climatic change has ensued as a result of the destruction of forests; areas that once had a measure of protection because they were inaccessible are now easily reached by road. The country lacks river transportation because the few rivers that exist are unnavigable.

The road from Mexico City to Veracruz served as the umbilical cord between Mexico and Spain and during the 16th century land links were also opened to the agriculturally rich Bajío region north of Mexico City and to the mining district of Zacatecas. But when new mines were discovered in what is now southern Chihuahua and an attempt was made to colonize what is now New Mexico, it didn't work. It took more than a year to make the 2,600-km (1,600-mile) round trip from Zacatecas to New Mexico and neither Spain nor Mexico had the money, skill or resources to integrate the great northern reaches of the land, which the conquistadors had so arrogantly claimed. When the time came, Anglo-Americans took over what was then northern Mexico. They had the men; they had the money; and, most important of all, they had an overriding determination to overthrow Mexican rights.

Eager investors: During the Díaz dictatorship foreign capital poured in and helped finance the building of roads and railroads to the north and develop untapped natural resources. It then became economically worthwhile for American companies to begin bulk ore mining. Foreign capital also financed the exploration for oil. In the aftermath of the 1910 Revolution the government expropriated some foreign holdings, and by then a basic communications system was in place.

If many areas are still isolated and hard to reach, at least it has allowed much of the country to be preserved, a boon to nature-lovers. How refreshingly remote are the vast deserts of Baja and the mountains of central Mexico and the jungles bordering the Bahía de Campeche where a marvelous variety of flora and fauna thrives. Some are protected in national parks; others in wildlife refuges.

Left, Tarascan girls tending sheep in Michoacán.

But although the government has done well, it has not yet done enough, for only a tiny portion of Mexico boasts protective areas, and many of the parks are in the mountains and less accessible. Popocatépetl and Iztaccíhuatl are the best-known mountain peaks, but they can seldom be seen from the city itself because of the pervasive smog.

Volcanic spectacles: In geological terms, Popo (altitude: 5,452 meters/17,887 ft) is a child. The "smoking mountain" (which is what its Nahuatl name means) is now dormant but once it put on spectacular shows, erupting in 1519 to greet – or perhaps protest – the arrival of Cortés. It is said that of the 10 men Moctezuma sent to the top to view the eruption only two returned. Iztaccíhuatl (altitude: 5,286 meters/17,342 ft) means "sleeping woman", because its somewhat flattened top resembles such a figure. A paved road goes to the base of the two mountains.

Pico de Orizaba, or Citlaltépetl (Star Mountain) is 5,700 meters high (18,750 ft) and can be seen clearly by those driving along the road between Mexico City and Veracruz, as well as sailors out at sea. West of Mexico City, the Nevado de Toluca or Xinantécatl (Sacred Bar) stands 4,680 meters (15,354 ft) tall. A dirt road, passable most of the year, leads to the crater and the Lake of the Sun and Lake of the Moon. These lakes, sacred to the Indians, are stocked with rainbow trout.

Paricutín, the youngest of Mexico's volcanoes, was born on February 7, 1943, when farmer Dionisio Pulido witnessed its emergence from a cornfield in Michoacán. Awestruck, he returned with his compadres the next day to discover a cone 6 meters (20 ft) high. Soon after, Paricutín exploded, hurling great chunks of molten rock 100 meters (328 ft) into the air and putting on a fiery display of orange lava. During Paricutín's nine active years it poured out a billion tons of lava, covering the village of Parangaricutiro, drowning 10 other hamlets and creating a mountain 427 meters (1,400 ft) high. Visitors can reach the site from the village of Angahuan. En route they will pass the steeple of the late Parangaricutiro's church, sticking defiantly out of a black lava bed.

Toward the western edge of the volcanic axis, the Nevado y Fuego (Snow and Fire) crater in the state of Colima is not unusually

Left, the village of Tapalpa, in Jalisco, at dawn.

high (3,326 meters/10,912 ft), but it is topped by two cones, one of which is snow-covered and the other which periodically emits fumes. The last major explosion occurred in 1913, although in 1973 the mountain rumbled and spewed lava and ashes. Some 575 km (357 miles) off the west coast of Mexico is the Mexican-owned archipelago called the Revillagigedos, where, in 1952, the Mariano Barcena mountain blew its top. The Chichonal volcano in Chiapas exploded in 1982, causing many deaths.

Agricultural erosion: Experts estimate that about two-thirds of Mexico's land has a slope of more than 10 degrees, beyond the limit that agronomists claim makes for efficient agriculture. Many farmers, of course, are more concerned with survival than efficiency and thus it is not unusual to see an absurdly angled rocky slope sown with corn. Erosion, as a result, is inevitable.

Mexico's flatland is generally found either in the north or in the Yucatán, and as much of the land in the north is desert or semi-desert and much of the Yucatán has only thin soil, just about all the land with agricultural potential is already under cultivation. Only with proper planning, research and huge investment, could the amount be increased.

The most productive region in Mexico is the northwest, particularly the narrow fringe between the Sierra Madre Occidental and the sea, which though semi-desert is blessed with several rivers and flat land. Under the regimes of President Obregón and Calles, both of whom came from the northwest, a system of dams was built and the area is now Mexico's most productive agricultural region. About one-fifth of Mexico's agricultural land is irrigated, almost half of it in the states of Sonora and Sinaloa, and the Río Colorado district of the otherwise mostly arid Baja California. These irrigated lands yield big crops of alfalfa, wheat, safflower, soybean, cotton and tomatoes.

Other areas of the north raise cattle. A large market for beef has grown in Mexico itself indicating a move into middle-class affluence by a substantial portion of the population. Much of the rest of Mexico's farm areas concentrate on corn and beans, the eternal staples. The population increase, formerly a threatening 3.5 percent, one of the

Left, The Christmas lights go up over the capital.

world's highest, has been brought down to 2.5 percent. But cities are big and getting bigger, and even rural areas have felt the pressure of more mouths to feed. Subsistence plots grow smaller and with over-use the land becomes less fertile.

Ubiquitous corn: But for Mexicans, corn is life and has been the basic staple for hundreds of years. The *tortilla* is Mexico's bread and the average Mexican consumes almost half a kilo of it (over 1 lb) every day. In many of the rural areas consumption can be double that amount. Indians attach a mystical importance to corn, because of its close association with their religions. They grow corn despite government advice to introduce other crops as well. The corn yield could be improved but it means additional expense for irrigation and fertilizer and unfortunately corn has been less receptive in research projects than wheat. Outside Mexico City at the Rockeller Center research facility, plant-breeding programs for wheat have been spectacularly effective but the center has not had the same good luck with corn.

Until the once-rife malaria was eradicated, coastal Mexico used to have a reputation for being unhealthy but today tropical plantations in the region produce most of Mexico's sugar, cocoa beans, henequen and coffee. Unfortunately, world prices have been unstable in recent years and the country has to compete with the rest of the world.

Minerals: For centuries the export of minerals, especially silver, dominated the economy. There was so much silver in colonial times that in some places it was cheaper to use it for shoeing horses than to use iron imported from Spain. Mexico, still a major producer of silver, also exports lead, zinc, copper, sulphur, antimony and mercury. The first high-temperature furnace for refining iron in Latin America was built in Monterrey in 1903. Mexico is now self-sufficient in most types of steel and exports steel to Caribbean and Central American countries.

Until 1939, Mexico's exports comprised roughly two-thirds minerals and almost one-third agricultural products. By 1950, mineral exports had fallen to about half of the total, while agricultural products had climbed to 55 percent. Today, oil and its by-products

Left, a *charro* gallops at full speed – just before reining in his horse to stop on a centavo.

account for 25 percent of the nation's exports; almost two-thirds of exported goods are manufactured.

Wildlife: Though there is not enough prime land for agriculture, there are vast amounts of land in which wild animals can roam. Mexico is a great place for the nature-lover. It has 2,896 species of vertebrates, including 520 mammals, 1,424 species of birds, 685 different kinds of reptiles, and 267 amphibians. Of these, 16 mammals, 13 birds and 9 reptiles are on the endangered list.

The most spectacular of the mammals is the gray whale, which migrates yearly to Baja California's Pacific bays to mate and calve. Almost extinct a few decades ago, it has made a strong recovery thanks to the government's protective policies. At Scammon's Lagoon, their breeding ground on the Pacific coast, only 250 gray whales were counted in 1937: by 1975 there were 18,000.

Guadalupe and the San Benito islands off the Baja coast are a refuge for elephant seals. Male elephant seals can reach over 6 meters. The biggest ones lead a vigorous life; marine biologists estimate that just 4 percent of the males impregnate 85 percent of the females. These maritime machos have done their duty well. At the beginning of the 20th century their number was close to zero in this part of the world, but by the late 1970s elephant seals on Guadalupe alone exceeded 47,000.

Tough hikers can sight great horned sheep in the San Pedro Martir national park in the mountainous interior of Baja. In the Cumbres de Monterrey national park there are black bear, as well as unconfirmed reports of grizzlies in the wildest reaches of the Sierra Madre Occidental mountains.

Because Mexico is the winter terminus for many species of birds, it is a bird watcher's as well as a hunter's paradise. Most species seem to favor the Pacific coast, reputed to be a duck hunter's nirvana. On the other side of the country, the Rio Lagartos area of northern Yucatán is graced with thousands of pink flamingos. And a year-round fairyland of bright fish and corals can be explored in the Caribbean waters of the Yucatán. But perhaps the most spectacular gift of nature is the Monarch butterfly, which brightens eastern Michoacán by the thousands in winter.

Right, a spectacular natural arch at Cabo San Lucas at the southernmost tip of Baja California.

Mexico has been inhabited for 21,000 years, measured by the radioactivity of the carbon content of organic material. It all began in Siberia, with ancient peoples crossing the Bering Strait in quest of meat. Their trek started perhaps 70,000 years ago and they moved south at a rate of about 27 km (17 miles) per generation. From Alaska they went south into Canada and the United States, and eventually reached Mexico. Some hardy sojourners went on through Central and South America, eventually down to the end of the

shores of what was once Lake Texcoco, now the site of Mexico City, confirms. In this case, they were helped by the animal being stuck in the mud.

Traditions continue: In the late Cenolithic Age (9000–7000 BC), long after mammoths became extinct, people in what is now Mexico used a crude stone implement to grind grain. This was the forerunner of the *metate,* the slab upon which Mexicans in Indian villages still grind their corn today.

Some dates are helpful. In about 6000 BC,

line, the south of Chile, which they reached some 13,000 years ago.

They came in small groups – two or three or perhaps as many as five families at a time – and probably took with them a rudimentary religion. The different groups had to adapt to weather ranging from the bitter cold of the tundras to tropical forest and jungle and to arctic conditions at Patagonia.

These ancients were animal and wild plant eaters, usually hunting small or medium-sized animals. Seemingly foolhardy, they also hunted mammoths, teaming up for the attack, as the discovery of a mammoth skeleton killed by men and buried along the

agriculture is believed to have started in Mexico – compared with 13,000 BC in the Thai-Burma border region and 10,000 BC in the Middle East – a tardiness attributed to the groups' millennia as nomads.

In Mexico the first cultivated species appear to be the avocado pear and the squash. Sometime around 5000 BC they began to grow maize and beans, which have since been the staples of Mexican diet. The first ears of corn were just 3.81 cm (1½ inches) long. You can see specimens in the Museum of Anthropology in Mexico City. About 3000 BC people began to grow cotton, weave textiles and irrigate the land, and in about

2000 BC they learned to make pottery. In about 1500 BC they began to fashion gods.

Olmecs were first: The first and most mysterious of Mexico's great ancients were the Olmecs of the regions now known as Veracruz and Tabasco. They might be called "the Sumerians" of the New World because, as in Mesopotamian culture, they provided artistic, technical and religious instructions for the civilizations that followed them. They were skilled in agriculture, adept in building canals, and artistic in fashioning pottery, jewelry and weapons. However, it took the publication, in 1926, of *Tribes and Temples*, a book by Frans Blom and Oliver LaFarge, to call attention to Olmec achievements. The book included the revelation that La Venta, an island near Villahermosa in Tabasco, was the site of an Olmec ceremonial center.

It is difficult to reconstruct the nature of the Olmec culture (*circa* 1000–400 BC), for there are virtually no written records. It is known that they were great stone carvers, however; few other pre-Columbian cultures of the New World achieved their mastery. They created 30-ton basalt heads, exquisite jadeite miniatures and paper-thin obsidian jewelry. It is through these carvings that the Olmecs speak to us. The motif that recurs most often is the jaguar, the tawny-coated big cat known in Mexico as *el tiger,* the "tiger," which ruled the jungles and played a leading role in Olmec religion.

Artist-writer Miguel Covarrubias, known as "the last of the Olmecs" for his analyses of Olmec culture, has shown in a series of drawings of pre-Columbian sculpture how the jaguar mask was gradually transformed into a rain god. Covarrubias said that some of the faces display "a haunting mixture of human and feline characteristics… It is often difficult to guess whether a given carving was intended to represent a man disguised as a jaguar or a jaguar in the process of becoming a man."

Those massive Olmec heads seem to have

negroid features, but at the same time the eyes are mongoloid. Two small statues have earned the distinction of sobriquets: "The Wrestler" (probably a player in a ceremonial ball game) and "Uncle Sam" (probably on account of the shape of the man's beard).

Study of Olmec heads, if in fact they represent true portraits, suggests that there were two physical types in the Olmec culture: some with negro traits, some without. Did the negroid features come from across the Bering Strait? We can tell nothing from

skeletal remains: high humidity and the acidity of the soil have obliterated the evidence.

Revelation came slowly. Sixteen years after Cortés conquered Mexico in 1521, the Pope of Rome (Paul III) acknowledged in a papal bull that indeed the people of Mexico were human beings who must have originated from the Old World and were descendants of Adam and Eve.

Little writing: Gaps exist in the story telling. There was little phonetic writing before the Spanish conquest. Though the Mayas and others wrote in glyphs, these are only slowly being deciphered.

One of the most remarkable legacies of the

Preceding pages: Temple of the Bearded Man at Chichén-Itzá. **Left**, a depiction of early settlers spearing a mammoth. **Right**, "The Wrestler," an Olmec sculpture.

Olmecs is the pit at La Venta in Tabasco. More than 7.6 meters (25 ft) deep, it was dug out and lined with 480 blocks of semi-precious serpentine stone, forming a mosaic. Naturally, it is jaguar-shaped. The pit was filled with colored sand and clay and covered. Thus protected, it remained undisturbed until archaeologist Matthew Stirling and his crew dug it up 3,000 years later.

The Olmecs spread their civilization. In their search for semi-precious stones, they established colonies in central and southern Mexico, thrusting their culture upon less advanced peoples. They influenced art forms and introduced their religion, the ritual calendar, glyph-writing, technology and cere-

During the 1,700 years between the demise of the Olmecs and the arrival of the Aztecs many cultures developed, flourished, then faded in Mexico. The best known of these was the Mayan culture, which dominated the Yucatán peninsula and areas south, including what is now the state of Chiapas, and into Guatemala and Honduras.

Other cultures developed for a time: the Teotihuacán of central Mexico and the Gulf coast; the Zapotecs and the Mixtec in southwestern Mexico and at Monte Albán (whose tombs yielded jewelry and carvings); the mysterious Tarascans of Michoacán, who twice inflicted defeat upon the haughty Aztecs; and the Totonac group of Veracruz,

monial centers. All the civilizations that followed in Mexico are indebted to them.

The Olmecs cultivated the soil and harvested water resources by digging ditches and channeling the water to the growing crops. Doubtless they also knew how to use water for transport, else how could they move the immense basalt blocks?

Mysterious conclusion: The Olmec civilization came to a violent end around 400 BC, as indicated by the mutilation of Olmec stone sculptures at that time. We can only hazard a guess at what happened. Did the lower classes rebel against their rulers? Or was there a devastating invasion from outside?

who built the niched pyramid at El Tajín.

The lives of many of these ancient peoples are shrouded in mystery. The Xochicalco ruins in Morelos, southwest of Cuernavaca, for example, stretch for 1,544 hectares (6 sq. miles) and include a palace, ball courts, a network of caves and passageways, and a restored pyramid. On the walls are elaborate carvings of serpents and humans. The features seem Mayan, but they could be Toltec, or possibly Zapotec. The ethnic identity is still unknown but since Xochicalco was a meeting place of various peoples, all of these influences could be present.

Monte Albán, which the Indians changed

to suit their purpose, is the oldest site of post-Olmec culture. The mountain top was leveled, a monumental feat which lopped off an area 610 by 245 meters (2,000 by 800 ft).

From an archaeologist's point of view, the history of Monte Albán divides into five distinct periods. The first, 500–550 BC, is represented by a series of bas-reliefs known as "The Dancers" (in fact, the contorted bodies may represent medical specimens, jesters or acrobats).

Around 300 BC, an evolution of the people in the Oaxaca region touched off the second phase of the Monte Albán story. These people built great stone tombs that are works of art. Perhaps their attention to burials stemmed

their gods. The architecture favored a baroque style.

The fourth period of Monte Albán, from 1000–1250 AD, saw new tombs laid out and old ones enlarged. The fifth and final phase of Monte Albán lasted until the Spanish conquest. During this period the Zapotecs, no longer at the top of the hierarchy, were supplanted by a people called the Mixtecs, who came from the Cholula-Puebla area in the north, invaded Monte Albán and mixed with the Zapotecs, taking it over as their own necropolis. A talented people, they produced fine metal and stonework and carved wood and bone objects.

Mayan influences: The Zapotecs built the

from their belief that their ancestors came from the depths of the earth and hence must return in proper style.

The next period (Monte Albán III-A and III-B, in archaeological terms) began at the opening of the Christian era and continued for 1,000 years. The Zapotecs, who lived in the Valley of Oaxaca, arrived at the beginning of this period. These early Zapotec practiced confession as part of the ritual of purification and offered human sacrifices to

Left, a Mixtec skull with overlaid turqoise mosaic, from Monte Albán. **Above**, a sculpture of the Toltec god Quetzalcóatl.

long, low "palaces" at Mitla whose facades are decorated in raised stone mosaic. The geometrical patterns suggest textile designs and resemble the Mayan stone latticework at Uxmal in the Yucatán. The Mixtecs, punctilious keepers of manuscript records of their gods and the genealogies of their nobility, also took care of their dead rulers. Taking over the tombs of the Zapotecs, they threw out the bones of the occupants and replaced them with the bodies of their own nobles.

The best known of the Mitla graves, Tomb 7, was excavated in 1932 by the Mexican archaeologist Dr Alfonso Caso. The grave was a treasure house containing more than

500 pieces of exquisite Mixtec art, much of it gold jewelry.

El Tajín, in Veracruz, is another cultural site whose construction began during the latter part of the Olmec era. The first occupants were Huastecs, a branch of the Mayas but separated geographically from their better-known cousins. Through the science of glottochronology (time-analysis of two related dialects), it has been determined that the Mayas and the Huastecs, who once spoke the same language, split into two groups around 3,200 years ago – when the Olmec culture began.

Naked warriors: The Huastecs developed on their own, not nearly as refined a culture pletely ignored for the next seven centuries.

In 1811 the intrepid German traveler-naturalist Alexander von Humboldt visited El Tajín and described it in detail. In 1836 the traveler Carlos Nebel published in Europe a series of splendid lithographs of the ruins. Much later (1934) the Mexican government ordered the first excavation work on the site, directed by archaeologist Gracía Payón, to whom we owe much of what we know about this important cultural center. Recent extensive excavations have revealed a great deal more information.

Unfortunately, we know much less about the cultures of western Mexico. Its people left us only scant clues, some shaft tombs and

as the Mayan, but valiant and able to resist Aztec attack. They shocked the enemy by facing them totally naked, with filed and colored teeth and deformed heads.

The ritual center of El Tajín covers 1,012 hectares (2,500 acres), much unexcavated. The Pyramid of the Niches which dominates the site was probably begun by the Huastecs who, in turn, were pushed out by the Totonacs. The pyramid is obviously an edifice of ritual. The Totonacs completed the central structure and built other highly decorated stone buildings and a ball court with magnificent bas-relief carvings. El Tajín was destroyed around the year AD 1100 and was almost com- pieces of pottery. Colima, Jalisco and Nayarit never merged into unified kingdoms but remained under chieftains who controlled small areas. They apparently never developed urban centers and there was little cultural exchange between groups. Our knowledge about them, which comes from their pottery, tells us merely that at one time they came under the influence of the central highlands cultures. We glean from their clay figurines that they believed in life after death. Thus a man was buried with ceramic replicas of his wife, servants and slaves to enhance his life in the afterworld. The clay figures are full of life and are among the most charming art of Mexico. They depict religious and social scenes; a ritual ball game with a crowd of spectators, women wrestling, lovers embracing, phallic dances, musicians, warriors and animals, especially dogs.

Thanks to the Spaniards, we know a good deal about the Tarascan culture of Michoacán. Shortly after the Conquest, the first viceroy ordered Vasco de Quiroga – later to become a priest – to compile a history of the Tarascans. *Chronicles of Michoacán* gives us a start in understanding Tarascan culture. The Aztecs claimed that the Tarascans were part of the Chichimeca group of tribes, saying they and the Tarascans had a common origin, emerging from seven caves in the north.

meters wide (1,400 ft by 800 ft), with a stairway 91.4 meters (300 ft) wide.

Ancient crafts persist: Except for the *yácatas*, the Tarascans built in wood. They left few stone buildings and carvings but excelled in pottery, woodwork, copperware, and especially in featherwork (modern Tarascans still excel at all of these crafts except featherwork, an art form that has been abandoned). The ancient Tarascans knew how to organize for battle and had well-trained military forces. Tariacuari, the first legendary king, welded the rival clans into an alliance. So well-knit was this confederation that they twice defeated the Aztec juggernaut.

The story of the end of the Tarascan king-

Michoacán means "Place of the Fishermen," and the state of Michoacán is bordered by the Pacific ocean. However, the ancient religion of the inhabitants was based not on the ocean, but on volcanoes. The cult of fire was central to the Tarascan religion. The chief deity, Curicáueri, the "Great Burner," represented the young Sun. In his honor the people kept fires burning constantly on top of stone ceremonial structures called *yácatas*, the largest of which, at Tzintzuntzan, consists of a platform 427 meters long and 244

dom is a sad one. The last of the Tarascan kings converted to Christianity and went humbly, feather hat in hand, to pay homage and submit to Cortés. Debasing himself, as was the Tarascan custom, he wore soiled and torn clothing, but it did not help. Later Nuño de Guzmán, the most brutal of the Conquistadors, had the king burned alive on the pretext that he had taken part in a conspiracy against Spanish rule but in reality because he was unable to produce enough gold.

The peoples of the central highlands provided our most detailed knowledge of Mexico's history. The last people to dominate the highland plateau were the bold Aztecs, who

Left, Mayan painting of dignitaries found in Bonampak. **Above**, Rivera mural depicting Tajin.

assimilated the civilizations they found. Teotihuacán, which began some 200 years before the beginning of the Christian era, was a ghost town when the Aztecs arrived in the 1300s. Nevertheless, the ruined city (it had been burned and abandoned in the 8th century) was so imposing that the Aztecs believed the Sun and the Moon were created there. They called the site "The Place of the Gods" (Teotihuacán).

Teotihuacán is bisected by "the Street of the Dead," and dominated by the Pyramid of the Sun, 65.5 meters high (215 ft).

Rainy paradise: The rain god, Tláloc, was one of the principal deities of Teotihuacán. Rain gods dominated ancient Mexican cultures – consider the Mayan Chac rain god, and Cocijo, the Zapotec rain god. Tláloc was amply rewarded by his followers, both in this world and in the next. There is a well-preserved mural painting of Tláloc's paradise, in which people are frolicking, singing and dancing, and the land is lush.

Quetzalcóatl, the god of the Toltecs, the deity known as the Plumed Serpent, was the most important god in Meso-America. His cult developed in Teotihuacán, where the most important structure is dedicated to him. Quetzalcóatl was a complex god. King of the legendary city of Tollan, he strove to enforce the highest code of ethics as he pursued his love for the sciences and the arts. But, so the story goes, jealous enemies schemed for his destruction, giving him and his beautiful sister *pulque* to drink. Brotherly love thus changed to carnal desire with its inevitable consequences and when Quetzalcóatl woke up the next morning he fled to the coast, built a funeral pyre, and threw himself on it. His body was destroyed but his heart turned into the planet Venus.

There are a number of variants to this tale. According to one version, instead of casting himself into the flames, he built a raft and left for the east, promising to return. When Cortés came to Mexico, the Indians believed him to be an envoy of departed Quetzalcóatl.

A busy god: Other myths about Quetzalcóatl tell how he descended into the Land of the Dead, found some bones, sprinkled them with blood and thus created the human race; how he stole maize from the ants and thus introduced food to mankind; how he taught man astronomy; how he invented the calendar; how he taught man to cut and polish jade, to weave and make mosaic paintings with feathers. The Quetzalcóatl cult emphasized peaceful living; there were no war gods in his cult. The people of Teotihuacán were governed by priest-kings, who were interested in commerce, not conquest.

Teotihuacán grew in an orderly fashion. At one time the urban area's population of 100,000 even included a ghetto of "foreigners." Once more we lack the knowledge about how it all ended. Was the destruction of this peaceful city through rebellion or invasion? Some Teotihuacán people resettled at Azcapotzalco, now a suburb of Mexico City. The cult of Quetzalcóatl has been kept alive in the central highlands, especially at Cholula, near Puebla.

Possibly the Toltecs destroyed Teotihuacán. According to one story, a group of Chichimecas, nomadic hunters, came to central Mexico under the leadership of their king, Xolotl. They settled down and founded Tula in 856 AD and became Toltecs. (The term Toltec means "master craftsmen.") There were plenty of these in Tula: masons, stone and jade carvers, weavers, metalsmiths, featherworkers. The Toltecs were good warriors and at one time controlled much of central Mexico. It is likely they became soft and quarreled among themselves. Whatever the reason, the time came when they could not resist invasion by other and tougher Chichimecas, who torched Tula in 1168, dispersing the population into central Mexico.

Indian culture: The Spanish conquerors of Mexico were not much interested in the Indians' culture, except insofar as it could advance Spanish economic and political ends. A few missionaries studied the indigenous cultures and left valuable information, but they were looked upon with suspicion and their work was stored away. It is said that most of our knowledge of the Mayas comes from Friar Diego de Landa, bishop of Yucatán. However, even he burned most of the Mayan codices; only three Mayan pre-Columbian codices survive.

The publication in 1831 of Lord Kingsborough's book, *Antiquities of Mexico* spurred interest in the Mayas and marked the beginning of serious efforts to study Mexico's past. And an American, John L. Stephens, published the first widely distributed, popular work on Mayan ruins. Accompanied by draftsman Frederick Catherwood, Stephens spent almost two years (1839–41) seeking out Mayan ruins in Honduras, Guatemala and Mexico. His book, *Incidents of Travel in Central America, Chiapas and Yucatán* contained Catherwood's accurate drawings. Partly because of Stephens' work, Mayan studies became an almost complete monopoly of the United States until the recently established Center for Mayan Studies at Mexico's National University.

As the American consul in the Yucatán from 1885 to 1909, Edward Thompson devoted his free time to archaeological exploration. He even bought a tract of land, which included the ceremonial center of Chichén-Itza. Thompson's discoveries include sev-

rial, and in general the buildings are of harmonious proportions, often beautifully decorated with stone carving or stucco. The Mayas excelled in portraiture and detail. The main sites are dominated by pyramids which sometimes contain burial chambers. Although the Mayas never discovered the true arch, they invented the corbelled vault of fitted stones, each of which projects slightly farther than the stone underneath.

All-important time: The dominant theme of Mayan civilization was the passage of time. No other culture was so obsessed with recording time. They calculated the solar year at 365.2422 days and the moon's period at 29.5209 days. Both figures are so accurate

eral old Mayan ruins and the Sacred Cenote (a huge well), which contained the bones of human sacrifice, gold and precious objects, which he obtained by diving to the bottom.

Specialists divide Mayan history into three time-frames: the Formative (*circa* 200 BC–300 AD; the Classic (300–900); and the Post-Classic (up to the Spanish conquest). Mayan civilization reached its peak during the Classic period. In the lowlands of the Yucatán, limestone provided the craftsmen with first-rate building and sculpture mate-

that it was only in the 20th century that scientists came up with figures infinitesimally more exact. The Mayas calculated time from a date zero – August 13 in the year 3113 BC – and believed that the universe would end when the Great Cycle of the Long Count ran out on December 24, 2011.

The Mayas needed a precise calendar because coordination of the heavenly bodies determined everything they did, beginning with the agriculture cycle. Since the universe moves in cycles, they knew that past movements of stars and planets would be repeated and thus priests could take appropriate action to forestall disaster. It took centuries of

Above, a Frederick Catherwood drawing of a corbelled arch.

work to coordinate data and it was not until the year 750 AD that the eclipses of the sun and moon were worked out by astronomers meeting in Copán. A sculptured monument there marks the great event. To work out these accurate predictions, the Mayas made amazing advances in mathematics. Even today some highland survivors of the Mayan culture still guide their lives by elements of the classic Mayan calendar.

The Mayan pantheon was just as complicated as their calendar. We know of 166 named deities, each with four different representations corresponding to cardinal direction. There are also counterparts for the opposite sex. Moreover, every astronomical

creature. Some crippled horses were left behind by the Spaniards and they became cult figures to some Mayas. When Cortés' horse died, its skeleton was worshipped.

For a long time it was believed that the Mayas were peaceful, and non-violent worshippers of the gods, but now we know this was not true. Mayas sacrificed their children, tearing out their hearts and offering them to the gods. They cut their own ears; slashed their tongues and arms, used a stingray's tail on their bodies. And there was the gory practice of self-mutilation. A man would pierce the head of his penis, pass a cord through, and douse the statue of a deity with blood. Mayas fasted and abstained from sex

god had an underground avatar, or incarnation. The chief of the gods seems to have been Itzamna ("Lizard House"), often represented as an old man with a Roman nose. Credited with the invention of writing, he was patron of arts and sciences. In his embodiment as the Sun, he was the husband of the Moon, Ix Chel, the Rainbow Lady, benefactress of weavers, doctors and women.

Cultish horses: The Chacs (rain deities) were among other important Mayan gods. The mounted Spaniards with their firearms became associated with the Chacs, the firearms representing thunder and lightning. Horse and rider were thought to be one

before and during religious rituals and during the planting and harvesting seasons. They had a ruthless code of morals – adulterers, for example, were disembowelled.

No central capital: The Mayas had a structured and disciplined society, as proved by all the ceremonial complexes. They were governed by priest-rulers. Instead of a central capital they had a series of autonomous city-states which enjoyed friendly relations with each other. None of the classical Mayan sites was protected by fortifications for evidently none was needed. Between the 3rd and 6th centuries, they had considerable contact with other parts of Meso-America, especially with Teotihuacán and Monte Albán.

The Mayas engaged in trade, moving goods by water in large sea-going canoes. They exchanged textiles, tools, feathers, pottery, precious stones, medicinal herbs, incense, farm products and especially salt. Cacao beans were used as a form of currency.

Meanwhile as time went by the Toltecs at Chichen-Itzá became more and more Mayan in speech and outlook. They retained only the boast that they were descendants of the warriors of Tula.

Toltec domination over northern Yucatán lasted some 200 years. It was ended by an intrepid Maya named Hunac Ceel Cauich. The Mayas at times cast humans into the Sacred

Well at Chichen-Itzá to see if the rain gods had a message to impart. Few of these sacrificial victims survived, but when Hunac was thrown into the well he emerged with a message from the gods: "Throw the rascals out!". Inspired by those words, the Mayas crushed the people of Itzá and the descendants of the Toltecs. Hunac set up his capital at Mayapan, near present-day Mérida. This was a true city, unlike the ceremonial sites which were inhabited only by priests. Hunac started the Cocom dynasty, which partially

Left, date glyphs from Palenque. **Above**, a stucco head from Palenque showing the Mayan profile.

restored Mayan culture. Around the middle of the 15th century, the Tutul Xiu family led a revolt against the Cocoms and Mayapan was destroyed.

The Aztecs: As for the Aztecs, their culture was in full bloom when the Spaniards arrived, and we have accounts of the conquest in works by various missionaries.

The rise of the Aztecs took place over about a century. No other group in Mexico rose so quickly from savages to imperial rulers. At its apogee, the Aztec court even laid down guidelines on the proper way to smell flowers, a ritual as stylized as wine-tasting is today.

According to legend, the Aztecs and other Nahuatl-speakers came from the seven caves called Chicomózoc, in the north of Mexico. The Aztecs claimed to have migrated from Aztlán (hence their name), perhaps a temporary home after they left the seven caves. One of their legendary leaders was Mexitli, who may have given his name to the Mexicas, another name for the Aztecs, and thus to the Spanish name Mexico.

The Aztecs were led by their tribal god, Huitzilopochtli. When they arrived on the shores of Lake Texcoco, site of modern-day Mexico City, they were rude barbarians with no technical skills and dressed in animal skins. But they were tough and had faith in themselves. On an island in Lake Texcoco, they saw a sign which their priests had prophesied would end their wanderings. It was an eagle, perched on a cactus and devouring a serpent (now the emblem of modern Mexico).

Here they were to build their city, Tenochtitlán, named for Tenoch, one of their leaders. They were not welcomed, and when they asked permission to settle in the area the ruler of Azcapotzalco gave them a snake-infested marsh. For 75 years the Aztecs learned from their advanced cousins, but never abandoned faith in their destiny. Keeping their spears sharpened, they hired themselves out as mercenaries. They lived off snake meat, fish, ducks, and even mosquito larva, slowly developing agriculture skills. They built *chinampas,* floating gardens anchored to the shallow lake bottom.

Rise of the Aztecs: At last, in 1428, Tezotómoc, the tyrannical king of Azcapotzalco, died. Allied with other tribes, the Aztecs defeated Tezotómoc's son, thus winning their independence. Next they formed a triple alliance with the towns of Tlacopan and Texcoco, then ruled by the poet-architect-engineer king, Netzahualcóyotl. Slowly the Aztecs began to dominate. Itzcóatl, the first ruler of the independent Aztecs, governed from 1428–40. In typical dictator style, he set about revising history by ordering all the codices painted before his reign to be burned. Now his appointed historians could glorify the Aztec past.

By now the Aztecs were on the march. Used to drumming up wars, they were adept at provoking pretexts for belligerence. They still kept their two allies, the Texcocans and the Tlacopans, but only the former were permitted to furnish warriors. The Tlacopans

supplied *tortillas* and porters.

In 1473 the Aztecs established absolute control at home by defeating a faction of their own tribe who controlled the great market at Tlatelolco. In their capital of Tenochtitlán the Aztecs built imposing structures and turned out well executed sculpture. They were often brutish but still they had a sense of the artistic. According to some accounts, during the dedication of the temple-pyramid of Huitzilopochtli, they sacrificed 20,000 prisoners of war, who were marshalled, four abreast, in a 5-km (3-mile) long file, then driven to the sanctuary on top of the pyramid where priests tore out their hearts.

The ritual went on for three days and nights. Then there was a great feast, during which the Aztecs consumed parts of the bodies.

The last and best known of the Aztec emperors, Moctezuma II, began his career as a general. He was renowned for his courage. However, in time the warrior-king began to mellow, devoting more and more time to his priestly duties and less to gory war. This change of character was partly responsible for the Aztecs' defeat by Cortés.

Good administration: Obviously there was a lot more to the Aztecs than blood and guts. Their social system elevated the common citizen, making him feel he was playing a vital role. The government was free of corruption, administrators were excellent and the Aztecs provided a system of education unprecedented in Mesoamerica. What is most striking about the Aztecs is their capacity for abstract thought.

The Aztecs differentiated between concepts based on observation and experience, on the one hand, and magic-cum-superstition, on the other. They had a popular religion, worshipping a symbolic reference to natural phenomena in the form of over 2,000 gods. There was also an official state theology, separate from the philosophical religion, wherein intellectuals sought answers to eternal questions about man's purpose.

The founder of the universe was called Ometéotl. Under him many gods fought for supremacy, which would permit them to rule men's lives and direct the destiny of the world. In Aztec belief, there were five time-spans, or Suns. The First Sun lasted 676 years. This was the god Tezcatlipoca, the Sun of Night and Earth. During his reign, the land was inhabited by giants who lived on acorns. The First Sun was vanquished by Quetzalcóatl, who struck him a tremendous blow with a club. He fell into the water and was transformed into a jaguar that ate the acorn-fed giants.

The Second Sun, Quetzalcóatl, God of the Wind, lasted 364 years, a period that ended when the aforementioned jaguar clawed Quetzalcóatl and overthrew him. A great wind arose and everyone perished except for a few monkeys.

The Third Sun was Tláloc, the Rain of Fire, whose domination lasted 312 years and ended when Quetzalcóatl conjured up a day-long rain of fire which killed everyone except a few who survived as birds, chiefly turkeys. The Fourth Sun, Chalchiuhtlicue, controlled the world for 676 years. The end came when Tláloc sent a great flood in which all drowned except for a few, who became fish. The Fifth Sun, the Sun of Movement, is the contemporary ruler. His era started at Teotihuacan, when the assembled gods decided that he who was brave enough to cast himself into the fire would be the next Sun. Eventually an unassuming deity called Nanahuatzin leaped into the flame.

Symbolic suns: The reason that each Sun reigned for a period of time defined right down to an exact number of years was that each of their eras had to be divisible by 52, a

they admired. The new chronicles also depicted their tribal god Huitzilopochtli as a major god associated with the Sun, a god who led Aztecs to greatness.

The official state doctrine decreed that the noblest form of death was in childbirth for women (the making of warriors), and on the battlefield or as a human sacrifice for men. According to state doctrine, the souls of such dead would bask in glory and accompany the Sun on his daily journey.

It is plain that the military dominated Aztec culture. Soldiers who won fame were given land and positions of wealth and influence. Even when there were no major campaigns underway, the Aztecs carried on "wars

sacred number. The Aztecs interposed themselves in the struggle of the gods so that the world would not come to an end at the close of any 52-year cycle by fortifying the Fifth Sun. How? By giving him the most sacred and life-giving of food – living human hearts.

Less than 100 years before the Spanish came, there lived a nobleman among the Aztecs named Tlacaelel. He was responsible for the destruction of the ancient codices which allowed the Aztecs to claim close relationship with the Toltec nobility, whom

<u>Left</u>, Moctezuma II. <u>Above</u>, Aztec warriors and men of rank.

of flowers" with their own allies, capturing soldiers whom they put to death. They considered soldiers the best of all sacrifices to strengthen the time-span or Sun.

The Aztecs were not interested in occupying the lands of the vanquished – they had too few warriors to spare for armies of occupation. They left the conquered peoples with their own leaders and government but demanded heavy payment. Their arrogant tax collectors could always summon the military to punish those who did not produce on time and in large enough quantity. Such a people as the Aztecs were bound to incite hatred among the subject tribes.

The Spanish conquest of Mexico is one of the most exciting adventure stories of mankind, at least from an outsider's point of view. Four and a half centuries have gone by and still there is the great question: how could a tiny army led by a law-school dropout conquer the mightiest tribal nation of Mexico's military culture?

Against the tens of thousands of Aztec warriors and allied tribes, Hernán Cortés, the Spanish leader, had fewer than 400 Spanish soldiers in the beginning and later some 7,000 Tlaxcalan enemies of the Aztecs. The Spanish also had 16 horses – "fearsome beasts," they were called – and 10 heavy guns, four lighter pieces and plenty of ammunition. The sound and fury of those artillery pieces initially terrified the Aztecs.

Cortés was just 19 when he arrived in Hispaniola in 1504. Strong, intelligent and ambitious, he was restless and craved adventure. Under Velasquez, the governor of Cuba, he organized an expedition to Mexico, sailing in 11 ships. After a battle in Tabasco, he landed at Veracruz, 312 km (195 miles) east of Tenochtitlán, the Aztec capital, on April 22, 1519.

Burned his ships: The first thing Cortés did was to order all but one of his ships destroyed. It was daring to cut himself off from the line of retreat, but a smart move, militarily. His men now knew beyond doubt that they were on their own: they had to conquer or die. They began the march inland.

The Aztecs would soon learn how cruel the Spanish could be. At Cholula they invited the nobles to a religious ceremony. An old woman informed the Spanish that the nobles were plotting against them. Suddenly without warning, the Spanish attacked with "knife strokes and sword strokes and death." Everyone in sight was slaughtered.

When the invaders finally reached the outskirts of Tenochtitlán, what they beheld was a marvelous city set in a lake with a wide main street, temples, terraces, gardens and snowcapped blue mountains in the distance. Throngs of the curious beheld the Spanish and their armor, cannon and horses. The Spaniards looked at the people, the canals, the bridges and the boats gliding in the water,

carrying produce to market. They saw huge causeways, miles long, wide enough for 10 horses to ride abreast.

Bernal Díaz, a soldier in Cortés' army, described the wonder he felt when he and his comrades first saw the shining Aztec capital. "[The city] seemed like an enchanted vision from the tale of Amadis," he wrote. "Indeed some of our soldiers asked whether it was not all a dream." They visited the great market of Tlatelolco, patronized by some 70,000 people a day, with row upon row of every kind

of merchandise laid out for sale.

Moctezuma came out to meet Cortés. The king was about 40 years old, tall, trim, with a wispy beard, his face lighter than the faces of his copper-hued subjects. He greeted Cortés courteously, thinking he was a divine envoy of the god Quetzalcóatl, gave Cortés gifts and arranged for the Spanish to quarter in a palace built by his father. They spoke through the interpretation of a woman named Malinche, a Mexican Indian. That night when the Spanish fired their cannon, the Aztecs shuddered.

There followed a week or so of palaver between Moctezuma and Cortés, but nothing much was accomplished. The king remained polite; Cortés became increasingly bold. By then the Spanish were growing restive and so Cortés decided on a daring stroke. He and his cohorts took Moctezuma captive, claiming he was merely a hostage. Although Moctezuma could have ordered his people to resist, he chose not to.

Cortés wins battle: Governor Velasquez back in Cuba had heard the reports. He feared and hated Cortés and feeling he was too ambitious, sent an expedition from Cuba to arrest

not do well." As word of the killings spread, the Aztecs rose in rebellion and attacked the Spanish. Cortés pressed Moctezuma to cool down his warriors. The king tried but the Aztecs reviled and wounded him, calling him a coward and a woman. The king's spirit was crushed. He refused to talk or eat and he died soon after.

The Aztecs blockaded the palace, destroyed the bridges over the canals, and cut off the Spaniards. The Spanish had to get out of town. After midnight on July 1, 1520, they

him. Ever the strategist, Cortés sallied forth to meet his countrymen, defeated them, and incorporated them into his army.

While he was away an ugly incident occurred at the palace at Tenochtitlán. The Spanish troops under Capitán Alvarado who were guarding Moctezuma gave permission to the Aztecs to hold a religious festival, during which the participants were slaughtered. That massacre shook even Cortés and he rebuked Alvarado and told him he "did

Left, Hernán Cortés. **Above**, matchbox art depicts human sacrifice (left) and the meeting between Moctezuma and Cortés.

slipped out of the palace, hauling a portable bridge to span the canals. They were weighed down with Aztec gold.

The populace was sleeping, but a wild running battle ensued as the Aztec battle whistle sounded in the night, summoning the warriors. The Spanish wielded their trusty swords. The Indians thrust with their copper-tipped long spears, threw stones, hurled darts, and fired volleys of arrows. They were experts with the sling and also welded the *maquahuitl,* a paddle-shaped club inset with razor-like pieces of obsidian.

Greed for gold: The Spanish were running for their lives. The Aztecs no longer feared the white invaders and harassed them along their road of retreat. Many Spaniards died from greed; carrying so much gold they could neither fight nor move effectively. Bernal Díaz wrote that during this *Noche Triste* ("Sad Night"), as it became known, the Spanish lost more than half their army, all their artillery and munitions, and 57 of their 80 horses. "We fought very well but they were so strong and had so many bands which relieved one another by turns, that if we had been ten thousand Trojan Hectors and so many Rolands, even then we should not have been able to break through."

When the surviving Spaniards finally escaped, they ran out of food and had to live on

On their final assault the Spaniards had 86 horsemen, 700 foot soldiers and 118 crossbowmen and musketeers. The footmen discarded their metal armor and wore the quilted cotton protection of the Aztecs. Again the Spaniards had thousands of Indian allies.

The Spanish victory: The following year, 1521, a reinforced Spanish army laid siege for almost three months to Tenochtitlán. They conquered the causeways first, then the city, street by street. Besides Spanish arms, the Aztec defeat was caused by widespread smallpox brought in by a black slave from Cuba and many died from lack of fresh water as the lake around them was brackish. The Spanish naval siege of the Aztec capital

wild berries and the few ears of corn they could glean from the fields. If a horse was slain or died, it became a nourishing dinner. The Aztecs should have followed up their victory and rushed the Spaniards but they let the remnants get away. Thus Cortés was able to reach Tlaxcala, and there he received reinforcements of men and arms for the final assault on Tenochtitlán. Again he devised a superior strategy, ordering 13 war sloops to be built and armed with cannon. These were hauled to Lake Texcoco, allowing him to control passage on the water, thus cutting off Aztec supplies. He also severed the freshwater pipelines supplying Tenochtitlán.

proved a major success, cutting off food and other supplies. The Aztec resistance ended when the Spaniards captured the new emperor, Cuauhtémoc, as he tried to flee Tenochtitlán in a canoe.

Consider the story of the conquest of Mexico from the Aztec point of view, as described by the Mexican scholar Miguel León-Portilla in his book *The Broken Spears*. For years before the Spanish came, a miasma of doom hung in the air with a series of omens portending disaster. One night, the sages said, a huge, flaming ear of corn appeared in the sky, dripping blood. Comets flared, trailing tails of fire. A man with two heads was reported walking the streets. On a windless day, the waters of Lake Texcoco rose and flooded the city. A strange bird was captured that had a mirror set in his head. The bird reportedly was brought to Moctezuma, who looked in the mirror and, though it was daytime, saw the night sky and stars reflected. Clearly something was wrong. He took another look and saw a strange army advancing on his capital. The soldiers were mounted on animals that looked like deer.

It was about this time that reports came of the Spanish landings on the coast. The king's fortune tellers prophesied that these strangers would rule the land. Aroused, the king ordered the bearers of these ill tidings to be strangled – but the memory of the tale haunted him. And, of course, Moctezuma knew the legend foretelling Quetzalcoatl's return. The description of the Spanish fitted the story of the legend. They, too, had white skin and black beards.

So the invaders arrived and Moctezuma tried to win them with gold. Miguel León-Portilla wrote that they "picked up the gold and fingered it like monkeys… they hungered like pigs for that gold."

Path of broken spears: The destruction of Tenochtitlán was dreadful, the author said. "The cries of the helpless women and children were heart-rending. The Tlaxcalan and the other enemies of the Aztecs revenged themselves pitilessly for old offenses and robbed [the people] of everything they could find… The anguish and bewilderment was pitiful to see. The warriors gathered on the rooftops and stared at the ruins of their city in a dazed silence and the women and children and old men were all weeping."

How did the Spanish win with so few combatants? León-Portilla says it is true their arms were superior; the noise and flash of their artillery frightened the Aztecs. But after a while the Indians got used to the noise and they soon discovered that even the fearsome horse was mortal. It was the Spaniards' bravery and expert military tactics that proved as important as their armor or weapons.

Treacherous La Malinche: Cortés' most valuable aide was his Indian mistress and interpreter, Doña Marina, who was known as "La Malinche." Presented to Cortés after his first

battle in Tabasco, she was the daughter of a Mexican nobleman, who spoke both Maya and Nahuatl, the language of the Aztecs. She had learned Spanish from a seaman who had been shipwrecked off the Yucatán coast. She gave Cortés advice on strategy and on the psychology of the Aztecs. Cortés was shrewd in the ways of diplomacy. He often took La Malinche's advice. (Mexicans understandably consider her the arch traitor.)

The Spanish not only lusted for gold, for they also had a sense of divine mission, wanting to win land for their monarch and aggrandize his realm. Also they wanted to convert the Indians to Catholicism – they believed God to be on their side.

Bernal Díaz said the Spanish triumph was achieved "not of our volition, but by the guidance of God. For what soldiers in the world, numbering only four hundred – and we were even fewer – would have dared to enter a city as strong as Mexico, which is larger than Venice and more than 4,500 miles away from our own Castile?"

The Spaniards fought valiantly but not only for ambitious reasons. Indeed, they were sincerely shocked by human sacrifices and other Aztec rituals. The defeat of Tenochtitlán ushered in the colonial period: a time of good or evil, depending on a person's point of view.

Left, Moctezuma is taken prisoner. **Right**, Cortés during the night of his defeat.

COLONIALISM AND INDEPENDENCE

For three centuries Spain ruled Mexico. It was hardly an enlightened rule, and often harsh colonialism at its worst. Rebellion flared from time to time, but the rebels, including in 1562 Hernán Cortés's son Martin and a group of his allies, were always swiftly crushed.

Spain ruled with an iron hand. After defeating the Aztecs, the Spanish consolidated their power, subjugated the Indian tribes, and reached out for new riches. At the beginning of the 16th century Spain was one of the most dynamic countries in the world. United after finally driving out the Moors, it was now ready for new adventures. At home the Church reigned supreme, while small groups of nobles held staunch political power. A rigid hierarchy prevailed; not a breath of democracy was permitted.

Quickly recognizing the importance of Mexico, or "New Spain" as it was called, Spain would not permit the rule of a semi-autonomy overseas. The conquistadors were not only neglected but the Crown eventually took away many of the land-grants which Cortés had given his stalwarts, and dispatched a nobleman to rule New Spain as the viceroy. The soldiers who had fought so bravely came away with little more than their wounds. "We ought to call ourselves, not the victors of New Spain, but the victims of Hernán Cortés," Bernal Díaz commented bitterly.

Encomiendas and haciendas: The land-grant system had worked this way: the holder of the grant – called an *encomienda* – was allocated a number of Indian workers, whom it was his duty to protect and convert to Christianity. Most of the *encomiendas* were too small to be economically viable and fewer than 2 percent of the holders could make a living out of them; the rest had to find other jobs to supplement their income. As agriculture developed, the *encomiendas* gave rise to *haciendas,* larger extensions of land bought from the Crown.

Nobody was much troubled by the master-servant relationship between Spaniard and

Preceding pages: the Independence, depicted in a mural by Juan O'Gorman.**Left**, the Palacio de Iturbide in the 19th century.

Indian. The Church heartily supported the philosophy that each person had his assigned station in life and only by humbly accepting his place could he reap his reward in the next life. It took decades to Christianize the Indians. Did they possess a soul which could be saved? Finally, it was decided that, yes, the Indian was a human being.

The Spanish missionaries concentrated their initial proselyting efforts on teaching the children of the native aristocracy. In 1528, the College of Santa Cruz de Tlatelolco was founded for this purpose. Many of the students aspired to the priesthood but a decree in 1555 prohibited the ordaining of Indians, *mestizos* or *negros.*

But religion was secondary to the fact that the native community was being wiped out, chiefly through disease. With no immunity against the white man's diseases and especially hard hit by smallpox, almost 90 percent of the population disappeared in the decades after the conquest. Moreover, some of the proud Indians refused to accept Spanish rule and there were even instances where whole groups of disenchanted people committed suicide. Others refused to produce offspring, not wanting to bring up their children as slaves in their own land.

Silver, cattle and land: Nor did the Spanish find the great riches for which they hungered, although the discovery of silver at Zacatecas, Pachuca and Guanajuato stirred fresh hope. By 1548, more than 50 silver mines were in operation. But even with the forcible recruitment of Indians to work in the mines, the labor force was insufficient, so black slaves were imported. By 1800 Mexico was producing 66 percent of the world's silver.

Spurred by the shining metal of Zacatecas, adventurers pushed into the far north, looking for buried riches. These independent men, being several months' journey from Mexico City and thus well out of the reach of the ruling hierarchy, developed an open society. Usually *criollos* (Mexican-born Spaniards) or *mestizos* (of Spanish and Indian blood), they were brazen as brass cymbals, self-reliant and full of hell, much like the pioneers of the American West. The semidesert and wide-open lands they settled, useful for cattle-raising but not much else, extended into what is now Texas, Arizona, New Mexico and California. Large tracts were taken over for grazing.

There was now a new hunger – for land. Obviously accumulation of land led to power, so ruthless men seized Indian farmland. Endless disputes about land and water rights followed and sometimes the bitterness led to killing. The Indians came out the losers. Kept in servitude because of the accumulation of debts, an Indian family was often compelled to remain on the same *hacienda* for generations, never catching up with their debts. Thus while slavery was officially abolished in the New World in 1548, many Indians

The Church also had inevitable clashes with the viceroy, who represented the king of Spain and thus had absolute authority in the colony. That the Church was wealthy no one could deny. It received a 10 percent tithe from agriculture, from commerce, and from the wealth of the mines, as well as its cut from the native economy, such as it was. It owned sugar mills and well-run haciendas and loaned money. But on the other hand, it stood resolutely for moral authority and somehow succeeded in maintaining the peace.

What mattered most of all to the Spanish Crown was how well New Spain was paying off; it always needed money. Hence it introduced special laws to help maximize their

remained in bondage. Sometimes the Church sought to protect them. Priests of conscience, such as Fray Bartolomé de las Casas in Chiapas and Bishop Quiroga in Michoacán, set up organizations to help the Indians.

Church versus victory: The Church itself had its own problems, including internal politics and conflict with civil authorities. Several religious orders sent disciples to convert the Indians and by 1559 there were 380 Franciscan monks, 210 Dominicans and 212 Augustinians. Other orders, including the Jesuits, followed, each with its own style of evangelizing and different assigned area but at times there was acute rivalry among them.

profits from the colony. For example, the planting of grape and olive trees was forbidden in Mexico in order to protect Spain's export monopoly in wine and olive oil. Intercolony trade was also banned since it would compete with imports from Spain. In fact, Mexico could not trade with any European country except Spain. Naturally, contraband trade flourished and a good proportion of Mexico's silver was smuggled out. From Acapulco, on the west coast, a galleon departed once every year or two, laden with silver and bound for Manila.

Corn favored: Sugar cane did well in Mexico but as early as 1599 a decree was passed restricting the planting of cane in favor of corn and wheat. In the states of Tlaxcala and Hidalgo, haciendas produced *pulque,* an alcoholic drink made from the fermented juice of a species of cactus called the maguey. The Yucatán peninsula specialized in the production of cotton and indigo; Oaxaca produced cochineal (a red dye from the blood of a cactus grub) other places raised vanilla, cacao and tobacco.

Obviously the Indians did most of the sweat labor. Still there were also many poor Spaniards – artisans, small-scale farmers and ranchers – for by the 1570s there were around 60,000 Spanish settlers in New Spain, where only Spanish people (and for a time Portu-

New Spain to dream of independence, and a few years later Napoleon looked at Spain, decided it could serve as a useful springboard for an attack on England and so invaded. Charles IV abdicated in favor of Ferdinand VII, who gave way to Napoleon. Bonaparte placed his brother, Joseph Napoleon, on the Spanish throne.

Far off in Mexico City the elite of the ruling class met to decide what to do. Up rose Francisco Primo de Verdad, a lawyer, and as his name implies, he spoke the truth. He said that the king of Spain had been overthrown, that a usurper had taken over, and that the sovereignty of the people of New Spain should be returned to its rightful heir, the

guese) were allowed to settle. Meanwhile, a medley of new peoples was being born: the *criollos,* or Spanish-born Mexicans; the *mestizos*; and the *castas,* of varying degrees of Spanish, Indian, black and Oriental blood. The authorities kept bureaucratic note of these mixtures and had a name for each particular mix. By the 18th century the *mestizos* and Creoles accounted for around half the population.

The French Revolution, which began in 1789, encouraged the beleaguered people of

people themselves, as represented by the town magistrates. The assembly exploded. Primo de Verdad was called a "heretic" and "Lutheran" and sent to prison, where he died.

Thoughts of independence: In 1808, a group of committed men met in Valladolid (today's Morelia in Michoacán) to talk of independence. The French Revolution, which began in 1789, led the beleaguered people of New Spain to dream of independence; events in war-torn Europe helped nourish the dream. Proceeding from the middle-class, they were the type of people who had the most to gain by a change in the establishment. The archbishop of Mexico, who was also the viceroy,

Left, a painting of the National Palace by Casimiro Castro. **Above**, 17th-century view of Acapulco.

discovered the plot and quelled it. But a spark had been struck.

A group of people with the same thought had been meeting in Querétaro, the neighboring state, in the house of Miguel Domínguez, the magistrate, and his wife, Josefa. Always present was the quiet Father Miguel Hidalgo y Costilla, parish priest of the town of Dolores. Captain Ignacio Allende was also there. Father Hidalgo's thesis was plain and simple: New Spain should be free. The friends planned an uprising. They thought they might begin in San Juan de los Lagos in Jalisco toward the end of 1810. They could take advantage of the crowds who would come to the fair and to the religious ceremandedequalityamong men and land for the landless. It was, in fact, the battlecry of the ages. The revolution had begun.

Father Hidalgo carried a painting of Our Lady of Guadalupe, dressed in native garb, which served as the flag of the rebels. Armed with spears and sticks, Hidalgo's band marched from town to town and wherever they went more men joined. From a few hundred they became thousands. Freedom was on the march, as they triumphantly advanced through the countryside.

Bitter battles: The government commissioned General Félix Maria Calleja to halt the rebels. A capable leader, he set out implacably to do the job. And now the horror

mony honoring the Virgin Mary.

But before it could take place word leaked out. Doña Josefa heard of the planned treachery and warned the conspirators. Captain Allende speedily rode to Dolores to warn Father Hidalgo, who seemed unperturbed.

On the morning of September 16, 1810, however, Hidalgo made his famous *Grito de Dolores*, the Shout of Dolores, the most famous outcry in Mexican history. Arriving at dawn to say Sunday Mass, he spoke to a filled church of insurrection: of killing *gapuchines* (a term of contempt for those born in Spain), the only ones legally permitted to hold the highest offices. Hidalgo debegan. Both sides committed atrocities, shot prisoners and pillaged, an oft-repeated pattern in the bloody history of Mexico.

Hidalgo arrived with his men in Morelia where he had been rector of the seminary. By now he had changed completely. No longer the subservient priest, he was now a fierce and bold combat leader. He went on to Guadalajara, where he formed his first administration. To this day Tapatios (the people of Jalisco) rejoice in the knowledge that the first seat of an independent Mexican government was set up in their state.

In Guadalajara, Hidalgo either ordered, or at least tolerated, the assassination of hundreds of Spaniards. Captain Allende, his chief lieutenant, was revolted and even thought about doing away with the priest. But Hildalgo's plans had taken fire. He issued an edict abolishing slavery and sent his cohorts on missions all over Mexico to whip up revolutionary fervor. In the meantime, General Calleja had arrived with an army and laid siege to Guadalajara.

Then in January 1811, the rebels came out to do battle at Puerte de Calderón, some 40 km (25 miles) east of Guadalajara, and were crushed. Hidalgo and his chieftains fled north, hoping to reach the US, but were betrayed and captured. Hidalgo was imprisoned in far-off Chihuahua to await his fate, and on

ess, Our Lady of Guadalupe. Among the new rebel leaders was José María Morelos y Pavón, a rural priest and former student of Hidalgo, who began with just 20 men, but with his shredness and knowledge of the terrain soon attracted some natural leaders.

Morelos seized Acapulco. Wherever he went he installed a government and – revolutions costing money – collected taxes. He sponsored the Congress of Chilpancingo which wrote a constitution with a bill of rights, forming the basis of Mexico's legal code. Morelos's idealism, however, helped undo him. Soon he was quarreling with Congress and was deposed. After losing a battle, he was taken prisoner and executed. The

July 30, 1811 he was shot by a firing squad. He faced death with dignity and impassiveness. The crowning insult came when the Church repudiated him. But he didn't die in spirit; Father Hidalgo lives on in the hearts of Mexicans, as the father of the nation.

The next stage: Nor did the movement die. New leaders sprang up and the armed revolutionaries enlisted intellectuals and even rich ranchers. In Mexico City, a secret society was founded, called the "Guadalupes," adopted from the name of Mexico's patron-

Left, the lobby of a colonial building in Campeche. **Above**, a colonial bedroom in Morelia.

revolution was now practically leaderless, except for one man and he was on the royalist side: the rich and able Agustín de Iturbide, a Creole who hungered for power.

In the south only one strong rebel remained: Vicente Guerrero. After trying unsuccessfully to capture him, Iturbide asked Guerrero to join him. Thus the royalist Iturbide and the rebel Guerrero embraced, and parleyed, marking the end of a 10-year struggle. They developed the Plan of Iguala, which demanded independence. The newly arrived viceroy, Juan O'Donojú, signed the Treaty of Córdoba which converted New Spain into Mexico on September 27, 1821.

The first half of the 19th century was a time of bloodshed in Mexico, leaving the country exhausted and drained, commerce ruined and the land devastated. Thousands lost their lives. From the time the Creole priest Hidalgo y Costilla shouted his *Grito de Dolores* (Cry of Dolores) on September 10, 1810, until the triumph of the liberals under the leadership of Benito Juárez, the country was in turmoil. Hidalgo cried out for racial equality and for distribution of the land among the peasants. Revolution broke out. The liberals were finally beaten. Hidalgo was taken captive, shot, and his head was put on display.

For the next three decades, the charismatic Mexican general-politician Antonio López de Santa Ana dominated the political scene earning the title of "perpetual dictator."

Mexico's major problem was the distribution of power and money based on race, with whites holding both. Of roughly 6 million inhabitants at the beginning of the century, 60 percent were Indians, 22 percent were of mixed race, and 18 percent were white. Small but powerful selfish interest groups dominated with two political groups struggling for power. Liberals preached the growth of the state and the weakening of the Church, touted laissez-faire economics and held up the United States and Republican France as their political models. The conservatives, meanwhile, wanted a well-ordered monarchy that would follow the example of the great European kingdoms. The liberals usually won on the battlefield but the conservatives were the ones who ended up in power.

The great *mestizo* and Indian majority lived in poverty and were apathetic about politics. Mexico was a disunited, troubled land. There was the vastness of the country; the lack of roads, railroads and communications, and insidious foreign influence, as well as the eternal problem of State versus Church.

Fight for independence: Santa Ana, a shifty opportunist, joined the Mexican revolutionary Augustín de Iturbide in a fight that led to Mexican independence in 1821. Santa Ana, who was elected president in 1833, loved the trappings of power and became a dictator but, despite his many faults, he was the only politician who could rally his countrymen in time of crisis. His massacre of the Texans at the Alamo earned the hatred of Texans in perpetuity. In turn, he was badly beaten by Sam Houston at San Jacinto in 1836 and Texas, which had belonged to Mexico, became a republic.

The 19th century was a time of both internal and external struggles: long and bitter contests between liberals and conservatives weakened the country and tempted ambitious foreign powers to intervene (thanks to popular myths about boundless mineral riches

BENITO JUAREZ, PRESIDENT OF THE MEXICAN REPUBLIC.

in Mexico). European powers harassed the weak, young Mexican republic. Many Europeans were influenced – and misled – by the now classical *Political Essay on the Kingdom of New Spain* written by the German aristocrat-scientist Alexander von Humboldt who had explored the country.

During this period Mexico also became entrapped in more immediate disputes: the American South, for example, wanted the then Mexican Texas to become a slave-keeping enclave, and when Mexico, by constitutional prerogative, said that slavery was forbidden, there was great consternation among the anglo population of Texas. Added to these troubles was Santa Ana's ambition, which caused his country numerous problems. His greatest prank was to sell a portion of Mexico to the US, under the conditions of the Gadsden Purchase of 1853. This sale of 77,000 sq. km (30,000 sq. miles) of southern New Mexico and Arizona for $10 million proved to be Santa Ana's final undoing.

Santa Ana commanded the Mexican forces in the disastrous war with the US (1846–48), and lost half his country's territory in the process. But, like the Indian rubberball, he wouldn't stay down. Back he came again and was elected president. Finally, the Juárez revolution drove him into exile in 1855 and off the stage.

Mexico City. In the final stage of this fighting, the cadets who garrisoned the castle in Chapultepec Park fought to the last boy. At the end, 16-year-old Juan Escutia wrapped himself in Mexico's flag and jumped off the rampart rather than be taken prisoner.

Following Santa Ana came Benito Juárez, an Indian from Oaxaca often likened to Abraham Lincoln as one of his country's great leaders. A man of brooding, dark features, he was implacable and could be ruthless but was also courageous and honest. Born in 1806 in a village in the Sierra de Oaxaca, he spoke only Zapotec as a child.

Indian patience: Taken in as a boy servant in a Creole household, he so impressed his

The war with the US was a classic example of the old saying: might makes right. The Americans were well organized, tightly disciplined, and had ample logistical support. The Mexicans, lacking all three of these ingredients, fought bravely but lost to superior forces. American troops moved south from New Mexico and captured Chihuahua; more came from Texas and captured Monterrey, Coahuila and points south. The bulk of the American forces under General Winfield Scott marched inland and captured

Left, Benito Juarez. **Above**, though a full-blooded Indian, Juarez was acclaimed by all racial mixes.

master that he helped the boy get an education and eventually Juárez became a lawyer. He was a man with a cold but logical legal mind, and incorruptible. He had the patience of the Indian and in his long and strife-torn life he needed it. He also had a dream and he achieved it: to lead the liberal revolution that would change Mexico forever.

Juárez served as governor of Oaxaca from 1847 to 1852. Opposing Santa Ana, he was imprisoned, then exiled, spending some time in New Orleans. Back home he became the prime mover in the drafting of the liberals' Plan of Ayutla (named for a mountain village), and in the overthrow of Santa Ana.

Under the new regime he became minister of justice and drew up the *Ley Juárez*, the Law of Juárez, which attacked the privileges of the Catholic Church and the military, the two untouchable bastions of power in Mexico.

The Juárez Law, an outgrowth of the liberal constitution of 1857 which Juárez had drafted, emphasized human rights and agricultural reform. The Lerdo Law, which followed, offered church lands for sale, with preference going to tenants who were working the land. A prospective buyer might have a problem: should he seek material gain but risk excommunication? This appeared to be no problem for wealthy speculators, who snapped up the land at bargain prices.

As is readily understandable, the Juárez venture was revolutionary, bound to stir up enormous resentment on the part of the conservatives. It meant the whites sharing power with the *mestizos* and Creoles. When the conservatives contested the new constitution, the liberal president Ignacio Comonfort, with no stomach for battle, resigned and the man of iron, Juárez, took over as president. The bitter and savage War of Reform (1858–61) broke out. Hostages and prisoners were executed; civilians were massacred. Historians refer to those bloody days as the time of "the brush fire sweeping the land."

On January 1, 1861, the liberal forces marched in triumph into Mexico City and a few days later Juárez came from Veracruz. There were endless problems to be faced. Because the treasury was bare, Mexico was compelled to suspend payment of its debts to Spain, Great Britain and France. That gave Napoleon III an excuse to invade – he had long dreamed of adding to France's overseas empire. The French, although defeated by the Mexicans under General Zaragoza at Puebla, were able to take over most of the country. Allied with them were the conservatives who hated Juárez more than they hated the idea of foreign rule.

By 1863 Napoleon talked Maximilian, the young archduke of Austria, into becoming emperor of Mexico, under French protection. Though repeatedly beaten by the French, Juárez refused to surrender. The Mexican forces turned north, pulling back to the US border at a place now called Ciudad Juárez.

Maximilian ironically acted much more like a liberal than a conservative, restricting working hours and child labor, cancelling all debts over 10 *pesos*, restoring communal property to Indian villages and forbidding corporal punishment. In addition, he broke the monopoly of the *hacienda* stores and decreed that henceforth peons could no longer be bought and sold for the price of their debt. Thereupon, he lost the support of the conservatives and in time also lost the support of Napoleon, who withdrew his troops. The US, which had finally finished its bloody civil war, decided that France had no business being in Mexico and strongly protested. Still, Maximilian hung on, refusing to leave and was captured. The archduke was a well-meaning ruler but he had been manipulated and then deserted by his ambitious sponsors.

Juárez was not a bloodthirsty man but he wanted respect to be paid to Mexico. So he decided to set an example for the world to see. Mexico was a sovereign state; no one could violate its territory with impunity. Juárez cast his ballot – the deciding ballot – for death for Maximilian. On June 19, 1867, the 35-year-old prince was put against a wall. A brave man, he gave each of the members of the firing squad a gold coin and as the rifle shots rang out, he shouted: "*Viva Mexico! Viva la Independencia!*"

Left, Maximilian of Habsburg. Right, an Indian girl of Oaxaca, photographed by Desiré Charnay.

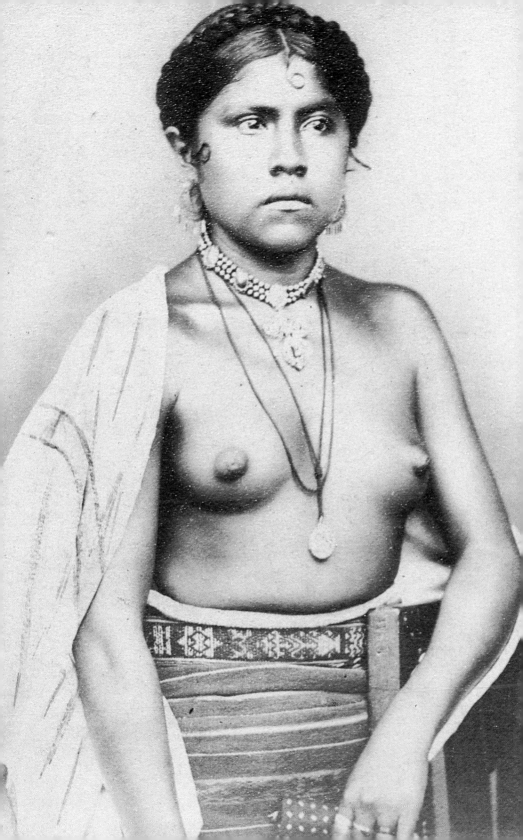

For more than three decades, President José de la Cruz Porfirio Díaz reigned in Mexico, presiding over a long regime that has come to be known as the *Porfiriato*. He was ruthless but his rule was effective. Díaz snuffed out the *revolución* and doled out land to his henchmen and supporters. Capital poured in from abroad with three-quarters of the nation's mineral rights being sold to foreigners. Roads were built, railroads were laid.

Díaz was a *mestizo* who originally supported Juárez, the reform movement and the fight against Maximilian. When he ran for president against Juárez in 1871 and was beaten, he claimed that the election was fraudulent and led a long revolt against the government. No one had the right to keep running for office forever, he said, a statement that was surely ironic in his own case, for once he became entrenched, Díaz felt no compunction against running, again and again. After successful armed intervention during the 1876 elections, he had himself proclaimed President.

Strict administration: In the beginning of his rule, Díaz stressed the pacification of his strife-torn country. Pacification extended to both the war-like Apache Indians and the peaceful Yaquis, both of whom greatly resented having their lands taken away by politicians. Once he had things under control, Díaz pressed for modernization of the traditionalist land of Mexico. Political liberty, he promised, would be granted if and when Mexico reached the point where it was compatible with discipline and development. What the country needed, Díaz claimed, was lots of strict administration and very little politicking. He used his army to enforce his program ruthlessly.

Don Porfirio was a railroad buff and thus the prices paid and the subsidies granted seemed outrageous at the time. Nevertheless Mexico wound up with a sound railroad system that endures today. Of course, one of the consequences of an efficient network of rail lines was that Díaz could move his troops with alacrity. But the rail system also revolutionized the transportation of goods in a country where there were no inland waterways to do the job properly. Now steel mills

could be built in Monterrey and iron ore railed in from Durango. It suddenly became economically feasible to ship cotton by rail from the fields of the north to textile plants in central Mexico.

Railroads also made it possible to develop mining, not only gold and silver but also coal, lead, antimony and copper. American companies made big investments – and subsequently big profits – in mining. By the end of the Porfiriato (1910), foreign investment amounted to $1.7 billion, mostly American

(38 percent), followed by British (29 percent) and French (19 percent).

Wealthy *hacendados*: Mining, banking and the oil industry all fell into foreign hands, but basic agriculture by the Mexican landowners was generally neglected with the unfortunate result that in a land where corn is the staple, it had to be imported. During the Porfiriato anyone who did not have legal title to his land – and very few did because of the complicated bureaucratic system – had their land taken away. This applied particularly to the Indian communities.

Most of the productive land was in the hands of some 6,000 *hacendados*, whose holdings ranged from 2,500 acres to areas the size of a small European country. William Randolph Hearst, the American publisher, bought 2½ million acres for a song, in return for supporting Díaz in his newspapers. Governor Terraza of Chihuahua controlled 15 million acres, it was said.

These landowners raised cattle and grew exportable cash crops such as mahogany, sugar, coffee, tobacco, rubber and *hennequen,* a cactus fiber used to make rope. Cotton was grown primarily for domestic use. Foreign-

Left, Porfirio Díaz in his youth. **Above**, a Siqueiros mural of Porfirio Díaz.

ers invested in coffee and cotton plantations. Mexico's chief exports during the Porfiriato were gold, silver, copper, oil and agricultural products. A few wealthy Mexicans controlled the economy, while rural dwellers and most people in the cities barely survived.

Díaz shrewdly sought a rapprochement with the Church and, though he did not allow it to regain its once formidable holdings (which at one time had included half of settled Mexico), he restored some lost powers and privileges. Knowing that if he ap-

peared to be tolerant toward the Church he would gain a number of influential conservative adherents, he allowed the Jesuits to return and offered no objection when the Bishop of Querétaro started the custom of an annual pilgrimage to the shrine of Our Lady of Guadalupe, Mexico's patroness.

He even married so as to benefit his regime, taking a bride who was the daughter of a religious politician. Díaz helped seal the union between army, Church and landed aristocracy. All economic interests in the country were beholden to him. Don Porfirio was even a phrase-maker of note, or rather, what seems more likely, a man who recognized a catchy phrase and borrowed it for his own. Hence to Díaz is attributed a famous saying about Mexico: "Poor Mexico! So far from God and so close to the United States."

Díaz's talkative end: Díaz, however, managed his American affairs quite well by simultaneously catering to his powerful neighbor of the north while giving himself elbow room by dealing with the French and the British. He cultivated American politicians and, chiefly through William Randolph Hearst, won over American public opinion.

Díaz ruled with an iron hand. His police were effective; their long arm sometimes reached even into the United States. The only real opposition came from radical liberals who fled to the US and under the leadership of Ricardo Flores Magón took to armed rebellion. The US offered a haven to Mexican politicos out of favor, some of whom escaped across the Río Bravo (the Rio Grande), which marked the border.

Oddly, Díaz's end came because he granted an interview to an American magazine writer. In the interview he declared that Mexico was now ready for democracy – an honest election – and that he would welcome real opposition. Francisco I. Madero, a wealthy vineyard hacienda owner in Coahuila, read the story and thought it a good idea. Indeed he wrote a book, *The Presidential Succession of 1910,* in which he, too, called for a genuinely free election offering himself as a candidate. The book became too popular; Díaz arrested Madero, who fled to Texas disguised as a railroad worker. The chips were down.

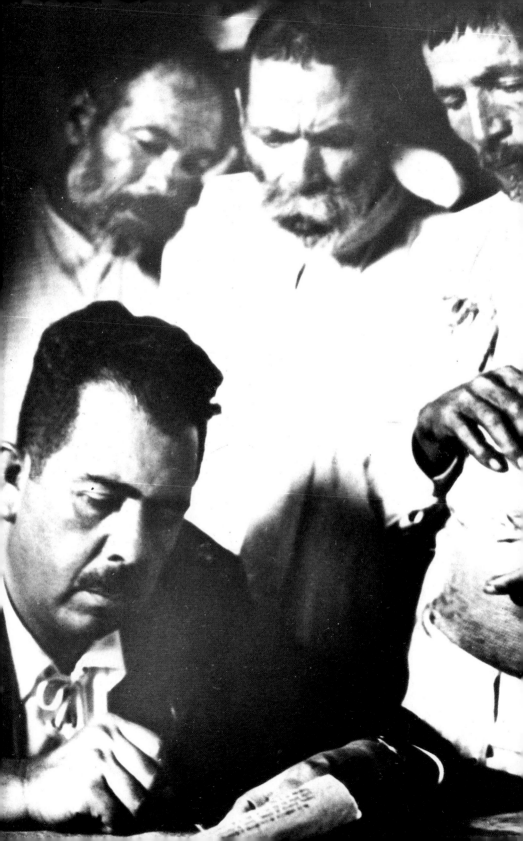

Between the years 1910 and 1920 the whole world was watching Mexico. They were hard, bitter years of war, revolution, uprising, revolt, murder. People went hungry, were tortured and shot, and as many as a million died (one out of every 15 people).

Consider the dramatis personae: Díaz, Madero, Huerta, Carranza, Obregón, and the two *guerrilleros* who caught the imagination of the world, the flamboyant Pancho Villa in the north, and the silent Indian Emiliano Zapata in the south.

Díaz was ousted, to be followed by Francisco Madero, a cultivated man with a degree from the University of California. He championed democracy and wanted an end to social injustice, but he lacked conviction. Honest but weak, Madero was the kind of man to put relatives on the government payroll. Instead of making a clean sweep of the Díaz sycophants, he tried unsuccessfully to bargain with them.

Tierra y Libertad: Madero tried to convince Zapata that he, too, wanted land reform, but Zapata's creed was a simple one to which he remained forever loyal: throw out the landlords and divide the land among the landless. A born leader, Zapata felt the injustice suffered by his people. In 1910 when he had taken up arms against the government with the cry of *Tierra y Libertad* (Land and Liberty) his men began to seize land, killing anyone who got in the way. So Zapata's support for Madero disappeared when he thought Madero was dragging his feet on land reform.

Zapata, illiterate but very intelligent, knew exactly what he wanted, and instructed a schoolteacher to write down his land reform project, called the Plan of Ayala. He took control of most of Morelos and (with Villa) occupied Mexico City. To this day, he is the hero of the Mexican agrarian movement to most Mexicans. Villa, a *bandido* from Durange, was a horse general in the tradition of the great cavalrymen of history. Villa's admirers looked on him as a Robin Hood.

Madero came to a bitter end. Victoriano Huerta, commander of government troops, bore Madero a grudge and plotted against him, first capturing, torturing and killing Madero's brother, Gustavo, then arresting Madero himself. With the backing of US ambassador Henry Lane Wilson, Huerta had Madero assassinated.

Huerta had one break: a mistake by President Wilson. Wilson sought to cut off Huerta's supplies and sent American troops to occupy Veracruz. Mexicans meanwhile had bad memories of the American intervention of 1847. Huerta seized on the incident to prop up his sagging popularity. He proclaimed himself defender of the nation's sovereignty.

Huerta formed a government, essentially with the goal of restoring the old regime of Díaz, whom he admired. Huerta, too, emphasized concession to foreign investment but immediately ran into trouble: the unplacated Zapata of the south; the rambunctious Villa in the north and Venustiano Carranza, the governor of Coahuila who had joined Madero against Díaz, and General Alvaro Obregón, all teamed up against him.

Implacable opposition: Carranza took over but although Obregón supported him, Zapata and Villa refused to acknowledge Carranza as chief, and more fighting broke out. The north where Villa and his men reigned was in chaos. Carranza promised land reform and an end to social injustice, trying to weld together all the factions that had fought Huerta. He called a convention at the town of Aguascalientes but the delegates agreed only to disagree.

In December 1914, while the world's attention was riveted on the war in Europe, Villa and Zapata occupied Mexico City sending Carranza and his government scrambling to Veracruz. The Zapatistas came in from the mountains; then came Villa's men in boxcars, with their horses, and their *soldaderas* (camp-followers). The two rebels weren't in agreement, however, and their men didn't mingle.

But though the rebel chieftains were in the capital they were men of action who didn't know how to run a government. Meanwhile in Veracruz, Carranza and Obregón made use of their time to refit. A month later Zapata and Villa left Mexico City and Carranza and the army returned.

Obregón pursued Villa and mangled his followers in Celaya by digging trenches, lacing the ground with barbed wire and setting up machine guns. The lesson of the war in Europe had not been lost on him. He knew that Villa loved to charge with his horsemen, and, according to script, the rebel chief led a reckless charge into the teeth of those defenses. Most of his men were slaughtered.

New liberal constitution: Carranza tried to consolidate his power and in 1917 wrote a new constitution. A very liberal document for that era, it included a number of pro-labor

dered General John J. "Black Jack" Pershing to capture Villa, dead or alive, and the US Army pursued the revolutionary for 11 months. It was a lesson in futility with some Americans killed or wounded and only a few *guerrilleros* captured.

What led to Carranza's downfall was that, like Madero, he lacked a sense of urgency. Time ran out on him. An election was coming up; he had hand-picked a successor but when it appeared that the popular Obregón would be the winner, Carranza turned on his old commander and had him arrested. Obregón escaped, disguised as a railroad worker, and since Carranza was trying to perpetuate his own rule, Obregón, as the new

items, such as the right to strike, an eight-hour work day, equal pay for equal work, housing for employees, and accident insurance. It also aimed at breaking up the haciendas and distributing the land among the peasants, taking away the Catholic Church's wealth. It touched off a wave of anti-clericism, which even resulted in the slaying of priests.

Villa, much less powerful but still the gadfly, tried to involve the United States in a war with the Carranza government. His men murdered 16 American engineers in Sonora and raided the New Mexican border town of Columbus, killing a number of people and destroying property. President Wilson or-

president, had to depose him. Carranza boarded the train for Veracruz but on the way heard that government forces were on his trail. He got on a horse and rode north and was shot and killed as he slept in the village of Tlaxcalantongo.

Rebels terminated: Zapata and Villa also came to violent ends. In 1919 a colonel in the federal army sent word to Zapata that he and his detachment were anxious to defect to his side. He offered proof of his sincerity in blood, ordering the slaughter of fellow government troops. Then the colonel invited Zapata to a parley. The normally shrewd Indian didn't smell a rat, went and was assassinated. Villa mellowed with age, stopped riding on his raids and settled down on a hacienda in Parral. Then one morning in 1923 his Dodge car was ambushed and he and his bodyguard and assassinated.

General Obregón took over an exhausted country, drained by revolution, ravaged by conflict, plagued by foreign debt and sunk in economic morass. Clever, resourceful, ambitious and tough, he imposed order and reasserted the power of the central government. Obregón's first job was to make himself secure. Needing foreign capital, he was forced to come to terms with the International Committee of Bankers through which he renegotiated his country's 1.5 billion *peso*

Jalisco and Veracruz, and, as the historian Nicholas Cheetham put it, "there was plenty of work for the firing squads."

Obregón began land reform, pushing it enthusiastically in Morelos and the Yucatán where there were no American landowners, but being very circumspect in his native northern Mexico. There his personal interests and those of the Americans more or less coincided. Nevertheless, he is credited with distributing 2.5 million acres, a fairly modest amount, but still eight times more than Carranza had achieved.

Educational progress: Corruption thrived under the cynical Obregón. A new class grew up, *los politicos* – men of wealth and

debt. Then, in violation of the constitution, he granted rights to foreign oil companies to continue exploration.

For economic reasons Obregón cut down the size of the federal army from 100,000 men to 40,000, a decision that spurred the ambitions of a group of military men who led a revolt. Once more rifle fire resounded in the land. But Obregón obtained arms, ammunition and even a few planes from the US. His government forces beat the rebels in

Left, Pancho Villa sits in the presidential chair, with Zapata to his right. **Above**, an execution during the Cristero Revolt.

position. Nevertheless he made at least one commendable appointment – that of José Vasconcelos as minister of education. A man of profound insight, Vasconcelos built schools all over the country and imbued schoolteachers with a sense of purpose.

During the Obregón regime the civil government's never-ending fight with the Catholic Church escalated. During the Porfiriato, the Church had regained some of its power but now the military and civil leaders were more fanatically anticlerical than ever and had the legal support of the constitution itself. They harassed the Church, setting obstacles in its course. In 1923, the Vatican's

Apostolic nuncio was expelled and so were foreign-born priests. Convents and Church schools were closed. A running battle went on for three years extending over into the presidency of Obregón's successor, Plutarco Elías Calles.

The opposition included Catholic guerrillas, the *Cristeros*, whose war cry was *Viva Cristo Rey* ("Long Live Christ the King"). They clashed with the *federales* in Jalisco, Michoacán, Guanajuato and Colima, battling for a pro-cleric constitution. At one point in the fanatical struggle the Church was driven underground and priests had to conduct mass by hiding in cellars. Eventually a compromise was reached: religious services

El Jefe Máximo: President Calles became known as the biggest power broker in the history of elected officials of Mexico. He was more intelligent than Obregón and a much better administrator and in his regime schools were built, miles of road were carved, and irrigation projects were started. He renegotiated his country's debts and gave guarantees to private enterprise. He distributed 7 million acres. He named the labor leader Luis Morones as his secretary of labor and industry and thus just about eliminated strikes.

But under Calles political and moral standards fell. His detractors likened him to a Fascist dictator. He founded a political party, the PNR, or National Revolutionary Party,

were restored and the government, while not rescinding the decrees repugnant to the Church, agreed to apply them in a conciliatory way.

In 1926, Obregón, hungry for power, convinced the Mexican Congress they should amend the constitution and allow him to run again for president. He had his way and was re-elected. On July 17, 1928, he was shot dead by a young man who was allowed to approach to show him a portfolio of cartoons. The man was a fanatical Catholic and apparently acted on his own but many people didn't believe it. They thought they detected the hand of Calles in the act.

the forerunner of today's PRI party, and through it he controlled his own and subsequent elections (he named his successors). He brought diverse factions under the PNR umbrella, such as labor, the farmers, the military. The *Callistas*, a tight little group of financiers and industrialists, pledged allegiance to him and he was their *Jefe Máximo,* the top leader.

Calles' presidency ended with the election of General Lázaro Cárdenas in 1934. A mestizo, Cárdenas was a refreshing change: a chief executive who was honest, austere and impeccable. He did more for the common man than any president in the history of modern Mexico. A Socialist, deep in his heart he was more importantly a Mexican nationalist, gutsy and full of pride and spirit.

Between 1934 and 1940, he distributed 45 million acres. Perhaps this was too fast; some of the biggest, but most efficiently-run haciendas were broken up, which understandably led to a fall in agricultural output. The farm cooperatives Cárdenas sponsored were not efficient enough to make up the loss, so he had to slow the drive down. The government issued certificates of exemption (from appropriation) to landowners who ran very efficient operations.

Supporting labor: Cárdenas encouraged the labor unions. In 1936, Vicente Lombardo

Also in 1936, the CTM demanded pay raises and fringe benefits from the foreign oil companies. The companies – American and British – agreed to talk, but were not about to give in. Six months of bickering went on and then the union called a strike. Cárdenas stepped into the strike, appointed a commission and the companies were ordered to grant a 27 percent wage hike. They appealed to the Mexican Supreme Court. Another six months went by before a ruling was handed down. The court granted the workers' demand and gave the companies a week to pay off. More maneuvering went on. Finally, Cárdenas had had enough.

He broadcast on public radio that he was

Toledano, a Marxist, founded the CTM, the *Confederación de Trabajadores Mexícanos*, or Confederation of Mexican Workers. Cárdenas welded the agrarian movement into one big, government-sponsored group, the *Confederación Nacional de Campesinos*, or National Federation of Farmers. With those two organizations behind him, Cárdenas had a broad political base. Though he listened to Marxists, he took orders from no one.

Left, General Obregón and his wife. **Above**, the whole country mobilized resources to pay for the nationalization of the petroleum industry, including these women donating chickens.

appropriating the oil companies' property and nationalizing the industry. Mexicans cheered; the British were incensed and Mexico broke off diplomatic relations. President Roosevelt, being the chief advocate of the "Good Neighbor" policy with Latin America, had the US State Department present a comparatively mild note of protest, pointing out that it was Mexico's duty to pay fair compensation. Implementation was long delayed: a settlement with the US oil companies amounting to $24 million, plus interest was not concluded until 1942. Payment to the British took even longer. It amounted to $81 million.

Between World War II and the beginning of the 1990s, Mexico's population jumped from 22 million to 85 million. Such demographic growth is awesome: it means that the Mexican economy needs to provide 800,000 new jobs a year.

In addition to the *Distrito Federal* or Mexico City, the nation's capital, the Mexican republic comprises 31 states. Its constitution was modelled on that of the US and the congress consists of two houses: the senate, with 64 seats, and the chamber of representatives, consisting of 500 members. In reaction to Porfirio Díaz's 35-year dictatorship (1876–1911), under the constitution, the president is allowed to serve only one six-year term in his lifetime. However, during his administration he is endowed with almost unlimited power.

Each *sexenio* (six-year period) is an almost independent unit, with major changes in government functionaries and objectives, which rather inhibits long-term planning. It is said, jokingly, that some politicians perceive their life-spans totally in terms of how many *sexenios* they have left.

Manuel Avila Camacho (1940–46) was president during World War II. A middle-of-the-roader, he stressed economic growth. With the world in flames, it was clear that Mexico had to learn to stand on its own feet, so he encouraged the building of light and heavy industry.

Permanent "revolution": It was Miguel Alemán, a wealthy lawyer but a champion of labor, who changed the name of Mexico's ruling political party to the Institutionalized Revolutionary Party (PRI) during his presidency (1946–52). His reasoning was that the revolution was permanent: the seed planted by the original revolutionaries was still thriving but the goal had not yet been reached. Alemán, the former governor of Veracruz, had resigned that post to run Avila Camacho's political campaign, stressing foreign investment, improved communications and education, and generally raising the standard of living. With an eye on President Roosevelt's

"Brain Trust," he drafted bright young men into government service, modernized the railroad system, tied the nation together via a highway network and started the vast Papaloápan Valley project.

However, his biggest achievement was the construction of University City. The National University of Mexico is the oldest university in the New World, created by an edict of Charles V of Spain on September 21, 1551. One of the most impressive university campuses anywhere, it covers almost 8 sq.

km (3 sq. miles) of modernistic buildings adorned with murals by Mexican artists such as Diego Rivera and David Alfaro Siquieros.

The next president, Adolfo Ruíz Cortínes (1952–58) tried to consolidate Alemán's gains. He enfranchised women and encouraged foreign investment. American corporate business hurried down to Mexico – everybody from Nabisco to Sears. But domestic responsibilities continued to grow: in 24 years the population had doubled.

Adolfo López Mateos (1958–64), the next president, was a man of energy, verve, and personality. Under Ruíz Cortínes, the revolution had stagnated; under López Mateos it

Left, Monument of Mexico's constitution. **Right**, oil reserves provided an unexpected bonanza.

came alive again. He realized there was trouble in the land and that the great promises had gone unfulfilled. His forthrightness won the support of the young. Encouraging industry, he sought foreign capital but also distributed 30 million acres to the landless, the most since Cárdenas. He bought out American and Canadian industrial interests. Social welfare projects were stepped up with expanding medical care and old-age assistance programs, and public housing was built.

"I lean to the left, but within the constitution," were his famous words. But at the same time he was harsh on politicos who were to the left of the constitution. He jailed the Communist muralist Siquieros and kicked

70), a conservative from Puebla, was president during a time of stress. The PRI didn't realize trouble was brewing and how widespread it would be. In 1968 student rioting broke out. The leaders were well organized and aggressive and could call out half a million people at a rally. In response, the government ordered out troops to maintain order. It was inevitable that clashes would take place and that people would be killed.

There were a number of preliminary skirmishes but just before the opening of the Olympic Games which Mexico was hosting the big battle took place on October 2, 1968, in the Plaza of the Three Cultures in the district of Tlatelolco, in central Mexico City.

out the Communist leadership in the railroad and the teachers' unions. Although he called out the troops to put down a railroad strike, he also pushed through a law calling for profit-sharing for workers. Eventually workers covered by the law won annual 5–10 percent bonuses from their employers.

After Fidel Castro came to power in 1959, López Mateos voted against Cuba's expulsion from the Organization of American States and maintained diplomatic relations, thereby arousing American annoyance. Yet he condemned Castro in 1962 for permitting the Russians to bring missiles to Cuba.

Troubled times: Gustavo Díaz Ordáz (1964–

It was a relatively small demonstration. The police ordered the demonstrators to disband; they refused. Police and army units moved in with clubs and tear gas. What happened then is speculation. Many people were caught in the crossfire. Newspaper stories quoted the government as saying 43 people were killed. Government critics placed the number at 200–400. Two thousand demonstrators were jailed. It has never been forgotten.

Ordáz's successor, the energetic Luis Echeverría Alvarez (1970–76), roamed the country before his inauguration, visiting hundreds of communities, talking to farmers in the fields and workers at their lathes. He put great stress on helping the rural communities, even, if necessary, at the expense of industrial progress. Echeverría was well aware of the volcanoes smoldering; in fact, he had served as secretary of interior during the campus rioting and the bloodshed at Tlatelolco. Because of inflation, he put a tax on luxury items.

Echeverría brought young people into the government and during his presidency the voting age was lowered to 18. But there were still problems: the population was growing and inflation was roaring along at a rate of 20 percent a year. In September 1976, the *peso*, which had been 12.5 to the dollar, was devalued for the first time in 22 years, first by 60

and knew at first hand the financial condition of the country, which is why inflation and unemployment frightened him. On becoming president, López Portillo tried to bring a sense of calm and purpose, setting the pattern for his administration early on. Suddenly, a bonanza – new and great reserves of oil were discovered. Mexico, the geologists said, was sitting on an ocean of oil.

The economy grew by almost 8 percent in 1979 and by 7 percent in 1980. New industries sprang up and a new "industrial area" took root along the Mexican-US border. However, a glut on the world oil market in 1982 cut the demand and price of Mexico's principal export. To obtain loans from the International

percent and soon after by another 40 percent. Toward the end of Echeverría's term, peasants in Sonora seized private lands in the Yaqui Valley. Echeverría declared the seizure legal. His presidency marked a return to Mexico's revolutionary tradition, sometimes at the expense of efficiency and production.

Oil-rich Mexico: José López Portillo (1976–82) was far more determined than his predecessor in applying the laws governing foreign investment. A law professor, he had served as finance minister under Echeverría

Left, the Aztec Stadium, built for the 1968 Olympics. **Above**, Carlos Salinas on walkabout.

Monetary Fund, Mexico was required to adopt strict fiscal measures. People began to send their money abroad for safekeeping. The value of the *peso* plummeted to 150 per $US and subsidies for staple foods were drastically reduced.

Although the PRI remained the ruling party through all these years there were other political parties to present at least symbolic opposition, although until recently they held no seats in either of the two houses of congress or state governorships. In 1988, in a much-disputed election, Carlos Salinas de Gortarí was elected. With a master's degree from Harvard University like his predecessor, Salinas was a technocrat who achieved a single digit inflation rate and generally created a sense of renewed confidence in the country's economy. Elected with a bare 50.1 percent over Cuauhtémoc Cardenas, son of President Lázaro Cardenas, there was widespread tension and claims that he had in fact not actually won the presidency. To avoid losing further credibility, the PRI conceded several governorships to opposing parties, for the first time since it came into power in the 1920s. Considered a very effective head of state both in Mexico and abroad, Salinas was very much behind the North American Free Trade Agreement with Canada and the US and its passing has been one of the

with the beginning of NAFTA and as the campaign of the new PRI candidate for the presidency, Luis Donaldo Colosio Murrieta, was about to begin, trouble broke out in the southeastern state of Chiapas. Armed and masked Indians who had complained for years of unemployment, poverty and exploitation took temporary possession of several towns before being ousted by a massive government response. Army planes bombed what they termed rebel outposts and numerous human rights violations were alleged. Negotiations were conducted in San Cristóbal between representatives of the rebels, the local bishop and – on behalf of the government – the former mayor of Mexico City,

milestones of his administration, making Mexico a major player in the largest existing world market.

Refugees and migrants: Refugees from wartorn Central America pose problems for Mexico. Seeking sanctuary from brutal repression in their own nations, refugees flock to Mexico's already over-burdened cities and have added their numbers to Mexico's indigent and homeless. In addition, thousands of Mexicans cross over into the US in search of work that isn't available at home or is much better paid, touching off tensions with the US.

On New Year's Day, 1994, coincident

Camacho Solis.

Even before these were concluded, tragedy struck in Tijuana when Colosio was felled by an assassin's bullet while addressing an election rally. President Salinas was quick to name a successor, Ernesto Zedillo, as the PRI candidate for the forthcoming August election but clearly major changes in the Mexican political scene had become more than a cloud on the horizon.

Above, Cuauhtémoc Cárdenas is mobbed by reporters. **Right**, Ernesto Zedillo shouts the name of his predecessor, Luis Donaldo Colosio, during the March 1994 election campaign.

ELECTING A PRESIDENT

After one of the most dramatic political years since the Revolution itself, Mexico elected a new president in 1994. Despite considerable skepticism and two serious challengers, it chose, once again, the candidate of the Partida Revolucionaria Insticionale (PRI), which has held office without interruption since its inception in 1929. There was one apparent change: the new president, Ernesto Zedillo, will probably be the last under the country's increasingly reviled system known as *el destape* ("the unveiling") under which the sitting president has anointed his successor without input from the country at large. Zedillo himself was chosen by the previous president, Carlos Salinas de Gortarí, after the PRI's original candidate, Luis Donaldo Colosio, was assassinated at a rally in Tijuana.

Elected with barely half of the vote in a poll that produced the largest turnout in Mexican history, the PRI's Zedillo promised more democratic reforms to quell misgivings about the way the entrenched ruling party conducted the electoral process. For the 1994 election, voters were issued with photo identification cards and were obliged to dip their thumbs in ocher-colored indelible ink. Nevertheless the opposition, particularly the two other leading parties (there are eight in all) alleged fraud – just as they had in previous elections.

A large group of international poll watchers concluded that despite observing "irregularities" they had not detected evidence of such widespread fraud as ballot-stuffing and intimidation that had characterized earlier elections. Opponents, however, pointed to the late opening of polling stations in many rural areas, names missing from electoral rolls and the thousands who had been unable to vote because the supply of ballot forms had ran out in many places. And the provision of transparent ballot boxes might well have cut down on ballot stuffing, they agreed, but had failed to eliminate the old custom of *"taco"* voting (a second ballot slipped inside the first).

Control of the electronic media by the ruling party is widely recognized as the most unfair aspect of the electoral process. The biggest television network, Televisa (the choice of 80 percent of the viewers) noticeably favors the PRI in its coverage and charges advertising rates well beyond the budgets of the smaller parties. A pre-election study by the Federal Election Institute,

created in 1990, revealed that Televisa's main nightly news show devoted 41 percent of its coverage to the ruling party, only 8 percent each to the PAN and the PRD.

The 1994 election occurred after a turbulent eight months which had seen not only Colosio's assassination but the murder of a high-ranking police chief in Baja, the killing of a Roman Catholic cardinal at Guadalajara airport and the mysterious highway death of an opposition candidate in Chiapas. None of these killing has been satisfactorily solved and theories that they were political, and possibly connected with drug trafficking, have abounded.

The southeastern state of Chiapas has been a major scene of unrest since the well-timed emer-

gence of the Zapatistas coincided with the enactment of the NAFTA trade agreement on January 1. Spokesmen for the ragtag Indian fighters who called themselves the Zapatista National Liberation Army (after Emiliano Zapata, the Indian champion of land reform whose troops occupied the capital in 1914) demanded a rewriting of the constitution, a fairer distribution of land and provision of better educational and health services to eliminate the ingrained poverty of the region.

The new president, Ernesto Zedillo, born in Mexico City in 1952 and educated at Yale, vowed to change the system during his six-year term. "This is a victory for the PRI of tomorrow," he proclaimed on the day of his election victory. ∎

Nine months after the first Spanish conquistadors set foot on Mexican soil, the first *mestizo*, Spanish-Indian, was born. The majority of Mexico's 72 million people are now *mestizo*. There's also a large number of Indians, a comparatively small number of Spanish and other Caucasians, and a sprinkling of blacks and Orientals. And there are the combinations of all these races.

Central Mexico was the melting pot. The Spanish moved whole communities – Tlaxcaltecans and Tarascans – north to act as a buffer against hostile Indians. Some of the northern Indians fiercely resisted the intruder, and still do. The Tarahumaras, the Mayas and the Yaquis, in particular, hang on to their old traditions and their tribal lands. In the fastness of the Chiapas highlands the Tzotzils and the Tzeltals also retain their old way of life. The Huastec Indians survive in the mountains. However, most of the descendants of the original tribes of central Mexico live in scattered villages around the Valley of Mexico. They include the Nahuas, the Otomí and the Mazahua tribes.

In southern Mexico, in the lands that no one else covets, live many groups, in the eroded highlands of Guerrero, Oaxaca and Chiapas, and on the thin limestone plateau of the Yucatán peninsula.

How many full-blooded Indians are left? According to official census figures, between 3 and 4 million. But that number represents just the core, those who speak their native Indian tongue at home, have retained their racial purity, and their traditions. They live mostly in the marginal lands, the "zone of refuge." They are of infinite variety and of marked cultural differences. Some have been assimilated by Christianity; others have not. Most of them have learned to exist in tandem with Christianity; a sort of *modus vivendi*, partly Christian, partly Indian. They worship the saints along with their old gods.

What has survived might be said to be a primitive religion with overtones of Catholicism and with emphasis on a harmonious relationship between the physical and the spiritual world. Perhaps what distinguishes most Indians from *mestizos* is their orientation toward the community and not toward the individual. The *mestizo*'s attitude is exactly the opposite; he and his family come first, with the community a distant second. Naturally, the Indians who have kept their culture alive are the ones who are most isolated from the rest of the country.

In the essays that follow we discuss a few of the 50 or more tribes who are among the most authentic descendants of the Indians of old. Their way of life and the things that motivate them make these tribes the most fascinating people of Mexico.

Preceding pages: Independence parade crowd gathers; a young Huichol signals with a horn to announce the return of Peyote pilgrims; Mardi Gras celebrants pause for a breather. **Left**, a Nahua girl, Cuetzalán.

The 50 or so Indian groups in Mexico represent a remarkable contrast to their mixed-blood countrymen, the *mestizos*. There are great differences among the Indians, yet at the same time great similarities. In many parts of Mexico, the *mestizos* and the Indians often look alike. But the difference is there for the perceptive to see: the difference in language, of course; the difference in clothing; but most of all, the difference in their basic attitudes toward life.

The Indian ideal is to come to terms with life and the universe. The *mestizo* ideal is to control life. The Indian tends to accept things passively; the *mestizo* tends to strive to dominate things. The Indian is community-oriented; the *mestizo* is aggressively individualistic. The Indian willingly subjugates his ego; the *mestizo* revels in machismo, and the vibrant personality.

Machismo of the *mestizos*: Mexicans have been examining themselves for generations. It was the Mexican intellectual Samuel Ramos who first took a penetrating look at his countrymen's culture. He said they suffered from a sense of inferiority which they responded to with "virile protest." They used their machismo as the "driftwood to salvation." He did not use the word "macho" but that's what he was driving at. He said the European glories in the pursuit of science, the arts and technology. The *mestizo*, he said, glories in the feeling that he has "a lot of balls."

Ramos blamed the Spanish rule for many of the attitudes still existent. The system of privilege, for instance. People get ahead in Mexico through their connections with a local boss or a powerful national politician. Ramos believed that this personality cult is "as bloodthirsty as the ancient Aztec ritual; it feeds on human victims."

The poet Octavio Paz presents his insight into the country's culture in the *Labyrinth of Solitude*, a book that is essential to anyone who wants to understand the psychological makeup of Mexico. Paz's thesis is that the conduct of the Mexican male is a mask to conceal his solitude. According to Paz, the

Mexican perceives that there are only two attitudes to take when dealing with others. Take advantage of them, or have them take advantage of you. "Screw or be screwed," in the violent language of the street. His honor requires him to face every adversity – even death – with a certain defiance. He must be aggressive and project an image of strength and devil-may-care. He must take the same arrogant attitude toward a business deal, as he does toward a woman. Machismo! To make money is not so important as to declare

his maleness and to exploit his associate. A "macho" must use his power arbitrarily.

The notion goes back a long time. After all, the country was born from the violent clash of Spanish warriors and Indian tribes. The conquistadors raped and pillaged. One woman was essential to their conquest – Doña Malinche, the interpreter-instructor-adviser. She is the Great Traitor – nationalist Mexicans revile her; her name has even entered the vocabulary: *malinchismo* means roughly the preference of all things foreign to anything Mexican. The two essential components of the *mestizo* culture can be summed up by machismo and *malinchismo*.

Left, a *mestiza* displaying the typical mix of Indian and Spanish blood. **Right**, macho man.

The Huichols: The ritualistic Huichol Indians of the rugged Sierra Madre Occidental of northern Jalisco offer a window to Mexico's pre-Columbian past. Anthropologists consider them among the Mexican peoples least affected by Western cultural influences. Their mountain home shut them off from the conquistadors, and missionaries arrived among them belatedly, 200 years after Cortés.

The Huichol have adopted Catholic rituals but with their own embellishment. Some, for example, choose to believe that the biblical Joseph won the right to marry the Virgin Mary by winning a violin-playing contest. Huichol beliefs reflect a Meso-American theology dating back to antiquity. The principal deities are the personalized forces of nature: Tatewari (fire); Nakawe (growth); and Kayaumari (the deer).

Clinging tenaciously to their lifestyle and customs, the Huichols earn a little money by working on the coastal plantations, through the sale of cattle, and by selling their handicrafts. Contact with others, however, affects them very little: they remain Huichols.

In the past, they planted corn and hunted deer. Settlements were generally far apart, sometimes as much as half a day's journey from one another. A myth claims that the gods ordered the Huichols to live apart so that their women wouldn't have the chance to quarrel. A more logical explanation is that they needed to live on slopes where they could plant their corn, beans and squash. Because such fields are scattered, so too are the settlements.

The Huichols hold their most important ceremonies – planting, harvesting, peyote gathering – in a centrally located *tuki*, or round temple. The *tzauririka (*singing shaman) leads the rites. He and the other temple officials are chosen for a five-year term, and almost every male Huichol holds several of these official positions during his lifetime. Besides being the heart of religious life, the *tuki* serves as the center of social life, where the Huichol can seek help and exchange ideas. Before a ceremony, there is often a ritual deer hunt.

There is little interaction between Huichols and *mestizos*, except during the big fiestas at San Andrés. *Mestizos* come to the festivals,

to sell things such as pottery and candy, play music and buy cattle. Huichols sometimes rent land to *mestizos*, who work the land as tenant farmers for half shares.

So far there has been no threat to the Huichol way of life – either from the *mestizos* or the many curious visitors. But the *mestizos* want land for grazing, lumbering and farming and this presents a challenge. To meet it, the Huichols need to find competent and strong leaders and hire the services of professionals, such as lawyers, surveyors and bureaucrats. What will eventually happen depends on the attitude of the government and the forces of economics. If the prices of timber and beef go up sharply, or if minerals are found in the land of the Huichols, then their way of life may be doomed.

There have been some signs of change, with different attitudes penetrating even the Sierra Madre. Some Huichols have picked up *mestizo* dress, and the use of Spanish. They are learning how to bargain shrewdly and even to affect arrogance.

Mexican officials would like to incorporate the Huichols into the mainstream of Mexican life, but they understand that to change the Huichol lifestyle would inevitably entail the disappearance of the culture.

The Huichols are most popularly known in and out of Mexico for their traditional ritual use of peyote (pronounced *pay-ó-te*), a species of thornless, spineless cactus well-known for its hallucinogenic effects.

Ironically, the Huichols can't grow peyote in their homeland; neither the soil nor the climate is right. So they make an annual pilgrimage northeast to the desert of San Luis Potosi to fetch it. A small "dose" – one to four buttons of peyote – takes away hunger, thirst, sexual desire and relieves tiredness. A larger dose – five or more buttons – produces hallucinations.

Before they go on their annual pilgrimage, the Huichol make elaborate preparations that go on for a day and a night. These include making offerings to the gods.

It is 500 km (312 miles) each way from the Huichols' Sierra homeland to the sacred peyote grounds near Real del Catorce in San Luis Potosi. This used to be a 20-day walk but nowadays the Huichol pilgrims walk for a few days from their home *caliguey* (temple), then take a bus or a truck, stopping off to pay tribute at sacred places along the way.

If a bus hurries past a sacred place, without a pause, the pilgrims will throw the offerings out the window as they pass.

One of the rituals of the peyote pilgrimage is the confession of carnal sins. On the fourth or fifth night of the journey, a Huichol pilgrim ties a series of knots in a string of *ixtle* (cactus fiber), one knot for every transgression, and then stands in front of the fire and confesses to any extra curricular sexual activities, detailing names, times and places and finally tossing the knotted string into the fire to gain forgiveness.

Other rituals and customs must also be followed. The Huichol are forbidden most food during the pilgrimage and subsist on

Before the pilgrims return to their families, tribute must be paid to many gods so that crops will bloom and life will be good. It is a small price to pay for the arduous yet exciting journey into peyote country.

Tourists have begun to turn up in Huichol country, especially during Easter Week, the only fixed-date festival in the Huichol calendar. Many are young people attracted by stories of exotic Indians and their peyote. Some of these strangers find the experience among the Huichols fascinating, but many are disappointed.

The Coras: For 200 years from the time of the fall of the Aztec empire, the fierce Cora Indians of Nayarit kept their loosely organ-

plain *tostadas* (dried *tortilla*), dried meat, oranges and generous slugs of alcohol.

It is not easy to find the elusive plant; only its tip peeps up from the ground and its color matches the color of the earth. It takes two or three days to gather some 10 or 15 kg (22–33 lbs). A little is eaten at the site to communicate with their gods; the rest is dried and taken home.

Everyone eats peyote at the homecoming – even the children, who wash it down with a chocolate drink. Shamans take peyote for wisdom to diagnose illness and it is connected with the ceremonies of planting and harvesting, the deer-hunt and the rain god.

ized tribal structure and refused to submit to Spanish arms or to missionary blandishments. Not until 1722 were they defeated. The inhospitable Sierra del Nayar, their homeland in the western range of the Sierra Madres, kept invaders out and allowed them to keep their independence. As the Jesuit missionary Father Ortega wrote: "It [the Cora country] is so wild and frightful to behold in its ruggedness, even more than the arrows of its warlike inhabitants, that it took away the courage of the conquerors, because not only the ridges and the valleys appear inaccessible, but the extended range of towering mountain peaks confused even the eye."

Nuño de Guzmán conquered the lowlands of western Mexico, but left the mountain areas untamed and they remained strongholds of Indian rebellion. Except for the Tarascans, there were no tightly organized political entities in western Mexico which could be quickly overcome by the Spaniards' superior arms. Guzmán had the Tarascan king murdered and the Tarascans accepted the Spaniards as their new tribute-greedy overlords; they were used to submitting. Not so the other tribes in western Mexico who could not be defeated so easily.

The Cora Indians became the most implacable of the rebels in this part of Mexico. Their nextdoor neighbor, the Huichols, hardly figured in this chronicle of resistance, perhaps because they dwelt in an even more inaccessible place and were even less closely organized than the Coras. During the 16th century much of western Mexico was in a state of rebellion and war and the untamed Indians frequently embarked on raids. As a countermeasure, the Spanish moved large groups of submissive Indians, including the Christianized Tlaxcalans, into new communities to act as a barrier against wild tribes. In 1616, the Coras joined in the great Tepehuan rebellion and carried out raids on an increasing scale through the rest of the century.

In vain the missionaries tried to tame the Coras but the Indians refused to give up their gods. Next, the Spanish cut off the Coras' salt trade and sent the Jesuit priest, Margil de Jesús, to make a peace offer. Their delegation was received by a group of musicians, warriors and elders led by Tonati, the sun priest. But though they were polite, the Coras refused to bend to Spanish authority.

Later, some Cora leaders offered to pledge allegiance to Spanish rule if they could keep their lands in perpetuity, pay no tribute and have the right to pursue the salt trade without

paying taxes. But not all Coras were in agreement even about this and the Spanish decided that they must resort to force to teach these rebellious Indians a lesson. The Spaniards' first large-scale expedition achieved only partial success, but in 1722, under Captain Juan Flores de la Torre, they won a clear-cut victory over the Coras. Some survivors fled into the remote mountains but large-scale resistance was over.

The missionaries who followed the army met with the same problems – how to cope with a recalcitrant people – a situation further complicated by the ongoing dispute between the Jesuits and the Franciscans over

Far left, peyote is hung out to dry. **Left**, an elder is honored with a gift of food. **Above**, music is provided by a miniature guitar and violin.

who had the right to save souls. The Jesuits won but only for a time. Less than half a century later the Jesuits were expelled from New Spain and the Franciscans took their place and set up missions in the religious centers. But, except at the time of the big fiestas, these locations were now avoided by the Indians.

The missionaries did succeed in fostering a Spanish-style civil government of sorts among the Indians and the titles that were bestowed on the officers – *gobernador, alcalde, alguacil* – are retained to this day. The missionaries also introduced Easter, but the adamant Coras converted it into something uniquely their own.

could understand only the Cora language.

Even today the Coras (only a few thousand of them remain) live a traditional life, working subsistence agricultural plots and practicing their own kind of religion. Their money comes from cattle and from the sale of their beautifully woven textiles. Like the Huichols, they engage in the ritual use of peyote. The shaman still invokes supernatural beings, and missionaries, who never give up, still try to influence them. The world has crept a little closer, on dirt roads and landing strips for small planes, but the Coras still go on being Coras, aloof, proud and independent.

The Totonacs: A man wearing a brilliantly colored suit is playing a flute and a small

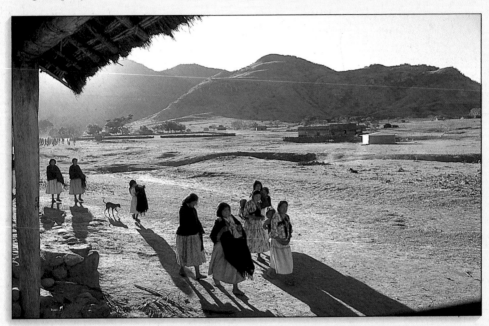

In the final analysis, the missionaries had scant success in taming the men of the mountains and when Manuel Lozada led a rebellion that almost captured Guadalajara, the Cora Indians joined in enthusiastically. At the turn of the century when the Norwegian explorer Carl Lumholtz visited the Coras, he found that to a large degree they still practiced their traditional culture. The Morning Star remained their deity, interceding with the other gods to help Indians in trouble. Lumholtz wrote that the Coras worshipped old stone figures and a large sacred bowl, which was considered to be the patron saint of the community, a mother of the tribe. It

drum at the same time. He is dancing and leaning precariously backwards close to 25 meters (80 ft) up a narrow pole. The trunk sways in the breeze and there is a dramatic moment as the flutist regains his balance.

What is the man doing up the tree? He is the captain of a team and he represents the Sun. He gives a signal and four men who have been sitting at his feet drop backwards. Wait a minute. They do not fall; they are securely tied with a stout rope around their waists. They represent the four essential elements: earth, air, fire and water. They glide 13 turns around the pole, moving out farther and farther, until they reach the ground, flip themselves erect, and land feet first. Four men do 13 circles each. That adds up to 52 turns, the magic number, and the number of years in the sacred pre-Columbian century.

This ritual is known as "Voladores de Papantla." It was started by the Totonac Indians and has been adopted by other Indian tribes. The Totonacs, who number perhaps 150,000, have maintained much of their rich cultural tradition. They live in the tropical coastal lands of Veracruz and in the cool highlands of the Sierra Madre of Puebla, lands where irrigation is not needed but a lot of hard manual labor is.

The Totonacs trace their ancestry back to one of the most distinguished of the ancient

cannons over the mountain passes. Because they aided the Spanish, the Totonacs were given a small measure of autonomy during early colonial rule. They kept their communal lands; their leaders were permitted to exercise some power. During colonial times the land of the Totonacs yielded much wealth: they grew sugar cane, tobacco, coffee and vanilla. But eventually they were forced into labor on the Spanish-owned estates.

They were converted to Catholicism, but they reinterpreted its rituals. "Voladores de Papantla," for example, is performed on the anniversary of St Francis' birth but involves pre-Christian rituals. Ancient ways still dictate how the tree is chosen, cut and trans-

pre-Columbian civilizations. In ancient times they excelled at pottery-making, stone sculpture and architecture. It was they who built the graceful Pyramid of the Niches at El Tajín. They were subjugated by the Aztecs, to whom they paid heavy tribute, who took Totonacs for human sacrifice.

Cortés landed on the coast inhabited by the Totonacs and negotiated an alliance with their leader. Thus Totonacs served as porters for Cortés's army, lugging supplies and heavy

Left, Cora religious and civic centers lie in the few flat areas in the Sierras. **Above**, a group of Coras, painted black, celebrate Easter.

ported. But the blessing for the tree and the dancers is performed in church and often the tree, or pole, is set up just outside.

When the pole is erected the Totonacs combine Christian purification rituals with their own magical incantations and offerings of food and liquor. These precautions are to ensure that the pole will not take any performers as victims. As a final insurance measure, a live turkey is dropped into the post hole to "receive" the pole. This gobbling fowl is thus ritually crushed as a tree trunk is hoisted into its final position.

The ritual is considered a specialty of the Papantla area of Veracruz. It is a comment on

the times that the dancers have had to take steps to organize themselves into a union to protect their economic interests (they perform mostly for visitors) and to protect the authenticity of the performance. (One must regard skeptically the purity of the dance performed in, say, the Acapulco Center.)

Outside of Acapulco, your best bet to see a performance of the "voladores" is near Papantla (Veracruz), in the complex of ruins at El Tajín. A tall, permanent pole has been erected next to the Pyramid of the Niches and teams of Totonacs, usually from Papantla, perform whenever there are enough people to watch. For a reasonable amount of money, you can even arrange a private performance.

The Totonacs live a precarious existence, caught up between their traditional lifestyle and the intrusion of the modern world. The discovery of oil combined with large-scale cattle-raising has pushed them off the land. They live on the basic diet of the Indians of Mexico – corn, beans and chili, supplemented with vegetables and wild plants. Often wild plants are their only available medicine. They usually kill and eat domestic animals only during fiestas.

The Seris: Along with the Lacandones, the Seris are among the smallest Mexican Indian tribes. After centuries of catastrophic contact with the white man's civilization, most of the tribe has died off. In 1600, there were some 5,000 Seris living, but by 1930 only about 175 remained. At present there are approximately 500. The survivors have clung to some of their traditions in a part of their homeland on the Gulf of California in western Sonora.

Seris – the word means "those who live in the sand" – comprise one of six bands forming an ethnic group known as the Kunkaahac, meaning "our great mother race." They lived in the southern part of the Arizona-Sonora desert, along the Gulf coast, and on Tiburon island in the Gulf. Hunters and fishermen, they put out to sea in reed boats, killing giant sea turtles with ironwood spears.

In 1685, Father Eusebio Kino visited them on the shore opposite Tiburón island. He liked them and they liked him, but when he asked to be assigned to the Seris as a missionary he was sent instead to the Upper Pimas. A German Jesuit, Father Gilg, was given the

job of settling and converting the Seris, then calculated to number around 3,000. He was faced with many problems, not the least of which was the small amount of land suitable for agriculture in the semi-desert.

His efforts to convert them were also hard work: "They [the Seris] live," he said, "without God, without faith and without houses, like cattle. Just like they have no religious worship, so too one finds not even the shadow of any idolatry among them, since they have never known or adored either a true or a false deity." That was not quite true, of course. The Seris did have a local religion, built around animal deities, headed by the turtle and the pelican. Also, they worshipped the

sun and the moon.

Father Gilg denigrated the Indians for their lack of understanding of the Holy Sacrament and the Christian mysteries of faith, and had little success in teaching them to live like good, obedient subjects and work happily for their white overlords. In fact, the Seris, a proud people, rebelled. In 1662 a band of several hundred Seris fought the Spanish until the last Indian man and woman were killed. Their children were then distributed to the mission villages.

By 1742 only about one-third of the Seris had accepted a settled life in a mission. When the Spanish built a fort at Pitic in 1748 their

Left, Voladores in action. **Right**, a Seri woman.

efforts to persuade Seris to settle on land nearby met with a measure of success. But when the whites took the land from the Indians, the Seris protested, albeit peacefully. Thereupon the Spaniards arrested 80 families and shipped the women off to Guatemala and elsewhere. Inflamed, the Seris joined the Pimas and destroyed the mission at Guaymas, then carried out raids on Spanish settlements. However, by 1769 a shortage of food had weakened their will to fight and many Seris surrendered, agreeing to submit to Christianity and attend daily Mass.

In 1854, a Seri raiding party operating on the Guaymas-Hermosillo road captured a girl named Dolores Casanova, daughter of a prominent Guaymas family. Known thereafter by her nickname Lola, she took up the Indian way of life and became known as the "Queen of the Seris." She was the subject of many tales. Even though the shaman Coyote-Iguana had killed her father, Lola followed him to Tiburón island and had several children by him.

Near the end of the 19th century there were only some 500 Seris still carrying out raids. The government mounted a campaign against them and rounded up about 150. A rancher named Encinas set up a large cattle range and provided jobs and instruction for the Seris. Unfortunately, the ranch happened to be in a place where the Seris had traditionally hunted deer and rabbit and they felt that they could now "hunt" cattle, too. That was the background of the 10-year Encinas War between cowboys and Seris. Heavy penalties were set: for every head of cattle the Seris rustled, a Seri was executed.

By 1920, only a few of the remaining Seris were nomad hunters. Some settled temporarily outside a small Mexican village on Kino Bay and became fishermen. There was a boom in the market for shark livers in the 1930s, so the Seris went shark hunting.

Then came the 1950s and another source of income: wealthy Americans who had discovered the great sports fishing off Kino Bay. By then many organizations were taking an interest in the Seris. Anthropologists began to study them; linguists translated the New Testament into the Seri language; and Protestant missionaries made nominal Christians out of them, prohibiting their custom of painting their faces in the process – much to the dismay of visitors and anthropologists.

Slowly the Seris appeared to prosper and increase. These days they earn money by selling fish, shell necklaces and beautiful ironwood carvings of animals.

The main group of Seris (about 300 people) lives at Desemboque. They still weave heavy, decorative baskets from a fiber called *torote* and fashion pottery and ceramic figurines. They are also good mechanics. It is said that a century ago they could shape a piece of equipment for their Mauser rifles, using only a file for a tool. Their skill is still alive and they use it to keep their outboard motors in good repair.

The Lacandones: Another tribe that has retained its cultural identity is the Lacandones,

who up until comparatively recently escaped the influence of Western civilization by living in the Chiapas jungle. However, over the years, lumbermen, hunters, merchants and researchers traded with the Lacandones, exchanging alcohol, firearms, food and clothing for precious wood, tobacco, and chicle. These days tourists pay the picturesque Indians to pose for photographs.

The Lacandones live in two- or three-family units, worshipping their old gods and eking out a living from the jungle. Though the tribe is very small, it is still somewhat protected by its formidable surroundings.

The Lacandones were hardly heard of until

the French anthropologist Jacques Soutstell and his wife, Georgette, visited them in 1933. Soustelle called their habitat a green hell, hard to get into and equally difficult to get out of. Soustelle reported that no sun penetrated the thick carpeting and the ground was a mass of rotting vegetation that made even walking a struggle. Yet the Lacandones moved about easily. The trees looked tortured, something out of a nightmare, and over all towered the giant mahogany. There were innumerable pools of water which never gave off a reflection because the sun rarely penetrated below and few animals, except for chattering monkeys. Strangely, there were very few insects, except on river banks.

tant deity is the Sun God, who is accompanied by other gods in a complex mythology which father passes on to son. They believe the Sun passes the night in the subterranean world, in a house of stone where he eats and drinks like a human being. They perform rituals and give offerings to ensure that the he will appear promptly next morning.

To the Lacandones the old Mayan ceremonial centers are objects of special veneration. Because they believe that the god Atchakyum lives in the Yaxchilan complex, small groups go there to offer incense and food.

Soustelle found the Lacandones living in small clearings, walled in by jungle, with never more than a dozen people to a commu-

Because the Lacandones fended for themselves for so long, they are well adapted to their environment. They know which plants are beneficial and which are harmful. By the time a boy is 12 years old, he knows how to survive in the jungle.

The word Lacandon comes from *Lacantun,* meaning Great Rock, an island in Lake Miramar and the home of the Lacandones' ancestors, who were a branch of the Itzae Mayas. To the Lacandones the most impor-

Left, a Lacandone smokes a home-made cigar. **Above**, a photograph of Lacandones taken by 19th-century French explorer Desiré Charnay.

nity. They planted cotton, tobacco, chili, corn, yuccas and bananas, using the destructive slash-and-burn technique to clear the land, on which they then grew crops for three or four years before it was exhausted and they had to move on.

The Lacandones looked for places in the jungle that were thought favorable for women's fertility, but because of a lack of womenfolk there were few children. Even today men sometimes "marry" infant girls, with the husband living in his father-in-law's house and working for him for a number of years. As soon as the child grows up, she cooks for her husband. The Lacandones' concept of wedded life is more about eating together than sleeping together.

The Lacandones used to do a lot of hunting with bow and feathered, silex-tipped arrows. Their quarry was usually monkeys, wild turkeys or wild pigs. The jungle not being the healthiest place in the world to live, the Lacandones suffer from malaria and rheumatism induced by the dampness. They also succumb readily to white man's diseases and germs, often dying of influenza and even from a common cold. No visitor with a cold is allowed into their country.

Their contact with white men began in earnest during the latter part of the 19th century, when mahogany became a sought-

nimble fingers, the soft clay quickly took shape. Soon a jolly demon appeared under her subtle touch, to take his place in her work: five devils having a party. Later she painted and fired the sculpture in her backyard kiln and took it to market.

The Tarascan village of Ocumicho specializes in making clay devils in great variety: devils riding motorcycles, devils shaped in the form of a fish, devils fighting with snakes. Tarascans have been renowned artisans since pre-Columbian times.

Their home is in northern Michoacán around Lake Pátzcuaro and to the west on the *meseta* (plateau) of Tarasca. Census figures vary widely but there are probably around

after material and access roads were built. Some Lacandones worked for lumber companies to earn money to buy axes, machetes, firearms and liquor.

The few Lacandones who have managed to survive to the present day have seen dramatic changes during the last few years. A dirt road (dry-season only) gives them access to Palenque. They were given legal *ejido* title to vast tracts of their jungle by former president Luis Echeverría. With money received from lumbering concessions, they have bought trucks, clothing and other manufactured goods.

The Tarascans: Deftly handled by the girl's

80,000 who still speak their native language.

Today, Tarascos are known as fishermen and, particularly, as craftsmen, making pottery, copperware, lacquered bowls and trays, wool weavings, guitars, leather goods, wood masks, hats, mats and furniture. Many villages have a specialty: Santa Clara, copperware; Ihuatzio, rush mats; Patamban, green pottery; Paracho, guitars.

Prior to the arrival of the Spanish, the Tarascans had welded together a militaristic empire strong enough to check the Aztec war machine. Perhaps because they were a hardy people, the Aztecs considered them as relations but, in truth, the Tarascan language is like no other Indian language. Some people have tried to trace them to a Peruvian tribe, but this seems unlikely. What we do know comes largely from *The Chronicles of Michoacán,* an illustrated document by a Franciscan monk.

Shortly after the Spanish conquest, the Tarascans found a great friend and protector in Don Vasco de Quiroga. A lawyer and personal friend of the Spanish monarch, he was appointed to Mexico's Royal High Court of Justice, which had condemned Nuño de Guzmán for his assassination of the Tarascan king, Tangaxoan. Consecrated as priest and bishop on the same day, Quiroga went to Michoacán to Christianize the Tarascans and

pursue their crafts. They created intricate feather mosaics for him and modeled figures of their deities from a paste made of pulverized cornstalks and orchid extract, so light in weight they could be carried into battle. Perhaps it was Father Quiroga who encouraged the Indians to fashion corn paste figures of Christ.

During colonial days the Tarascans were forced to adapt, caught between Christian strictness and Spanish greed. Trade was controlled by Spanish merchants, and no direct exchange of goods between Indian villages was permitted. All goods had to pass through markets in white-dominated towns.

Carl Lumholtz, a Norwegian explorer and

protect them from the Spanish landlords.

Father Quiroga organized hospitals in the missions. He took some Tarascans to Spain to show people they were human beings and deserved humane treatment, always acting with kindness and courtesy towards them. They have never forgotten him. He was awarded the affectionate nickname "Tata" (father). Only one other white man has earned that mark of respect: former president Lázaro Cárdenas, himself from Michoacán.

Tata Quiroga encouraged the Tarascans to

Left, a Tarascan market. **Above**, Lake Pátzcuaro has many Tarascan villages along its shores.

chronicler of Indian tribes, traveled through the Tarasco land at the beginning of the 20th century. He noted how the Tarascans had adapted to their new religion. Farmers, for example, buried stone replicas of their old deities in the fields to ensure a good crop, while at the same time appealing to San Mateo (Saint Matthew), who was responsible for fruitful harvests.

Lumholtz observed that the Tarascans were not able to live solely from the land. Many had to devote themselves to making handicrafts, which was exhausting and poorly paid work. There were no buying and selling cooperatives and the artisans had to pay a high price for supplies. Yet the Tarascans persisted with their crafts, and today they continue to demonstrate their skills. A common aim of Tarascan craftsmen is to have enough money to fulfill what is called their "cargo," a post of honor bringing prestige to the holder, who is responsible for arranging and paying for fiestas. In order to finance such activities, craftsmen usually step up production prior to a celebration.

In his effort to help the Tarascans, President Cárdenas tried to foster a sense of self-sufficiency. His idea was that villagers could participate in the national economy while retaining their traditional way of life. It was a dream that for many reasons has not worked

Spaniards, the Tarahumaras learned about the white man from Jesuits at the beginning of the 17th century. At first the Tarahumaras were curious and meetings were peaceful, but in 1631 silver was found in southern Chihuahua and, inevitably, the rush was on. The Spaniards needed labor for the mine and forced the Tarahumaras to work. This triggered a series of revolts that were to last for decades.

Some of the bloodiest revolts and reprisals in the history of Mexico took place in Tarahumara country. The first rebellion was led by Teporaca in 1648 and the first victims were missionaries. The Jesuits had tried to stop mistreatment of the Indians but had had

out satisfactorily. Many Tarascan men must seek work outside their villages in order to make a living. Some even make the long trek across the border to seek work in the US.

Tarahumaras: Chihuahua's sierras provide a place of refuge for the Tarahumara Indians who refuse to accept the Mexican way of life. For the Tarahumaras, who wanted to keep their own culture, there were only two choices when the Spanish invaded: to fight and die, or retreat into the mountains. There are now about 50,000 Tarahumaras living in a 50,000-sq. km (19,3000-sq. mile) region of the Sierra Madres in northwest Chihuahua.

Aside from fleeting contact with a few

little success. To the Tarahumara, however, the enemy was the white man and missionaries were white. In the intensity of their hatred, the Indians slew the missionaries and mutilated their bodies.

There was constant war. Many bands of Indians preferred death to surrender; others retreated into the sierras. To survive, some accepted a superficial form of Christianity and were partially assimilated into the white man's culture, at the lowest rung.

Mexican independence brought no relief to the Tarahumaras. Spanish power was gone but the Mexican government didn't have the funds to help and was preoccupied elsewhere. Thereupon the Apaches began to raid Tarahumara settlements. More trouble came. A law of 1825 opened unused land to colonization and onto the best lands of the Tarahumaras poured an army of landless.

The Norwegian explorer, Carl Lumholtz, reported that the missionaries' efforts to induce the Tarahumaras to live in communities were largely unsuccessful, explaining that they exerted only slight influence on the Indians, since many areas received only one visit by a priest each year. The Tarahumara ritual adoption of Christianity retained an aboriginal flavor, with Christ and the Virgin Mary simply becoming another important male and female in the Tarahumara pantheon.

arduous feat is by abstaining from drinking their favorite *tesguino,* a corn brew.

Magic also plays a role. According to their unusual pharmacopoeia, the best remedy for a weakened spirit is to smoke a mixture of tobacco, dried turtle and bat blood.

Tarahumaras are also a betting people: old men may risk their meager flock of goats, sheep or cattle on the outcome of a race.

As with other Indian groups in the north of Mexico, the Tarahumaras still make ritual use of peyote. Lumholtz was told that when God left the earth to live in Heaven, he left peyote as a remedy for his people and as a safeguard against witchcraft. When applied externally, it was considered to be a good

theon. The Catholic calendar was tacked on to the aboriginal calendar.

The Tarahumaras are known as great runners – not sprinters but long-distance runners, some running 180 km (100 miles) nonstop (it's no surprise that the Tarahumaras should call themselves *Rar'amuri* meaning "The People With a Light Foot"). Races are held between two teams of up to 20 runners, who kick a wooden ball as they run, day and night. One of the ways they train for such an

Far left, a Tarascan woman mending nets. **Left**, some Tarahumaras still live in cave dwellings. **Above**, two Tarahumara men celebrate Easter.

treatment for snake bite, burns, wounds and rheumatism. The plant was held sacred and offerings had to be made to it to ensure that it would not provoke insanity.

At present, most Tarahumaras live in an enclave in the Sierra Madre Occidental, with perhaps 20 percent of them retaining their traditional way of life. Their basic difference from other Mexican Indian types is their desire to isolate themselves.

There is now a National Indian Council, and thousands come to large congresses organized by the government. Some of the local leaders demand legal titles to their land and request schools and teachers, better roads, telephones, doctors and medicine, legal help, control over their forestry resources and self-determination on a local level. But other community leaders have no desire to integrate and don't even want schools or roads.

Tzotzils and Tzeltals: In the highlands of Chiapas, near San Cristóbal de las Casas, some 200,000 Indians live, divided almost evenly between the Tzotzils and the Tzeltals, who both speak Mayan dialects. They have been able to keep aloof from other Mexicans and retain their old way of life because they are stubborn, tough-fibered and committed.

Theirs is marvelous country. A writer speaks of passing through "layers of cold before entering the cool mountain sunshine

of the Chiapas highlands." The Tzeltals live on the lower slopes of Chiapas's central mountains while most of the Tzotzils live in the same area above the 1,500-meter (5,000-ft) line. Both tribes keep their distinctive style of dress and cultural and social traits.

Since there is no tribal consciousness, identity and a sense of belonging are imparted by the community, which is made up of a central village and outlying farms, often a steep climb, several hours away. The civil officials reside in town with their families, while most of the others live in the nearby hills. The village comes noisily alive only for Sunday market and the periodic fiestas. The key to

this harmony is that each individual has status in the community. An individual lives on good terms with his fellows and all supernatural beings – the traditional gods, ancestral spirits, and saints that the Spanish introduced. The villagers offer food, incense and flowers to these gods. If someone leaves the community, he is considered a traitor.

The Spaniards savagely exploited these Indians. Their lands were seized and they were forced to work on plantations. During colonial times, when no proper roads existed, the Tzeltals were used as porters. They would carry heavy loads to Veracruz, almost 1,000 km (625 miles) away. Many died from the debilitating heat of the lowlands. If they rebelled they were put down ruthlessly.

Relations between the Indians and the Catholic Church were often strained and marked by intolerance. Few of the early missionaries tried to understand the traditional Indian rites; they sought to break up the Indian idols, baptize the heathens, and convince them to accept an inferior status and serve the Spanish. Their reward would come, they said, in the hereafter.

Such treatment was bound to spark rebellion. With only a few exceptions, the Church backed the exploitation of the Indians. There was, however, the great benefactor, Father Bartolomé de las Casas, who defended the rights of the Indians. By and large, the missionaries led a life of ease, even of luxury, and sometimes they paid for their indolence. Priests were killed during bloody rebellions which flared periodically in Chiapas.

These uprisings were always local affairs – Tzotzils and Tzeltals could never get together and wage military action on a large scale. The uprisings of 1994 may have more impact for they have at least shown the world how badly many Indians are still treated. Most of the time, however, they have meekly followed the orders of the Church. In public, the Tzeltals venerate Christ as God, but in their homes they sometimes also worship Chulmetic, goddess of earth. They also believe in Uch, a supernatural being who helps make the corn grow. The Tzotzils believe in Hz'k'al, a phantasm who is black and has a penis 1 meter (3 feet) long. Both the Tzeltals and the Tzotzils have established a *modus vivendi,* with Christianity a live-and-let-live philosophy.

Some Tzotzils believe that the saints and

the gods hold periodic meetings at which time they decide whether to punish human beings by visiting upon them an ailment or by bringing on a bad crop. The Indians believe that the celebration of Mass is a community obligation to the saints. Their civil authorities visit the dwelling places of the supernatural beings – the mountains, caverns, springs – where they pray, play music and appease the gods with food and drink. A man's first and foremost obligation is to plant and care for his field of corn, for it is his relation with corn that distinguishes him from the animals. These Indians consider it a waste of time to try to grow anything other than corn and despair of agronomists who

for these people. Sometimes the Indians seek to emulate the culture of the *ladinos*, who once exploited them. Some rural Indian schoolteachers serve as examples of this disturbing phenomenon. Often a teacher denies knowledge of his own language and refuses to wear native clothing or to keep the Indian faith. But even though he may be barely literate, a teacher exudes an aura of prestige, for reading and writing are magical arts to the Indians. So the ill-taught teacher is respected, even venerated, and provides a model for other Indians.

It is once again a repeat of an old fallacy: whatever comes from the "outside" is better than the indigenous. Still, there are Indians

want them to raise a variety of crops. The Indians believe that a man must provide sustenance for his family from his corn crop, with enough left over to contribute to fiestas.

In the Chiapas highlands the visitor will see some of the most gorgeous costumes in Mexico, such as finely embroidered blouses and soft woolen shawls. The Zinacantec men wear red cotton ponchos and straw hats festooned in ribbons. The women go barefoot. None like to be photographed.

Cultural assimilation is an acute problem

who see for themselves the flaw in this reasoning and recognize and cherish the value of their traditions. Thanks to them, the Tzotzil and Tzeltal communities survive.

The author B. Traven wrote with great sympathy for the Mexican Indians. He said they still recognize that "certain immaterial matters such as the infinite beauty of wild flowers, or the possession of a little desert-like place, or riding an Indian pony into the rising sun early on a tropical morning, or journeying at night by a creaking *carreta* with a full moon popping up between the large horns of the bullocks... are worth more than certain amounts of money."

Left, A Tzeltal official. <u>**Above**</u>, drinking is an essential part of Tzeltal rituals.

The art produced in Mexico before the conquest (1521) remains one of the most fascinating branches in the vast realm of man's imagination. Ancient and exotic, yet at the same time refreshingly contemporary and attractive to modern taste, Mexican art of the Indian times is both visually handsome and conceptually intriguing. Both the art lover and the historian-archaeologist find it an endless source of wonder.

Created in isolation, with no close connection to external influences, Mexican Indian art offers a remarkable level of quality and unity. Like Egyptian and Chinese art, it has a feeling of permanence.

Pre-Columbian art is widely accepted today but this was not always so. At first Europeans misunderstood Mexican art and were even horrified by it. The Spanish conquerors believed it to be the work of the devil and had no qualms about destroying it. They appreciated only jewelry, for obvious reasons. Mexican art, they felt, was inferior, childish and ugly to the point of monstrosity.

The appreciation of pre-Columbian art was part of the process of the growth of nationalism. Both national identity and cultural pride found a prestigious symbol in the neglected art of the Indians.

Miracles of the Gods: Indian shapes are found universally in Mexico today – in interior decoration, architecture, jewelry, coins, clothing design, even in advertising. But that does not necessarily mean that pre-Columbian art is liked and enjoyed. However, it does have a growing acceptance and has ceased to be a "curiosity." The people of Mexico are discovering this rich treasure of beautiful and meaningful, though strange, shapes – homages paid to forgotten old gods with unpronounceable names. Almost all Mexican pre-Columbian art is religious. Its purely visual and formal values are rich and its power of suggestion is strong.

Acceptance of this art is first credited to eccentric foreigners who fell under its spell, one of the earliest of whom was Sir Edward King. Obsessed with the codices, or books,

made by the Indians, he spent his fortune reproducing them. The American journalist John Lloyd Stephens and the British artist Frederick Catherwood teamed up to record their experiences of exploring the Mayan cities in the classic *Incidents of Travel in Central America, Chiapas and Yucatán.* Many other writers have also visited the ancient sites and left their impressions, including Aldous Huxley, André Malraux, D.H. Lawrence, Jacques Soustell, B. Traven and Evelyn Waugh.

Mexican Indian art is the product of small, isolated tribesmen who inhabited a difficult country. Although the highland area, the *altiplano* of central Mexico, seems suitable for human survival, in actuality it does not have rich soil and the primitive agriculture of the day could not provide sustenance for a growing population. Yet against all odds, many cultures did flourish and left countless monuments as tribute to their genius. Art flourished after an agricultural base was established to support the society.

Consider the technique of producing pre-Columbian art. Working without shaping tools or machines, they produced some of the most polished and spectacular works of art in the world. There is nothing "primitive," technically speaking, about pre-Columbian art. Sometimes the virtuosity, such as that exhibited by the crystal rock jewelry or obsidian mirrors, is incredible. No wonder skill in the arts was considered one of the moral virtues, one of the ways to religious fulfillment.

The Olmecs were the first Mexican artists. Their development dates from 1500 BC. The colossal heads they produced – strong, silent, expressive – present the earliest portrait of American man. Although they have negroid features, the Olmec figurines represent an Asiatic-looking people, which serves to compound the mystery of the Olmecs.

According to Laurette Séjourn (*Burning Water*), symbolic language was first developed by the Olmecs, and, afterward spread all over Mexico. The Olmecs developed a strong, centralized organization closely identified with religion. The chief god was the Jaguar, which apparently served as a symbol of the Earth. It is abundantly represented as

Preceding pages: a Huichol Indian concentrates on a yarn painting. **Left,** a huge Olmec head.

a combination of man and beast, and was the first in the fantastic gallery of Mexican gods, hybrids of man and animals.

Consider the pyramid. This beautiful, simple and strong architectural shape that is so assertive and forbidding among the Aztecs, so eloquent and spiritual in Teotihuacán, and so exquisite and baroque among the Maya, is an Olmec invention. In the beginning a pyramid was a simple mound covered with roughly cut stone. It was placed in front of an open square, a bulky pedestal to elevate a small temple where the priests could pray and perform their rituals.

These Mexican temples were simple rooms which sometimes also served as astronomical observatories. It was in the temples that human sacrifice took place, making the steps ascending the pyramid slippery with blood.

The pyramid also performed a symbolic function. It represented a mountain, one of the universal symbols of mankind. In primitive religions the mountain has often had a strong symbolic appeal. Even in the Judeo-Christian tradition there is Sinai, Zion, Tabor and Golgotha. The mountain is the point of contact between earth and heaven, the doorway to the sky, and the natural dwelling place of the gods. Hidden sometimes by cloud, every now and then it erupts unpredictably. So, in Mexico, great efforts were made to construct artificial mountains.

The Indians built thousands of pyramids, some plain and homely, some proud and magnificent. They built them in the jungle and up high valleys. These pyramids were not primarily burial places and do not seem to possess the same precise and meaningful geometry of the great Egyptian pyramids. Nor are they very sophisticated from an engineering point of view, being little more than huge mud mounds covered with stone. Nevertheless they are among the most intriguing buildings of mankind.

The first Mexican pyramid was built by the Olmecs at La Venta, which, though not a very impressive or beautiful place, is a good example of a city with a ceremonial center.

Mexican cities were built in accordance with a precise astronomical layout. Around these sophisticated centers people lived in humble, makeshift towns. The tradition seems to endure: Mexicans often combine a penchant for making their public buildings rich and impressive, while at the same time disregarding personal comfort.

The Olmecs started the art of sculpture in stone. They also developed the "mirror" arts which Mexicans so cherish, the making of fine jewelry and ceramics. In Mexico some of the most beautiful creations of art are the work of the potter or the goldsmith. The Olmecs were the first to use the "green stone" we call jade – translucent, mysterious, spiritual.

The Olmecs carved the jade figurines with mask-like faces on exhibit at the National Museum of Anthropology in Mexico City. The mask is another Mexican art specialty. Produced most likely for funerary use, it does not portray a person, nor is it a playful variation of the human face, but rather it is something like a portrait of wisdom. For centuries stone carvers endeavored to reproduce, not human features, but a spirit of serenity, a man who has struggled to become his own master.

Ancient, abandoned cities: Mexico is a country of ancient, abandoned cities, the most famous of which is the great ceremonial center of Teotihuacán. The city was built along a wide street, or succession of plazas, known as *Micaotli*, or the Avenue of the Dead, one of the most beautiful urban axes in the world. The Avenue starts at the huge square known as the citadel, with the pyramid of Quetzalcóatl covered with masks. At its other end is the Pyramid of the Moon and the Quetzalpapalotl palace, an ornate building that has been restored.

Centrally located along Micaotli is the sovereign of all Mexican pyramids, the Pyramid of the Sun, a perfect example of classical pre-Columbian architecture which manages to convey a feeling of grandeur that no other pyramid in Mexico can match. Perhaps this is due to its clever design of inclined planes and proportions. In contrast to the rich and refined art of the Mayas, or the strong, almost brutal art of the Aztecs, the art from Teotihuacán achieves the perfect simplicity associated with classicism.

After the fall of Teotihuacán, around AD 800, came a period of decline in central Mexico life which lasted until the Aztecs founded their capital city, Tenochtitlán. During that period other centers prospered, then

Left, Coatlicue, the Aztec goddess of the Earth and mother of the ferocious Huitzilopochtli.

fell. Such was the fate of Tula, Xochicalco and Texcoco. Tula, 128 km (80 miles) north of Mexico City, is particularly attractive. The main building, the Temple of the Warriors, is crowned with four Atlantean figures, almost 3 meters (10 ft) high. These warrior figures, which are among the most famous examples of pre-Columbian sculpture, are supposed to be the entrance columns or caryatids of a long-destroyed temple. They represent a remarkable accomplishment, blending sculptural expression with the simple geometry of the column.

From the sculpture we learn how the men of Tula dressed: in loincloth, sandals and a feather hat. (In winter, a toga-like cotton cape was added.) The simplicity of their dress contrasts with their elaborate jewelry.

The Aztecs were not only brave warriors and competent merchants; they were also among the most sensitive of artists. The great paradox is that they blended the soul of the poet with the heart of the barbarian. They were devotees of the cruel ritual of human sacrifice, tearing out the hearts of humans to appease the gods. The Indian religions believed in human sacrifice as a bribe to induce the gods to stay on the job and keep the world spinning. This horrific custom is expressed in their arts: Aztec architecture and sculpture convey a disquieting strength, verging at times on brutality.

In contrast with the happy beauty of the Mayas or with western Mexican art, the Aztec forms portray deep, violently moving beauty with undeniably barbaric undertones. The Aztec gods were doubtless among the ugliest in the world. Gaze, for example, upon Coatlicue, mother of the Aztec god of Sun and War, Huitzilopochtli. Her monumental stone portrait, more than 2½ meters (8½ ft) high, an Aztec masterpiece, was found in the 19th century as workmen dug a ditch for a water main.

Coatlicue's statue depicts the quintessential Aztec monster-god, basically the body of an old woman with flaccid breasts, which is all we can see of her body. (Mexican art is not concerned with the human body as an object of beauty.) The rest is covered with an arrangement of symbols. Instead of a head, there is a face formed by a pair of rattlesnake heads, the rattlesnake being a symbol of changing Earth, a creature that changes its skin regularly. Coatlicue's chest is covered with the hearts and hands of those who were sacrificed on the altar. Her arms are in the shape of serpents; her navel is hidden behind a skull. She is known as Our Lady of the Serpent-Skirt.

The strength of Aztec art is exemplified by two sculptures at the National Museum of Anthropology in Mexico City. They are minor works of art and not famous, but they are superb. One is a receptacle shaped like a jaguar. Its Aztec name is Ocelocuauhxicalli, or jaw-breaker. On the back of the sculpture is a cavity in which sacrificial hearts were placed. The stone carving is about 1 meter (3 ft) high, the body smooth and rounded, incredibly strong and simple. Yet the jaws, which bare enormous teeth, inspire the same sense of terror and awe that one feels when viewing the Coatlicue sculpture.

Xiuhcóatl, housed in the same museum, is a fire-serpent crowned with stars who escorted the Sun on his daily rounds. Three meters (10 ft) tall, Xiuhcóatl is a strong and skillful composition of rounded shapes creating circular movement. At its center is the circle of the serpent's eye whose geometric simplicity emphasizes the abstract quality of the sculpture.

Strength is also the predominant element of the most celebrated of Aztec works of art, the Sun Stone or Aztec Calendar. This giant monolith (almost 4 meters/13 ft in diameter) is the distillation of Aztec astronomic knowledge and there are countless interpretations of its hidden meaning. At the center it exhibits the face of the impassive Sun God surrounded by successive rings containing astronomical symbols. The last ring is formed by two fire-serpents facing each other.

Apart from being skilled sculptors, the Aztecs were extraordinary potters, jewelers and painters whose books – the codices, on deer skin – are among the most beautiful ever produced. But perhaps the greatest masterpiece of Aztec art was the city they built in the middle of the lake, the proud center of their empire.

Gifted western ceramicists: The Indians of western Mexico left little sculpture or architecture, no painting and no ceremonial centers of importance. Indeed western Mexican art is just a collection of pots and small sculptural ceramics. Lacking the refinement of the Mayans or the technical sophistication of the Oaxacans, the work of the potters of the west is distinctive, thanks to simplicity and cleanliness of design and to the joyfulness expressed – a feeling absent from earlier Mexican art, which devoted itself to religion and cosmic preoccupations. The art of the west is concerned with everyday life and the small joys and pleasures inherent in everyday living. Some primitively sculpted figurines depict scenes from the daily life of common people in the villages: a house, a fire, and people gathered around, obviously engaged in that most human of occupations – gossiping.

Erotic art is virtually absent in old Mexico. No sculpture or figure of Venus or Apollo is to be found. Sex was obviously a strictly controlled commodity. One of the most com-

ultimate purpose of these niches is unknown but they were used to house wood-burning braziers which, when lit, must have given the pyramid a fantastic look.

Little is known of the Huastecs and the Totonacs, but the art objects they left are both mysterious and magnificent. These are the so-called "palms," "axes" and "yokes." The palms were breastplates, cumbersome and uncomfortable, while the taxes and yokes relate to a ball game, a mixture of ritual and sport, played at practically all ceremonial centers in ancient Mexico. The best preserved field – it is shaped like the letter "H" – can be seen at Chichén-Itzá in Mayan country. The players used a heavy rubber

mon models for western Mexican art was the dog, or rather the native Mexican dog, the *itzucuintl*: plump, hairless, and said to be very tasty. Being the chief attraction at many a banquet, the *itzucuintl* is almost extinct.

Tajín's pyramid: The Huastecs, who inhabited the northern half of the Gulf region, left one of the most magnificent sites of pre-Columbian Mexico: Tajín. Now covered in jungle, it was a major metropolis around AD 500. The main surviving structure, the Pyramid of the Niches, was around 18 meters (60 ft) high and indented in 365 places. The

Above, Toltec carving of Chacmool.

ball slightly larger than the modern-day softball. The ball, which could be propelled only with knees, hips and elbows, had to be passed through a stone ring, placed high on one of the walls surrounding the grounds. The ball game, it is assumed, was a symbol of astronomical movement and the losers are believed to have been enslaved or even sacrificed to the gods.

Also at the National Museum of Anthropology is the masterpiece of Huastec sculpture: the tall, slender figure of a young man, believed to be a portrayal of Quetzalcóatl, the ancient deity. There is a delightful contrast between the parts of his body that are

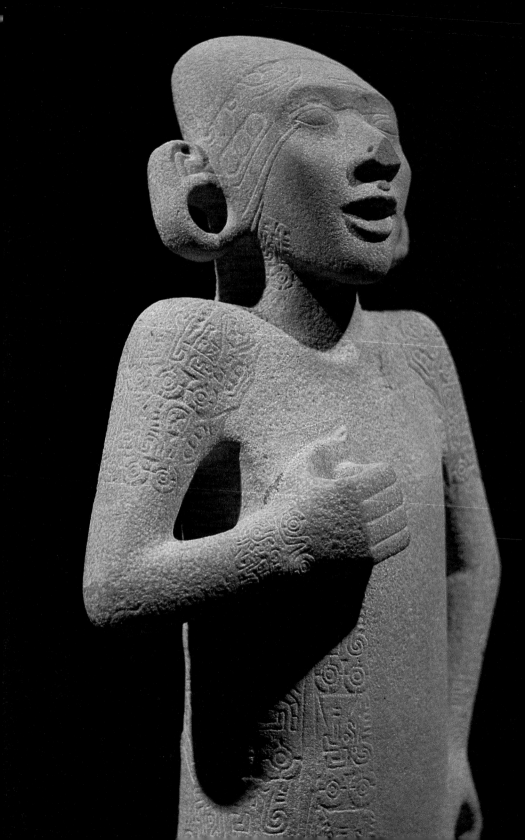

completely naked, and those that are adorned and delicately carved.

The Totonacs lived in the southern half of the Gulf region (present-day Veracruz). Though no major ceremonial center survives, they left an impressive contribution to the art of Mexico, especially in their smiling figurines. These are 30 cm tall (1 ft) and are among the enigmas of Mexican art because nobody is sure what these little men – not unlike the dwarfs of European folklore – are supposed to represent.

The ceramists of Veracruz had great skill. At the National Museum of Anthropology is the magnificent sculpture in clay of the oldest god in the Mexican pantheon: Xiuhtecuhtli or the old god of fire, sometimes known as Huehuetéotl. He is hunched over, weary perhaps from toting an enormous brazier on his head, and a good example of the grace and skill typical of the Gulf coast. It is in marked contrast to the rigid, solemn architectural design of most of the stone sculpture of the Aztecs.

Oaxaca is one of the poorest and most Indian of Mexican states yet also one of the most colorful. It is the seat of two major pre-Columbian cultures: the Mixtec and the Zapotec, who together make up the art of Oaxaca and especially that contained in the mountain-top ceremonial center of Monte Albán. The architecture is of a refined classicism. No ornamentation was added to the precise geometry of the pyramids and platforms forming the city. Though the buildings of Monte Albán may seem less picturesque than those of Teotihuacán, the blend of sky, mountain and architecture is impressive. The contents of the burial places that Alfonso Caso unearthed here show that the Mixtecs were probably the best jewelers of old Mexico. The treasures of Monte Albán can be seen in the museum of Oaxaca, housed in the old Dominican monastery of Santo Domingo. Here the art of Mexico perhaps even comes up to the level of achievement of the art of China and India.

On display in another of Oaxaca's museums is an attractive collection of Mixtec and Zapotec funerary urns. Nearby is another major center, Mitla, built by the Mixtecs and celebrated for the cut-stone mosaics covering its walls. The mosaic design is apparently geometrical, but actually deals with that most important of Mexican themes: the feathered serpent.

Pyramids and palaces: For the hurry-up-and-see-it-all-quickly visitor, the Mayan world can be compressed into three all-important centers: Palenque, Chichén-Itzá and Uxmal, which sum up the features that make Mayan art so distinctive and different from the rest of Mexican art. The Mayan pyramid is considerably steeper than its counterparts in other parts of Mexico, its verticality emphasized by the temple built at the top, which the Mayans usually crowned with a tail and an elaborate crest.

Mayan "palaces" are habitable buildings placed in the ceremonial centers. One feature of Mayan construction is the decorated wall in which a small door is the only opening; another is the remarkable sculpture known as *stelae*. Tall and free-standing, the *stelae* were "milestones" raised periodically to mark the passage of time which, along with its measurement, was the great obsession of this culture. The Mayans developed a complex double calendar to pursue their calculations of time, back into the distant past and forward into the far future. Astronomy and the measurement of time were important to all Mexican cultures, but to the Mayans it became the main concern of the privileged and sophisticated priestly caste.

The Mayans excelled in all artistic techniques. They produced some of the most exquisite ceramics of old Mexico: elaborate funerary urns, delicately painted vases and figurines with almost a Chinese refinement. To experience the greatness of Mayan art one must go to Chichén-Itzá, Uxmal and particularly Palenque, which is the most accessible of the old empire sites. It has a remarkable beauty, both architecturally speaking and on account of its tropical setting. Palenque offers some of the best Mayan buildings, palaces and pyramids. Its "Palace," perhaps the most complex of antique Mexican buildings, contains vaulted galleries, open courts and a four-story stone tower, which was probably used for astronomical purposes. The most important pyramids are those of the Sun, the Cross and the Inscriptions, all of which exhibit the peculiar verticality of Mayan pyramids and the richness of design of the temples. Though small (usually

Left, fine Huastec image, believed to be of the young Quetzalcóatl.

one to three chambers), the Mayan temple is elaborate in form with a sloped roof, a crest or comb crowning and delicate carving.

The Palenque cross: The Temple of the Inscriptions yielded a surprise when in 1952, by chance, Mexican archaeologist Alberto Ruz discovered a burial chamber in the temple. That led to the speculation that Mexican pyramids were, like the Egyptian pyramids, a place for burial and not merely the base for a temple, as had been thought previously. The treasure in the burial chamber contained two marvels. One is the tomb slab itself, which is beautifully carved; the other is a masterpiece of sculptural portrait, showing a young man with a long and aristocratic Palenque nose. He is wearing a lovely feather hat. This sculpture is in the National Museum of Anthropology.

In the Temple of the Cross archaeologists found a giant carving of a cross much like the Christian Cross. Naturally, this led to speculation that somehow Christianity was being preached many years before the Spanish conquered Mexico – perhaps even by Quetzalcóatl himself. In any case, the Palenque Cross is one of the most beautiful carvings left by the Mayans.

Uxmal, in the flat Yucatán, is an open city and it contains two of the jewels of Mayan architecture. One is the Pyramid of the Magician, so-called because of the tale that a magician built it in a single night. The other is the adjoining Nunnery Quadrangle.

Uxmal's pyramid is a majestic structure, more than 38 meters (125 ft) high, with oval ground plan ends and a proud, soaring staircase that leads to the elegant temple on top. It has an unsurpassable elegance, balanced between stark classicism and excessive baroque. The Nunnery was named by the Spaniards because it reminded them of a convent, with its spacious central court flanked by four long galleries. Each gallery has several doors leading into dark, undecorated rooms. The exterior is formed by two horizontal stripes. The lower one is plain; the upper one is highly decorated with abstract-looking serpentine motifs. The Nunnery reaches perhaps the perfection in this balance between the simple and the ornate. It has been influential in modern architecture. The American architect Frank Lloyd Wright designed several houses in this Mayan style.

Chichén-Itzá in northern Yucatán is the best example of a curious cultural cross-breeding. The Mayas were invaded by a group of Toltecs from central Mexico; thus Mayan art absorbed all the characteristics of simplicity and roughness of central Mexican art. The hybrid style that resulted might not please the purist but it is certainly attractive. The outstanding structure in Chichén is the Castle, a pyramid in strong and simple central Mexican style but with the verticality and grace of Mayan architecture. It was built in honor of Quetzalcóatl, who is known in the Yucatán as Kukulcán.

Another structure in Chichén, the Warriors, is also particularly worth mentioning, for it contained two of the most famous pieces of Mayan/Toltec sculpture. One is the so-called *chacmool*, a reclining figure, upon whose chest offerings were placed. This sculptured form came from central Mexico, as interpreted by the skilled hands of the Mayans. The *chacmool* is flanked by the other masterpiece: a pair of sculptured columns of feathered serpents.

Of course, Chichén-Itzá had pure Mayan structures before the arrival of the Toltecs. The large sacred cenote (well), for example, had already been a sacred pilgrimage site for centuries. The *caracol* (snail), thus named for its spiral interior staircase, was an astronomical observatory with precisely located windows which corresponded most exactly to sacred positions of celestial bodies, especially the sun and Venus.

Astronomy and astrology probably lost some of their importance with the arrival of the Toltecs, who placed more value on warfare and sacrifice, in curious contradiction to Quetzalcóatl-Kukulkán's original teachings. Excellent bas-relief sculptures at Chichén-Itzá show an eagle and a jaguar, each devouring a human heart (the most appreciated offering to the gods). This blood and sacrifice is carried on in low-relief sculptures that flank the ceremonial ball court at Chichén-Itzá, the largest and best restored of its kind in Mexico. According to the most acceptable interpretations, the carvings depict the decapitation of the captain of the losing team. The pre-Columbians took their ball games seriously. Indeed, life, art and religion were inseparable elements of Mayan life.

Right, a head from one of the *atlantes* stone sculptures at Tula.

Mural painting is Mexico's greatest contribution to contemporary art. It was a cultural product of the Revolution, flourishing in Mexico well into the 1950s when the dramatic work of Diego Rivera, David Alfaro Siqueiros and José Clemente Orozco astounded the world.

Murals have been painted in Mexico as far back as pre-Columbian times, but the murals of the Revolution were an explosive new departure. Most, though impromptu expressions of passion, were probably influenced

regime of Porfirio Díaz was overthrown. At least a few members of the new Alvaro Obregón cabinet were ready to experiment and Jóse Vasconcelos, minister of public education, offered the walls of a number of centrally located public buildings as canvases for murals. Among the buildings was the Escuela Nacional Preparatoria, the testing-ground for the first phase of Muralismo.

In Europe, Rivera had been in touch with avant-garde movements such as Cubism, although curiously the most important influ-

by the work of José Guadalupe Posada (1852–1913), whose stark engravings have been described by author Kate Simon as "masterly fierce." Posada's macabre *calaveras* (skulls) for the popular press were authentically Mexican, a far cry from the way artists of that era used foreign models. Posada employed black humor and incisive line, laying the groundwork for a whole school of artistry which was vigorous, obsessively nationalistic, and an unusual blend of the simple and the baroque.

The fiery founder: The movement began with Diego Rivera (1886–1957) who had just returned from Paris when the turgid

ence on him was not contemporary at all, but came from Italian Renaissance painting. Paolo Uccello's *La Battaglia di San Romano* is one of the most important influences on Mexican mural painting.

Rivera was a contradictory painter who aroused deep feelings. Though an ideologist (he was a Communist, but was expelled from the party), his work is less political than sensual in style, in the tradition of Paul Gauguin, Henri Rousseau and even Pieter Brueghel the Elder. He was also influenced by Aztec and Mayan sculpture.

Notwithstanding all these influences – hotly denied by nationalist critics – Rivera was deeply Mexican in his love of color and soft shapes and in his strong identification with the Mexican Indian. An excellent draftsman and watercolor artist, he created an image of a sweet, primitive Mexico, inhabited by brown, tender-loving girls and dreamy children carrying huge bouquets of flowers. Naturally, there was a degree of nostalgic sentimentality in all of this.

Rivera himself was also colorful, a source of gossip and a natural tabloid subject. According to his detractors he was an accom-

which he called the Anahuacalli, a sort of Aztec-surrealist building which housed his studio and collection of pre-Columbian art.

The ideologue: In contrast to Diego Rivera, Siqueiros (1899–1974) was a strong man of action. A participant in the Revolution, he was a political activist who was involved in a failed attempt to assassinate Leon Trotsky. Siqueiros volunteered for the Spanish Civil War, took part in labor struggles and was imprisoned several times. His paintings reflect his ideological drive, his taste for bold

plished liar and womanizer (though married to fellow painter Frida Kalho). He loved to shock. On his mural *Sunday Reverie in the Alameda*) gracing the now demolished Prado hotel in Mexico City (the mural is now contained in a special museum on Avenida Juárez, behind the Alameda Park) he wrote: "God does not exist." The words caused such an uproar they had to be expunged.

With a portion of the millions he made he built one of Mexico City's strangest homes,

Preceding pages: *Catharsis* by Orozco. **Left**, Rivera's *Liberated Earth* eulogizes Mexico's land reform. **Above**, Siqueiros' self-portrait.

action, and even for violence. They are so massive and muscular that they become a sort of imprisoned sculpture. Indeed, he experimented with a combination of painting and sculpture which he called *esculptopintura*. A constant innovator, Siqueiros was always trying new materials and techniques. Perhaps his best murals are those in Chapultepec Castle, which offer a baroque and powerful interpretation of Mexican history. His works at the Palace of Fine Arts are among the best of his easel paintings.

Orozco (1883–1949), a tragic and passionate artist, is often considered the best of the big three. He was a political skeptic, a biting satirist but also an idealist who was deeply disturbed by the sordidness of history, using the mural to convey his troubled feelings. In a sense, he is the *true* muralist of Mexico, although ironically the least Mexican in that his message transcends the national picture and can be understood by everyone. He can be compared to such German artists as Max Beckmann, Otto Dix, and Käthe Kollwitz. Orozco, always an outspoken man, denounced the Mexican Revolution as a bloody farce that would result in new servitude for the masses.

The first important Orozco mural was painted in the early 1920s at the National Preparatory School. Stark and simple, it showed some influence from early Italian Renaissance painting. At the Escuela Preparatoria, he nonetheless achieves moments of grandeur, especially in *The Trench*, a powerful image of war and human struggle. On the staircase of the same building, Orozco painted *Cortez y la Malinche*, depicting the naked bodies of the conqueror and his woman. The painting makes a clear statement about the relationship between Spain and Mexico, between conqueror and conquered, a theme to which Orozco returned many times.

From 1927 to 1934, Orozco lived in the US and painted murals for Pomona College, Dartmouth, and the New York School for Social Research. He described the cultural life of the times in his bitter *Autobiography*, and in letters to his friend and fellow artist Jean Charlot. Back in Mexico, he painted – at the Palace of Fine Arts – *Catharsis*, whose central figure is a colossal whore, the symbol of corruption. Orozco also produced many paintings, drawings and watercolors on the subject of prostitution viewing the brothel as a place of ultimate horror.

In the late 1930s his greatest works were produced in Guadalajara – in the Palacio de Gobierno, the Paraninfo and on the walls and ceilings of the Hospicio Cabañas. Here he is at the peak of his power, covering straight and curved surfaces with fiery reds and stark blacks, paying homage to Father Hidalgo, denouncing political manipulation, searching for deep and universal symbols.

Jean Charlot, born in Paris in 1898, another of the early muralists, left an interesting body of work. His *Massacre in the Main Temple*, a mural completed in 1923 on the stairway of the west court of the Escuela Preparatoria is regarded as the first fresco painted in Mexico since colonial times. Charlot was interested in archaeology and he collaborated with the great historian of the Mayan culture, Sylvanus G. Morley. He also produced fine field studies of archaeological finds at Chichén-Itzá, Yucatán, and at Cobá, Quintana Roo. Before his move to Hawaii, Charlot painted in the US, helping, with his works and writings, to popularize mural painting during Franklin Roosevelt's early days as president.

Juan O'Gorman, a painter and architect, transformed the mural into a sort of panorama of miniature scenes. Though modern, his paintings are anchored in Mexico's 19th-century popular art. He is famous chiefly for his murals decorating the Central Library Building of University City in Mexico City. Constructed with colored stone, these giant mosaic-murals describe the culture of the world in a baroque texture that is surprisingly innocent and fresh.

Other muralists: Beside the grand three, there are others of note, one of whom is Rufino Tamayo, who died in 1991 at the age of 92. Never political, he soon abandoned realism for poetically simplified forms. Tamayo's murals are unabashedly decorative, dealing with cosmic and domestic symbology (the stars, cats, women) and indifferent to the interpretation of history.

Pedro Coronel explored much the same ground as Tamayo. His murals are perhaps the best of those painted in recent years. Other mainline Mexican mural painters never far removed from realism include Fernando Leal, Xavier Guerrero, José Chávez Morado, Roberto Montenegro, Raúl Anguiano, Manuel Rodríguez Lozano, Alfredo Zalce and Jorge González Camarena.

The contemporary mural in Mexico seems to be trying to follow the many paths of modern art, with different degrees of success. But, in truth, the Mexican mural sprang forth out of passions engendered by the Revolution and, for all practical purposes, that emotion is gone and done with. The followers of the three great muralists keep repeating the same old formula but what – in Rivera, Siqueiros and Orozco – was a statement delivered in heat and passion, is now through repetition, sheer rhetoric.

Right, Orozco's portrait of Hidalgo.

CRAFTS

When does a craft become an art? When it is unique? When it sells for more than $10,000 at a New York art auction? When you put a frame around it and distinguish it with a spotlight? As a very loose definition, let us say that it is a craft so long as it is intended for common people's daily use and, incidentally, may even be good to look at.

The first crafts of Mexico were weapons used for hunting, and baskets for carrying wild edible plants. Archaeological excavations show that thousands of years ago man used a variety of interlaced fiber with which to carry things. Around 6,000 BC, man first planted corn and used stone implements to crush it. Those were the crude antecedents of the *metate* and the *mano,* still used today to grind corn. Man also began to improve the quality of the baskets in which he carried the corn, weaving vegetal stands so tightly that they could hold water without leaking.

Perhaps around 4,500 BC someone with great imagination covered a basket with clay, then hardened the clay in fire, and made pottery. That was quite a creative leap forward. You could cook with pottery; it could hold liquid indefinitely. It seemed almost inevitable that man would then begin to decorate clay vessels, thus adding a non-utilitarian charm to a household item. Admiring his work, a neighbor would naturally try to improve on it.

Soon man began to make weavings from maguey fiber, tree bark and native cotton. Many of the techniques and designs used in basket-making, pottery and weavings are still in use today, even the same materials, which date back to before the first complex Mexican civilization (2,500 BC).

The discovery that wet clay could be shaped, then fire-hardened, led to the making of the first religious figurines, replicas of naked women with huge breasts found in great quantities in Tlatilco, outside Mexico City. All the while new crafts were springing up, most concerned with things needed for daily use but also luxury items for the leisure class: gold jewelry, feather mosaic "paint-

ings," fine cotton weaving, exquisite lacquered vessels, beautiful figures of polished jade, and monumental stone and clay representations of the deities.

When the Spaniards came to Mexico, they found the native artisans well organized, selling their wares at great Indian markets called *tianguis,* a word still in use today. Among the profound changes wrought by the newcomers were the introduction of the wheel in pottery-making and the use of metal tools. The Spaniards needed items which

were too expensive to import from Spain: furniture, saddles and bridles, woolen weavings, household items. In 1529, a lay brother, Pedro de Gante, established an arts and crafts school in Mexico City for the Indians and in Michoacán Bishop Vasco de Quiroga introduced new techniques for working copper. He also showed the Indians such new products as ironware and lacquer.

On the heels of the conquistadors came Spanish craftsmen who taught their specialties to Indian apprentices, who learned quickly enough to compete with their former instructors although initially native craftsmen were scorned. Everything Spanish was

Left, a mask from Guerrero reflects Indian and Spanish roots. **Right**, devil image.

considered superior. But then came Mexican independence with its spirit of nationalism, and the creative pendulum swung the other way. Now for a while Indian craft was exalted and Spanish work was denigrated. Cuauhtémoc, king of the Aztecs, was a hero; Cortés, a villain.

Humble artisans: In 1921, President Alvaro Obregón opened a crafts exhibition, the first such official recognition given to the native artisan. The great muralists, David Siqueiros, José Clemente Orozco and Diego Rivera, praised the humble crafts. All of this hype had its effect. Middle-class Mexicans started to buy it; so did the American visitors. They still do, although the picture is not as rosy as it might seem: so many middlemen get their cut that the craftsman seldom fares well.

Artisans in Mexico might be divided roughly into four classes. The majority are farmers or laborers who work at their craft part-time to supplement their income and usually make everyday things. Then there is the full-time craftsman who either has his own shop or works for someone who does. He fashions items that are both decorative and useful, but also supplies the souvenir trade with cheap stuff that appeals to visitors. Next come those engaged in large-scale commercial production who study the market and mass-produce their work to fill a need. Finally there is the unemployed city worker who lives by his wits. He uses the cheapest of materials – paper, wire, wood, cork – to make toys, trinkets or geegaws. But his endeavors are not insignificant: often he is amazingly skilled, marvelously imaginative and ingeniously effective.

Mexico's various regions specialize in particular craft items. Sometimes the same village has made the same item since pre-Columbian times. If it catches the public's imagination, then it is mass-produced. The biggest concentration of craftsmen is found in central and southern Mexico. In many state capitals there is a *Casa de Artesania* where you can buy the specialties of the region, albeit at higher prices than is customary in the marketplace. The north of Mexico is not known for its crafts, but exceptions include the ironwood animal carvings of the Seri Indians, the wide woolen belts of the Tarahumaras and the sarapes made in Saltillo, Coahuila and Zacatecas.

In Tepic, Nayarit and Guadalajara, the Cora and Huichol Indians sell woolen belts and bags, embroidered clothing and yarn paintings. Tlaquepaque, a suburb of Guadalajara, offers ceramics, including fine copies of pre-Columbian pieces, blown glass and furniture. The town of Tonalá, near Guadalajara, specializes in pottery with its market days on Thursdays and Saturdays. In Guadalajara, the huge market of San Juan de Dios sells all kinds of handicrafts, with prices open to bargaining.

Aguascalientes is known for its *deshilados* (hemstitch) and embroidery, the best time to buy being at the yearly wine festival, from April to early May. San Luis Potosí is famous for its fine silk *rebozos,* so delicate and

compressible you can slip the shawls through a wedding ring. In the area known as La Huasteca (part of San Luis Pososí, Puebla and Veracruz), Indians weave a white traditional woman's cloak (*quechquémetl*) with cross-stitch embroidery. They also weave rugged and inexpensive wool bags and cactus fiber items. Guanajuato offers fine pottery; San Miguel de Allende sells sarapes, cane containers, piñatas for children's festivals and paper masks; and Querétaro is famous for its semi-precious stones and silver jewelry. In nearby Tequisquiapán, craftsmen make baskets, stools you can take apart, and sarapes. It can all be bought in the colonial town of San Juan del Río. In Mezquital valley in Hidalgo, the Otomí Indians use backstrap to weave rebozos and belts. They also make reed containers. The town of Ixmiquilpán makes bird cages in the shape of cathedrals. The town and state of Tlaxcala, where wool was first woven in New Spain, is still a center of weaving. Sarapes are a specialty of the house. Coastal Veracruz, meanwhile, produces silver and coral jewelry, and woven palm-leaf items.

Puebla state boasts riches in the variety and quality of its crafts. Talavera ceramics, household crockery and faience tiles are made in the capital. In Tehuacán and Tecali onyx is cut. The "Tree of Life" baroque ers for casting spells. Reed baskets – made in Puebla – are the most frequently purchased tourist items with 30 to 40 boxcars laden with baskets going to Tijuana each month.

Michoacán probably has the greatest variety of crafts in Mexico, many of its craftsmen and artisans living near Lake Pátzcuaro. Most of the villages in this region can be reached by car or bus and most of the crafts are available in Pátzcuaro town. On November 2, the Plaza de Don Vasco becomes a center for craftsmen. Artisans work year-round in the nearby House of the Eleven Patios, a former convent.

Certain towns have their specialties: Santa Clara del Cobre (also called Villa Escalante),

ceramic decorations, often seen on travel posters, are made in the town of Acatlán, especially by Heron Martínez, and in Izúcar de Matamoros, by the Flores and Castillo families. Pueblo is also famed for its textiles; over the centuries the Indians have continued to make their traditional clothing. The embroidered blouses of Cuetzálan and the bead-decorated blouses of San Pablito Pahuatlán are the best examples. Just as in ancient times, a kind of thick paper, *amatl,* is made from tree bark, a paper used by sorcer-

Left, a 19th-century water jug with pre-Columbian influences. **Above**, a Huichol woman weaving.

copperware; Paracho, guitars; Tzintzuntzán, burnished ceramics; Quiroga, painted wood bowls and household items; Ihuatzio, reed mats and basketry; Patamban, exquisite green-glazed pottery; and Uruapán, masks and lacquerware. There are two places in Morelia, capital of Michoacán, where you can also buy some of the best of the state's handicrafts: the Casa de Artesania, located in the former convent of San Francisco, and the convention center, a typical Tarascan wooden house.

South of Mexico City, the state of Morelos concentrates the sale of its craft production in Cuernavaca, a tourist-oriented town. Here for sale is locally made, colonial-style furniture, wooden bowls, combination jewelry and sarapes, and palm-leaf strip basketry. The village of Huejapan, in the municipality of Tetela del Volcán, produces wide, embroidered shawls. The adjoining state of Guerrero specializes in pottery. Olinalá produces the most beautiful lacquerware in Mexico – gourd bowls, wooden trays, jaguar masks. Taxco is world famous for its silver jewelry. In the tropical towns of Xalitla, Toliman and San Agustín de las Flores, the Huapanec Indians paint flowers, animals and abstract designs, using bright, fluorescent paint on the bark paper which is made in San Pablito Pahuatlán, in the state of Puebla.

Over the border in Oaxaca, the Zapotec Indians make elaborate blouses with tiny flowers and miniature dolls which hold the pleats together. So intricate is the work that the artisans say, as a challenge: "*Hazme si puedes*" – that is, "Make one like me, if you can." The blouses and wrap-around skirts of Yalalag are dyed with natural colors. No analines for them. Yalalag also produces silver crosses.

The Mixtec coast is known for its carrying nets. Cuilapan produces wooden animals in bright colors and assorted shapes. Near the city of Oaxaca, the village of San Bartolo Coyotepec makes a traditional burnished black pottery. From Santa María Atzompa come ceramic animal figures. Teotilán del Valle produces Mexico's best sarapes, either in traditional pre-Columbian designs or as copies of famous modern art paintings. In the town of Oaxaca, artisans create exact copies of the intricately beautiful Mixtec jewelry found in the tombs of Monte Albán. Oaxaca's handicrafts can also be found in the markets, where the prices are cheaper. There are important fiestas in December where much local craft is sold.

Chiapas produces woven wooden clothing, worn by the Indians of the highlands. The clothing is for sale in the villages and at market on Sunday in San Cristóbal de las Casas as well as in the cooperative of San Jolobil in the former convent of Santo Domingo. The town of Chiapa de Corzo is known for its lacquerware, especially the masks used in the festival of San Sebastian. Amatenango produces traditional pottery, which is fired without an oven. The Tzotzil village of San Juan Chamula makes much of the woolen clothing sold throughout the state, as well as guitars and harps. Yucatán produces the county's best hammocks, made either from sisal or from cotton. The best Panama hats come from Becal in Campeche. Quality mahogany and cedar furniture is made in Mérida, Valladolid and Campeche.

The state of Mexico also has many crafts. The town of Metepec produces the polychrome ceramic "Tree of Life." Wool sarapes are woven in a number of villages. Lerma produces baskets. Using orange-tree wood, Ixtapán de la Sal carves household utensils and decorative animals. Toluca is known for silverware, chess and domino games, made of leather, bone or wood.

Mexico City produces modern jewelry. The capital has many gifted craftsmen. They produce art objects from plastic, bottle caps, rubber bands or wire. Popular TV characters are made from foam rubber and painted in garish colors. A model of a children's hero comes with rubber-ball springs emerging from his head. There is also the work of the Linares family, who make figures of Judas that are burned on Holy Saturday. They also make sophisticated papier-mâché figures.

Left, a ceramic "Tree of Life" from Metepec. **Right**, a *mestizo* shapes a hat from a rolled cactus fiber called *ixtle*.

To understand the Mexican fiesta think of Mexican history and its mix of peoples. Mexican history is full of blood and tears. Mexico's people are partly *mestizo*, partly Indian, partly Spanish. The culture is old, yet new; it has retained to some degree the traditions of the past. The background of fiesta is Indian and Spanish, but condiment and spice have been added. There is some modern influence, chiefly from America; some folklore influence, from places as far away as France and even China.

On the whole, the Mexican is not a happy *hombre*. At least not in the effervescent way that the Cariocas of Rio de Janiero are said to be. Generally, the Mexican is grave and sedate and life for him is serious. Sometimes he even verges on the gloomy.

Sacred theatrical performances: The Indian fiesta was once religious in character. Not until the conquest did things liven up. Somberness dominated, which was only natural considering that the Indian festival revolved around human sacrifice. Pre-Columbian man lived in a hostile world, ruled by gods who were indifferent to man's fate. Like the gods of ancient Greece, they needed bribes to keep them content and not vindictive. Unfortunately, the Mexican gods were addicted to human blood. The Indians of ancient Mexico performed human sacrifice in a most ritualistic way. It almost verged on the artistic – a sort of sacred theatrical performance – but the blood was real. At some of the celebrations the people ate the flesh of the humans they had sacrificed. But drink was forbidden – only senior citizens were permitted to get drunk. Perhaps it was construed as a reward for longevity.

When the Spanish arrived they brought pleasures: bullfighting, horse racing, sports, dance, gambling, drinks. These same revelries are ardently pursued at fiesta time today.

Mexican fiesta is associated with Catholic festivities. Indeed, fiesta has two sides: human enjoyment and religious practice. There are the masses, the religious processions, the reciting of rosaries, the chanting of novenas. As an example, the Feria de San Marcos is celebrated for 10 days every year, starting on St Mark's Day, April 25. San Marcos is the patron saint of Aguascalientes city. This *feria* has been celebrated there since 1604 and apart from religious rites includes musical serenades, flower battles, bullfights, *mariachis*, cockfighting, and much drinking of the wines of Aguascalientes.

Mexicans like to gamble, and fiesta offers the chance to win or lose. At the *palenques* (palisades), where cockfights are held, the doors are closed as soon as a match starts so that bettors can't duck out if they lose. And, of course, there's the betting on horse races, often a primitive affair with just two horses running along an improvised dirt track.

The bill for a fiesta is usually paid by a person chosen by the community. A fiesta patron is called a butler, a deputy, or a district attorney. Whatever his title, it costs him a substantial sum of money; but in return for his largesse, he gets the gratitude of the people and a lifetime of prestige.

Fiesta-goers wear their best traditional dresses. The women adorn themselves with big gold earrings, bracelets, rings, ribbons, lace, and brightly colored silk. They do it up big, especially in Oaxaca where an affluent woman might sport pounds of gold. Generally speaking, Mexicans are indifferent toward comfort and not much concerned about saving *pesos* for a rainy day, but they love the displays of riches.

Fiesta takes place in midtown, in the church, main square and the surrounding streets. A marketplace springs up, someone installs a wheel of fortune, or a merry-go-round and the *lotería* and *los antojitos* make an appearance. The *lotería* is a Mexican version of bingo. The cardboards are decorated with traditional figures: the devil, the moon, the soldier, the drunkard, the dandy, the watermelon, death. The man in charge *(el gritón)* calls out the name of the card from a stack he has shuffled and the first person to complete the figures on his cardboard cries out "*Lotería!*" and all the others groan. It is a game played all over the world – from Europe to the Orient.

Preceding pages: Maardi Gras in La Paz. **Left,** a *conchero* dancer performing in a festival for the Virgin of Guadalupe.

What makes the *lotería* creative is the way each *gritón* describes the figures. Death, for example, becomes "the one that will take us all." The moon is "the one who goes out by night." The drunkard is the "chap who does not give a damn." The descriptions vary with the imagination of the caller.

Los antojitos mexicanos, which enliven every fiesta, are the favorite dishes of Mexican cooking. Most are made of corn, cooked in many ways. *Antojitos* are deeply fried and heavily spiced and calorie-laden. Among the most popular dishes are *tamales, buñuelos, sopes, atole, tacos, tostadas, pozole, enchiladas, menudo, mixiotes, quesadillas, memelas,* ad infinitum.

as the breaking of *piñatas,* (a clay pot filled with candy and fruit which is broken by a blindfolded child wielding a stick). The *piñata* may be beautifully decorated with colored shreds of paper and hanging ribbons.

Nowadays the *posadas* have become more sophisticated. The procession is now followed by dancing and drinking. Some families are doing their best to preserve the old traditions which were meant for the enjoyment of the children.

At Christmas, Mexicans hold a big dinner, attend midnight Mass, and nowadays, because of the influence of the US, decorate Christmas trees and exchange gifts. In the old days they put up a *nacimiento* – a mini-

Among the patriotic fiestas the most important take place around September 16, Independence Day. There are the parades, the *Grito* (proclamation), speeches, fireworks, etc. Religious celebrations are more elaborate, though they are beginning to lose their clout in the big cities.

The *posadas* are fiestas preparing the way for the biggest celebration of all, Christmas. *Posadas* (inns) commemorate the journey of Mary and Joseph to Bethlehem. At one time people used to join informal processions behind the images of the holy couple, chanting songs about their quest for a room (*pedir posada*). Afterward, there were games, such

ature clay replica of Bethlehem and the stable where Christ was born. Gifts were given, but only to the children, and on January 6 rather than Christmas Day, because this is the day the Magi are supposed to have offered their presents to Jesus. At dinner on that day a huge doughnut-shaped cake is served, inside which is hidden a figurine. The person who finds it has the honor of paying for the fiesta held on February 2, the *Candelaria* feast.

New Year's Eve used to be a sort of Thanksgiving day for Mexicans and was usually characterized by melancholic nostalgia. It has since become a happier day, even a bit boisterous. There is dancing and drinking and the air is full of great expectation for the year ahead.

Lent and Holy Week: The beginning of Lent in February or March is preceded by *Carnaval* or Mardi Gras. Traditionally it was important only in the port cities – mainly in Veracruz and Mazatlán. It is marked by parades, all-night dancing, drinking and masked balls. More seriously, everyone repents and goes to church to be reminded that man is mortal.

Lent also offers a chance to savor new dishes and to enjoy the splendors of the usually dry and sunny Mexican spring. The Holy Week used to be tightly controlled: noise was forbidden and people stayed home

villain of the moment is portrayed in the Judas head: Adolf Hitler, for example, during World War II.

Corpus Christi day was one of Mexico's most important fiestas in colonial times. The processions were elaborate; the preparations lavish. Children were taken to church, dressed as Indians and carrying tiny straw donkeys. Feasts are held to honor other saints: Joseph, Francis of Assisi, Anthony of Padua, John the Baptist, Philip of Jesús. The latter is the first Mexican saint. In addition there are celebrations in honor of the Virgin: the Assumption, the Immaculate Conception, and local celebrations, such as Guadalupe, Talpa, Zapopan, de la Salud de Pátzcuaro, de los

and attended religious functions. They were required to visit seven churches on Maundy Thursday, and Good Friday was traditionally a day of fasting and silence. On Saturday, an effigy of Judas was burned. Mexicans used paper figurines, wrapped in firecrackers, which they would light at precisely 10 in the morning, the presumed hour of heaven's opening. The Judas replica can be tiny and toylike, or big and sculptured. Judas is painted in bright colors. Sometimes the

Left, a Nahua wears a headdress to honor St Francis of Assisi. **Right**, the Crucifixion is re-enacted at Ixtapalapa on Good Friday.

Remedios, and so on.

November 2, the Day of the Dead, is a religious ceremony of special importance. People go to the cemeteries to visit their *muertitos,* to put flowers on the graves, pray and weep. Indians symbolically place food on the graves for the dead, and the living drink to their memory. This day brings forth all sorts of things related to death: primarily skulls and skeletons – painted, drawn, sketched or made in sugar candy or of pastry. These *calaveras* (skulls) might seem grotesque, but Mexicans do not think of them in terms of the macabre. They look upon such things calmly and with a touch of wry humor.

THE DAY OF THE DEAD

Antonio, a full-blooded Tarascan Indian, stood up in the round-bottomed canoe, with his trusty spear in his hand. The slightest indiscreet move would tip the canoe over into the cold water. Lithe as a ballet dancer, Antonio moved quickly and let fly his spear at a wild duck about to land on the surface of the water. The spear hit home – the duck fell thrashing into the water. Antonio paddled over and retrieved the bird. Smiling, he said, "Now when my father comes home from the land of the dead, he will be happy." When

a bullfighter, a bicyclist, even a bride. Children are given toys that familiarize them with death. At the fiesta people exchange candy skulls. Death often bears a title. In folk songs and popular poetry, Death is referred to as "the bald one," "the slim one," or "the one with his teeth always showing."

The Indian attitude toward the souls of the dead springs from the Nahua-speaking peoples of pre-Columbian Mexico. They did not think the skull was a symbol of death but a symbol of life. A skull did not inspire horror;

alive, Antonio's father loved baked duck.

The Fiesta of the Dead is one of Mexico's strangest rituals. Following Indian tradition it is celebrated in central Mexico, chiefly by Tarascan, Nahua, Totonac and Otomí Indians. The *mestizo* has a quiet defiance of death; he takes it in his stride. Mexicans look upon dying as one more misfortune to contend with, but they also regard it as the ultimate liberation. They joke about it. In popular art, the figure of Death is described with irony or sarcasm, which expresses the joy, the pain and the tribulation of humankind.

Death assumes human features – he is Don Quixote tilting his lance at a windmill; he is

it symbolized the promise of a new life. It was one of the most popular forms of ornament. In modern Mexico the skull is used in humorous drawing, in toys and candy.

Indians who celebrate the Fiesta of the Dead believe the souls of the dead return each year to visit their living relatives. The relatives provide a feast of the deceased's favorite food and booze.

At Antonio's house the table was set for the Fiesta of the Dead. Naturally, the baked duck had a place of honor – right below a photograph of the departed man. Candles were lit; there was a profusion of flowers, especially the yellow *cempoalzúchil,* which resembles the marigold. The night before Antonio had gone to his brother Pablo's house for the festival of the "little dead," dedicated to children who had died. An altar had been set up; there were toys and candy, so that the souls of the children, who had become little angels, would enjoy themselves on their visit.

At 6pm the next evening the bells of the church began to "call the dead." Every 30 seconds the bell rang, continuing until sunrise next morning. Just before midnight, cemetery stood an altar bearing a photograph of "Tata" (father) Cárdenas, the late President Lázaro Cárdenas, who came from this state and is much beloved.

At about 4am one of the candles fell over onto the baked duck. Probably a gust of wind blew it over. That served to reassure Antonio – it was proof that his father's soul had returned and accepted the offerings, especially the baked duck. Antonio smiled as he thought about it, but there were tears on his cheeks. At dawn, the people returned home,

Antonio and his brother's family left their homes. At the cemetery hundreds of candles glowed. Antonio and Pablo covered their father's tomb with offerings of food, drink, incense, candles and flowers. (It is believed that the returning soul will find his way back to the grave by the light of the candles and the smell of the incense.) The hours of devotion to a memory went by in silence, punctuated by the tolling of the church bells. Naturally, numerous toasts were drunk to the "health" of the departed soul. At one corner of the

Left, November 2 vigil. <u>Above</u>, sugar skulls, a sweet reminder of our mortality.

carrying the food which they had placed on the grave. They ate and drank heartily. They danced, and sang and got drunk. Having remembered the dead, they delighted in still being alive.

The ancients of Mexico believed in the indestructibility of a vital force and its transcendence after death. The Indians did not believe in the eternal life of the individual soul but in the survival of an abstract collective force in which humans as well as animals and plants participated. The world was conceived as an eternally repeated cycle of death-life-death where all destruction had in itself the seed of a new birth.

When the Spaniards arrived in Mexico they were shocked by its paganism, in particular the ritual offering of human sacrifices, in which still-beating hearts were ripped out of the victims in order to give strength to the Sun. To eradicate the old religion, the conquistadors tore down the temples and built churches, burning priceless documents in the process. They discovered, however, that an edifice does not guarantee devotion. Many of the Indians continued to worship their old gods, but gave them different names. Such theological eclecticism is still practiced by several Mexican Indian tribes, something that the priests understand and accept.

Homage to the Virgin: The sight was enthralling: on their knees in the plaza more than 100 young men moved haltingly along, pushing bicycles. They were engaged in an act of faith and self-mortification. They had ridden their bicycles for days to come to this place, and now, on their knees in supplication, they covered the last torturous stretch.

Why were they doing it? What could kindle such devotion? In Mexico, the answer is obvious. They were paying a call on the Virgin of Guadalupe, the country's patron saint. She is synonymous with Mexico. Born from the fusion of the Spanish and Indian cultures, she represents the Catholic as well as the pre-Columbian religions. She is the symbol of nationalism; the symbol of the racial and cultural mix that is Mexico.

Except for the Vatican, the Shrine of the Virgin of Guadalupe in Mexico City's Federal District is visited by more people than any other religious site in the Christian world. Some 6 million pilgrims arrive each year. The trail to the site is lined with orange peel and *taco* stands. The pilgrims carry wreaths and wax flowers.

Some 1,500 pilgrimages are made to the site every year. Business groups – ranging from General Motors of Mexico to Pepe's Clear Soups – send representatives. Sometimes a whole village will arrive. One day there may be just a dozen or so faithful – on another day, 100,000. An office in the ba-

Preceding pages: devotees of the Virgin. **Left**, a pilgrim celebrates.

silica directs the large-scale movements, coordinating things as meticulously as a military landing. Some of the faithful walk from remote parts of Mexico; they are on the road for days. Others walk only the last 5 km (3 miles), down the Calzada de Guadalupe.

Ask an old man why he has come and he says: "Señor, I have a hard life. A lot of work and very little money. But whenever I really need anything, I've always asked the Little Virgin and she has always helped me. I am grateful to her. Now that my wife is sick, I have come to ask the Virgin to cure her."

Tent in the Sinai: The original shrine of the Virgin was built in 1694 but its foundation was unstable and was beginning to crack. The new basilica was conceived by the architect Pedro Ramírez Vasquez, the same man who designed the National Museum of Anthropology in Mexico City, a building that has won the admiration of the world. The basilica is meant to convey the impression of the tent used by Abraham in the Sinai. It conforms to the directives of the Second Vatican Council under Pope XXIII and seeks to combine religious spirit and ritual. It took more than 20 months to build the imposing 11,000-sq. meter (36,000-sq. ft) temple and it cost over $10 million. The new basilica can hold 10,000 pilgrims, and with the doors open another 20,000 can watch proceedings.

The scene on the inauguration day of the new basilica (October 12, 1976) was hectic. More than half a million people attended. Many fainted from the crush. During the ceremony someone thoughtlessly slammed shut the doors, trapping people inside. Pilgrims became hysterical, begging the Virgin to save them. When the doors suddenly swung open people escaped with ashen faces and breathing hard.

In the 16th century, Father Bernardino de Sahagún set out to rectify what the Church considered a melancholy state of affairs. He reasoned that Catholicism could be implanted only by first understanding, then eradicating, the gods of the Indians. He found, of course, that the Aztec deities were complex. The most important of the goddesses was known by the names of Cihuacóatl (the Serpent Woman); Coatlicue (Serpent Skirt);

Chicomecóatl (Seven Serpents), or, as was most common, Tonantzín – Our Mother. She was the goddess of the earth, spring and maize. A temple was dedicated to her on top of a hill called Tepeyac on the outskirts of the Aztec capital of Tenochtitlán. Naturally, she became a rival of the Virgin.

The Spaniards themselves were also religious fanatics. Among the "gods" they brought along, none was more important than their own Virgin of Guadalupe who, according to legend, was carved by St Luke and appeared miraculously in Spain. She was associated by the Spanish with their reconquest of the Iberian peninsula from the Moors. Her shrine was built in Extremadura,

tary proof. Early one morning in 1531, a newly coverted Indian named Juan Diego, a simple man of the soil, was walking on the hill of Tepeyac when he heard a sweet voice calling him. It was the Virgin Mary. She said she wanted a temple built there so that everyone could worship and adore her. "Why me?" Diego asked boldly. "Why do you not ask one of the powerful Spaniards?"

The Virgin did not explain but told him to relay her message to Archbishop Zumaragá, which he did. As was to be expected, the archbishop scoffed. Next day, the Virgin appeared before Juan Diego again, and again the day after that. Finally she furnished Juan Diego with the proof he needed. She com-

Cortés's home. After surviving the sting of a scorpion in Mexico, the grateful Cortés presented the Spanish Virgin of Guadalupe with a scorpion of gold. Gonzalo de Sandoval, one of Cortés' captains, brought with him to Mexico a copy of the Spanish Virgin of Guadalupe. During the siege of Tenochtitlán, he set up camp on the bottom of the hill of Tepeyac where Tonantzín's temple stood.

The Juan Diego miracle: Not long after the conquest, all the Indians who lived in or near the capital had been converted to Christianity, peacefully, if possible, but by force, if necessary. What happened next is believed by the faithful, though there is no documen-

manded some roses to bloom – which of itself was a miracle since roses had never been seen there before – and ordered Juan Diego to gather them in his cactus-fiber mantle and take them to the archbishop, which he did. He threw down the roses at the archbishop's feet, and, miracle of miracles, the image of the Virgin appeared on the mantle. According to true believers, the mantle is the same piece of cloth that is preserved at the Basilica of the Virgin of Guadalupe.

Franciscan monks sought to dispel any confusion between the Virgin of Guadalupe and the old deity of the Aztecs, Tonantzín. There were several reasons why people might be confused, not least the fact that the Virgin's shrine was located at the site of Tonantzín's former temple. Also, the tone of the Virgin's skin was brown, almost an Indian brown. There was also the date of celebration: the pre-Columbian festival for Tonantzín was held on the first day of the 17th month of the Aztec ritual calendar. That corresponded to December 22 on the Julian calendar, which was used in Mexico until 1582. At that time Pope Gregory XXIII subtracted 10 days from the calendar date so that it should align better with the solar cycle. Thus December 22 became December 12, the day when all Mexico celebrates the Virgin of Guadalupe.

attitude of the Creoles (Spaniards born in Mexico), who had to take second place to Spanish-born subjects when it came to rank and prestige.

The Virgin of Guadalupe helped make amends. By her appearance before a humble Indian, she showed her favor to the entire Mexican nation. Now the people could lay claim to be the "chosen people." In the eyes of the Creoles this placed Mexico on an equal footing with Spain.

A venerated symbol: The Virgin of Guadalupe is held to have stopped the flooding of Mexico City in 1629. And in 1736, her image was said to have brought to an end a terrible epidemic that had already killed 40,000 peo-

Rays of divine love: The first written account of the miraculous apparition dates from 1648 – 117 years after it happened. This is a book by Miguel Sánchez, called *The Image of the Virgin Mother of Guadalupe Miraculously Appearing in Mexico*. It is based on a copy of the "Codex Valerianus," purportedly dating back to 1531 and written in the Nahuatl language, which recounts the Juan Diego story. But more important than "factual" evidence was the psychological

Left, a group of pilgrims complete the last leg of their journey on their knees. **Above**, floral offerings to the Brown Virgin.

ple. During the struggle against Spain, the Virgin of Guadalupe was awarded the rank of general. When Mexico won its independence, she became even more venerated (political leaders casually bandied her name to win regard); Emperor Iturbide founded the Imperial Order of Guadalupe; and the name of the first president of Mexico was Guadalupe Victoria. The dictator, Porfirio Díaz, had the Virgin crowned Queen of Mexico, and at the same time she was the patroness of Emiliano Zapata, who fought Días. Even today, no sensible politician would dare to utter the slightest criticism of the Virgin of Guadalupe.

You have probably heard of *mariachi* music, even if you've never been to Mexico. The players wear tight pants, dark jackets with silver buttons and decorations, and big felt hats. They play a variety of string instruments along with a trumpet or two.

You've also probably heard of *ranchero* music, which dates back to the Spanish romances or chivalric ballads. In Mexico they became *corridos*, about heroes and villains, *bandidos* and *pistoleros,* catastrophic events, politics, current affairs, and, of course, love. The themes are treated with varying degrees of stoicism, pathos, humor and mockery.

In popular music, machismo is usually muted. But in ballads about revolutionaries, such as Pancho Villa and Emiliano Zapata, the *machismo* is up front, where it counts. There are old favorites: the *hombre* who always does what he pleases because his word is law, or the *hombre* who tells about his forthcoming execution. The latter has killed his best friend and the woman who done him wrong with his best friend. He has no regrets and fears nothing. He says that in the afterlife he will seek out the pair he murdered – and kill them once again. A very macho man.

Noble musical traditions: Musical tradition in Mexico has its roots in both pre-Columbian Indian and Spanish cultures. Before the arrival of the conquistadors, the music of the Aztecs was an integral part of their religious rituals. Music in pre-Hispanic Mexico displayed unsuspected energy and variety. It had to be performed, like the dance, in a plaza, on a platform, or on a pyramid. Priests, nobles and even kings took part.

Netzahualcóyotl, king of Texcoco, near Mexico City, was a poet and a fine singer who encouraged the composers in his court to narrate the glories of his lineage and the history of his kingdom. Many of the songs dedicated to the gods have survived. Manuscripts and codices with rhythmic annotation were set down by the Spanish friar Bernardino de Sahagún in the 16th century and are the first examples of scored music in the Americas. The songs were generally accompanied by the *huehuetl* and the *teponaztli,* both of them percussion instruments, as well as by rattles, flutes, conch shells and grooved bones.

The *huehuetl* was a drum, supported on a tripod. It was made of a hollowed log, one end of which was covered by deerskin. The drummer, who was standing, played with his bare hands. The *teponaztli* was also made of a hollowed-out log. The player used two drumsticks, tipped with rubber. In some villages of Hidalgo, Veracruz and Tabasco both the *huehuetl* and the *teponaztli* are still considered sacred instruments and are used to accompany the old-time rituals.

The ancient wind instruments were sophisticated: reed and clay flutes, multiple flutes, ocarinas, whistle jugs and conch-shell trumpets. In funerary rites, the sound of the conch shells was associated with mourning.

Fray Juan de Torquemada left an excellent description of pre-Columbian song and dance that had been incorporated into religious rites. He wrote: "At the beginning of a dance three or four Indians blow shrill whistles. Other instruments come in, sounding a low tone, gradually growing louder. When the dancers hear the instruments play, they begin to sing and dance. At first the songs proceed at a slow pace, in a deep tone. When one song is finished (and it may seem very long because of its slow pace, although none lasts more than an hour), the instruments change their tone, and the leaders begin another chant, a little more lively, and rising in pitch. In this manner, the songs continue as though changing the voice from a base to a tenor."

Musical instruments for ceremonial use in Mexico-Tenochtitlán were kept in a sacred place called Mixcoacalli. A large number of musicians were employed in the service of the temples; men dedicated themselves to the study of song and dance. So important was music to the Indians that a missionary claimed conversions came about more readily through music than through preaching.

Colonial influences: Following the Spanish conquest, Musicians who had served in the Aztec temples were employed in the

Left, a violin player provides music for conchero dancers; his instrument bears the image of the Virgin of Guadalupe.

churches. The earliest school to teach music to the Indians was founded three years after the conquest by Friar Pedro de Gante. Soon after, New Spain started making its own organs and other secular instruments. Instruments used in the Renaissance and the baroque period were made in Mexico, starting in the 16th century. Some, such as guitars, violins and harps, became the specialty of certain villages. The Indians learned music surprisingly quickly. An early missionary marveled that "at the beginning they did not understand anything nor did the old instructor have an interpreter. In a short time they understood so well that they learned not only plain chants but also the songs of the organ

came the exciting rhythms of the tango, the rumba, the fandango, the *chaconne,* the *saraband,* the *cumbé,* the *habanera,* the bolero and the *danzón.*

During its 300 years as a colony, Mexico was treated to all kinds of music. In 1711, Mexico City played host to the first opera composed and performed in the New World, *La Parténope,* by Manuel de Zumaya. During late colonial times, the *corrido,* accompanied by guitar and harp, became the most popular musical form.

Mariachi groups were first formed in the 18th century and they now play all over the country but seem to be most popular in Jalisco and central Mexico. The name comes

and now there are many choirs and singers who are skillful in modulation and harmony, learning everything by heart."

The most prestigious job open to a musician in New Spain was that of musical director of the cathedral in Mexico City. Many of the directors were noted composers of religious music; competition for the job was intense. The first Indian to win the post was Juan Matias, who served from 1617 to 1667.

The secular music of the Renaissance arrived aboard the galleons from Spain. Out of the Caribbean came rhythms and musical forms that mixed Latin, Mediterranean, Arab, African and Indian music. From all these

from either the French word *marriage,* for wedding, or the Galician word *marriagero,* for a musician who plays at a wedding. At first the players used only string instruments. Later, trumpets were added for pizzazz.

During the 19th century the waltz became popular. The new music spoke of the triumph of the War of Independence. Major composers such as Macedonio Alcalá, Juventino Rosas, Ricardo Castro and Felipe Villanueva gave form to the Mexican version of the waltz. They combined originality, nostalgia and melodic imagination. The *jarabe* of Jalisco, the *sandunga* of Oaxaca, the *jarana* of the Yucatán, and the *pirecua* of

Michoacán accompany dances. The texts are in Spanish, Tarascan, Mayan or Zapotec.

The *marimba* is most popular in Chiapas, Oaxaca and Tabasco. These xylophone-type instruments with big wooden keys are played by up to four persons using rubber-tipped batons. The soloist carries the tune; the other three divide the secondary melody in counterpoint. It was traditional that all players came from the same family and could play waltzes, *paso dobles,* boleros and even excerpts from operas. The *marimba* is sometimes accompanied by a saxophone, gourds and percussion drums.

Wind instruments characterize the music of Indians from Oaxaca, Querétaro, Micho-

The bolero is probably the most popular type of music in the cities. Its origin goes back to the Andalusian bolero, but it is enriched by the beat of the tropics imported from Cuba. It takes pleasure in nostalgia. Agustín Lara, the most famous composer of boleros in this century, is able to combine clear and voluptuous writing with audacious rendering. The songs are often dedicated to the women in a gallant's life. Some of the best-known titles of the 1930s and '40s are "The Lady Adventurer," "Sell Dearly Your Love" and "I'm in Love."

Tropical bands often play in the dance halls. Usually the players play percussion instruments – bongos, *tumbadoras, güiros* –

acán and Morelos. Their repertory, aside from marches and waltzes, extends into the classical field, though at the same time keeping its solemn, traditional character. The musical bands of the far north are generally composed of guitars, accordions, contrabass and drums. Often you hear a central European flavor, which is evident in the waltzes, mazurkas and polkas. The repertory consists of popular music, *huapangos,* and even, these days, ballads which protest the treatment of wetbacks in the US.

Left, a *mariachi* singer concludes a heart-rending love song. **Above**, a twirling girl in a folk dance.

also rattle-gourds, guitars, pianos, marimbas and even electric organs. Rock from the US has gained popularity in recent years.

Perhaps as a reaction against this trendy American invasion there has been a recent revival of interest in folkloric music. This genre attracts a middle-class audience – sometimes appearing at concerts dressed in colorful Indian clothes – that favors genuine artists such as Cuco Sánchez, Chavela Vargas or Tehua. They appreciate nostalgic and rural musical forms such as the old *corridos* and sad love songs. They also like to relate to Mexican music as a part of an overall Latin American artistic expression.

To define the Mexican *charro* as merely a cowboy is to do him an injustice. Although there are some likenesses, there are marked differences between the two, in style, appearance, and how they perform. Naturally, the *charro* objects to a superficial comparison, and so probably does the cowboy.

The *charro* has his roots in Spain, whence came his horses, the cattle he works, and the dress he wears. When Hernán Cortés landed in Mexico, he was accompanied by a troop of 16 cavalrymen, which introduced the horse to Mexico. Those horsemen, Cortés's most effective strike force, made a tremendous impression. When Cortés led an expedition to Honduras, one of his horses died on the way. The Mayas thereupon deified the horse.

During colonial times, all Spaniards were obliged to own a horse, while a royal decree in 1528 forbade the Indians, under penalty of death, from even riding a horse. But over the years, as cattle were introduced into Mexico and Indians were needed to work the cattle, this law was abandoned. For both sport and exercise, as well as their daily work, men rode horses and cared for them. They had all the time in the world to practice with the lasso, and to teach their horse new tricks.

The Mexican horsemen developed a skill of their own – *colear* (grabbing the bull by the tail), a maneuver which showed the animal who was boss. That indefatigable chronicler of all things Mexican, Madam Calderón de la Barca, described in 1840 how "they [*charros*] proceeded to amuse us with the *colear* of the bulls, of which amusement the Mexicans throughout the whole republic are passionately fond. They collect a herd; single out several [animals], gallop after them on horseback; and he who is most skillful, catches the bull by the tail, passes it under his own right leg, turns it round the high pummel of his saddle, and wheeling his horse around at right angles by a sudden movement, the bull falls on his face. Even boys of ten years old joined in this sport."

As for the *charros*: "It is impossible to see anywhere a finer race of men than these

rancheros – tall, strong and well-made, with their embroidered shirts, coarse sarapes and dark-blue pantaloons embroidered in gold… their games of skill and trials of address are manly and strengthening, and help to keep up the physical superiority of that fine race of men, the Mexican *rancheros*."

Charros made very fine cavalrymen in Mexico's wars. At the battle of the Alamo, *charros* lassoed and captured Texans. In the fight against the French, galloping *charros* snagged cannon with their lassos and turned

them over. When Pancho Villa's "Golden Ones" rode into battle, however, General Alvaro Obregón, stopped them with trenches, barbed wire and machine guns.

The skilled work that the *charros* did in the field naturally led to competition, and then to sport. It all originated on the cattle ranges: roping, tying, riding, branding. Was there ever men with more endurance? They could work all day from sunrise to sunset, stay up all night dancing the *jarabe*, and be ready at dawn for another day's work.

For years bullfighting and *charrería* were intimately associated. Indeed, aficionados of both the *fiesta brava* and the *charros*

Left, a 19th-century engraving of a hacienda owner. **Right**, lining up for the off.

claimed as their own the great Ponciano Díaz, a bullfighter and *charro extraordinaire.* This famous torero was the first to charge admission for a *charro* performance. The earliest group of *charros* to travel abroad were the 12 men who took part in Buffalo Bill's Wild West shows in the US. Their leader, Vicente Oropeza, was known as the world's greatest artist of the lasso.

Urban *charros*: After the expropriation of many large cattle ranches during post-Revolution days, the *charro* lost status. Since then, the *charrería* has been developed in an urban setting by what one might call "the cowboys of the city" and has become what many consider to be the only truly national

within the rectangle. To top it off, he walks his horse backwards out of the ring.

Then comes the *coleadero,* the thriller. A bull comes charging out of a chute and down the passageway into the ring. Up gallops our hero, the *charro*, who grabs the bull by the tail and then tries to throw him off balance and roll him over on his back. Points are given for how swiftly the *charro* can perform the task and how neatly he makes the bull fall and roll over. Sometimes the rider ends up with a section of the bull's tail in his hand. He waves it at the fans.

The next series of events are performed in a circular space in front of the spectators. Aside from bronco-bucking and bull-riding

Mexican sport. The biggest *lienzo charros* (*charro* rings) are in Mexico City and Guadalajara where the city dudes hold weekly competition from 11am to 2pm on Sunday. The event is known as a *jaripeo.*

The show starts with horsemen riding abreast to salute the judges and the public, in a manner similar to the opening of a bullfight. The first event, called *cala de caballo,* demonstrates the mastery of rider over horse. The rider comes full gallop down a passageway and brings his horse to an abrupt stop inside a white, chalk-powdered rectangle. The rider turns his mount round and round – to the right, to the left – all the time staying

(the riders hang on with both hands), everything is now worked with the lasso. The *charro* is a magician with the rope. After making his flourishes with the lasso, the mounted rider throws down the loop in front of the bull. His teammates induce the bull to venture into the loop; thereupon the rider pulls the rope tight around the animal's legs and hauls him down.

The most spectacular event takes place near the end of the competition. Three riders drive a wild horse around the edge of the ring. The fourth member of the team stands about 3 meters (10 ft) from the side of the arena, leaving enough room to allow the wild horse and the riders to pass. After the riders and the horse have galloped a few times around the edge of the ring, the man on foot starts twirling his lasso. Then, with incredible, split-second timing, he jumps through a loop in his lasso and in the same breath drops a loop on the ground in front of the horse as it comes thundering by. When the hind legs of the horse are inside the loop, the *charro* on foot jerks his lariat, slips the knot tight, and wraps the rope around his back. The slack is hauled in; the *charro* leans back, digs in his heels, and brings down the wild bronco, who is not at all pleased with these developments. The crowd is, though, and goes wild.

Usually this performance is followed by a folk dance out of Jalisco, which is the favorite dance in *charro* country.

Charro chic: *Charros* tend to be romantic and conservative. They idolize women and are usually fervent nationalists. They are devoted to their horses and love to eat well and drink heartily. Teetotal *charros* are considered suspect.

Charros sometimes seem vain and often spend a fortune on their outfits. As they say in Mexico, they "throw the horse out of the window" in their splurging. There is a *charro* saying: "We're all made of the same clay, but a well-dressed dandy is not the same as a well-dressed *charro*."

There is an aura of nostalgia about the

the *paso de la muerte* (the pass of death) wherein a *charro* jumps off his horse onto the back of a wild horse. It is what is known in the trade as changing horses in midstream.

Women have their own events, called *escaramuza charra*. They dress, naturally, in *charra* style, and mount their horses sidesaddle, so as not to lose the "attractiveness of their exquisite feminity," as one gallant Mexican writer put it. The show sometimes closes with the dancing of the *jarabe tapatío,*

Left, a *charro* jumps through his looping lariat before lassoing a wild horse. **Above**, the felt hats worn by *charros* are immensely expensive.

charros, a wish to return to a golden past. Their machismo is up front – men with their horses perform daring feats to impress demure and well-made-up ladies.

Here are some *charro*isms, straight out of the horse's mouth:

"A horse to fill your legs, a fighting cock to fill your pocket, and a woman to fill your arms."

"A horse, a fighting cock and a woman should be chosen along blood lines."

"There are three kinds of idiots: those who drink with their employees, those who ride without a bridle, and those who dance with their own wives."

Many people are appalled when they see a bullfight for the first time. They say it's terribly unfair; the bull always dies. They think the bullfighter seldom loses, being unaware that one out of four bullfighters will be crippled in the course of his career, that one out of 10 will be killed by the bull, and that most bullfighters are gored, sometimes a great many times. Also, few who are not bullfight fans know that now and then a bull who has fought the good fight can be *indultado* – that is, pardoned and retired to

centuries may have introduced a form of bullfighting. During the Middle Ages, bullfighting was the sport of nobles, who rode horses and were armed with a short lance. One pope decreed that a bull could fight only once, reasoning correctly that a single encounter taught the bull something. In 1567, Pope Pius V threatened in vain to excommunicate all nobles who permitted bullfighting.

Some accounts say that the first bullfight in Mexico took place in 1526 to celebrate Hernán Cortés's return from his expedition

pasture, where he will spend the rest of his life eating, sleeping and at stud. It is hoped that his sons will inherit his courage.

Ernest Hemingway claimed there are two kinds of spectators at the bullfight: those who identify with the bull and those who identify with the bullfighter.

Bullfighting probably began in Crete where it is depicted in frescoes showing acrobats grabbing bulls by the horns and somersaulting over their backs. In the Middle East the bull was an object of worship and perhaps it is this concept which found its way to Spain through the Greek colonies established there. The Arabs who ruled parts of Spain for

to Honduras. There was certainly a bullfight on St Hippolyte's day, August 13, 1529, organized by that *bandido* of the conquistadors, Nuño Beltrán de Guzmán, to commemorate the Spanish capture of the Aztec capital in 1521.

Throughout the three centuries that Spain ruled Mexico, bullfights were held regularly to commemorate religious and civic celebrations; the canonization of a saint, the arrival of a new viceroy, the inauguration of the sanctuary of the Virgin of Guadalupe, the birthday and coronation of a Spanish monarch, the signing of a peace treaty. Although the Catholic Church often decried the spectacle, the clergy always occupied reserved box-seats at the corrida. They did not think the spectacle would damage *their* morals.

Bullfights were held in make-shift arenas until 1788, when the first permanent plaza was built in Mexico City. Originally, bullfighters fought on horseback. The first instance of someone dismounting was in 1680, and thereafter the bullfighters fought on foot as well as from a horse. In the Yucatán, mounted bullfighters used an enormous cape to taunt the bull. It was not until 1769 that

a bullfight with the help of the Committee of Patriotic Ladies to raise money for the resistance against the French and the imposed emperor, Maximilian, But after the Mexican triumph, Juárez prohibited bullfighting. That restriction was lifted by Porfirio Díaz, who knew he would win points with bullfighting fans. President Venustiano Carranza also banned the *fiesta brava,* but after he was assassinated, bullfighting resumed. No recent presidents have been rash enough even to consider prohibiting bullfighting. They

bullfighters were paid for their services: until then, apparently, they fought purely for the honor. Occasionally a spectator, caught up in the fever of the occasion, would leap over the barrier, into the bullring and square off vaingloriously in front of the bull. Strict laws were passed to discourage these interlopers: a year's exile for nobles, two months' imprisonment for common Spaniards, and 100 strokes of the lash for anybody else.

Valiant *tereros*. President Benito Juárez attended bullfights. In fact, his wife organized

attend enthusiastically at least one *corrida* a year, held in honor of the Mexican Army.

The first superstar among the bullfighters was Bernardo Gaviño. He caught Madame de la Barca's eye. She described his "dress of blue and silver which was superb and [which] cost him $500." Once, on his way to Chihuahua for a bullfight, Gaviño and his party of 64 were attacked by Comanches. The battle lasted from 9am to 4pm that day. Only three whites, including Gaviño, survived. But that did not deter the valiant *torero.* He kept his engagement and fought a good fight (the parish priest of El Paso del Norte who saw the performance died of a heart attack brought

Left, a young bullfighter with his impresario. **Above**, the anticipation of the crowds.

on by the excitement). Gaviño kept fighting the bulls for more than 50 years. In fact, he fought until the ripe old age of 75, when he was badly gored by a bull in Texcoco and died from the infection.

Torero Ponciano Díaz was both a great bullfighter and a superb horseman. He was able to work his fans up to such a frenzy of excitement that in 1902 they burned down the arena at Puebla. Díaz toured Spain in 1889. He used the Mexican method of placing the *banderillas* (the barbed darts thrust between the shoulders of the bull) with both hands. He delighted the Spanish crowd with his *charro* clothes. He was the only unshaven *torero* ever allowed in Spain.

to March or April. Some good bullfights are performed in the summer in arenas in cities along the US border because a few *nortéamericanos* have caught the fever.

The show starts promptly at 4.30pm, even if the clock has to be turned back. The opening parade is led by a bailiff who formally asks the authorities for permission to hold the *corrida*. Three *toreros* follow, resplendent in their *traje de luces* – suits of light – all silk and gold embroidery. Behind them come their assistants, then the picadors, and then the ring attendants with their mules, which will haul away the dead bulls.

The ring *presidente* waves his handkerchief and the first bull rushes in. He weighs

Mexico has nurtured a number of great bullfighters: Rodolfo Gaona y Jiménez, immortalized by his *par de Pamplona*, a perfectly planted set of *banderillas*; Fermín Espinosa Saucedo, who fought in the classical Spanish style, which is described as intelligent, dry and dominating; and Pepe Ortiz, who performed *à la baroque*, kneeling in front of the bull.

There's no denying the bullfight's popularity. There are 225 permanent arenas and 500 improvised ones in Mexico. Plaza de México in Mexico City, the biggest bullfighting arena in the world, can seat 50,000. The season runs from the end of November

upwards of some 500 kg (1,100 lbs) – a raging muscular combatant, moving along like an express train and itching to fight. The play unfolds in three acts.

Act 1: The *torero* watches while his assistants handle the bull with their capes. Then he takes a few turns himself to test the animal's behavior. How does he run and which way does he hook his horns? The *torero* uses a heavy gold-and-silk cape and will perform the best-known "Veronica" pass (named for the woman who wiped Christ's face). The picadors ride in. They push their lances into the big hump of muscle on the bull's back. The picadors usually stab twice to expose the "cross" where the bullfighter will thrust his sword in the death stroke. Exit picadors, leaving a raging but weakened bull.

Act 2: The *torero*'s assistants, or in some cases the bullfighter himself, then plant three pairs of *banderillas* into the bull's hump. The *bandillero* runs to the bull, plants the darts, leans on them, and dexterously gets out of the way of the charging animal. By this time the bull is bleeding profusely.

Act 3: *La Hora de la Verdad* (the Moment of Truth). The *torero* asks permission to kill the bull and dedicates the kill to his lady friend, or to another charming *señorita*, or to a *compañero*, or to the crowd, or to anyone else he chooses. He then has 16 minutes to

weakened that his head droops, the *torero* aims along his sword and plunges it between the shoulder blades, going over the horns and into the "cross," the place where the sword can penetrate cleanly and sever the artery to the heart or puncture the lung. The bull drops to his knees and usually dies at once. Sometimes, though, a *coup de grâce* has to be delivered by one of the *torero*'s assistants.

The *torero*'s reward depends on his performance. He can be awarded an ear, two ears, two ears and the tail, and sometimes even the hoof of the bull. If the bull has fought with customary courage, his body is dragged around the ring by a team of mules. Meanwhile the *torero* walks around the ring

dispatch the bull or be ordered from the ring in disgrace. The *torero* works his magic on the bull with his heavy cape, going through a series of daring passes, working even closer to the horns. That is when his capework is sternly appraised by people who are experts in the art of such an appraisal.

The *torero* then switches to a smaller flannel cape. (Bulls are color-blind; they go for anything that moves: it is a myth that the cape has to be red.) When the bull has been so

Above, the climactic moment, when the *torero* takes aim for the small spot between the bull's shoulders, the best place for a clean kill.

in triumph. He is showered with hats, flowers, cushions and wineskins, which his assistants toss back whence they came.

This performance is repeated six times. Two bulls are assigned to each *torero*. Aficionados and judges look for the following points: for *mandar*, the degree of mastery shown by the *torero* over the bull; for *parar*, how well the *torero* stands (is he straight, with feet firmly planted and not leaning toward the bull to fake audacity?); for *templar*, or the timing of the *torero*, the slow, rhythmic motion he uses to give the bull maximum time to hook him; and, of course, for the cleanness of the kill.

There's no way to see Mexico all on one vacation. The place is too big, too diverse. Consider just a few highlights: the world's most remarkable train ride, through a region bigger than the Grand Canyon, from Chihuahua to the Pacific coast; the 45-metre (150-ft) high dive off a cliff into Acapulco Bay; tumultuous Mexico City and its ancient pyramids in the valley to the north; the Mayan ruins in the southern and eastern regions.

From the arid desert landscapes of Baja California to the mountains of Chiapas and from the northern border skirting three North American states to the lush jungles of Yucatán and the turquoise waters off Cancún, Mexico boasts 9,650 km (6,000 miles) of coastline. Nearly half the country is more than 1,500 metres (5,000 ft) above sea level, bordered by mountain ranges dotted with still-smoking volcanoes. Mexico's rolling hills and snow-capped mountains are breathtakingly picturesque, its waters – from the Sea of Cortés in the northwest and the Caribbean in the southeast – are filled with some of the world's richest marine life.

The most practical plan is to settle for one region per visit and explore it thoroughly. Or maybe to concentrate on one theme – colonial architecture, for example, native handicrafts, marketplaces or perhaps just wonderful beaches. There's something for almost everybody in Mexico's 1,968,324 sq. km (760,000 sq. miles) – a country about one-quarter the size of its northern neighbor.

And Mexico is a year-round destination. The entire western coast, including the 1,770-km (1,100-mile) Baja Peninsula are bathed in sunshine for at least three-quarters of the year and the coastal area encompassing Acapulco, Ixtapa/Zihuatenejo and Puerto Vallarta thinks of itself as the Mexican Riviera, with all that entails. Even in the south, including Mexico City, the summer rains conveniently fall mostly in the afternoons, leaving the rest of the day clear. Many of the lovely colonial cities in the central part of the country – Guanajuato, Guadalajara, San Miguel de Allende, Morelia – are high enough up to be deliciously balmy on even the hottest days. They offer an adventure in history and an ideal climate in which to explore it. As for the Yucatán Peninsula, winter is the best time to explore the Mayan ruins but at any time at all the powdery soft beaches of Cancun beckon irresistibly.

Visitors mean a lot to Mexico; after oil, the tourist industry is by far the biggest money-earner and there can be very few natives who don't appreciate the fact. Not that they need any encouragement to be friendly. Try to acquire a little *español* for your visit and don't worry about being grammatically perfect. The Mexicans will applaud your effort. They'll smile and think of you as *simpatico* – an *amigo*, or friend. It's one of the nicest words in any language, and, indeed, Mexicans are among the most polite people on earth.

Preceding pages: a view of the river from Mission Mulege in Bajia; Popocatépetl looms above the cornfields of the central plateau; overview of Mexico City; a pristine beach at Quintana Roo. **Left**, in front of the Pyramid of the Moon, Teotihuacán.

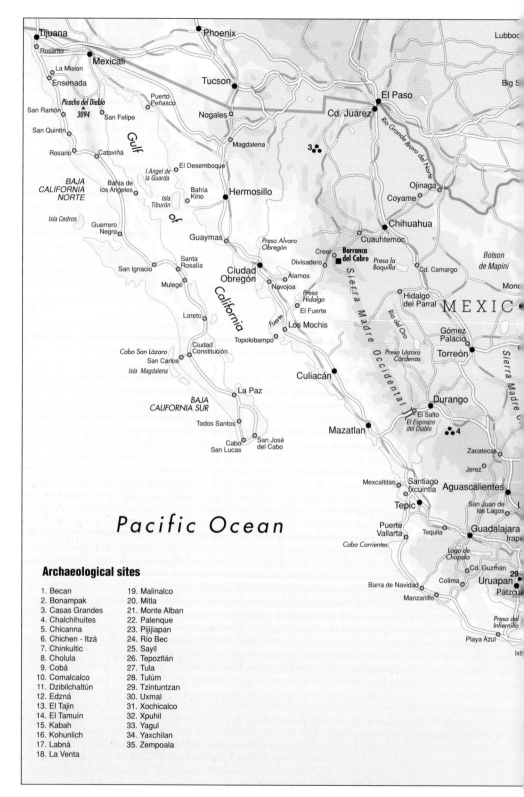

Tijuana
Rosarito
La Misión
Ensenada
Mexicali
Picacho del Diablo
3094
San Ramón
San Felipe
San Quintín
Rosario
Cataviñá
BAJA
CALIFORNIA
NORTE
Isla Cedros
Guerrero
Negro
Bahía de
los Angeles
I.Angel de
la Guarda
Isla
Tiburón
San Ignacio
Santa
Rosalía
Mulegé
Loreto
Cabo San Lázaro
San Carlos
Isla Magdalena
Ciudad
Constitución
BAJA
CALIFORNIA SUR
La Paz
Todos Santos
Cabo
San Lucas
San José
del Cabo

Gulf
of
California

Phoenix
Tucson
Nogales
Puerto
Peñasco
Magdalena
El Desemboque
Bahía
Kino
Hermosillo
Guaymas
Presa Alvaro
Obregón
Ciudad
Obregón
Navojoa
Álamos
Presa
Hidalgo
El Fuerte
Fuerte
Los Mochis
Topolobampo
Culiacán
Mazatlan
Mexcaltitán
Santiago
Ixcuintla
Tepic
Puerte
Vallarta
Cabo Corrientes
Tequila
Aguascalientes
San Juan de
los Lagos
Guadalajara
Lago de
Chapala
Cd. Guzmán
Colima
Uruapan
Pátzcu
Barra de Navidad
Manzanillo
Playa Azul
Presa del
Infiernillo
Ixt

El Paso
Cd. Juárez
Lubboc
Big S
Río Grande Bravo del Norte
Ojinaga
Coyame
Chihuahua
Cuauhtemoc
Creel
Barranca
del Cobre
Divisadero
Presa la
Boquilla
Cd. Camargo
Bolson
de Mapini
Mono
Hidalgo
del Parral
M E X I C
Río del Oro
Gómez
Palacio
Presa Lázaro
Cárdenas
Torreón
Sierra Madre Occidental
Durango
El Salto
El Espinazo
del Diablo
Zacatecas
Jerez
Sierra Madre O
Irap

3

4

Pacific Ocean

Archaeological sites

1. Becan
2. Bonampak
3. Casas Grandes
4. Chalchihuites
5. Chicanna
6. Chichen - Itzá
7. Chinkultic
8. Cholula
9. Cobá
10. Comalcalco
11. Dzibilchaltún
12. Edzná
13. El Tajin
14. El Tamuín
15. Kabah
16. Kohunlich
17. Labná
18. La Venta

19. Malinalco
20. Mitla
21. Monte Alban
22. Palenque
23. Pijijiapan
24. Río Bec
25. Sayil
26. Tepoztlán
27. Tula
28. Tulúm
29. Tzintuntzan
30. Uxmal
31. Xochicalco
32. Xpuhil
33. Yagul
34. Yaxchilan
35. Zempoala

168

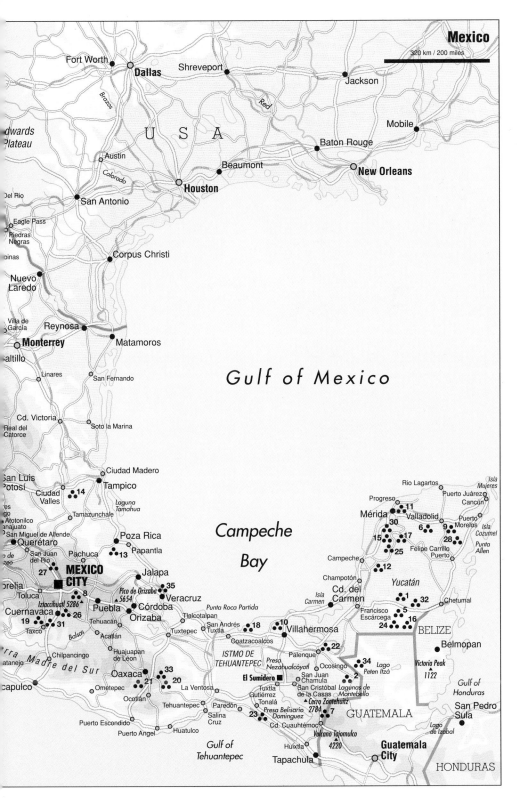

Mexico

320 km / 200 miles

Fort Worth · **Dallas** · Shreveport · Jackson

U S A

Mobile

Baton Rouge

New Orleans

dwards
Plateau

Austin · Beaumont

Colorado

Houston

Del Rio · San Antonio

Eagle Pass

Piedras
Negras

oinas · Corpus Christi

Nuevo
Laredo

Villa de
García · Reynosa

Monterrey · Matamoros

altillo

Linares · San Fernando

Cd. Victoria

Real del
Catorce · Soto la Marina

Gulf of Mexico

Ciudad Madero

San Luis
Potosí · Ciudad Valles · 14 · Tampico

es
go
Atotonilco
anajuato
San Miguel de Allende · Tamazunchale

Laguna
Tamahua

Campeche
Bay

Rio Lagartos

Progreso · 11

Isla
Mujeres

Puerto Juárez · Cancún

Mérida · Valladolid

Querétaro · Poza Rica

San Juan
del Río · Pachuca · 13 · Papantla

30 · 17 · 6 · 9 · Puerto
Morelos

Isla
Cozumel

15 · 28

Felipe Carrillo

Punta
Allen

Campeche · 25 · Puerto

de
zeo

27 · **MEXICO**
CITY · Jalapa · 12

orelia · Toluca · 8

Izttaccihuatl 5286 · Pico de Orizaba · 35

Champotón

Yucatán

Cuernavaca · 26 · Puebla · ▲ 5654

Córdoba · Veracruz

Isla
Carmen · Cd. del
Carmen

19 · 31 · Orizaba · Punta Roca Partida

Francisco
Escárcega · 1 · 32 · Chetumal

Taxco · Tehuacán · Tlalcotalpan

5

Bolsas · Acatlán · Tuxtepec · San Andrés
Tuxtla · 18 · 10 · Villahermosa

24 · 16 · **BELIZE**

Chilpancingo

Huajuapan
de Léon · Coatzacoalcos

22 · Palenque · **Belmopan**

atanejo

ISTMO DE
TEHUANTEPEC

Presa Belisario
Nezahualcóyotl · Ocosingo

34 · *Lago*
Petén Itzá

Victoria Peak
▲
1122

capulco · Oaxaca · 33 · 20

La Ventosa

El Sumidero ■

San Juan
Chamula

San Cristóbal
de la Casas · 2

Gulf of
Honduras

Ometepec · 21

Ocotlán · Tehuantepec · Paredón

Tuxtla
Gutiérrez
Tonalá

Lagunas de
Montebello

San Pedro
Sula

Puerto Escondido · Salina
Cruz · 23

Presa Belisario
Domínguez · ▲ Cerro Zontehuitz
2784 · 7 · **GUATEMALA**

Lago
de Izabal

Puerto Angel · Huatulco

Cd. Cuauhtémoc

Volcano Tajomulco
4220

Gulf of
Tehuantepec

Huíxtla · **Guatemala**
City

Tapachula · HONDURAS

169

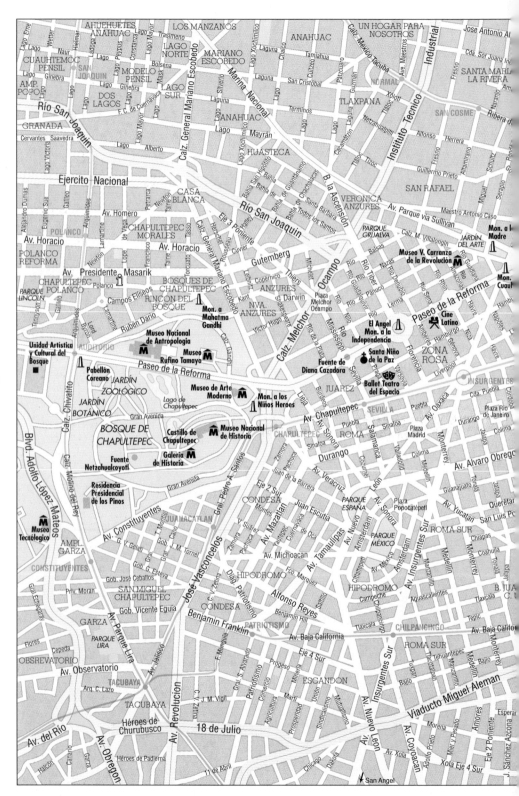

Mexico City Center

800 m / 0.5 miles

173

MEXICO CITY

Sprawling **Ciudad de México** has the finest restaurants, the best stores, the most luxurious hotels and the liveliest nightclubs in Mexico. In Mexico City is concentrated the nation's wealth and power. Here is the finest in cultural life: music, the arts, dance. It is a place of opportunity where Mexicans and visitors alike scent adventure in the air along the lovely Paseo de la Reforma. Yet Mexico City is very provincial still, preserving many of the ways of life of its colonial and Indian past.

Downtown corresponds roughly to the old Aztec and colonial capital. Small as old Mexico City is compared to the present-day megalopolis, it is big enough to wear you out if you walk. Basically, it comprises about 100 city blocks. Its boundaries are Repúblic de Peru to the north; José María Izazaga Street to the south; Circunvalación-La Viga to the east; and to the west what is now officially known as Eje Central Lázaro Cárdenas, but what everybody in town calls by its old names: San Juan de Letrán and Niño Perdido. (Some streets change their names every few blocks.)

The Centro includes the sordid and the majestic. It is Spanish, Indian, French romantic and modern. It is a business district, a marketplace, a colonial slum and a fancy shopping area. A good place to begin the day is a block east of the Alameda and Bellas Artes, with breakfast at the charming **Casa de los Azulejos**, a 16th-century house whose blue tiles were added 150 years ago when it was remodelled to house the exclusive Jockey Club. As **Sanborns** restaurant, it may be the best-known eating place in the city and has been famous at least since the days of Pancho Villa and Emiliano Zapata whose soldiers insisted on eating here.

A photograph of the revolutionaries dining can be seen down the block in the **Casasola photo store** where you can pose for a souvenir photo in a vintage costume from Revolutionary days and browse through archives of ancient pic-

tures. Opposite Sanborns, the **Torre Latino Americano** (176.5 meters/580 ft) with its panoramic 42nd-floor view is open until midnight.

The Centro's hub is the Zócalo, at the end of **Calle Madero**, once called *Plateros* (Silversmiths) but renamed by Pancho Villa in honor of his hero, the slain president Franciso Madero. Madero is still an interesting street and its occupants include the American Bookstore with a large array of English-language reading material, the **Museo Serfin** displaying colorful Indian costumes, and such famous landmarks as the sinking **San Francisco Church**, once part of the Franciscan monastery founded by Cortés himself three years after the Conquest, in 1524, and the striking **Palacio de Iturbide**. This is now owned by Banamex which stages art shows in the patio. Note also **La Profesa** church, which served as the capital's surrogate cathedral early in the 20th century and which has sunk at least a foot since it was built in 1720.

The **Zócalo**, which was the principal

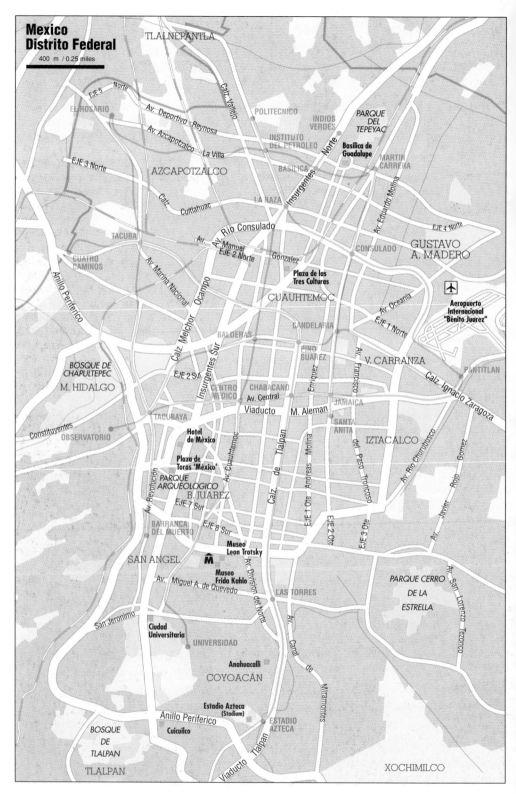

Mexico
Distrito Federal

400 m / 0.25 miles

TLALNEPANTLA

EJE 5   Norte

EL ROSARIO

Av. Deportivo   Reynosa

POLITECNICO

INDIOS
VERDES

PARQUE
DEL
TEPEYAC

Av. Azcapotzalco

INSTITUTO
DEL PETROLEO

Basilica de
Guadalupe

MARTIN
CARRERA

La Villa

EJE 3 Norte

AZCAPOTZALCO

BASILICA

Insurgentes

Norte

Calz.   Cuitlahuac

LA RAZA

Av. Eduardo Molina

EJE 4 Norte

TACUBA

Av. Rio Consulado

CONSULADO

GUSTAVO
A. MADERO

CUATRO
CAMINOS

Av. Manuel
EJE 2 Norte

Gonzalez

Av. Marina Nacional

Ocampo

Plaza de las
Tres Culturas

Av. Oceania

Aeropuerto
Internacional
"Bénito Juarez"

Anillo Periferico

CUAUHTEMOC

EJE 1 Norte

Calz. Melchor

BALDERAS

CANDELARIA

V. CARRANZA

PANTITLAN

BOSQUE DE
CHAPULTEPEC

INSURGENTES Sur

EJE 2 Sur

PINO
SUAREZ

Enriquez

Av. Francisco

Calz. Ignacio Zaragoza

M. HIDALGO

CENTRO
MEDICO

CHABACANO

Av. Central

JAMAICA

Av. Rio Churubusco

Gomez

Constituyentes

TACUBAYA

Viaducto

M. Aleman

SANTA
ANITA

Av. Javier Rojo

OBSERVATORIO

Hotel
de México

Calz.   de   Tlalpan

IZTACALCO

del   Paso   Troncoso

Av. San Lorenzo Tezonco

Plaza de
Toros 'México'

Av. Cuauhtemoc

Andreas

Molina

EJE 2 Ote

PARQUE
ARQUEOLOGICO

B. JUAREZ

Av. Revolución

EJE 7 Sur

EJE 1 Ote

EJE 3 Ote

BARRANCA
DEL MUERTO

EJE 8 Sur

PARQUE CERRO
DE LA
ESTRELLA

SAN ANGEL

Ⓜ

Museo
Leon Trotsky

Av. Division del Norte

Av. Miguel A. de Quevedo

Museo
Frida Kahlo

LAS TORRES

San Jeronimo

Ciudad
Universitaria

UNIVERSIDAD

Av. Canal   de   Miramontes

Anahuacalli

COYOACÁN

Estadio Azteca
(Stadium)

Anillo Periferico

ESTADIO
AZTECA

BOSQUE
DE
TLALPAN

Cuicuilco

Tlalpan

TLALPAN

Viaducto

XOCHIMILCO

176

Aztec ceremonial center, with open spaces, pyramids and palaces, has been transformed many times. Up to a few years ago it was a provincial square, with palm trees and a tram terminal. Now it is a huge open space, a convenient place for political rallies. (Old photographs of the plaza's earlier manifestations can be seen in he Zócalo metro station). The best view of the Zócalo is from the rooftop restaurant of the **Hotel Majestic** (entrance on Madero).

The Zócalo is full of history. On the north side are two vast churches – the **Cathedral of Mexico** and the **Sagrario**. The cathedral, supposedly the largest religious building on the continent, is an encyclopedia of Mexican colonial art. Construction took three centuries, beginning in Spanish Renaissance style and finishing in the French neoclassical style of the early 19th century.

Huge and impressive with a rich repository of decorative art, its somber but magnificent interior is softly illuminated through contemporary stained-glass windows that give off a mellow, golden light. Like all cathedrals of its time, it is a complicated building, 100 meters (328 ft) long and 46 meters (151 ft) wide. It is organized in five naves, the central one being reserved to house the choir and the main altars.

The main altars are El Altar del Perdón (the Altar of Forgiveness), which is used for the most important ceremonies; and, at the end of the nave, the magnificent **Altar de los Reyes**, one of the masterpieces of Mexican colonial art in *churrigueresque* style, named for the elaborate surface decoration favored by the 18th-century Spanish architect José Churriguera. Built and carved by Jerónimo de Balbas and finished in 1737, the altar is like a a large, over-decorated niche. It houses two paintings, one representing the Assumption of the Virgin and the other the Adoration of the Magi, flanked by golden columns, sculptures, moldings, angels, flowers and all the fantastic shapes of baroque imagination. This is the great Mexican *retablo*, all movement, color and madness. It was intended for the expected visit of

The cathedral at night.

the king of Spain (who never arrived).

The **Altar del Perdón**, located near the entrance, was so named because of the special benefits it is said to confer on people performing acts of devotion. Also the work of Jerónimo de Balbas, with a huge *retablo*, crowned by a festive arch framing a beautiful painting of St Sebastian, it is flanked by a majestic organ. The cathedral has 14 other chapels along the eastern and western walls, many of them unusually dark. The impressive, indeed elegant, main facade was finished by the sculptor and architect Manuel Tolsá, but the towers crowned with two original bell-shaped structures are the work of another artist, José Damián Ortiz de Castro.

Preserved by faith: The cathedral's neighbor, the 18th-century **Sagrario** is a graceful building with a highly decorated stone facade and a fanciful shape. Unfortunately, the constructor, the Andalusian architect Lorenzo Rodriguez, neglected to furnish the Sagrario with a robust foundation – hence the impressive cracks in the walls and an obvious tendency to lean. But in Mexico City, inclined or even half-sunken buildings do not necessarily collapse. Faith, perhaps, keeps them standing.

The beauty of the Sagrario is the way it harmonizes with the cathedral, though the two buildings are totally different in style and shape. The best view is from the center of the Zócalo. It's worth walking around the cathedral, especially toward the east where you will find a picturesque square with a fountain and a monument honoring one of Mexico's heroes – Fray Bartolomé de las Casas, the Spanish bishop who dedicated his life to defending the Indians. (He suggested, in good faith, that blacks be brought from Africa to do much of the hard labor, and that contributed to the infamous slave trade.)

Across the street from Fray Bartolomé's square, what were once deemed unimportant Indian ruins have been transformed into the ambitious archaeological project **El Templo Mayor**, an excavation of the area where the main Tenochtitlán pyramid once stood. These excavations have yielded rich treasures, the main piece being a great stone slab representing the Coyolxauhqui, goddess of the moon. Here, beside the entrance to the Templo Mayor, dances are held on summer afternoons.

On the Zócalo's east side is **El Palacio Nacional** (the National Palace) of Mexico, the seat of power in Mexico and once the site of an Aztec palace. (The president actually lives at Los Pinos near Chapultepec Park.) The palace contains two ministries – the Treasury and Presidential Planning – plus a rather somber and dull museum honoring Benito Juárez, Mexico's liberal hero. But most visitors to the Palace come to admire the Diego Rivera murals adorning the main staircase and first floor corridors.

Like all of Rivera's murals the ones here are both confusing and ambitious. The one on the staircase walls attempts to portray the entire history of Mexico, from the creation of the world up to a hypothetical Marxist revolution. The one on the staircase is a personal, naive, and charming vision of Mexican history

Detail on the cathedral's facade.

by a man in love with the Indian past. Rivera, a practicing Marxist though a millionaire – indeed he was expelled from the Communist party – hated the Spaniards to a ridiculous degree. But the mural, as a painting, is beautiful, full of soft and glowing colors, and somewhat like the church *retablos* except that instead of saints and angels Rivera painted all the heroes of Mexico that only a patriotic schoolboy would take the trouble to know.

Along the corridors, Rivera painted scenes that painstakingly represent pre-Columbian life. Utopian as they are, they reveal his great knowledge of Indian culture. The best of his works are in Mexico City. In the downtown area are two important murals, one in the Palace of Fine Arts, and the other, perhaps the better of the two, is in a special museum at the far end of the Alameda Park. But if you like Rivera, you should go to two other places. One is the Chapingo Agricultural School, in the city of Texcoco, some 48 km (30 miles) from Mexico City. The other place is **Anahuacalli**,

Diego Rivera's *The Great Tenochtitlán,* at the National Palace.

the exotic Aztec pyramid-palace Rivera built in the south of Mexico City to house his collection of Indian art .

El Grito Presidencial: The National Palace is the scene of one of Mexico's most popular festivities, *El Grito* (the Shout). This event takes place during the night of September 16, when the president of Mexico appears on the main balcony of the *palacio* to ring the bell with which Father Hidalgo summoned the people of his congregation in Dolores and thus started the War of Independence. El Grito is a short but emotional ceremony. The president proclaims once again the independence of Mexico and the crowd in the Zócalo shouts: "*Viva Mexico¡ Viva la independencial¡*"

The other buildings around the Zócalo are of minor importance. The one at the south end is the **City Hall**. On the west side are private buildings of lesser importance, with the exception of the one housing **El Monte de Piedad** (the Mount of Mercy), an enormous pawnshop founded by a millionaire miner of colonial days. He opened the institution in

1775 to help the needy and the Monte has since become an important part of the life of the city, especially prior to holidays, when long lines form and people drop off various cherished family possessions. Before leaving the Zócalo, look left for another landmark – the grey dome of the **Palacio de Hierro** department store, one block down Calle 20 de Septiembre. Inside you can gaze up at one of the most gorgeous stained-glass ceilings in existence.

South of the Zócalo are two buildings worth a visit. One is the **Museo de la Ciudad de México** (Museum of Mexico City) on Pino Suarez, housed in the former palace of the Counts of Santiago de Calimaya, with a fountained patio, corridors and an endless number of rooms. Across the street is the chapel of the oldest hospital built in the New World – **El Hospital de Jesus**, established by Hernán Cortés. It is located in the very place where he met Moctezuma for the first time. The church has a mural by José Clemente Orozco. All around are decaying colonial buildings.

To the southeast is the **Merced market**, near the metro station of the same name, an immense warren of activity with almost overpowering sounds and smells: chickens frying, radios blaring and men with loudspeakers peddling their questionable remedies alongside girls rolling, heating and filling *tortillas* from brightly colored plastic bowls.

Only a block or two away, on Fray Servando Teresa de Mier at Rosario, is the **Mercado de Sonora**, known for its wide array of medicinal herbs and alleged witches who sell some of them. The atmosphere in Sonora market is subdued, almost reverent: radios play more softly here, and even the babies cry less. At one end, past the shelves of garish religious figurines, is the animal market, with cage after stacked cage of rabbits, pigeons, doves, parrots, puppies, parakeets and canaries, and tanks of frogs, turtles and snakes.

North of the Zócalo is the former university area of Mexico City, now superseded by a newer campus in the southern part of the city. Two former

Rain pipes for sale.

schools are worth visiting: first, the **School of Medicine** (Venezuela and Brasil streets), and the Escuela Nacional Preparatoria, also known as **San Ildelfonso**, on the Plaza de Santo Domingo. In the portals here *evangelistas* ("gospel writers") write letters for illiterates on ancient typewriters. The preparatory school, a Jesuit school in colonial times, played an important role in Mexican culture. The old walls are covered with classic Orozco murals, and murals by Fernando Leal and Jean Charlot.

Near San Ildelfonso is the **Ministry of Public Education**, exhibiting exciting Diego Rivera murals, the first murals commissioned by José Vasconcelos, education minister after the revolution. An immense statue of him stands outside. Just inside this magnificent old building, which now houses the **Libreria Justo Sierra**, is a small (free) cinema (its schedule listed on a board). Two blocks down along Moneda is the **National Museum** (free), in an impressive 16th-century building whose patio is filled with trees, flowers and a fountain.

Before climbing to the second floor (where free cultural videos are shown on weekends) stop for a coffee in the cosy cafeteria.

A few blocks north, although more readily found by walking up San Juan de Letran past the post office and Teatro Blanquita, is the **Plaza Garibaldi**. This is a great place to return to at night when costumed *mariachis* gather with their instruments and the lively bars, nightspots and burlesque theaters are in full swing. Check out the long row of mini restaurants in the **Mercado de Alimentos San Camilito**, all serving *tacos* and other indigenous fast food. The square is dotted with statues of *mariachi* heroes, Pedro Infante and José Alfredo Jimenez (who had successful singing careers in 1950s movies).

By heading along Calle Honduras and turning left at Calle Allende and walking two blocks up to Rayon you will reach another of the city's major markets, **La Lagunilla**, which is in two sections, the one on the northern side of the street being the most interesting

A shoeshine dreams while he cleans.

with its *tortilla*-makers, clouds of aromatic steam and men with knives, choppers, and hatchets slashing, cutting and scraping countless pineapples, cactus leaves, carrots, and slabs of meat and fish. Scrawny heads of skinned ducks hang over the edge of a nearby counter, lifeless yellow claws scratch the air, chickens are eviscerated, their livers laid out in bloody lines, soup is ladled from giant enamel pots, a woman gurgles lovingly to her infant as she places him on the potato-weighing scales, and surely somebody will add a touch of nail polish to the manicured pink toes of the neatly arranged pigs' trotters?

The other market is mostly clothes, its aisles lined with embroidered *charro* hats, children's party dresses and scores of mannequins, gaudily draped with sequinned dresses or polyester suits, the whole effect resembling a walk through a Haberdashers' Hall of Fame. Outside Lagunilla, the sidewalks are a patchwork of stalls, blocks of ice, scavenging dogs. The stalls fill both sides of the street all the way along Rayon.

Back to **La Alameda** (literally Promenade of the Poplars), which in the beginning was a site for the burning of heretics, one of the few entertainments provided during colonial days. In the 19th century the Alameda was transformed into a romantic park full of fountains, sculptures, and the inevitable music kiosk. Every Mexican town has a central square with trees, flowers, a kiosk, and at least one monument to a national hero. In the middle of the noisy and chaotic capital is a fragment of laid-back provincial Mexico.

In the Alameda there is even a monument to Beethoven. Among the other monuments is the Hemiciclo, a tribute to Juárez in white Italian marble, and two charmingly erotic girls, also in marble, called *Malgré Tout* (In Spite of Everything) and *Désespoir* (Despair). One of the pleasures of La Alameda is to sit in a chair and have your shoes cleaned while you read a newspaper or gawk at the passersby.

At one end of the park is the **Palacio de Bellas Artes** (the Palace of Fine **Take a letter.**

Arts), which is Mexico's most important theater. Begun in 1904 by the Italian architect Adamo Boari, it was not finished until 30 years later by the Mexican architect Federico Mariscal. This time lapse explains the duel personality of the building: the white Italian marble exterior is pure art nouveau, full of flying sculpture and floral decoration, and the interior a sort of Aztec art deco.

Bellas Artes is a combination of theater and exhibition hall housing a permanent show of modern Mexican painting and murals. The Rivera mural was commissioned by John D. Rockefeller in 1934 for New York's Radio City, but the subject matter – a militant Marxist allegory – was deemed unsuitable for the center of capitalist endeavor and the mural was promptly rejected

The well-publicized stained-glass curtain, made by Tiffany of New York, and showing the volcanoes Popocatépetl and Iztaccíhuatl, is a masterpiece of high-class kitsch. On stage, performances by the **Ballet Folklorico** of **Amalia Hernández** are a durable tourist attraction.

Across the street, only a few steps from the Renaissance Venetian post office is Mexico's most beloved monument, **El Caballito**, or the Tiny Horse. The sculpture, which is actually huge and formal, depicts the Spanish king Charles IV. Though forced by Napoleon to abdicate in favor of Joseph Napoleon, Charles still had the good fortune to be immortalized by great artists. Goya painted a magnificent portrait of Charles IV's family; Manuel Tolsá sculpted the Mexican Caballito.

Tiny Horse has galloped all over Mexico City in search of a permanent stable, having adorned the Zócalo, the University's patio, and then the crossing of the Paseo de la Reforma, Avenida Juárez and Bucareli streets. But as the traffic grew heavier El Caballito became a nuisance and had to be moved. His current neighbors include the **Palacio de Minería** (School of Mining), also by Tolsá and one of the best neoclassical buildings in the country.

La Alameda is flanked by two important streets – **Avenida Juárez** and **Avenida Hidalgo**, the former lined with hotels, restaurants and stores catering to tourists. At the western end of La Alameda the former San Diego church houses a museum of colonial painting, the **Pinacoteca Virreinal**. Included are works by colonial masters such as Echave, Juárez, Cabrera and López de Herrera. Mexican colonial painting, derivative from Spanish and Italian models, is not to everyone's taste. Always religious, it tends to be somber.

Avenida Hidalgo has a completely different atmosphere from cosmopolitan Juárez. Two small colonial churches, **San Juan de Dios** and **Santa Veracruz**, face a tiny square and preserve some of the flavor of old Mexico City. Nearby is the **Hotel Cortés**. This was not Hernán Cortés's residence, but an inn, once Santo Tomás de Villanueva, built by the Augustinian fathers in the 18th century and now offering a pleasant patio.

On Hidalgo check out the incredible **Franz Mayer Museum**. A German-born financier and an inveterate collector, Mayer, who became a Mexican citizen, assembled a rich collection of pe-

The domed Palacio de Bellas Artes.

riod furniture, stylish pottery, tapestry, rugs, silver objects and paintings, all laid out in a manner that must have delighted its benefactor as much as today's visitors.

To the west, at Avenida Hidalgo and Paseo de la Reforma, the colonial church of **San Hipólito**, stands on the spot where the Spaniards were defeated by the Aztecs on the *Noche Triste* (the Sad Night), August 13, 1521. This small church is the only landmark commemorating the Spanish conquest.

The grand **Paseo de la Reforma** ranks as one of the world's more charming boulevards. To the northeast the Paseo is less fashionable, with traffic circles that are often clogged, undistinguished monuments and a huge housing development called **Nonoalco-Tlatelolco**. Otherwise unimpressive, this is worth a visit on account of the **Plaza de las Tres Culturas** (Square of Three Cultures), which marks the site of an Aztec temple. Also in this square, in 1968, in the shadow of the colonial **Church of Santiago** and the rather bland **Ministry of Foreign Affairs** building, police and army troops shot and killed a number of students and others protesting police brutality and lack of democracy.

At the hectic intersection of the Reforma, Juárez and Bucareli is the tall tower of the **Loteriá Nacional** (National Lottery Building), where public draws take place three nights each week. From the crossroads the Reforma marches grandly along. Bucareli is the centre of the newspaper industry, and Avenida Juárez becomes **Ejido**, at the end of which is the massive Monument to the Revolution, perhaps the biggest art deco building in the world.

The **Monument to the Revolution** began as the huge central dome of the never-completed legislative palace, part of Porfirio Díaz's plan to transform Mexico City into a sort of Latin American Paris. But the revolution interrupted that grand scheme and the gigantic, empty iron structure was left to rust for years until an enterprising architect transformed it into the imposing monument you see today. Below it is a fasci-

On the Zócalo.

nating (free) museum which includes a collection of cartoons in which the building assumes many amusing forms.

Across the street is the **Frontón México**, venue for jai-alai, a Basque ricochet ball game that is one of Mexico City's great passions. It is interesting to watch in small doses – unless you participate in the betting, when it becomes much more interesting. Three blocks northeast on Alvarado, the **Museo de San Carlos** houses a collection of fine European paintings and some interesting 19th-century Spanish paintings.

Seine in cement: During the Díaz regime the Paseo was a grand promenade, full of shade trees and monuments, culminating in Chapultepec Park and its romantic castle. The Mexican writer Octavio Paz said the Paseo was Mexico City's river, a sort of Seine in cement, majestically crossing the best part of town. But, alas, the Paseo's success and Parisian appearance was also its undoing. As the horses and carriages were replaced by automobiles, the French-looking mansions were torn down and replaced by skyscrapers. But even today the Paseo is a beautiful street. Its monuments include **Columbus**, and, at the crossing of the Reforma and Insurgentes, **Cuauhtémoc**, the last Aztec emperor and first Mexican hero, who ruled during Cortés's siege of Mexico City. Cuauhtémoc became the perfect romantic hero, valiant and doomed, and this monument to him seems like something out of an opera; he stands like a Roman senator wearing a feather hat at one of Mexico City's busiest intersections.

The next monument, the glittering **El Angel**, is perhaps the most beautiful of all, standing gracefully atop a tall and elegant column and commemorating the country's independence. It is surrounded by grand buildings, such as the **María Isabel Sheraton Hotel** and the **American Embassy**.

The Zona Rosa: South of Reforma and between Cuauhtémoc and the Angel is a district formerly known as the Colonia Juárez but gradually transformed into **La Zona Rosa**, or the Pink Zone, a

Independence Day parade.

neighborhood crowded with fancy boutiques, expensive restaurants, hotels and stores. Deep down, La Zona Rosa harbors international aspirations – hence such street names as Hamburgo, Niza and Copenhague. In reality, it is colorful, chaotic and very Mexican.

The area is crammed with eating places, the most interesting being the cafés on Copenhagen or Genova. Local residents go to the Zona specifically for eating, shopping and people-watching, and long lunches are a Mexican institution, so take your time and unwind.

Check out **Amberes Street**, chic since the 1960s and known for its exclusive goods. In particular, look out for the whimsical, tinted sculptures and jewelry of **Sergio Bustamante**, a Mexican artist of Indian and Chinese origin. **Gucci** is at the corner of Hamburgo; **Los Castillo** has intriguing silver inlay chinaware. The entrance to the glitzy **Plaza Rosa** mall is across the street. Londres has the **Plaza Angel**, a mall specializing in antiques, some with a Mexican motif, such as quaint pictures of saints and miracles on tin and sculptural colonial furniture. Its central patio and walkways are filled on Saturday mornings with a popular flea market. Across the street is the **Mercado Insurgentes**, with its extensive array of silver, serapes, embroidered clothing and all kinds of souvenirs. One side is lined with cheap but clean food counters.

One of Zona Rosa's curiosities is the huge circle on which the **Insurgentes Metro Station** is located. It is packed with stalls of every type. In other cities, subway stations are just subway stations; no more, no less. In Mexico, they are grand exhibition spaces. One called **Pino Suarez** boasts an Aztec pyramid – the real thing. It's no trouble getting around on the metro: wall maps are clear and easy to follow. (A detailed metro line map is reproduced in the Travel Tips section of this guide.)

Chapultepec Park is not only the largest wooded area in Mexico City, but one of the few places in the capital where you can relax in the open air. It is also a place of great historical importance. In pre-Columbian times, the city's

drinking water came from Chapultepec because the lake that surrounded Mexico-Tenochtitlán was salty. Mexico's rulers have lived here for centuries (it is believed, for example, that the famous Indian king Netzahualcóyotl had a palace there.) The summer home of Viceroy Matías de Gálvez eventually became Mexico's military academy.

During the Mexican War the invading Americans attacked the military school, known as **El Castillo**. The young Chapultepec cadets who were defending it chose to die rather than surrender to the US forces, and thus became national heroes, *Los Niños Héroes*. A monument at the entrance to the park commemorates them.

Chapultepec Castle is inhabited by the ghosts of Maximilian of Austria and his empress, Charlotte, whose story reads like a 19th-century popular novel. Maximilian was the prince who became the tragic, short-lived emperor of Mexico, under the auspices of France. But after the French army left for home in 1867, the forces of Benito Juárez

A Zona Rosa jeweler.

186

defeated Maximilian, who was captured and shot. Charlotte went insane and died years later in Europe, forever dreaming of the adventure in Mexico that went wrong.

The castle, a steep 20-minute hike up from the park, houses a **Museum of Mexican History**, whose artifacts include Maximilian's carriage. It is a good place from which to see Mexico City in all its grandeur provided there isn't too much smog. Also, Chapultepec boasts some fine murals, notably in the Siqueiros hall, which is painted with themes of the revolution. Chapultepec houses a zoo, botanical gardens and a lake. There are also theaters and museums including the **National Museum of Anthropology**, one of the outstanding buildings of the world. Designed by Pedro Ramírez Vásquez, it offers a spectacular arena with a patio half covered by an immense sculptured umbrella.

Fine gifts at Sergio Bustamente.

The seemingly unfinished statue outside the museum, standing on Reforma, is Tlaloc, the rain god, who was brought here in the 1960s amid continuous downpours, which some said was due to his protest at being moved from his previous location. The museum's magnificent interior court of pink stone with water falling down the single column holding up the striking roof canopy, was inspired by the Mayan ruins at Uxmal.

The museum is extremely large and takes time to savor. Its highlight is the marvelous **Sala Mexica**, dedicated to Aztec art and history. This hall includes the famous **Aztec Calendar**, the heroic sculpture of the goddess of Earth and Death, **Coatlicue**, as well as a most entertaining group of models of life in pre-Columbian times.

The museum is organized as follows: Introduction to Anthropology, Meso-América, Origins, Preclassical, Teotihuacán, Toltecs, Mexicas, Oaxaca, Gulf Cultures, Maya and Cultures of North and West. All these halls are on the patio level but there is another museum on the second floor, the **Ethnology Museum**, describing the life of Indians and decorated with contemporary murals.

The **Museo de Arte Moderno**, a

round glass building, exhibits easel paintings by some of the best-known muralists and other Mexican masters, including Frida Kahlo. Especially notable are two small but beautiful permanent exhibits, one dedicated to the great Mexican photographer, Manuel Alvarez Bravo, and the other a collection of landscape painting by the 19th-century Mexican José María Velasco.

The **Tamayo Museum**, housed in an ingenious building conceived by designers Zabludosky and González de Léon, has a rather nondescript collection of contemporary art, but also some beautiful Tamayos, including a splendid portrait of Tamayo's wife, Olga.

Outside the museum the Paseo de la Reforma continues west to enter residential areas occupied by well-to-do Mexicans, neighborhoods such as **Lomas de Chapultepec**, **Bosques de las Lomas** and **Polanco**.

The southern half of Insurgentes is a commercial street, lined with tall buildings. Landmarks to look out for are the huge **Hotel de México**, which has a re-volving restaurant on the top floor; the **World Trade Center**, a highrise being outfitted as offices, and, on the same block, the **Poliforum Cultural de Siquieros**, a multi-faceted building covered with dramatic murals painted by Siquieros, with *The March of Humanity*, the world's largest mural on an adjoining fence.

A few blocks south is an uncompleted project for what was intended to be the **City of Sports**. Among the finished structures is the **Plaza de México**, the world's largest bullring. (On the south side of Mexico City on the Calzada de Tlalpan is another enormous sporting arena, the **Estadio Azteca**, one of the biggest soccer stadiums in the world where the famous "Mexican wave" originated.)

Ten blocks before San Angel you'll spot the mosaic facade, Mexican mural-style of the **Teatro Insurgentes** on the right (lots of people): its theme is the theater in Mexico and the work was created by Diego Rivera. The striking red laquered fingernails of the enor-

Entrance to the Tamayo Museum.

mous hands partially covered in crimson lace seem to hold up the composition of the world-famous Mexican comic actor Cantínflas, taking from the rich and giving to the poor.

The fashionable village of **San Angel**, once some distance from the city and now encompassed by its sprawl, has managed to retain much of its charm, with crooked, cobblestoned streets and secluded mansions, many hidden behind high walls. The charming **El Carmen** church has tile-covered domes and a serene cloister. Be sure not to miss the spectacular **Casa del Risco** fountain – a national monument – composed of hundreds of gaily colored plates, cups, saucers and vases, most of them centuries-old, set into the wall of the *casa*.

Every Saturday a handicraft market, known as the **Bazar Sabado**, fills San Jacinto square. Usually packed, which makes getting around a squeeze, this bazaar is attractive because the salespeople are often the artists who created the crafts for sale. The **San Angel Inn**, a former *hacienda* with bags of aristo-

cratic appeal, is a fine restaurant frequented by wealthy Mexicans.

Other interesting little villages in Mexico City's southern suburbs include **Coyoacán**, where you shouldn't miss the **Frida Kahlo Museum**, the home of Diego Rivera and his last wife, Frida, a surrealist painter. It contains all kinds of memorabilia, including the couple's love letters and Frida's Indian dresses.

Coyoacán also has a museum dedicated to the first great heretic of the Communist faith, **Leon Trotsky**. It was in his home in Coyoacán in August, 1940, that Trotsky was assassinated by a Spanish Communist, apparently at the instigation of Joseph Stalin.

South of San Angel **Insurgentes Sur** crosses the big campus of Mexico's **National University** (UNAM). Constructed in the 1950s, it was for a long time an architectural wonder, dazzling in its bold use of color, murals and sculpture. Nowadays its prestige has waned, partly because unappreciative students have daubed the walls and statues with their own brand of graffiti. The

Rivera mural on the Teatro Insurgentes.

campus is still worth a visit, if only to admire the central library, where Juan O'Gorman covered the four huge walls with stone mosaic; and the stadium, which is decorated with a brutal stone mosaic by Diego Rivera.

The campus was built on top of a lava field, part of which, known as the **Pedregal**, is one of the city's poshest residential areas. At the bend of the campus, Insurgentes crosses the **Periférico**, a freeway decorated with modern sculpture. Nearby is a huge shopping center, **Perisur**, as soulless as any to be found in an American suburb.

Not far from here, almost isolated by the busy highway, is the oldest structure in the valley: the round pyramid of **Cuicuilco**, built perhaps as long as 1,000 years before the Christian era.

A mile or two to the east is **Xochimilco** (take the light rail from Tasquena metro station), a floating village which is the only remnant of the old lake city of Tenochtitlán. It used to be the favorite promenade of local residents who came here to eat and drink and ride in the flowery boats, but is now an overrated tourist attraction. A US$250 million renovation program should restore the gardens to their former glory. Bargain fiercely if buying a boat ride, and bring along a picnic, as the eating places are around the main embarkation point beside the parking lot at the foot of Ave Nativitas, which is not necessarily the dock where the bus will drop you off.

When you leave the boat, walk back up to the street and turn right, making a left turn on Nuevo Leon. This will bring you to a market full of exotic fruit, such as persimmons, guayaba, papaya and tamarind, all impeccably arranged as if for a competition. Further along, opposite the town plaza, is the 16th-century former convent of **San Bernadino**.

Although they are geographically close to each other, and each about a 45-minutes ride south of the city, it is almost impossible to go from the University to Xochimilco except by taxi (expensive). Buses along Insurgentes or the metro to Copilco station will take you close to the university.

Rent a boat at Xochimilco.

HOW TO BARGAIN

The first rule of bargaining for goods in Mexico is: there *are* no rules. In the past, conventional wisdom dictated that prospective buyers offer half the asking price for any item or items they wished to buy. The quick-witted locals soon caught on to that ploy; after all, some of them read the same guidebooks in which tourists found that advice. In any event, the word got around, so, as a countermeasure, the routinely quoted prices soared.

In the larger cities more and more shops are offering merchandise at fixed prices. Nevertheless, it doesn't hurt if you find something you really want, to try a tentative, *"Es possible un poco menos?"* ("Is is possible to have it for a little less?") It doesn't usually bring an affirmative answer, and certainly won't in the more elegant shops, but occasionally it does and the thing to remember is "nothing ventured, nothing gained," particularly if the time is right, such as off-season in a resort.

If prospective buyers have the time (and the energy), they can test the waters and check several shops or market stalls before deciding which item or items they absolutely cannot live without, and then proceed from there to haggle with the proprietor. It is rarely sensible to rush into buying anything until you have looked around to see what prices are being offered elsewhere. In Mexico City, for example, there's an official government store (with fixed prices) on Juarez opposite the Alameda. Check that out first – and then go to markets, such as as La Merced or Sonora or the Artesianas de la Ciudadela, and see if you can find the same items for less. (You usually can.)

The important factor that people should always keep in mind is that bargaining is a *game,* a game that at its best can be enjoyed by both the buyer and the seller. So, it is essential to play the game with good grace. If, in response to your inquiry of *"Quanta costa?"* a price is quoted that seems too high but not absolutely outrageous, you might try making a counter offer. And, if in turn that counter offer brings another counter offer, that's the equivalent of an invitation to proceed. If the initial offer is considered by the seller as too low to allow for a negotiated settlement, it will probably elicit no more than a shake of the head... or a simple "no."

Even here the buyer has a choice: to smile and coax a bit and test the reaction again, to raise the offer, or simply to leave. Then the game may conclude, or begin again. The important thing is to leave the seller with a sense that he or she has not lost face. So, even as a deal is in progress, the buyer may have to give up an extra *peso* or two to finalize a bargain and leave both parties feeling good. When, however, the potential buyer becomes abusive or rude, nobody wants to play and the fun is gone.

So, whether or not people speak Spanish (or at least know the numbers, which is a prerequisite for serious bargaining) or use pen and paper to write down their changing offers, they should remember to keep their manners intact. And especially to smile, even in the thick of hard bargaining. A teasing attitude is often much better than a serious demeanor when trying to consummate a sale, particularly for an inexpensive item. It's frequently much more effective too. Try it and see. ∎

The hard sell.

DAY TRIPS FROM MEXICO CITY

East, north and west of Mexico City is the state of Mexico; to the south is Morelos. Just a weekend trip away are Hidalgo to the north; Puebla and Tlaxcala to the east. This is historic Mexico, the heart of the country, comprising a mosaic of peoples and offering a geography ranging from cool but stately pine forests to hot and humid valleys bursting with plant life.

Let's follow six routes out of Mexico City and try to make as few detours as possible. It's appropriate to remember that the really important things in Mexico are frequently those that require the most effort to discover.

Tepotzotlán: Querétaro Road, an extension of the busy freeway known as the Periférico, starts in the northwest of the city, near the bullring known as **Cuatro Caminos**, and crosses the sprawling industrial and middle-class northern surburbs. Along the way **Satélite Towers**, five tall, slender and brightly colored structures designed by Luis Barragán and Mathias Goeritz, are surely among the world's most attractive water towers.

About 26 km (16 miles) further north, right at the toll gates, is **Tepotzotlán**, famous for its magnificent church and monastery, one of the jewels of colonial art and chosen to house the national museum of the art of the viceroyalty. In the 16th century the monastery was designed to serve as a school for the Indians, later becoming a Jesuit seminary before being converted into a museum and cultural center. It is about 90 minutes by bus from the capital.

Tepotzotlán is one of the masterpieces of Mexican baroque style, a genuine, native product. Baroque goes well with Mexican sensitivity: its lavish use of color and movement, its excesses and its unbounded imagination are the soul of Mexican art. Perhaps Mexicans are a baroque people at heart, helplessly in love with color, with murals, with ornament. Tepotzotlán is noted for its fine baroque and *churrigueresque*, which is the name given to late baroque in Spanish-speaking countries.

The main **church of Tepotzotlán**, completed in 1762, has a lavishly decorated facade carved in light-colored stone. It is typical of Mexican colonial churches: flanking the door and central window are four richly decorated columns framing niches containing sculptures of saints. Tepotzotlán has a single deliciously carved and graceful belfry and the interior is a medley of golden *retablos*. The *retablo*, a gilded wooden structure, appears to grow and multiply like an exotic tropical plant, covering the walls and transforming them into a mysterious, glittering surface. It provides an inspiring frame to paintings and sculpture. The striking *retablo* of Our Lady of Guadalupe boasts paintings by Miguel Cabrera, one of the masters of the colonial era.

Each *retablo* tells a religious story, with each saint and image organized as precisely as guests at a banquet: obviously it helps to know who the saints are, and their particular significance. Those in Tepotzotlán are all related to the Jesuits and their history, with the church itself dedicated to St Francis Xavier, the great friend and follower of St Ignatius of Loyola, the 16th-century founder of the Jesuit Order. The church is flanked by chapels, one of which – dedicated to Our Lady of Loreto – contains a replica of the house in Nazareth where the Virgin Mary is supposed to have lived.

The chapel of Loreto has an eccentric neighbor, the **Camerino** (the term for a dressing room in a theater), in which the clothes of the Virgin's images were changed according to the time of the year. Its ceiling is decorated with angels, flowers, shells and paintings.

The monastery at Tepotzotlán houses the **Museum of the Viceroyalty**. Among the favorite halls is No. 15, which has a colorful carving of St James (Santiago), patron saint of Spain and one of the most popular saints in Mexican colonial art. In hall No. 19 is a wondrous painting of the Virgin of Bethlehem, attributed to the Spanish master Murillo. Hall No. 20 houses *The Wed-*

Preceding pages: a service at the Basilica of Guadalupe. **Left,** gilded interior, Tepotzotlán.

ding of the Virgin, by one of the best colonial painters, Juan Rodriguez Juárez; halls 32–42 are devoted to a rich and varied collection of ornaments, jewelry and other *objets d'art*.

About 50 km (31 miles) north of Tepotzotlán is **Tula**, an archaeological center which played a major role in Mexico's pre-Columbian life. Tula dates from the beginning of the 10th century, when Teotihuacán had already been destroyed and Tenochtitlán had yet to be founded. Thus Tula is another link in the chain of cultured settlements that preserved the spirit of civilization in the Mexican highlands. Tula was founded by King Ce Acatl Topiltzín (Our Lord One-Reed), who was a member of one of the nomadic tribes known as Chichimecas. Tula became the capital of the Toltecs, a cultured people. Ten Toltec kings ruled Tula for 312 years –until Tula was destroyed by Chichimecas. No written history of Tula exists but myths are abundant.

An important building here is the **Temple of the Morning Star**, Tlahuiz-calpantecuhtli. Behind the lower gallery, covered in pre-Columbian days by a roof supported by columns, is a pyramid, some 9 meters (30 ft) high. It supports *atlantes*, or columns, Tula's most important contribution to Mexican art. They represent Quetzalcóatl as the morning star. He is dressed in warrior garb, wearing a pectoral in the form of a butterfly. On his back he carries a round shield in the form of the setting sun and in the center of the shield is a human face.

Of the other structures in Tula that have survived the centuries, perhaps the most interesting is the **Coatepantli**, or Wall of Serpents, raised along the north and west sides of the pyramid. Almost 2 meters (6.5 ft) tall, it is crowned with the universal motif of ancient Mexican art – the serpent in motion. In what is known as the **Burnt Palace**, near the pyramid, is the Chac Mool, another typically Mexican art form. The Chac Mool is the reclining figure of a priest. On his chest is a receptacle in which were placed offerings to the gods.

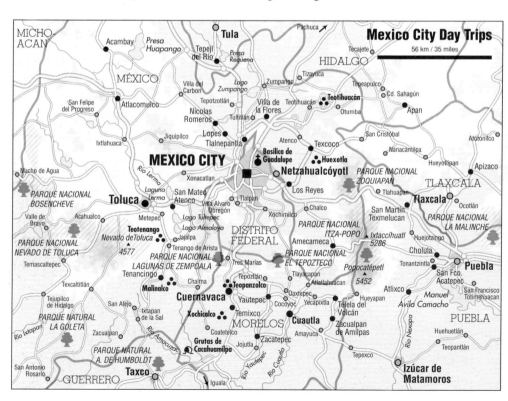

Basilica of Guadalupe: A trip to the Basilica of Guadalupe can easily be fitted into a half day, but car drivers might want to continue on to Teotihuacán. The metro station at La Villa is actually a closer stop to the basilica than the station of that name. As you depart from the station, you will see the curved roof of the new basilica, with the old one it replaced a few blocks to the north. Designed by Mexico's top architect, Pedro Ramirez Vasquez (who was responsible for the acclaimed Museum of Anthropology), it is regarded by some as a *monstruosidad*, but it has been hugely popular from the day it was completed in 1976.

It contains the image of **Our Lady of Guadalupe**, the Brown Madonna, a great national religious symbol. History relates that in 1531 an Indian named Juan Diego believed he saw the Virgin on top of a hill nearby. Miraculously, she left her image in his *tilma,* a sort of fibrous cape worn by Indians. This image became the symbol that is found in most Mexican homes, stores, places of work, even buses, trucks and taxicabs. She is not only the Madonna, but the Mexican Madonna. Mexicans have adopted her as their fighting flag, and even hard-bitten politicians who are known as anti-clerical tread softly when speaking of the Brown Madonna.

On December 12, a national holiday, thousands of penitents make the pilgrimage to Guadalupe for the anniversary of her 16th-century apparition. At any time of the year you'll see penitents crawling up the approach on their knees, and quite often you will witness chanting, banner-waving processions filing into the enormous square.

There is almost always a service taking place in the vast basilica itself, but people are constantly wandering in and out, admiring the stained glass windows, the marble stairs, latter-day chandeliers and fluted ceiling of burnished wood. A slow-moving pedestrian walkway carries an endless stream of admirers past the giant-sized portrait of the Virgin high up on one wall. The spacious building can hold as many as

Atlantes at Tula.

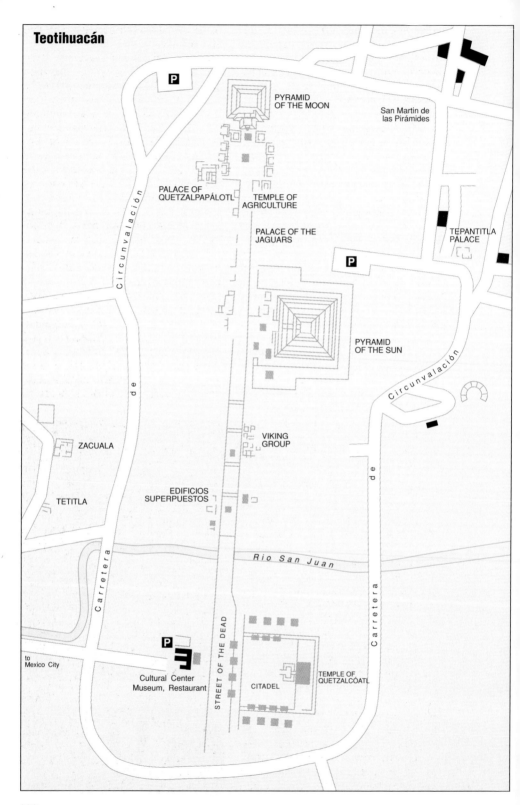

Teotihuacán

PYRAMID OF THE MOON

San Martin de las Pirámides

PALACE OF QUETZALPAPÁLOTL

TEMPLE OF AGRICULTURE

PALACE OF THE JAGUARS

TEPANTITLA PALACE

Circunvalación

de

Circunvalación

PYRAMID OF THE SUN

ZACUALA

VIKING GROUP

de

EDIFICIOS SUPERPUESTOS

TETITLA

Carretera

Rio San Juan

Carretera

to Mexico City

STREET OF THE DEAD

Cultural Center Museum, Restaurant

CITADEL

TEMPLE OF QUETZALCÓATL

10,000 people at a time. The old basilica, much more aesthetic, dates back to 1533 but had become too small to accommodate the enormous crowds. Besides, it was beginning to list noticeably as – like many other buildings in the capital – it gradually sank into the ground. For some years the old basilica served as a museum, with a fine collection of colonial paintings, but at present it is fenced off and undergoing renovations. Behind it, on top of the hill, is a small chapel, and in front, beside the pedestrian bridge, is a string of shops and stalls selling religious images, incense, food, toys and lottery tickets.

The pyramids: This northbound road from Mexico City, the continuation of Insurgentes Norte, leads to the exit of Teotihuacán and Acolman, 50 km (31 miles) northeast of the city. **Teotihuacán** is known as Meso-America, the city chosen by the gods as the place from which to create the universe. Teotihuacán, the City of Quetzalcóatl, is a major archaeological center, one of the best preserved in the country. It is not as spectacular as the Mayan cities, which are lost in tropical green, for its beauty is subdued, even sober. Even the landscape is simple and serene; not too dry, not too fertile. The hills are softly contoured and the valley is high and typically ample.

A few minutes before the turn-off for Teotihuacán keep your eyes open, on the left, for the fortress-like **San Agustín de Acolman**, an attractive 16th-century church and monastery with a delightful medieval interior. The church is located in a large atrium; large enough to accommodate the great number of converts who would come here for instruction but could not be received inside the church itself. In the center is a remarkable mission cross, carved by an anonymous Indian sculptor who interpreted the symbols of Christ's Passion in an Aztec style. The bus does not stop at Acolman; you'll need the Indios Verdes bus for that. There are many 16th-century churches and monasteries all over Mexico, but few can be visited as easily as Acolman. In no other place are a major archaeological center and a

beautiful colonial monument to be found side by side.

At **Teotihuacán**, the bus drops you at Gate 1, where you pay the admission charge and a fee for any cameras you are seen to be carrying. Walk up past the multitudinous stalls (none sell anything but clothing and souvenirs) to the museum which contains a scale model of the site and some reproductions of items found here (the originals are in the Teotihuacán Hall of the Museum of Anthropology).

Upstairs is a small café and an exorbitantly expensive restaurant, so it is advisable to bring fruit and sandwiches with you. There are restaurants in the area but virtually none of them can be reached without a car.

Teotihuacán, the city of Quetzalcóatl, is one of the best-preserved archaeological sites in the country. Beginning as an agricultural settlement several hundred years before the Christian era, it became one of the biggest cities in the world with a population of around 200,000. Around 600 BC it began to

decline and was soon after abandoned. Whether this was due to a shortage of wood and building materials in the days before the invention of the wheel, or perhaps as the result of a successful invasion, nobody knows for certain. When the Aztecs arrived in the 14th century it had long been deserted.

The site is huge (13 sq. km/5 sq. miles), so it becomes "crowded" only in a relative sense. In fact, there seems to be as many people selling things as visitors. These peddlers are amiable but a pest, like mosquitoes that must constantly be fended off.

The **Temple of Quetzalcóatl** is nearest to the entrance and thus best dealt with first. Filled with exquisite sculptural decoration, based on the theme of the serpent in motion, and with masks of Quetzalcóatl and Tlaloc, the god of rain, it was discovered covered by a pyramid when the back of another pyramid was demolished. Archaeologists aren't sure why the builders of Teotihuacán hid such marvels away but such was the custom in ancient Mexican architecture; many pyramids hide earlier ones.

A causeway, about 2-km (1-mile) long, runs between this rectangular complex – named by the Spaniards as the **Citadel** although it was never a fortress – and the Pyramid of the Moon to the north. The causeway, which has been named the street of the dead on account of the many skeletons discovered along its length during excavations, runs in a straight line but actually consists of a series of semi-enclosed spaces. Occasionally there are frescoes to be seen in covered spots along the walls.

Just over halfway along you'll pass the gigantic **Pyramid of the Sun** (base 222 by 225 meters/728 by 856 ft). Even without the temple that once adorned the top, the pyramid is more than 65 meters (200 ft) high – less than half the height of the Great Pyramid of Cheops in Egypt, which stands on a comparable base. Like its Egyptian counterpart, it is riddled with tunnels and secret chambers but these have never been open to the public. Behind the pyramid, more frescoes can be seen in the **Tepantitla** Pyramid of the Sun at Teotihuacán.

Palace. Teotihuacán and its Pyramid of the Sun are simply expressions of the importance given by an agricultural society to astronomy and the measurement of time.

The **Pyramid of the Moon**, completed at a later date than the Pyramid of the Sun, overlooks a plaza at the northern end of the avenue, surrounded by a dozen small temples, including the Palace of Quetzal-Mariposa with well-preserved murals and bas-reliefs of *mariposas* (butterflies) and *quetzals* (tropical birds) nearby. Noteworthy is the **Palace of the Jaguars**, which has been well restored and still bears traces of the red, green, yellow and white symbols that represent birds, maize and water. Though smaller (52 meters/150 ft) than the Sun pyramid, the Pyramid of the Moon is built on a higher base and is therefore about the same height above the ground. It is also easier to climb.

You could spend a whole day wandering around the complex, but you'll probably find a couple of hours is enough. Although most guidebooks advise you to arrive early, the pyramids actually look their most impressive at sunset. The grounds close at 6pm.

Don't fail to explore the surrounding countryside. Nearby is **Otumba**, where the Aztecs were defeated by Hernán Cortés in one of the decisive battles of the Spanish Conquest. Farther to the northeast is **Ciudad Sahagún**, one of Mexico's industrial experiments.

The region is typical of central Mexico; desert plains and hills, in which the main vegetation is the cactus plant from which *pulque*, the national beverage, is extracted. Peculiar-tasting, frothy, beerish and loaded with vitamins, *pulque* is said to be very nourishing (the best excuse in the world for a favorite drink). During colonial times and in the 19th century, big *pulque* plantations were developed. The manor houses of such plantations were magnificent. Some survive – such as **Xala**, near Ciudad Sahagún, which has been transformed into a hotel and preserves something of its earlier grandeur.

Puebla and the volcanoes: Built in an

Teotihuacán's Avenue of the Dead and the Pyramid of the Moon.

area of frequent earthquakes, Mexico City is surrounded by volcanic peaks such as the majestic **Popocatépetl** (5,452 meters/17,886 ft) and beautiful **Iztlac-cíhuatl** (5,286 meters/17,342 ft) as well as a dozen minor mountains. But the temblors of modern times have usually been mild and modern Mexican architects are famous for their engineering skills. The famous volcanoes can be seen on the way to Puebla, the road to which is a continuation of the great avenue called **Calzada Ignacio Zaragoza**, the backbone of proletarian Mexico City that begins near the airport in the unattractive eastern section. This traffic artery runs by a sprawling community, **Netzahualcóyotl**, a bedroom suburb with a working-class population of more than 2 million, sometimes called "Mexico's third largest city."

Once the *calzada* leaves the urban area behind, the road to Puebla enters a beautiful but cold and rainy mountain area. The volcanoes loom very close. The route to those snowcapped wonders, **Popocatépetl** and **Iztaccíhuatl**, is via the Amecameca road through a pleasantly pastoral land.

After crossing the mountains, the road descends into the ample valley of **Puebla**, a city founded during colonial times and the capital of the state with the same name. Now a growing industrial center, Puebla has nevertheless preserved some of its old character and possesses some of the most important colonial works of art in Mexico. One such gem is Puebla's elegant and majestic cathedral, regarded by some as the finest in Mexico.

It was built from 1588 to 1649 in the most refined architectural style of the Spanish renaissance, the *Herreriano* (named for Juan de Herrera, the architect of the Escorial, the classic monastery and palace in New Castile, near Madrid). The style is severe and elegant, paying its respects to Roman architecture. The fine main altar is the work of the famous neoclassical artist, Manuel Tolsá.

On Calle 5 Oriente, beside the cathedral is the tourist office almost next door

Beetling along the streets of Puebla.

to the **Casa de Cultura** where cultural events are held. Once a seminary, founded in 1646, it now has a sculpture garden and tiny coffee shop, and serves as a community center with its open-air theater. Up the stone stairs is the splendidly ornate **Palafox Library**, the oldest in America, with its 50,000 volumes nestled on shelves of carved and gilded woodwork. There is a small admission charge but you can peek in through the open doorway.

On Calle 2 Sur is Puebla's newest uncharacteristically high-tech attraction, the **Amparo Museum**, whose computerized catalog and interactive videos provide further amplification of the art therein. Spanning several centuries, the art was the personal collection of the late Manuel Espinosa Iglesias whose (colonial-era) house this was. The museum is free on Mondays, closed Tuesdays. Three blocks away the distinctive **La Compañía** church, with its elaborate facade, is said to be the last resting place of China Poblana, the 17th-century Asian princess whose statue surmounts a fountain at the east side of town. Her costume of frilly blouse atop embroidered skirt has become a characteristic cliché of Mexican peasant garb. Adjoining the church, bordering a pleasant, cobbled alley is the **Puebla University**, housed in a 16th-century building which once served as a Jesuit college.

Excluding the cathedral, the architecture of Puebla might be regarded as a Mexican version of Spanish baroque, interpreted through a great profusion of tiles and plaster decoration. The best example is perhaps the **Casa del Alfeñique**, now the regional museum and containing good examples of ceramics produced in the state, along with memorabilia from that great event in Puebla history, the battle of Cinco de Mayo (May 5) in 1862.

Puebla's remarkable colonial architecture includes lavish churches, such as the church of La Compañía, and mysterious convents, such as **Santa Monica**, which operated secretly and unknown to the secular authorities until 1934. It is now the **Museo de Arte**

Girls' talk.

Religioso. Inside the 16th-century **Santo Domingo** church, with its tiled dome, is the famous gilded **Capilla Rosary**, altar to the Virgin.

The extensive use of Talavera tiles on Puebla's church domes has given rise to its reputation as "the city of tiles", and the characteristic blue Talavera pottery which has been produced since the 16th century, with designs reflecting Asian, Spanish-Arab and indigenous influences, can be found at **El Parian**, the central market aimed at tourists whose stalls sell everything Mexican, from serapes to sombreros.

At the end of this block adjoining the so-called "artists' quarter" of craft workspaces is the **Teatro Principal** which was almost 150 years old when it suffered a disastrous fire in 1902, after which it was fully restored.

Looking west up 6 Oriente you can see the cast-iron structure of the old **Mercado Victoria**, abandoned some years back for still-to-be-completed renovations. It was one of the last of the grand old markets, built by Porfirio Díaz who sought to transform Mexico into a carbon copy of France. The surrounding area is a warren of activity, especially **5 de Mayo**, which is lined with sidewalk stalls. Almost every town in Mexico has a Cinco de Mayo, but Puebla is where the day first assumed its national importance. It marks the date when a Mexican army, led by General Ignacio Zaragoza and including battalions of Indians, defeated a French army. The victory boosted Mexican morale, but was unable to prevent the French occupation.

Puebla is associated in Mexican minds with colonial grandeur, with General Zaragoza, with the start of the Revolution of 1910, and also with three culinary specialties: *camotes* (sweet potatoes prepared with fruit and sugar), *rompope* (a sort of eggnog, said to be a child's introduction to alcohol) and *mole* (a dark sauce whose ingredients include chili peppers, spices, chocolate, nuts and bread, all finely ground and then mixed with tomato sauce and chicken or turkey broth and served over cooked **Ploughing in the highlands.**

chicken or turkey). Like any great dish, good *mole* requires a lot of work. It is sometimes referred to as the national dish, though it has a number of competitors for that honor. The sauce is said to have been invented in the kitchen of the **Santa Rosa Convent** (No. 3 Nte, near No. 14 Pte), which is now an excellent handicraft museum.

Cholula is a Puebla suburb which in pre-Columbian times was a major center of religious cult. During the conquest, Cortés, fearing an ambush at Cholula, set up an effective counter-blow which resulted in the killing of some 3,000 people. Then, after decimation by plague, Cholula, once a city of great importance, became an impoverished village. The main attraction is the **Santuario de los Remedios**, a tiny church placed on top of what looks like a hill, but in reality is a pyramid. It is the largest pyramid in Mexico, one of the most ambitious constructions ever undertaken. The successive building phases are documented.

Two other remarkable churches among the scores to be seen in Puebla are the **Convento de San Gabriel**, with its beautiful 16th-century temple and vast chapel, and the **Capilla Real**, which was inspired by the mosque of Córdoba.

In **Huejotzingo**, about 40 km (25 miles) east of Puebla, is a 16th-century Franciscan monastery. It preserves one of those curiosities of Mexican art – the **Capillas Posas** – literally, inn-chapels. Built in the corners of atriums, they were places where pilgrims could rest during long and tiring religious processions. Those at Huejotzingo are among the best in Mexico. The town is also famous for woolens, sweaters and *sarapes*, or blankets.

San Francisco Acatepec and **Santa María Tonantzintla**, two villages on the road to Oaxaca, both have remarkable churches in the popular Mexican baroque style. The interior of the church at Tonantzintla is covered with playful plaster decorations, a splendid example of how Indian artisans adopted Spanish techniques and iconography.

The neighboring state to Puebla is

Selling the end result.

tiny **Tlaxcala** with a capital of the same name. It has another beautiful baroque church in the village of **Ocotlán**. Perched atop a hill, the 18th-century church seems as lightly spun as sugar candy.

Tlaxcala's other famous religious building is the **Convento de San Francisco**, which has a wooden roof in the Moorish style (*mudéjar*). Tlaxcala is famous historically because the Tlaxcalans helped Cortés conquer Mexico. Brave soldiers, they served gladly in the Spanish forces because they hated the Aztecs. A mural in the **Palacio de Gobierno**, painted by Desiderio Hernández Xochitiotzin, tells the story of these Indians.

Other historical landmarks are the *pulque* haciendas that prospered until the revolution. Among the best are San Bartolomé del Monte, Ixtafiayuca, San Cristobal Zacacalo and San Blas.

Toluca: Several roads connect Mexico City with Toluca, capital of the state of Mexico and an hour's bus journey due west of the capital. A direct road leaves from Mexico City's Chapultepec Park via the Avenida Constituyentes. Once it leaves Mexico City behind, the road goes through surprising countryside: tall pine forests reminiscent of Germany.

But once across the mountain range into **Toluca Valley**, typical Mexican landscapes reassert themselves in dry, golden fields, cacti and adobe houses. **Toluca** is a typical provincial city with colonial churches, 19th-century buildings, a large central square, narrow streets and the usual *portales*, or arcades. These are the hub of town, especially at dusk, when everybody seems to be idly walking about, flirting, gossiping and window-shopping.

Toluca has its own food and drink specialties. The drinks, called *moscos*, come in bottles with long spouts and are famous because, like all street liquor, they are *muy traidores* ("very treacherous"). Toluca is also celebrated for its fruit jam, excellent candy, and spicy *chorizos*, or Spanish chili sausage, which are all sold at the *portales*. Meanwhile, Toluca cathedral is an unmitigated horror. Don't miss it! A block away, on the **Plaza Garibay**, where the market used

to be, is an attractive botanical garden.

Out of Toluca you have two options: keep going south to Ixtapan de la Sal, or west to **Valle de Bravo**. The road to Valle de Bravo crosses a flat valley with a snowcapped volcano to the left. The landscape changes constantly, from European-type forests to typically Mexican valleys. Valle de Bravo is a picturesque mountain settlement.

The road to Ixtapan de la Sal crosses the same sort of landscape but one rich in history, a land of Indian tradition blended with colonial. A good example are the ceramics produced in **Metepec**, a village near Toluca. The pottery shows imagination, especially those with the *Arbol de la Vida* or Tree of Life theme. This is a simple interpretation of the tree in the Garden of Eden, with all the *dramatis personae* of that great tale.

Farther south, **Tenango** has an interesting archaeological center that includes the remnants of a palatial temple, once the dwelling of the rulers of the valley. **Ixtapán de la Sal** is a bathing station, semi-tropical and flowery. The

Sailing at Valle de Bravo.

main hotel, the **Hotel Ixtapan**, which describes itself as the "Shangri-la of America," is worth visiting. Its waters are said to be rejuvenating. The hotel is in fantastically bad taste. The bathing area is in classical style, with Greek and Roman goddesses officiating over the private hall. The food here is good, and the service even better. The main building produces a certain sense of nostalgia among older visitors from the US and Canada because it reminds them of the 1940s, when the place was built. An amusement park adjoins the spa.

Near Ixtapan de la Sal is the village of **Malinalco**. Built in a ravine, Malinalco was a resort in Aztec times and is the site of an impressive mountain temple. The main structure, the **Cuauhcalli**, or House of the Eagle, is carved out of the rock. There is a circular chamber with an eagle marking the center of the floor. Near Malinalco is the **Church of Chalma**, a place of pilgrimage. During the first five days of the year **Chalma** village is crowded with thousands of pilgrims, who worship a miraculous Black Christ. Once the worshipping is over the revelry begins, with penitents dancing and drinking. From Chalma, you can return directly to Mexico City, reluctantly back to the 20th century.

Cuernavaca: Mexico City's Insurgentes Sur leads to the highway to **Cuernavaca**, the busiest thoroughfare in Mexico. Cuernavaca is *the* weekend resort for the capital. That's where the *capitalinos* go for pure air, pleasant weather, privacy: an escape from the cacophony of Mexico City. At an altitude of 610 meters (2,000 ft) lower than the capital, Cuernavaca has always attracted the capital's elite. Aztec emperors built palaces in Cuernavaca; Cortés built a pleasure dome there.

The **Cathedral de la Asuncion**, built like a fortress in a garden, is rather plain except for some curious frescoes depicting the persecution of Christian missionaries in Japan and believed to have been done by a convert from that country who lived here in the 17th century. A rare statue believed to be of Cortés sits in the church at the entrance. At one

Snowcapped Nevado de Toluca.

time the Franciscans had a monastery on the precincts; the skull and crossbones above the portico is the symbol of their Order. In the Franciscan cloister, the fairly new **Museo Casa Robert Brady** has an interesting collection of Mexican art and Asian handicrafts. An interesting group of paintings of Indians at work in pre-colonial days can be seen in the nearby **Palacio Municipal**.

Because so much of Cuernavaca's beauty lies behind the high walls of private gardens, the town can be disappointing for the visitor, but the nicest of all its gardens, the **Jardin Borda**, which once surrounded the 18th-century home of Taxco's richest silver magnate, happens to be public. It was restored a few years ago and is exceptionally pleasant with fountains, artificial lake and outdoor theater.

Adjoining the **Jardin Juarez** (designed by Gustav Eiffel) is the larger Jardin de los Heroes, or **Alameda**, at whose eastern end is the **Palacio de Cortés**, which the Conqueror built as a summer home on the ruins of an old Indian temple. Now a museum, with a strong colonial component, it boasts a spectacularly interesting mural by Diego Rivera depicting almost 400 years of Mexican history with all its famous heroes and villains. For more than half a century before the *Where's Wally?* concept it has been challenging Mexican children to identify the participants in their national saga.

Apart from the market, across the ravine to the east, and the not especially impressive **Teopanzolco Pyramid**, in a park even further east (you'll need to take a taxi), that's it for Cuernevaca. It does have some excellent hotels of which the most famous is possibly **Las Mananitas**, half a dozen blocks north of the city center on Calle Ricardo Linares. If you've ever dreamed of staying in a beautiful, flower-filled garden in which fountains tinkle and peacocks strut, sleeping in a room filled with period furniture and eating first-rate food, now is the time to indulge. If Cuernavaca is somewhat disappointing, the state of Morelos, though one of the **Jardin Borda.**

smallest in Mexico, is beautiful and full of surprises. One of these is **Xochicalco**, an ancient hill fortress (Place of the House of Flowers), set amidst wonderfully green landscape. The main structure, the remarkably well-preserved **Pyramid of the Feathered Serpent**, is a decoration full of writhing life. If you like caves, the most famous, **Crutas de Cacahuamilpa**, is in Morelos. They are enormous, intriguing and frightening for the claustrophobic.

Taxco, Mexico's famous silver-working town, is near Xochicalco, some 72 km (45 miles) south of Cuernavaca and about a third of the way between Mexico City and Acapulco. One of the few Mexican towns to have been declared a national monument, Taxco is about as picturesque a place as you will find anywhere: narrow, cobblestone streets twist up and down hills, all eventually leading to the Zócalo (main square) overlooked by the colonial church of **Santa Prisca**, completed in 1758 and dominated by twin baroque, 40-meter (130-ft) towers. Its timely carved stone facade is more than matched by its gilded interior and paintings by Miguel Cabrera, Mexico's most famous artist of colonial times. Take special notice of the organ and the excellent carvings on the wooden pulpit. This church was paid for by José de la Borda, the French silver miner who became one of the richest men in Mexico.

To the right as you leave the church, still in the plaza, a plaque marks **Casa Borda**, where the town's rich patron once lived, and through the adjoining arcade and downstairs is the **Silver Museum**, which contains a rich selection of work (including a chess set with pieces matching the Indians against the Conquistadors) of Antonio Pineda, who in 1953 won the first of the annual contests now staged by local silversmiths. Señor Pineda was the first apprentice of William Spratling, the Tulane University professor who arrived in Taxco in 1932 and created the local silver industry by hiring local youths and teaching them silversmithing skills. He integrated pre-Columbian designs into the jewelry.

So good and unusual were Spratling's pieces that clients such as Neiman-Marcus and Bonwit Teller competed to buy his output. Eventually, many of his former student-craftsmen set up their own shops, now represented by more than 300 shops in the town itself. There are no great bargains as the prices quoted are about the same as in Mexico City. The advantage here is that you can see a tremendous variety of silverwork and also watch the artisans handcraft their exquisite products.

Spratling invested much of his well-deserved riches in a collection of pre-Columbian art, housed in the **William Spratling Museum** (Spratling's home until his death in a car accident in 1967). Down a flight of narrow steps behind the cathedral is the **Mercado de Artesians**, scores of market stalls selling almost everything.

On Ruiz de Alarcon (named for a local playwright who was the contemporary of Cervantes) is the **Casa de Humboldt**, where the noted German explorer/scientist Baron Alexander von

Santa Prisca, Taxco.

Humboldt (1769–1859) stayed in 1803, during his travels in Central and South America. Large enough to have once served as a convent and hospital and later as a guesthouse owned by a local architect, it now exhibits a miscellaneous collection of religious artifacts and other items. Most interesting, perhaps, are the bust and portraits of von Humboldt himself and a reproduction of a painting of a somewhat grandiloquent José de la Borda in a costume that must have amused even his friends.

The steep hill leading off the eastern side of Plaza Borda leads down to the shabby Plaza Bernal at whose corner can be found the seldom-open **Museo Grafica de la Historia Social de Taxco** which displays early photos of the town and illustrates its development as an overcrowded tourist center. Residents and developers are forbidden to build in any non-local style or to change the character of the town in any way. It has understandably become a big favorite of the foreign community. A Mexican comic once drew applause by saying

he'd refused an invitation to visit Taxco because he didn't speak English.

The town proper has more than 10,000 residents and about five times that number live in scattered communities on nearby hills. Houses are of stucco-covered adobe, roofed in red tile, their balconies overflowing with flowers.

During Easter, when there are processions, penitents and a re-enactment of Christ's last hours, you need to have confirmed reservations to stay in Taxco. The rest of the time, the town makes a good overnight stop on your way to or from Acapulco. It is also a good place to take a break from your explorations around Mexico City, and it's only a hop away from the state of Morelos.

Morelos is the sugar-bowl of Mexico. Cortés brought sugar cane here, along with black slaves. The slaves were rebellious and instead of sugar planted the seed for the agrarian movement in Morelos. Zapata was the great leader and his battle cry, *Tierra Libertad*, has echoed throughout the land. Every village displays Zapata's portrait: the huge bristling mustache, the *charro* (rancher) attire, the sombrero, and the deep, sad look in his eyes.

Morelos is rich in old monasteries, most of them built in the 16th century in fortress style. Time has dealt gracefully with them. After years of exposure to tropical rain and wind, they now look like old and peaceful castles.

Tepotzlán (not to be confused with Tepotzotlán, mentioned at the beginning of this chapter), 26 km (16 miles) northeast of Cuernavaca, has a 16th-century convent, primitive and charming, nestling in a beautiful landscape. An odd-looking group of hills make up the **Sierra**, the most important being the **Tepozteco**, which serves as the base for a temple dedicated to Tepzotecatl, god of crops and drunkenness.

East of Tepoztlán are Oaxtepec and **Cocoyoc**, Indian villages and vacation towns both with big hotels. There are monasteries in **Oaxtepec** and in the neighboring villages of **Tlayacapan** and **Atlatahuacan**. Perhaps the best is in **Yecapixtla**, a short distance east. It resembles a proud Moorish castle.

Left, painting ceramics. **Right**, the highly decorated San Francisco Acatepec.

GUADALAJARA, JALISCO

Jalisco, northwest of Mexico City, is a fascinating state, one of the most important in the country. It has agriculture, a booming industry, and a coastline that beckons visitors. Its capital is **Guadalajara**, the second biggest city in Mexico, with a population of 3.2 million. Jalisco is also the home of *mariachi* music. The bubbly musicians so characteristic of Mexico have a square of their own in Guadalajara, the Plaza de los Mariachis, near the Libertad Market.

This city, perched on a "mile-high" plain (actually 1,524 meters/5,000 ft high), is crowded and bustling and yet in many ways a provincial metropolis that still manages to retain the atmosphere of a small town. Guadalajara has the best climate in North America. Clear, dry and mild, it is over 20°C (70°F) all year round. Ah, those lucky *tapatiós*, as they are called. (Their name derives from an old Indian expression meaning "three times as worthy." It's a boastful nickname that captures Guadalajara's proud character.)

Quaint trolleybuses: Guadalajara is a city of parks and monuments; flower filled lanes, nice old plazas and gracious old buildings; as well as supermarkets that are as fancy as any in North America. There are art galleries and bookstores; gourmet restaurants, luxury hotels, lovely parks with fountains and the best murals in the country (Orozco's). The quaint white *trolebuses* glide along on rubber tires.

Guadalajara was founded in 1542 and was meant to be the capital of the kingdom of New Galicia, independent from New Spain. That was the dream of Nuño Beltrán de Guzmán, the conquistador who took the place. A man of soaring ambition and savage disposition, Guzmán never attained his dream, yet Guadalajara managed to remain independent of Mexico City and its archbishopric was as rich and powerful as that of the capital. In fact, Guadalajara always retained some political and judi-

Preceding pages: quiet Tapalpa town.

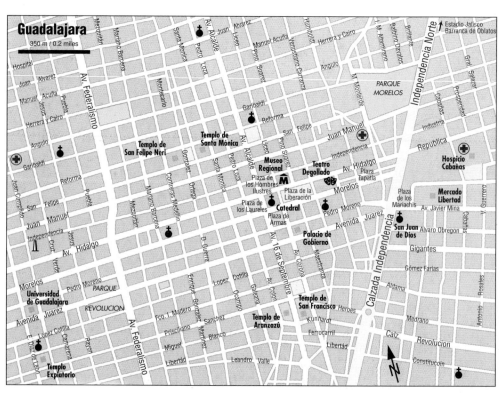

cial autonomy. Early on, the city also boasted its own university, and students were drawn from as far away as southern Texas, then part of New Spain.

From the beginning, Guadalajara enjoyed a regional importance. It is situated near one of the few passages through the mountains leading to the fertile Pacific coast. It became the 'capital' of the vast Mexican west. Though Guadalajara is a big city, most of its points of interest are downtown.

Gothic landmark: A huge religious building, the cathedral is the symbol of Guadalajara, with its twin Gothic-style towers (covered with unlikely yellow tiles) comprising the city's central landmark. Surrounded by four plazas, it provides a welcome oasis amidst the bustle of a big city.

The square in front of the cathedral, **Plaza de los Laureles**, contains a fountain commemorating the city's founding and a Greek-looking enclosure, the **Rotonda**, which is the burial place of Jalisco's famous men, some of whom have their own monuments along the path of the **Plaza de los Hombres Ilustres**. To the south is **Plaza de Armas**, originally Guadalajara's main square, marketplace, and long ago the site of executions. Now it is a pleasant square with a bandstand adorned with an attractive sculpture imported from Paris. The most unusual plaza is the one to the east, Plaza de la Liberación/Plaza de los Tres Poderes.

In spite of these serious-sounding names this square is almost always referred to as the **Plaza del 2 de Copas**, from the two fountains in the shape of champagne glasses which adorn it. This beautiful square, designed by the contemporary Guadalajara architect Ignacio Díaz Morales, blends in a dignified manner with the colonial buildings framing the rear of the cathedral and the facade of the 19th-century **Degollado Theater**. Recently restored, this theater has a wonderful decorated ceiling.

A handsome late baroque building in gold-hued stone, the **Palacio de Gobierno** (Place of Government) faces the Plaza de Armas. Its facade is in a festive military style; its central patio enclosed by classical arcades. But the chief attraction is a magnificent mural painted by the late **José Clemente Orozco**, Jalisco's foremost modern painter. The mural is a homage to Father Miguel Hidalgo, the priest who triggered the Revolution. It is perhaps the most passionate statement made by any Mexican mural. One side of the huge triptych is known as *The Clowns* – a savage satire on exploitative ideologies.

Facing the Hombres Ilustres plaza is a former seminary, a pleasant baroque building with lush garden surrounded by Roman arches and now housing the **State Museum**. Behind the adjoining Degollado Theater is an expansive pedestrian precinct known as the **Plaza Tapatía**, built in an affected style and looking a little contrived. It leads to one of Mexico's most important colonial buildings – the **Hospicio Cabañas**. Founded and financed by one of Guadalajara's great benefactors, Bishop Juan Ruiz de Cabanas, it was built around a series of patios. At the center is a magnificent chapel, decorated in the

Cathedral in Guadalajara.

late 1930s by Orozco with murals depicting the ties between Spain and Mexico. He could not resist adding a series of political satires.

Orozco's murals at the Hospicio – designed by Manuel Tolsá, Mexico's best-known colonial architect – are generally regarded as among the masterpieces of modern art and are the crown of Mexican mural painting. Four giant male figures decorate the dome. Orozco, a harsh and silent man, never explained them but some think they are supposed to represent the four elements: earth, water, wind and fire, which also symbolize stages of spiritual development.

The colorful, bustling **Mercado Libertad** is a neighbor of the Hospicio and close to the market is **San Juan de Dios Church**, the core of the city's traditional center, outside which musicians play their traditional *corridos* (street ballads).

Calzada Independencia, on which the Mercado Libertad, the church and the Plaza de los Mariachis are located, is the backbone of popular Guadalajara. It is not by any aesthetic standards a beautiful street, but it is bustling and full of life. Due north of the Calzada is a huge soccer stadium, the **Estadio Jalisco**, a shrine to the most popular sport in Mexico. Guadalajara is a *futbol* fan's dream city with four major league teams (there used to be five). Workers here spend much of their meager salaries on tickets for the two or three games that take place weekly during the season. They also gamble on regular soccer sweepstakes called *pronósticos*.

All Mexican kids worship the players, many of them imported from South America's two soccer superpowers, Brazil and Argentina. Unfortunately, Mexico's passion for *futbol* is an unrequited love. No matter how many times Mexico has attempted it, she has never won the coveted World Cup.

A few kilometers further north along the Calzada, Guadalajara offers a nice bonus: the majestic **Barranca de Oblatos**. At the bottom of this canyon the **Río Santiago** slides into the tropics and the distant Pacific. The Barranca has strong, sculptural stone walls softened by lus-

cious, green vegetation. During the rainy season, there is an impressive – if temporary – waterfall. There's a spectacular view of the Barranca from **Huentitan Park**, which also features a zoo, amusement park and planetarium.

San Francisco and **Aranzazú** are two remarkable colonial churches in the southern part of the downtown area, survivors of a group of churches and monasteries built by the Franciscans in their ambitious attempts to extend their missions all the way to the Californias. Both churches face pleasant *jardines* and once formed the heart of one of the city's best neighborhoods, which is now a financial district. Aranzazú is the more beautiful; its diminutive but elegant golden *retablos* are the only ones left in town. The *retablos* in the San Francisco church were destroyed in an arson attack in the 1930s.

On the west side of downtown are the **Santa Mónica** and **San Felipe Neri** churches, the former a convent church whose facade is enhanced by a prodigious carving done in the late baroque

Potter at work.

216

style. In a niche in one corner is a giant sculpture of St Christopher, to whom the local women still pray to help them find a man (or to help them get rid of the one they have). San Felipe is a very grand church with an exotic-looking belfry and well-proportioned dome.

The **University of Guadalajara**'s central building is a comparatively recent addition, dating from the 1920s. Here again are splendid Orozco murals, with one in particular showing Orozco in his most biting and bitter mood. It is a big fresco showing rogues leading the masses along the road to hell. Behind the university the big Gothic church modeled on the cathedral of Orvieto in Italy is known as the **Expiatorio**. Don't fail to take a stroll along Avenida Vallarta, west of the university.

Southeast of Guadalajara is **Lake Chapala**, Mexico's biggest lake. The comfortable weekend homes of wealthy *tapatiós* and retired *norteaméricanos* line its north shore.

Three small villages in Jalisco are famous in their own fashion. Two have been swallowed up by the city's suburbs – San Pedro Tlaquepaque and Zapopan – and the third is the village of Tequila (*see page 218*), 80 km (50 miles) north of Guadalajara.

San Pedro Tlaquepaque is nationally famous for its ceramics. In the good old days, pieces produced here were known for their remarkable quality and simple elegance. But with the arrival of tourism the quality of much of it has deteriorated. But some nice traditional pieces are still made here; the best are colorful geometric designs typical of the region, examples of which are on show in the local museum. Modern ceramic forms have been introduced by artists such as the renowned Jorge Wilmot and Ken Edwards. To avoid the junk, head for shops such as **La Casa Canela** and **Antiqua de Mexico**; the latter is located in one of the magnificent homes built here during the 19th century by Guadalajarans escaping the city.

San Pedro Tlaquepaque is also interesting to visit because it looks the way all Mexican villages once did, with

Fishermen, Lake Chapala.

cobblestoned streets, spacious and secretive houses and noisy central square. The **Parián**, the old covered market, is especially favored by *tapatiós*, who flock here to listen to *mariachis*, drink beer, eat a kid-goat barbecue dish called *birria,* and watch passersby. San Pedro's best restaurant, **Sin Nombre** ("without a name"), is located in one of the town's fine 19th-century mansions.

Zapopan is a famous pilgrimage center. Every summer the town takes an image of the Virgin to Guadalajara to protect the town against floods, and then, on October 12, in what must be among the best-attended pilgrimages in the world, brings the image back home again to Zapopan. Its **basilica** belongs to the heavy baroque style common in rural Mexico.

Then there is **Tequila** (population 17,740), famous, naturally, for its drink extracted from a blueish-green pulse plant that is a variety of *maguey*. Similar to vodka in color but stronger, tequila grows yellow, or golden, as its proud producers claim, with age. It is an aperitif and knowledgeable tequila drinkers never suffer it to be mixed. That is considered sacrilegious. Good tequila drinkers use the liquor in moderation; they have a healthy respect for it and invariably recount how their grandfather never missed his daily *fajo* (the cup in which you drink tequila) until his departure from this world at age 92.

Though every Mexican touts his own special brand of really good tequila, frequent nominees for the *best* commercial tequila are Herradura, both in its normal and well-aged varieties (*añejo*), and the tequila brands Tequileño, Centinela, Cuervo and Orendain. Herradura, a family-owned company headed by Guillermo Romo, is distilled in Amatitan (a self-contained walled village with adobe houses, old ladies with shawls and unpaved streets. Here agave plants are cooked in old adobe brick ovens and filtered through cellulose filters (the company reverted to these when more modern German filters took much of the taste away). In Guadalajara, on Avenida Vallarta, the Tequila Sauza bottling plant offers morning tours every weekday, and free tastings afterwards.

In a perfect world the perfect vacation would combine an inland site followed by a few leisurely days at a beach. It's as easily done as said: **Puerto Vallarta** – Jalisco's sophisticated Pacific Coast resort – is just minutes away by plane and five hours by car. For those who prefer less activity and more privacy, there are long stretches of creamy sand beaches north of Puerto Vallarta and romantic rocky coves to the south. (See *The Glamor Coast, pages 279–87*).

Jalisco is a state with strong rural traditions and a rich folklore. In this fascinating part of the country, the *charros* and *mariachis* thrived. Jalisco's traditional music, the *son jaliscience,* is almost a second national anthem. Jalisco is the home of Mexican *machismo*. Think of the mustachioed *charro*, riding his horse, singing a Jorge Negrete song, and shooting from the hip. He never misses. At least that's how Mexican movies portray him. Jalisco is a Mexican's Mexico. It is also a place where myths are born and take wing.

Imitation *charro* trappings for sale.

TEQUILA

Like Jerez, Curaçao, Champagne and a handful of other places, Tequila has achieved a reputation far out of proportion to its size. Millions of drinkers who might not even dream of ever going to this small town wax rhapsodic about its name. Less than an hour's drive northwest of Guadalajara on Highway 15, Tequila lies almost under the shadow of an extinct 2,950-meter (9,700-ft) volcano. It is surrounded by thousands of acres of spear-like cultivated agave plants.

Although there are hundreds of different species of the maguey plant, under Mexican law at least 51 percent of any tequila must be from a specific variety, the tequila weber agave, which grows only here and in a nearby region. The best kinds of tequila use pure juice; cheaper brands supplement their liquor with cane juice.

After growing for eight to 10 years, the tequila maguey is trimmed down to its 50-kg (100-1b) heart or *pina,* which is steamed then shredded and squeezed. Sugar is added to this liquid, which is then allowed to ferment for four days before undergoing two distillations. Most of this colorless liquid is then bottled, the rest aged in oak casks for anything up to seven years, during which it assumes a golden color.

Like tequila, the popular drinks *mescal* and *pulque* are also derived from the maguey cactus, but they are fermented rather than distilled (before the Conquest, the distillation process was unknown). These two drinks – whose origins go back at least 1,000 years – have retained their mass popularity. *Pulquerias,* with their sawdust covered floors and predominantly blue-collar clientele, tend to the exclusivity found in the Public Bar (as opposed to the more family-oriented lounge) of English pubs.

Tequila, on the other hand, has taken its place with top-flight liquors, especially in the US, which, by the late 1980s was importing 5 million cases a year from its southern neighbor. As long ago as the 17th century, tequila became popular with silver miners in nearby Bolanos but its reputation got its major boost from American servicemen on leave in border towns during World War II. Now more than 600 million *margaritas* are reportedly drunk in the US every year – that's about 1½ million every day.

Hueblein is the market leader in the US. When the company launched a big advertising campaign in 1989, its public relations director Steve Goldstein said that the drink "always had something of a bad boy image and we wouldn't want to lose that even though we are promoting its mixability."

This theme was paralleled by Seagrams, whose first ad campaign for its Herradura brand included billboards adorned with graffiti and an 800 telephone number. A raspy voice asked callers to leave their addresses, to which were sent boxes containing spray cans and Herradura brochures.

The ritual of correct tequila drinking begins with placing grains of salt on the top of the fist, licking them, then, after sucking some drops of lemon, taking a drink from a *fajo* (the cup from which you drink tequila). This is followed by a sip of sangrita. The idea is to establish a precise and satisfying balance of strong flavors in which tequila's pure, sweet fire is complemented by the hotness of sangrita, the acidity of lemon, and the relief given by those grains of salt. ∎

Taking a tequila break.

SIX CENTRAL STATES

A big highland block of central Mexico – almost as big as France – takes in six states which offer much for the traveler who has the time, patience and curiosity to explore: **Zacatecas**, **San Luis Potosí**, **Aguascalientes**, **Guanajuato**, **Querétaro** and **Michoacán**. Starting in the center with the state of Guanajuato, we'll work our way around. There are many roads to follow, and the region is earmarked for Mexico's first chain of inexpensive highway motels. Sleep Inns is a division of the country's Calinda Hotels Group, which already has hotels throughout Mexico. The first Sleep Inns will be built in the region between Guadalajara and Queretaro.

Guanajuato city, the capital of the state, is one of Mexico's most famous tourist spots and in colonial days it was the center of a rich mining area and one of the greatest producers of silver in the world. The mines were flooded during the wars for independence; but reopened again under Porfirio Díaz, bringing new prosperity to the area. Abandoned again in the Revolution, they were reopened in recent years as the price of silver escalated. Guanajuato, like many once-prosperous cities that stagnated, is remarkably well preserved and is now a national monument.

Built in a ravine and on the banks of a river that from time to time flooded the town, the city is quaint, charming, romantic and sometimes eerie. It does not have a single street that runs in a straight line. All go their crooked ways, up hill and down dale, some falling into an abyss. In some houses the entrance is through the roof. The old river that once ravaged the town has been re-routed and the ravine through which it once flowed is now Miguel Hidalgo Avenue. A mixture of tunnels and streets meanders along the basements of the town's old buildings, intermittently offering an exit into a shady square or busy street.

Los Callejónes (alleys or lanes) are like an urban canyon, a circulatory system through which flows the life of the city. In Guanajuato people *callejonear*, that is, they walk around with no particular goal in mind, going up and down the crooked valleys in search of a friendly door, a flowery balcony, or an inviting girl. The *callejónes* have intriguing names: "Shell," "Moon," "Bronze," "Lion," "Backbone," "Grave," "Mandate," "Angels," "Holy Child," "Hell." Perhaps the most famous is the "Kiss" (Callejón del Beso), near the steps of the Plazuela de los Angeles, an especially narrow alley, which is said to have acquired its name from the plight of ill-fated lovers kept apart but able to kiss each other while sitting in their windows on opposite sides of the *callejón*.

Starting place: Begin your tour at **Jardín de la Unión**, the central square, with its remarkable neighbors, **San Diego** church and the **Teatro Juárez**. The former is delightfully *churrigueresque,* but the interior is mediocre. The tiny theater is unique with a "French-Moorish" appearance.

Almost all of Guanajuato's sights are strung out to the west of the Jardin

Union, with the exception of the **Don Quixote Museum**, which is a few blocks to the east. A wealthy advertising executive and avid Quixote-phile donated his collection (which ranges from time-store junk to a Picasso) to the city.

Two blocks west from Jardín de la Unión is a narrow square known as **Plaza de la Paz**, which is more like a monument imprisoned between two busy streets. Nearby buildings include the old homes of silver millionaires and the remarkable **Basilica of Our Lady of Guanajuato**, whose image is worshipped in an interior chapel. King Philip II of Spain offered the image of the Virgin to Guanajuato. Another fashionable building, in neoclassical style, is the **Casa de Rul y Valenciana**, designed by Eduardo de Tresguerras, a great 18th-century Mexican designer and architect. Today it is the home of the Supreme Court.

The University building, huge and white, is an outstanding example of Moorish-inspired architecture only half a century old. It is the pride of Guanajuato

and the centerpiece of the Festival Cervantino, an international cultural festival which takes place in late October. Its neighbor, the **Church of the Company**, is the grandest church in town with a beautiful dome and an impressive interior. Nearby is the house, now a museum, in which **Diego Rivera** was born. Guanajuato's **market**, in a French wrought-iron structure, is large, noisy and full of good and bad smells.

Plaza de San Roque is a church that has become famous for its presentation of *Entremeses Cervantinos*, the famous farces of the renowned Spanish writer Miguel de Cervantes. Lighthearted and funny, the *Entremeses* became a tradition in Guanajuato and with official support have been expanded into an international cultural festival.

La Alhóndiga is an impressive building, originally a grain store. During the War of Independence, it was converted into a fortress by its Spanish defenders before being captured by the rebels after an incident famous in Mexican history. Protected by a slab of stone which he **Guanajuato.**

carried on his back, a miner called the Pípila rushed the door of Alhóndiga, set it on fire, and the rebels poured in. Today the place is a museum with murals by Chávez Morado and a collection of paintings by the 19th-century artist of Guanajuato, Hermenegildo Bustos. A grandiose monument to pipila sits on a ridge overlooking the city from which there is an excellent view. Carved in the statue's plinth is a revolutionary text.

The best panoramic view of Guanajuato, a short bus ride from the plaza, can be found at **La Valenciana**. Here a rich baroque church sits beside the mine which, under its Spanish colonial masters, produced a large quantity of the world's silver. On the way you may (or may not) want to stop at Guanajuato's most famous attraction, the **Museo de las Momias**, west on Juarez, which has become closely associated with visitors' memories of the town. It is devoted to grotesque corpses found to be mummified when an old cemetery was extended in 1865. The combination of mineral-rich soil and exceptionally dry air tends to mummify bodies, as the space-saving practice of exhuming and cremating bodies after five years has revealed. (It is possible to pay for a body to stay undisturbed.)

The beautiful 17th-century **Hacienda San Gabriel Barrera**, about 2km (1 mile) out of town on the road to Marfil, may not be completely authentic, but it does give visitors an idea of the opulence of the wealthy during the colonial era.

San Miguel de Allende, east of Guanajuato, was just another quaint colonial town until a man named Sterling Dickinson founded an art school here in 1938. Soon after the town began to attract artists and writers, tourists too began to descend, as they so often do. The school, the Instituto Allende, now run by Nel Fernandez, remains one of the town's chief attractions. Some famous artists have lived here, including the muralist David Alfaro Siqueiros who studied mural painting here at the Bellas Artes, a former convent.

The **Parroquia**, an astonishing 19th-century church, designed by an unschooled Indian in impure Gothic style, stands white and enormous in the center of town. It looks down on the central plaza, the *jardin*, and dominates the entire town.

Ignacio Allende, for whom the town was named after Mexico gained its independence, was a 30-year-old officer in the army garrison here in 1810. This was the year he conspired with Father Hidalgo to rebel against Spanish rule. The plot was uncovered prematurely and the rebels joined the garrison and took over San Miguel. A year later, the premature fight for independence collapsed and Hidalgo and Allende were executed. (Independence was finally won a decade later.) Allende's house, on the *jardin*, is now a museum.

Also on the plaza is one of the palatial *casas* of the aristocratic Canal family, the rich and devout "Medici" of San Miguel. It was Canal money in the 1730s that paid for **La Santa Casa de Loreto**, part of the multi-towered church of **San Felipe Neri** a few blocks northeast. The chapel is a copy of one in Loreto, Italy, dedicated to the Virgin Mary, and con-

Statues of Don Quixote and Sancho Panza, at Guanajuato.

tains a lavish and whimsical *Camerino,* or dressing chapel.

South of the town, on Anchas de San Antonio, in what was the 18th-century home of the Conde de Canal, is the popular art and language center, the already mentioned **Instituto Allende**.

Two blocks west of the *jardin*, on Calle Canal, is the church and convent of **La Concepción** whose huge dome was inspired by that of Les Invalides in Paris. The convent belongs to the government which has transformed it into **Bellas Artes**, a cultural center. A major attraction of San Miguel is the shopping. Art galleries and handicraft shops line the streets around the main square. Many of them carry top-quality merchandise, including the hand-loomed tablecloths and tin and brass items produced in the region.

The newest addition to the city is a botanical preserve, **El Charco del Ingenio**, a series of rock pools ranged over a 65-hectare (160-acre) site about 15 minutes from town by taxi. Here you can explore long stretches of peaceful pathways, admire cacti and many other plant species and overlook San Miguel in the valley below.

Near San Miguel, in the village of **Atotonilco**, is a baroque pilgrimage church whose sanctuary is decorated with frescoes painted by the colonial artist Miguel Antonio Martínez de Pocasangre.

Dolores Hidalgo, in north central Guanajuato, is the cradle of Mexican independence and earned its name from Father Miguel Hidalgo who, late on the night of September 15, 1810, proclaimed his *Grito de Dolores,* the "shout" for independence from Spanish rule. His audience was a sleepy congregation which had gathered for Mass. Hidalgo, a smoldering Creole, a man of learning and an activist, became the moral and political leader of the independence movement. He had no military training but at one stage his forces – peasants out of the villages and hills – controlled a large part of western central Mexico. In the end he was imprisoned, then shot.

Lovingly preserved are the beautiful

Rancheros **chew the fat, Atotonilco.**

Parroquia where Hidalgo uttered his *Grito* and the house (now a museum), at the corner of Hidalgo and Morelos, where the plotters met. Dolores, to which expedient Mexican presidents return to repeat Hidalgo's inspiring proclamation, is a typical Mexican town with a rough but luminous landscape so far undiscovered by artists or writers. The houses are solid and secretive, with shady patios, and there are many lovely, simple churches.

Celaya, **Salamanca**, **Irapuato** and **León** are four Guanajuato cities located in central Mexico's largest valley, the **Bajío**, a prosperous agricultural area stretching from coast to coast and sometimes called the "breadbasket of Mexico." Founded during colonial times, these cities are growing rapidly yet none is much favored by visitors. **Celaya** has some elegant late-colonial architecture and the neoclassical **Church of el Carmen**, another building by the 18th-century Mexican architect Eduardo de Tresquerras.

Salamanca, once a sleepy and dull agricultural town, has become prosperous and chaotic since PEMEX, the national petroleum company, chose the place as the site for a huge new refinery. One of its redeeming qualities is the church of **San Agustin**, which possesses some of the most beautiful retablos in Mexico. South of Salamanca, the farming village of **Yuriria** boasts a 16th-century convent with an ornate facade done in Plateresco style.

Neither Irapuato nor León is particularly interesting to the tourist. Lively **León** is Mexico's shoemaking capital and some of its rich cobblers have built elaborate houses with enormous gardens. Its **Plaza de León** is a pleasant square. The town has hotels, and good places to eat, such as the **Circulo Leones**, half a block from the Plaza, and the fantastic **Panteón Taurino**, decorated with the paraphernalia of bullfighting. León is known for its meat, cooked in the Argentine style (a number of Argentinian soccer players belonging to the city's two professional soccer teams opened restaurants in the city when they

Throwing a bull by its tail.

retired). Near León is **Cubilete** (the dice-box), a mountain marking the geographical center of Mexico. On top, blessing the valley, is a monument of Christ with open arms.

Alongside Guanajuato is the state of Querétaro whose capital, the city of **Querétaro**, is known for its colonial art. It also has a good bullring and its *feria* attracts famous *toreros* and enthusiastic fans. Querétaro has been a stage for some of the greatest episodes in Mexican history, including the events that accelerated the proclamation of Independence. Though now industrialized, it is both a city of religion and history; every block has a convent or a church. It was here that the pretender king, Maximilian, was executed and the Constitution was signed.

The clerical and monastic Querétaro and the secular and political Querétaro are intertwined, giving the city a unique character and flavor. The city is notable for its 1,170-meter (3,840-ft) aqueduct whose 74 magnificent arches were built more than 250 years ago.

The chief historical monuments are the **State House**, the **Theater of the Republic**, the scene of passionate discussion about the writing of the Constitution of 1917 and the **Cerro de las Campanas** where Maximilian was shot. The **Casa de la Corregidora** (City Hall), which in colonial times was the residence of the local governor, is a proud building facing Querétaro's most charming square. In 1810 the governor's wife, Josefa Ortiz de Dominguez (later known as La Corregidora), was involved in a plot to proclaim the independence of Mexico from Spain. Although the plot was discovered, Doña Josefa was able to alert the other conspirators which triggered Father Hidalgo's *grito*.

Aristocratic memories: A plaque at City Hall commemorates this event, but curiously enough the monument in the adjoining square is not dedicated to Father Hidalgo but rather to an aristocrat, Don Juan Antonio Urrutia y Aranda, Marquis of the Villa del Villar del Aguilla, who built the magnificent aqueduct that brought water to Querétaro.

Making a song and dance.

Religious Querétaro is represented by a collection of churches and convents, the best of which includes the former monastery of **San Francisco**, a serene and happy structure with its tiled dome, wide-open courtyard, corridors, flowery arches and elegant stairways. It now houses the **State Museum**.

One block east, the **Federal Palace**, which used to be an Augustinian monastery, belongs to the late baroque style, with fantastically carved columns and arches. The leering gargoyles are said to be uttering the *Ave Maria* in sign language. **Santa Clara**, one of the many churches belonging to nuns' congregations, is simple on the outside but has a marvelous interior. The walls are covered by overflowing retablos and the grille separating the choir from the congregation is certainly a masterpiece. The outside fountain dedicated to Neptune is another work of the famous artist, Tresguerras.

Santa Rosa de Viterbo, another nuns' church, located about five blocks southwest of Santa Clara, has buttresses that seem more Chinese than European. It contains grand retablos and a splendid organ. The **Convento de la Cruz**, simple and devout, is reputed to be inhabited by the ghost of Maximilian, who was imprisoned there until he was shot.

Outside town, the **Cerro de las Campanas** is a low, barren hill where Maximilian went before the firing squad. Eyewitness accounts inspired the French Impressionist Edouard Manet to produce his famous painting of the execution. There is a huge and not very attractive sculpture of Benito Juárez, who confirmed the findings of the court-martial which pronounced the death sentence and a humble chapel dedicated to Maximilian.

About 61 kms (38 miles) south is **San Juan del Río**, a white village with narrow streets and solid provincial houses. It is not as aristocratic as Querétaro but offers the true atmosphere of rural Mexico. San Juan del Río has some interesting crafts, especially stone cutting and basket weaving. Nearby, on Highway 120, is the village of **Tequis-**

Toys for sale.

quiapán, famous for its thermal baths and a center of wine production.

Once a thriving mining center housing a royal mint and 40,000 inhabitants, **Real del Catorce** (pop: 800) is a ghost town today. It is located in the mountains west of Matehuala in desert land that produces another source of visions and euphoria – *peyotl*, the hallucinogenic cactus that still plays such an important role in the lives of many Indian tribes whose members pay an annual pilgrimage. Many of Catorce's homes are in ruins but there are rooms to rent, as well as stores, restaurants, silversmiths and mystics.

Mexican wine country: Although Mexico has a long tradition of wine-making (it was the first country in the Americas to plant vineyards), wine has not become popular until recent years. Demand is now growing steadily and the recent lowering of Mexico's trade barriers is creating strong competition for local products.

Mexican wine is unpredictable. A vintage may be good one year and inferior the next. A popular game is to discover which wine *esta saliendo bueno* (is coming along well). The wines of Tequisquiapán, especially the whites, are among the most dependable in Mexico. As a rule, the whites are good, the reds are a mystery, and the sherries, *oportos* and brandies tend to be a little suspect.

Near San Juan del Río is an old *hacienda* that has been transformed into a hotel. Known as the **Mansión Galindo**, it is one of the most beautiful hotels in Mexico. Like the wine, Mexican hotels and restaurants can be unpredictable. Mansión Galindo boasts striking architecture and gardens. The hotel is usually full and is expensive.

The capital of the state of **Aguascalientes**, the city of the same name, regards itself as Mexico's grape capital. Until recently the state was an important wine-producing region but the local vintners could not compete in either price or quality with imported wines. Today most of the grapes wind up as Mexican brandy, which bears only slight resemblance to Spanish brandy or

Aguascalientes is Mexico's grape capital.

French cognac, but is nevertheless the drink of Mexico's emerging lower middle-class. (Upper-class Mexicans never touch the stuff and the less affluent drink *pulque*, tequila or mescal.) The San Marcos Winery, north of the city, has weekday tours. Also north of town are the hot springs from which the town takes its name.

Aguascalientes is a pleasant spot. Its celebrated **San Marcos park** is described as a *jardín romántico*, a provincial garden laid out in the 19th century. On April 25, and running into May, San Marcos celebrates the famous **Feria de San Marcos**, with bullfighting, dancing, singing and brandy drinking. Though gambling is illegal in Mexico, there's plenty of that too.

On the town's main square is the **State House**, once the home of Mayorazgo de Rincon. It is an impressive 18th-century structure with two interior patios whose walls are covered with brightly colored murals painted by Oswalado Barra Cuningham and depicting the history of the city and the San Marcos Fair. The highlight of the town is the **Guadalupe Posada Museum**. Posada was perhaps Mexico's most famous lithographer and a great social and political critic of his time.

Marvelous Michoacán: Everyone has his or her favorite state in Mexico and many would choose mountainous **Michoacán**. With its lakes, rivers, Indian villages, volcanoes and colonial cities, it is like a miniature model of Mexico. Its capital, **Morelia**, formerly known as Valladolid but renamed for a hero of the independence struggle, is situated in the northeast part of the state. The road from Mexico City is marvelously scenic. Known as the **Mil Cumbres** (a thousand peaks), it meanders past pine-covered mountains and cool waterfalls.

Morelia is a colonial town, its walls built of pink-colored stone. Its climate is mild and life here moves at a slow tempo. The cathedral, built between 1640 and 1744, is a grand building in pure Mexican baroque style, with tall towers. At its side, by the Zócalo on **Madero Street**, is the baroque **Palace**

Morelia at dusk.

of Government, inside which is a colorful mural by Alfredo Zalce describing the beauties of Michoacán and outstanding events in its history.

Among Morelia's museums is the house, at Corregidora and Obeso, in which José María Morelos y Pavón was born. Later he studied under Hidalgo, became a parish priest and led some of the independence struggles before eventually being captured and executed. His life is depicted in the **Museo Casa de Morelos**, one block to the east. Just off the Zócalo is the **Museo Regional**, in which each room is devoted to handicrafts from a different village, illustrating the dazzling range of Michoacán village, and particularly Indian, craftsmanship.

The **Palacio Clavijero**, a former Jesuit seminary, now houses the tourist information office. Founded in 1660, it was named in honor of Francisco Xavier Clavijero, a Jesuit who taught here and wrote what many believe to be the best history of Mexico. **Colegio de San Nicolás**, where Morelos studied, is one of the oldest universities in the Americas. Even more attractive is the old convent of **Santa Rosa** which housed the first school of music in the Americas. It faces a peaceful plaza, which has a monument to Cervantes. Morelia offers good hotels, either in colonial buildings, such as the **Virrey de Mendoza** or the **Posada de la Soledador**, or in mountain-village-style structures, such as the **Villa Montaña**, straddling a hill overlooking Morelia.

West of Morelia, surrounded by Indian villages, is **Lake Pátzcuaro**, where the fishermen use distinctive butterfly-shaped fishing nets. In the middle of the lake is the island of **Janitzio**, with its giant sculpture of **José María Morelos**, described by the historian Nicholas Cheetham as "a stocky, bulldog of a man…an astute, tenacious *mestizo*." The statue's interior can be climbed: it offers a lovely panoramic view.

The cemeteries on Janitzio celebrate the Day of the Dead, November 2, with special panache: with floral displays, candles, and food offered to the de-

Fishing on Lake Pátzcuaro.

232

parted. People cry, sing, talk and get drunk and repeat the names and deeds of their loved ones, the *muertitos*, whom a good Mexican never, ever forgets.

Pátzcuaro, a town on the south side of the lake that is pure Indian, has a beauty of its own, with whitewashed adobe houses, overhanging roofs and cobblestoned streets. The Friday market is especially lively, although it gets harder and harder to find Indian wares among the TVs from Japan, knives from Taiwan and jeans from the United States.

There are remarkable buildings, such as the **Basílica de Nuestra Señora de la Salud** which has become a shrine for health-seekers from all over Mexico; the church of **St Agustín**, decorated with murals by the celebrated Juan O'Gorman; the **House of the Giant**, former residence of the Counts of Menocal; the **House of the Eleven Patios** containing craft shops, and the **Museo Regional de Artes Populares**, founded as a college by the revered 16th-century bishop Vasco de Quiroga, who dedicated his life to the welfare of the Tarascan Indians. On Wednesday and Saturday nights you can attend the Baile de los Viejitos at the Posada de Don Vascos hotel.

Near Pátzcuaro is a village with the catchy-sounding name of **Tzintzuntzan** (place of the hummingbirds). One of the chief archaeological sites in the state, it was the old capital of the Tarascans, an unconquered people until the Spanish arrived with their armor plate and cannons. The Tarascans have preserved their traditions, language and way of life to this day, especially in the mountain redoubts, where they preserve some of their *yacatas* or ancient temples.

Uruapán is not a fancy place but it marks the beginning of another Michoacán – the *tierra caliente*, or tropical lands. Uruapán is the center of a rich agricultural area famous for its avocados, located at the exact border between the mountains and the hills. The surrounding countryside is remarkable – witness **Tzaráracua**, a tropical park with lovely waterfalls.

Near Uruapán is **Paricutín**, a volcano

Paricutín erupts, circa 1944.

that came into being as recently as 1943 and is now sleeping, or perhaps just taking a siesta. All around is evidence of its power: the fields covered with black-sand ashes are slowly producing green life again.

The area is dotted with Indian villages which are known for their handicrafts, their cooking, or the beauty of their surroundings. They include **Paracho**, **Santa Clara**, **Charán**, **Cotija**, **Zira-huén**. The state of Michoacán is full of surprises, and full of contrast. Consider the **Ciudad Lázaro Cárdenas**, which was once a distant coastal village and is now the site of one of Latin America's biggest steel mills.

To the north is **Zacatecas**, which is the point of contact between two areas as different as two countries. The highland region of Central Mexico is green and densely populated, of great historical significance, and rich in archaeological treasure. In contrast, the north is huge, barren and empty. Life there has always been hard; its inhabitants have never enjoyed the refinements found in the central highlands. Even the cooking is elementary.

In pre-Columbian times Zacatecas was an important cultural area, and it boasts one major archaeological site: **Chal-chihuites**, in the northwestern part of the state. Protected by fortifications, Chalchihuites flourished from the year AD 900 to 1200. It has yielded ceramic treasures that suggest contact between the Mexican art style of the highlands and the simpler geometric art style of the American West.

Though geographically part of the north, Zacatecas became, culturally speaking, part of the highlands because it was rich in minerals – notably silver – which attracted settlers and produced wealth. For this reason the spectacularly sited city of Zacatecas, surrounded by dry and forbidding mountains, boasts some of the best colonial architecture in Mexico. (It is also one of the cleanest and friendliest cities.) The facade of its cathedral is delicately carved in filigree patterns. Zacatecas has a curious atmosphere, combining the vigor and rough-

A horse takes a break.

ness of a border town with architectural refinement. The houses, which can only be described as aristocratic, are graceful, with their fancy wrought-iron balconies and window grilles. The hard, gray stone of Zacatecas is sculpted with sober elegance.

Within a 12-block area, best explored on foot, are the cathedral, the state house, the Calderon theater, the Gonzalez Ortega market and a turn-of-the-century structure that has been converted into a shopping center. Here La Quija restaurant is a good place to sample local and international fare. Also in this area are the San Agustín and Santo Domingo churches. Next to the latter is the **Pedro Coronel Museum**, housing the enviable personal collection of the noted Zacatecan artist. Rafael Coronel, the artist's brother, donated the collection of 5,000 masks and 19th-century marionettes and pre-Hispanic pots to his native city. The collectio is displayed in the magnificently restored **Convent of San Francisco**.

It is interesting to take a tour of the

Eden mine, which functioned as such from 1586 until the beginning of this century. The tour can either be made on foot or in a small train. Your guide describes (in very broken English) the deplorable working conditions that existed in the colonial era. Leaving the mine, take the cable car up to **Cerro de la Bufa** for a thrilling view of the city. On weekends there's dancing in a discotheque that has been installed inside the entrance to the mine.

In **Guadalupe**, a suburb of Zacatecas, is a remarkable convent which has been transformed into a museum with a large collection of religious paintings. In **Jerez**, about 45 km (28 miles) west of Zacatecas, is the horseshoe-shaped **Hinojosa Theater**, a replica of Ford's theater in Washington, DC.

Similar to Zacatecas is the western part of the neighboring state of **San Luis Potosí**, which is large and diverse in character: to the east (Huasteca Polosina) it is hot and tropical; the center is full of dry plains; and the west is mountainous. Visitors initially encounter a grandiose but harsh vista of rocks and mountains and a lunar landscape, empty of human presence. Then, suddenly, as in Zacatecas, out of nowhere springs a thoroughly civilized city: **San Luis Potosí**, the state capital and the seat of Benito Juarez's government before the defeat of Maximilian. It is a 19th-century city with the air and feel of a city in Europe – witness the main square and buildings such as the **Casa de Cultura**, once the residence of a wealthy British mining family and now the site of daily activities.

The city's pre-eminent jewel is the church of **El Carmen**, adorned with shells and multi-colored tiles and a retablo of highest quality. The **Teatro de la Paz**, undistinguished but pleasant, is surrounded by a square. Across the street is the **Mask Museum**, displaying about 1,500 masks from pre-Hispanic to modern times. Four blocks southwest of the Plaza de Armas is the **Regional Handicrafts Museum**. There's also excellent regional and international food at **La Virreina**, one of the country's best restaurants.

Collecting peyote in Real del Catorce.

Although it saw the arrival of small numbers of settlers, the enormous northern region of Mexico was practically empty in colonial times. Indians were Christianized, exploited and dominated in the Mexican northeast, but it was a different story in the west. There the Indians rose in bloody revolt. The first uprising was the Tepehuan rebellion of 1616, in which hundreds of Spaniards were killed and thousands of Indians were put to death in revenge.

Then came the fierce rebellions of the Tarahumara Indians. The Spaniards, needing cheap labor, forced the Indians to work the land and to sweat in the mines. Indian settlements around the missions provided a concentration of manpower. The role of the missionaries is ambiguous – true, they often defended the Indians and protested their mistreatment, but they liked the idea of keeping the Indians in large communities where they could be easily controlled. It is no wonder that the Indians hated the whites, including missionaries.

The Spanish could not control the Apaches, who were thorns in their flesh for 150 years. The Apaches captured horses from the Spaniards, mounted constant raids, and conducted guerrilla warfare, hit-and-run style. They became experts at these tactics. They wisely refused pitched battle and established no bases that could be destroyed. They also operated in bands.

The Spaniards built a chain of *presidios* (forts) across northern Chihuahua to try to contain the raids but the Indians easily slipped past. Spanish settlers had to abandon their ranches; it was too dangerous to stay there. Finally, the Spanish found the solution. They first persuaded the Apaches to settle down near the *presidios* and then, luring the Indians with food, liquor and even some firearms, quelled the Apache fighting spirit, at least temporarily. During

Preceding pages: A Chihuahua landscape. **Left,** the long haul.

the Mexican War of Independence, the Apaches renewed their raids and when Mexico offered a bounty for Apache scalps some renegade Americans took up the offer.

Wars of intervention: By now American settlers had begun to occupy New Mexico, Arizona and Texas, where before long more than 20,000 anglos, as the whites were called, were living alongside a mere 3,000–4,000 Mexicans. That was the beginning of the end of Mexican Texas. The Mexican War (1846–48) began. Mexicans call it the War of Intervention, which it was. The Americans, for grievances both real and imagined, invaded all the key points in the north – Guaymas, Chihuahua, Saltillo, Monterrey – and Mexico was stripped of its territory north of the Rio Grande – in fact, half of the country.

Between 1864 and 1865 the Mexicans dealt with another invader, the French army supporting the Emperor Maximilian. President Benito Juárez fled to the north with his government, and remained across the Rio Grande in Mexico from El Paso, practically in exile. The US government was pro-Juárez, but was by now involved in its own Civil War. Nevertheless, for northeast Mexico the American war was a blessing. The American South was blockaded and could ship its cotton out only through Mexican ports. When the war ended, the US government brought diplomatic pressure on France to get out of Mexico, which it did, recalling the troops but leaving Maximilian to continue a futile fight to stay on the throne which ended with him being captured and shot. Porfirio Díaz brought relative peace and modernization to northern Mexico. The Apache problem was finally resolved when the US government herded them into reservations and a Mexican armed force under Colonel Joaquín Terrazas in Chihuahu defeated the last important band of Apaches.

If the War of Independence was largely a central Mexican episode, then the Revolution of 1910 was mostly a northern Mexican affair with almost all the major figures of the revolution coming

The gallant Villa leads his brave *Dorados* (the Golden Ones)

from the north: Francisco Madero and Venustiano Carranza from Coahuila, Alvaro Obregón from Sonora and Pancho Villa from Chihuahua. The exception to the rule was Emiliano Zapata, from Morelos.

Border towns: Mexico's north is vast, sparsely-settled, semi-desert or mountainous, and you must travel many a weary mile before getting to the population centers. For 3,200 km (2,000 miles), the US and Mexico share a common border and the towns on both sides of the border are unique, hybrids of the Yanqui and Latino cultures. Unfortunately, Americans who live on the border have often driven no farther and thus have an inappropriately negative view of the region.

Even if you have only a few days to explore, you can see a varied terrain ranging from mile-high mountains to deserts and unspoiled beaches with fine white sand. Also in the north are some important historic points of interest relating to Mexico's revolutionary struggle and the Mexican American War.

The Mexican northland contrasts markedly with the rest of the country. It looks different; its history is different; it is different. Most of the area south of the border, the states of Sinaloa, Sonora, Chihuahua, Durango, Coahuila, Nuevo León, and most of Tamaulipas, were once the domain of the Chichimeca Indians, an Indian tribe that lived mainly by hunting and gathering.

These days driving in the North is much easier than most people expect, with new toll roads similar to those in the US. A good driver's guidebook, such as the *Sanborn's Travelog* (available from any of their border insurance offices) is indispensable for learning about the tucked-away spots only drivers can find. From the towns on the southwest edge of Texas from Laredo to McAllen, Monterrey is the first logical stop. From Del Rio or Eagle Pass, Saltillo is the first stop. From Brownsville, you can beeline to Tampico. A circular trip is possible from any of these locations.

Monterrey is the third largest city in the country and an industrial and commercial center. Old guidebooks refer to it as the "Pittsburgh of Mexico," but that description is outdated, for its huge steel industry was shut down years ago. *Regiomontañas* (what local people call themselves) have an uneasy relationship with the federal government in Mexico City, and local businessmen seem to have closer cultural ties with the United States than with the rest of Mexico. They admire American know-how, marketing procedures and American business methods. This does not mean that they are not patriotic Mexicans and proud of their achievements, but it does mean that they often speak of government interference. Credit for Monterrey's industrial development is often attributed to the Garza-Sada family, free-enterprisers who emigrated to Mexico from Spain in the 19th century.

Bigtime manufacturing: Monterrey produces 25 percent of Mexico's manufactured goods, including half of the country's manufactured exports. The Alfa Group of Monterrey is Latin America's largest privately-owned company and the first in Mexico to be listed in *Fortune*

An area of heavy industry.

magazine's 500 of the largest non-US corporations. Dynamic Monterrey is the center of private enterprise. The Cintermex is one of the largest exhibition and trade show areas in the country. One of the best-known industrialists founded the Monterrey Institute of Technology which, patterned after the Massachusettes Institute of Technology, is probably Mexico's most outstanding university. (Nevertheless, many well-to-do Monterrey parents send their children to the US for schooling. Monterrey youth even play American-style football.)

In the center of town, **Plaza Zaragoza** is a large, baroque-facaded square bordered by a colonial cathedral with, nearby, a large free-form sculpture by Rufino Tamayo, one of Mexico's best-known artists. Dominating the plaza is the **El Faro del Comercio** (the lighthouse of commerce). This is a tall concrete structure with a laser beam that sweeps the city every evening, a beacon for commerce and entrepreneurs.

La Purísima Concepción church, a good example of modern, prize-winning architecture, contains a statue, which, it is said, once miraculously stopped the Santa Catarina river from flooding the city. This normally dry river was turned into a raging torrent in 1988 by Hurricane Gilbert, however, and hundreds died. The finest example of colonial architecture is the **Obispado**, the Bishop's Palace, located on a hill with an excellent overview of the city and an impressive mountain backdrop called **Cerro de la Silla** (Saddle Peak). The bullet holes and shellfire scars on the former church of the Obispado, now a museum, are souvenirs of the American invasion of September 22, 1846, when the US flag flew atop it.

A cheerful way to start or finish a tour of Monterrey, especially if you are thirsty, is with a tour of the **Cuauhtémoc Brewery**, Mexico's biggest and oldest brewery. The brewery produces fine Pilsner-type beer (Carta Blanca and Bohemia brands) and has led the way in providing good wages and benefits to its workers. Wage-earners of Monterrey tend to be envied throughout Mexico.

Coahuila vineyards.

They often benefit from free medical care, subsidized housing, 40 percent off their home-delivered groceries, and even free piano lessons.

Out of town: It's worth exploring the area around Monterrey. About 35 km (21 miles) or 40 minutes from town (toward Saltillo) at **Villa de García** is García Cave, which has spectacular formations of stalactites and stalagmites. The caves close at 4pm, so leave plenty of time to look around. The drive from the town is beautiful, but winding and narrow. There is now a little tramway to take you to the caves, as well as improved illumination. There is also a kids' playground and swimming pool.

Huasteca Canyon provides a spectacular drive, via paved highway, through the base of the canyon carved from the solid rock by Rio Santa Catarina (and the wind). It's only a 15-minute drive from downtown Monterrey, on clearly marked Highway 40 toward Saltillo outside suburban Santa Catarina. (Note: The road is good only as far as the Gruta de la Virgen; off-road vehicles are recommended from this point.) **Horsetail Falls** is a short drive away. You can picnic and look at the triple cascade called the Three Graces. En route you pass **La Boca** dam, where there is good fishing and water sports. For a spectacular view of the city, try **Chipinique Mesa**, where the well-to-do of Monterrey have homes.

Saltillo, capital of Coahuila state, at 1,598 meters (5,245 ft) above sea level, has a population of 650,000. This mile-high altitude has made it a favorite summer vacation spot for many years, especially among Texans. Presently it is an industrial and educational center, as well as a popular tourist stop. Saltillo's present boom started when US car manufacturers located huge plants here, bringing an influx of spin-off industries. The city also has a fine university to which many Americans come in summer for language courses.

Founded in 1575 by Captain Francisco Urdinóla, Saltillo was used as a base to explore the area and to control the Indians. In the 1700s, it was the headquarters for exploring and colonizing land to its north, and between 1824 and 1836 was the capital of a large area which included Texas. In 1847 one of the bloodiest and most decisive battles of the Mexican-American War took place at **Buena Vista**, half an hour south on Highway 54. Some 4,500 US soldiers, under General Zachary Taylor, fought 23,000 Mexicans commanded by General Antonio López de Santa Anna. Despite being outnumbered 5-1, the US suffered just 264 fatalities and 450 wounded, while the Mexicans suffered 2,500 casualties. Militarily the loss was attributed to General Santa Anna's poor preparation. Soon after this battle, the war ended. (To reach the battlefield, take Highway 54 south for 16 km (10 miles). On the left just past an Angostura sign is a small monument marking the site. There is a roadside rest area with parking space.)

Venustiano Carranza, governor of Coahuila in 1913, was the first to denounce Victoriano Huerta, who had orchestrated the murder of the populist president Francisco Madero. When his

At the Coahuila wine fest.

example was followed by the governors of Sonora and Chihuahua, these states became the cradle of the revolution against Huerta. Chihuahua also produced Doroteo Arango (Francisco "Pancho" Villa). From Sonora came Alvaro Obregón, who after starting life as a farmer became a soldier during the Orozco rebellion of 1912.

Saltillo is an interesting old city – a blend of "typical" and modern which maintains its colonial charm despite industrialization. Most important architecturally is the **Santiago Cathedral** on the main plaza. Finished around 1800, it is one of the northernmost examples of *churrigueresque* churches.

The governor's palace and city hall are fine examples of contemporary Mexican architecture. Museums include the **Juarez Archives**, where much of the early history of Texas is recorded and the **Ruben Herrera art gallery**. Popular local foods include *cabrito al pastor* (charcoaled young goat), *pan de pulque* (a delicious sweet bread made with the fermented sap of the maguey plant) and *huevoes con machado* (scrambled egg with Mexican-style dried beef and bits of pepper and onion). There is an excellent local wine, bottled at the **San Lorenzo Winery** (Mexico's oldest: founded in 1626), just off Highway 40 near Parras; tours are conducted. Nearby is **Rincon del Montero**, set in lovely grounds with a golf course and spring-fed pool.

Another specialty of Saltillo is Madero Brandy, said to be the world's best-selling brand. Saltillo's principal art work and a favorite of tourists is the sarape or blanket, used by Indians and ranchers alike and made by several factories here. Historians attribute the art of sarape-making to the Tlaxcalan Indians who were brought to the area by the Spaniards in the late 16th century to help defend them against other Indians. The traditional sarape was finely woven in a rainbow of colors.

If you enjoy a long spell of driving, head for **Mazatlán** on the Pacific coast, some 700 km (430 miles) west of Saltillo. By making a short detour on the way, you can visit **Parras**, home of Francisco Madero, leader of the 1910 Revolution. Farther on, the road goes by Torreón and La Laguna cotton districts. Push on and you reach **Durango**, a cattle and lumbering center where movies are often made. From Durango prepare yourself for what is probably the most spectacular drive in Mexico. From **El Espinazo del Diablo** (the Devil's Spine), the road winds like a top and drops down to Mazatlán.

The Gulf Coast: If you are heading for Yucatán or Belize or Guatemala, you will probably enter Mexico either from Brownsville or McAllen, Texas. Unless you are coming from Louisiana it is probably quicker to drive from McAllen. The highway from there (Mexican Highway 97) is only 8 km (5 miles) longer than Mexican Highway 101 from Matamoros and is often in better shape. The terrain changes from flat farmland to rolling hills after a couple of hours. The little town of **San Fernando** is a popular spot for a break with good restaurants and hotels. It is the center for hunting in the area; white-winged doves, ducks and geese being the attraction. During early November you must have a reservation.

About three hours south at **Soto La Marina**, make a one-hour detour to the east if you have time, to visit **La Pesca**, a sleepy little fishing village that was saved from being another Cancún only because of lack of resources. In 1991 the government designated it as a megaproject, the next touristic hot spot. A small airport was built, scheduled to be enlarged later; plans were laid for building 5-star hotels; the town's primitive *topes* (speed bumps) which were merely thick ropes were replaced by proper concrete ones; a new sewer was installed and land speculation became frantic. Fortunately for those who appreciate Mexico's natural charm, the project fizzled and there remain hotels in all categories except luxury, plus two classy hunting lodges and an RV park. From Soto La Marina to Tampico is about a three-hour drive.

Tampico, with its huge new harbor complex of Altamira, has a lively seaport atmosphere and some of Mexico's best seafood, especially crabs (*jaibas*) which is the town's symbol. An attractive beach can be found at the city's northeastern border, where the handful of seafood shacks may soon be joined by new hotels. The Tampico region has oil refineries, good hunting and fishing.

South of town is the vast **Tamahua Lagoon** whose islands and mangrove swamps can be explored in rented boats. The first scheduled airline flights from Mexico City came to Tampico, bringing payrolls for the oil refineries. Here you are a half-day's drive from **Papantla**, the center of Mexico's vanilla industry and famous for its *voladores,* who perform a daring pole dance.

Close to Papantla is the archaeological site of **El Tajín**, the most interesting structures of which are the Pyramid of the Niches and the ball court with its beautifully sculptured panels. El Tajín, an important ceremonial center of the Totonacs from AD 300 to 1100, is the largest ruin in Mexico.

If you head west instead of south from Tampico towards San Luis Potosí, you'll enter the region named Huasteca (for the Mayas' distant cousins who settled here). From **Ciudad Valles** drive through jungles of bamboo palm and banana trees, and just before reaching Tamazunchale take a short side-trip on a paved road to **Xilitla**, a genuine Huastecan village.

Tamazunchale has a fine 16th-century church and on Sunday the marketplace is crowded with Indians who come to do their weekly shopping. This area is also a paradise for the ornithologist and lepidopterist. In fact, you can buy well-mounted butterfly specimens in many of the town's shops.

From Tamazunchale there's a rough but scenic 320-km (200-mile) drive to **Pachuca** in the state of Hidalgo, not far from Mexico City. To the northwest, **Zimapán** has an unusual Moorish-looking church and a world-class spa.

Ixmiquilpán is an important Otomí Indian center with interesting colonial architecture. Stop off at the market where the best buys are wool weavings, pottery and silver jewelry.

García Caves, Monterrey.

CHIHUAHUA

Heading south from the Texas border, you will be confronted by two great mountain ranges, the Sierra Madre Occidental in the west and the Sierra Madre Oriental in the east. The former is by far the more rugged of the two; the latter does not present an imposing obstacle. Between the border crossing at El Paso-Ciudad Juárez and Guadalajara, in central-west Mexico, a 1,600-km (1,000-mile) stretch, there are only two ways to cross the mountains to the Pacific. That is, unless you want to hike it like Cabeza de Vaca, who, early in the 16th century, walked from Texas to the Pacific, through northern Mexico, an odyssey that took him seven years. Today's two routes are the railroad from Chihuahua city to Los Mochis on the Pacific coast, or the road from Durango to Mazatlán.

Northern Mexico, a vast expanse of land, is different from the rest of the country. The fiestas here are less colorful; there's not nearly as much production of handicrafts, and there is little colonial architecture left. But the Mexican wilderness ends with the states of Durango, Zacatecas and San Luis Potosí. There are two logical north–south axes: one from El Paso to Zacatecas and the other from Laredo on the border to San Luis Potosí.

Ciudad Juárez, just across the border from El Paso, is Chihuahua's biggest town and caters to millions of American tourists. Many see the city, go no farther, and tell people they've seen Mexico. It's an interesting town, where you can go to watch the bullfights, or to the greyhound races or the horse races and lose or win a packet. You can even go to the dentist (a surprising number of Americans do) because dental work costs a lot less here than in the US.

Drive straight down Highway 45 to Chihuahua city, or take detours and see a number of points of interest before reaching the capital city. Out of Ciudad

Chihuahua ranchero.

Juárez, swing right for **Casas Grandes**, home of several thousand Mormons whose ancestors refused to give up polygamy. At Casas Grandes archaeologists have found proof of an early race that knew how to irrigate the land, and build five-story-high adobe houses and water tanks. Casas Grandes combines elements of the Pueblo Indian civilization of the southwestern United States and the influences of Meso-America. Around the year AD 1300 the place was abandoned; nobody knows why.

Casas Grandes was deserted for centuries, until the explorer Cabeza de Vaca came by with two Spanish companions and a Moorish slave, and showed the Indians how to cure ailments. This ability made them supernatural in the Indians' eyes. Cabeza de Vaca told the Spanish of the fabulous wealth of Cibola as described to him by his Indian friends. Subsequent expeditions opened northwestern Mexico to colonization.

Another influential explorer, Francisco Coronado, debunked the de Vaca myth. He and his party set out from Compostela, walked across Sinaloa and southeastern Arizona and reached Cibola country, the land of the Zuñi Indians of New Mexico. But there was no gold in the Seven Cities of Cibola. Coronado sent some of his lieutenants farther along on the quest, and one of his lieutenants even reached what is now Kansas. But there was no gold, no silver. The north of Mexico, believed too poor to colonize, was subsequently forgotten.

Mennonite country: South of Nuevo Casas Grandes is **Babicora**, where William Randolph Hearst once owned a 354,000-ha (875,000-acre) estate, which was expropriated by the government in the early 1950s. Soon you come to Mennonite country, where some 15,000 German-speaking farmers work their land. It is the Mennonites who deserve credit for making the state a leading producer of oats, cheese and meats. Mennonites, the Mexicans say, do not mix much; few speak Spanish and they do not intermarry. As it is Mennonite custom to shun luxury and modernization, most still drive around in horse-

Mennonite gathering.

drawn carts. However, you may see a pickup truck or two, for not everyone follows the old order. Yet TV is still taboo in the homes, and 10-children families are not uncommon among these strange but fascinating people. Some tours from Creel include sharing a simple lunch in a Mennonite household.

It was a 17-year-old nobleman, Francisco de Ibarra, who led the expedition which opened up the silver-rich state of Chihuahua. In 1554 he set out with his party from Zacatecas, twice crossing the rugged Sierra Madre and discovering extensive silver deposits. De Ibarra showed tact beyond his years in dealing diplomatically with hostile Indians, pacifying them with words rather than weapons. His explorations led to the founding of New Spain's largest province, which included the present states of Durango, Sinaloa and Sonora. It was called Newe Vizcaya in honor of De Ibarra's home in Spain.

The last major exploration to the north set out from Santa Bárbara at the end of the 16th century and was led by Juan de Oñate. They went up Chihuahua, across the Rio Grande and into New Mexico. There they laid out a town, built a church and houses and began to till the land. The silver mines at Santa Eulalia (now known as Aquiles Serdán) are still being worked after 300 years.

Chihuahua city, founded in 1709, is worth more than a casual look. Its population is over 1.2 million. Leather is a good buy here, and there are several leather shops. One of the top attractions is Quinta Luz, the 30-room **Pancho Villa House**, which is now a museum housing assorted Villa memorabilia. Villa was at various times a bandit and a hero of the Revolution. Corral de Villa, one of Villa's wives, continued to live here until her death in 1981. Perhaps the most popular attraction in the museum is the bullet-riddled Dodge touring car in which Pancho Villa was riding when he was gunned down in 1923. There's a photo gallery that tells the history of Mexico during Villa's time, including the US Navy's uninvited "visit" to Veracruz.

The baroque **cathedral** on the main plaza is one of the North's few outstanding architectural gems from the colonial period. It was financed by the voluntary contributions of miners working in the nearby silver mines. An aqueduct and the church of **San Francisco** also date from colonial times. The state capitol is lined inside with paintings depicting the history of Chihuahua. In the inner courtyard is a monument to the memory of Father Miguel Hidalgo, whose *grito* aroused his countrymen to revolution and who was executed here. You can visit the grim dungeon in the federal building where he was imprisoned while he awaited his fate. **Quinta Gameros**, a Victorian manor house which dates back to the turn of the century, houses a regional museum.

Chihuahua is also famous for a couple of other things: Chihuahua dogs and Tarahumara Indians. Perhaps you're familiar with this popular breed of tiny dog: it's advisable not to buy one from a street peddler, because it might grow up to be a St Bernard.

You'll probably see a Tarahumara

A bride arrives.

Indian or two in Chihuahua. They are easy to spot: long, flowing black hair with colored headband; white *tapote* (over-sized loin cloth); and white shirt of rough cloth. For the most part, this shy tribe lives southwest of Chihuahua in the Sierra Madres, but they come to town on market days and on other occasions. They're very bashful, and unless married or in a close relationship, male and female Tarahumaras talk to each other at a distance, with heads turned. The men, fabulous long-distance runners, catch deer by chasing them for hours until the animals fall from sheer exhaustion. Two Tarahumara competed in the 1928 Olympics in Amsterdam. They ran the marathon (42-km/26-mile race) but did not fare well. "Too short! Too short!" they told their sponsors. Short races like these were only run by women and children back home.

Tarahumaras have no fear of cameras and you are welcome to take their picture, providing you ask first. Don't be surprised if they ask you for some money in return; they can certainly use it and they are "selling" something of value – a priceless picture. They have a hard-scrabble life and are cheated by merchants and traders who buy their artwork to sell. The mission store in Creel also has moderately-priced wares and the Indians benefit from all sales. There are about 50,000 Tarahumaras; they comprise one of the largest Indian groups left in Mexico.

Some tours of Copper Canyon, particularly those operated by Ecogrupos, devote some time to exploring San Ignacio, with its valleys of towering rocks and caves in which the Tarahumaras used to live. These tours include a visit to the school, to which the Indian children come from miles around.

If you want to go hunting, make arrangements through your hotel or one of the travel agencies. The best-known hunting lodges are the luxurious "La Estancia" in Mennonite country and "El Halcón." You can go horseback riding, play tennis, go swimming, or laze away time in a sauna.

Soldier settlers: A good paved road

The Quinta Gameros State Museum.

leads northeast towards **Ojinaga**. About 9 km (5 miles) before you reach the town of Aldama, you will see the mission church of **Santa Anna de Chinarras**, one of the few Jesuit-built churches outside the Sierras. Farther along, you pass **Pueblitos**, where some of Pancho Villa's fighting men were placated with 8 hectares (20 acres) apiece of irrigated farmland. They were also given farm tools and a year's grubstake.

Coyame, northeast of Aldama, produces rope, a spirited drink and wax – all derived from the various species of cactus plant that grow in such abundance here. This gives you an idea of what the countryside looks like. It was in 1880, in the desert country north of Coyame at Tres Castillos, that Coronel Terrazas finally defeated and broke the back of the Apaches. That marked the beginning of the end of the Apache raids in Chihuahua.

A few kilometers east of Coyame a dirt road leads to **Cuchillo Parado** (Standing Knife), a strange rock formation near the Río Conchos. Once the rock rose from the river, but, as has happened here, Mexico's rivers sometimes change course. About 18 km (11 miles) beyond the Cuchillo Parado turnoff, the road begins to climb until you come to a lookout at the Peguis Barranca overlooking the Río Conchos far below. You might as well picnic here before returning to Chihuahua since there's not much of any interest to see on the road to Ojinaga.

Driving south from Chihuahua city you will see the state's richest agricultural regions. It is here that they grow the famous chili peppers. From the city of **Camargo**, 157 km (98 miles) southwest of Chihuahua, you can zip over to **Boquilla Dam**, which is stocked with black bass from Canada. That is why the body of water is sometimes referred to as Lake Toronto.

Hidalgo del Parral is a thriving town with an active mine, called **La Prieta**, 149 km (93 miles) farther on. Once silver was the main support of the economy but now lumbering and commerce are also important. There is a fine

Desert cave paintings, Chihuahua.

old colonial church, dedicated to the Virgen del Raho, the Thunderbolt Virgin. It is said that the church was paid for in gold ingots by an Indian miner. He refused to reveal the location of the mine, even when tortured.

Another church, **Nuestra Señora de Fátima**, is built out of ore-bearing rock – gold, silver, copper, lead, zinc – with even the pews carved out of the rock. Obviously, the idea was to seek divine guidance and protection for the miners.

Parral is where Pancho Villa, driving his Dodge sedan, was ambushed by nine assassins, one of whom he managed to shoot before succumbing to the 16 bullets that hit him. There's a museum in town which contains old photos and a number of Villa mementoes. The man who led the assassination team spent only eight months in jail. One of the many stories engendered by the event was that Pancho Villa's head was dug up and sold for US$10,000. All that can be said for sure is that when the government decided Pancho Villa was an authentic revolutionary hero and his body was dug up for reburial in the Monument to the Revolution in Mexico City, the diggers couldn't find Pancho's skull. The central government's belated decision to rank Villa with the country's other national heroes did not settle the controversy that still surrounds the colorful Villa. Many conservatives still consider him an ordinary bandit, but popular songs and stories have made him the most widely known of Mexico's historical characters.

The town of **Cuauhtémoc**, about 95 km (60 miles) southeast of Chihuahua City, is the Mennonite center for commercial activity, though no Mennonites live here. They simply come into town to do their shopping. During the day you will see them, overall-clad men, married women dressed in black, and maidens in bright dresses.

From Cuauhtemoc a paved road leads to the waterfalls of **Basaseáchic**. Be sure to inquire about road conditions before venturing along this route, especially during the rainy season. There are a few cabins near the falls and two economny hotels. The falls plunge over 300 meters (more than 1,000 ft) but it's an easy walk up the road to the top. If you are in good shape, walk about halfway down for a spectacular view. It's best to hire a local guide as the path is not clearly marked.

In 1992, the the two-lane blacktop road between Tomochic and Hermosillo was finished. Basaseáchic is on this route and there are acceptable (but not luxurious) accommodations on the way. You can now visit the canyon by car, and then drive on to the Pacific coast.

Going south from Chihuahua city, it's another 800 km (500 miles) to Torreon, where you can head east to the coast. Or if you continue south it's another 320 km (200 miles) to Zacatecas where you can turn east. Not until you reach the central Mexican highlands will you have a wider choice of roads to pick from.

Copper Canyon: Chihuahua is also the jumping-off place for the **Barranca del Cobre** (Copper Canyon), which is even deeper than the Grand Canyon of Colorado. From **Creel**, you can take a second-class bus to **Batopilas** (luxury hotel

Basaseachic Falls.

plus two economy hotels), amidst semi-tropical vegetation. There is a steep gravel road full of switchbacks (you descend from 2,500 meters (8,200 ft) to 460 meters (1,500 ft) in about 90 km/56 miles). Only the foolhardy and adventurous should tackle it and then only in a pickup truck or 4-wheel drive.

Alternatively, take the highly recommended Chihuahua–Pacifico train ride (recommended even if you have your own vehicle). This has been called the "World's Most Scenic Railroad." It winds up, over, around and under the Sierra Madres mountains. The dry season is February until May; the rainy months, July through August.

If you are short on time, you can merely ride the train from Chihuahua (it runs every day) to Los Mochis or Topolobampo on the Pacific (make the trip during daylight hours to see the magnificent scenery of the Sierra Madres, with its 2,440-meter (8,000 ft) peaks). The best way, however, is to get off at Creel or Divisadero and explore some of the canyon on foot (there are special trails to follow). Three excellent hotels are available, but the Cabana Divisadero Barrancas hotel is the most scenic, perched right on the edge of the Barranca del Cobre. If you do want to get off the train and make a stop, make sure you tell the conductor when you buy your ticket. People who just ride the train will miss the Copper Canyon.

The construction of the splendid railroad was originally the dream of Albert Kinsey Owens, the founder of a utopian colony in Los Mochis, but it took very many years and many attempts to complete (finally in 1961 by Mexican engineers). The track, started in 1898 out of Chihuahua, reached Creel in 1912. Then came all the obstacles: revolution, lack of funds, and incredible engineering problems.

The final 160 km (100 miles) were the toughest, beginning in 1952 and taking nine years to complete. The last stretch has 39 bridges, 86 tunnels and many sections where the track switches back and forth as it descends a particularly steep grade. **Copper Canyon, the Sierra Madres.**

CHILI PEPPERS

hili peppers are everywhere in Mexico – more than 100 varieties. They're ubiquitous enough to be the subject of children's jokes ("What country can you fit into a piece of French bread?") and sometimes used by adults as a slang term for the male member. And, far from being alike in taste or spiciness, they are nearly endless in variety, depending on the specific climate in which they are grown, the chemical composition of the soil and even the characteristics of neighboring plantings.

Chilis are part of the nightshade family of plants which also includes tomatoes, eggplants and potatoes. Nevertheless, they elude strict description: chilis are horticulturally classified as fruits, although botonists refer to them as berries. Produce purveyors count them as vegetables but when they are dried, the world thinks of them as spices.

The Aztec Indians of Mexico and the South American Incas domesticated chilis about 7,000 years ago but it is only in recent years that their flavors and uses have been defined for people outside those cultures.

Columbus carried some back to Europe where Spain and Portugal adopted them for some dishes and passed them on to India and Africa, where they were eagerly incorporated into the native foods. Even then, the problems of identifying chilis was complicated by the changes in their characteristics when they were grown in different locales.

It becomes even more complex to attempt to define chilis by their "hotness" factor, because these perverse little examples of the *genus capsicum* vary from location to location and, oddly enough, occasionally from pepper to pepper on the same plant. Nevertheless, it isn't difficult to identify the ones most frequently encountered in the market.

Chile Serrano is the chili most common in Mexico. As a small green pepper it is used in fresh sauces and added to stews and soups for a touch of piquancy. When it turns red it loses some of its characteristic hotness. *Chile de Arbol* is occasionally used fresh but is predominantly grown for drying, to be used in table sauces and in cooking.

The *Chile ancho,* a chile used for its sweetish flavor, is a dried version of the green Poblano pepper which in its original state is stuffed with cheese or chopped meat, dipped in egg batter, fried and served with a tomato sauce as *Chile Relleno.*

Chile Chipotle is the same variety as a jalapeno pepper, only in this version it is first ripened, then smoked and dried. It is used to make a pungent sauce.

Chile Guajillo, the dried version of the Mirasol chili, adds bite as well as a yellow color to dishes in which it is cooked. *Chile Mulato* and *chile Pasilla* are similar. *Pasila* is used in one of the great dishes of Mexico City, *Caldo Tlalpeno,* a soup which includes chicken and avocado. *Mulato* is an essential ingredient for *mole* sauce.

Known in other cultures as "cayenne", *chile Pequin* is very hot in flavor, generally exceeded only by Yucatan's *chile Habanero,* which is said to be the hottest in the world. The *Pequin,* also known as *Chiltepin,* frequently grows wild throughout Mexico.

What to do if you find most Mexican food far too hot? If it's already in your mouth, reach for the bread, not the water. Beer also helps. If you are ordering a meal, the key word is *picante* – spicy – not *caliente,* which means hot only in temperature. ∎

Mexicans like it hot.

253

THE NORTHWEST

Northwest Mexico was neglected until the missionaries started to work among the tribes in the 17th century. The Jesuits were most successful with the Pimas and the Opatas; they achieved results with the Mayos and the Yaquis, but they made little headway with the headstrong Seri Indians. The priests introduced domestic animals, showed the Indians new crops, taught them better ways to farm and to build. Many Indians quickly took up the new life. Problems arose when Spanish colonists arrived and tried to take the most fertile lands and force the Indians into hard labor. Naturally, they resisted. Split into many tribes, spread out over great distances, the northern Indians could not be conquered in one blow. So rebellion flared, on and off, over the decades.

As more Spaniards moved in, resentment hardened. When the Jesuits were expelled from Mexico in 1767, the missions disintegrated and the northwest Indians lost their only protector. The whites brazenly encroached on tribal lands. The Yaquis, a fighting race, reacted angrily and the Spanish dealt with them harshly.

During the Revolution of 1910, the Yaquis joined General Obregón's forces, becoming excellent soldiers. But they wanted their tribal lands back, and when Lázaro Cárdenas became president in the 1930s, he ordered a dam to be built on the upper Yaqui river for irrigation, and set aside 4.5 million hectares (1 million acres) for the Yaqui tribes. It included the whole north bank of the river and part of the south.

The best deal: Much of the south bank was still held by the whites, but the Yaquis realised this was the best deal they could get. Setting up a reservation, they took over their own tribal lands, which they control to this day. Other northwest Indians did not fare so well. The Seri Indians, for example, were either killed or died of disease and their population dropped from 5,000 to less

Jet-skiing in tandem.

than 200. The Opatas, on the other hand, assimilated readily: they learned Spanish, intermarried and cooperated in the battles against the Apaches.

For centuries the tribes of the northwest were isolated in a rugged, remote corner of Mexico. They took little part in the life of the nation and were marginal to the independence movement of the 1810s. The region was weak and unprotected and practically invited invasion. The French, led by Gaston Raousset de Bourbon, captured Hermosillo in Sonora in 1852. Another adventure, led by Henry Crabb, an American from California, tried to capture northern Sonora in 1857. In both instances, the Mexicans reacted vigorously, defeating the invaders and executing the leaders. In time the Northwest developed muscle and conscience. When the 1910 Revolution broke out, the northwest took part wholeheartedly, providing troops and the general (Alvaro Obregón) who emerged after the inevitable internal power struggle.

For a decade, Mexico was ruled directly or indirectly by the "Northwest Mafia," first Obregón, then General Plutarco Elías Calles. Land reform was implemented slowly in the region. Large tracts were not taken over until President Cárdenas's program. By law, private land holdings are now limited in size, but there's a way to get around it: titles are registered under the names of relatives and thus large sections are controlled by a single person who has the capital and presumably the know-how to make the most efficient use of the land. The question naturally arises: should these tracts, acquired by amalgamation, be divided among the land-hungry who have neither the technical skill nor the capital to run a productive operation? It is a question that is never satisfactorily answered.

Varied crops: The Northwest is highly productive. Sonora leads the nation in cotton, wheat and soybean production. Sinaloa tops the other states in tomatoes – most of which go to the US – and also raises a hefty crop of wheat, cotton, sugar cane and chickpeas, which are exported chiefly to Spain and Cuba. Although the silver mines of the Northwest are practically exhausted, the mines of Cananea in northern Sonora make that state the leading producer of copper in the country.

The Pacific beaches are the main attraction of the route from the Arizona border to Mazatlán, but there are also interesting mountain towns and historical sights along the way. You can fly to Mazatlán from many US cities and although there are first- and second-class buses that can take you from the Arizona border to Mazatlán and anywhere in between, most people drive. There is a fine super-highway almost all the way. Completed in 1992, this magnificent tollway is equal to roads north of the border. But it is not cheap: tolls are about US$90 for a car and close to US$150 for an RV. An alternative is to take the longer *libre* (free) route but it has more traffic. Many of the resorts, particularly in the north, offer trailer facilities, with water and power hookups.

Many people begin with a short jaunt to **Pto Penásco** on the Sea of Cortés, in

Offshore
parasailing.

the far northwest corner of Sonora. This is a funky fishing village that has been "discovered," and is now a popular weekend retreat for Arizonans. Fishing and beaching are the main reasons for going there. If you take a boat out, be extra careful: tides are hazardous and winds are strong in the shallow waters at the head of the Gulf of California, or Sea of Cortés, its alternate name.

Twenty kilometers (12 miles) south of the junction with Highway 2 and Highway 15 is **Magdalena**, where the mortal remains of Padre Eusebio Kino, the Jesuit priest who helped to establish missions along the coast and later in Arizona and California, are enshrined. The history of the Jesuits, and that of the Yaqui Indians who were there when the Spaniards came, are intertwined. Kino, often crippled with arthritis, was a mathematician, astrologer, architect and economist who taught the Indians new farming techniques. He died in 1711 but his grave remained undiscovered until 1966. There is gold mining going on in the hills around Santa Ana but neither it nor Sonora's capital of **Hermosillo**, a thriving city with a Ford plant, have much of interest to tourists. From here, though, you can connect with Highway 16, which goes on to the Copper Canyon and Chihuahua. It is a lengthy one-day drive, with a moderately priced hotel and RV park at Yeócora and the the similarly priced Alma Rosa hotel at the Basaseáchic Falls.

Indian handicrafts: The next worthwhile stop is **Kino Bay**. It is a laid-back resort/fishing village that, while it has many *norteaméricanos* living there in the winter, still has an unsophisticated appeal. You can buy Seri Indian handicrafts such as ironwood carvings and baskets. These shy, nomadic people live in a small corner of the state, from Pto Libertad in the north to Bahia Kino. They were moved here from Isla Tiburón, which is now a wildlife sanctuary. They have been fishermen for centuries, though fishing is now pretty well played out on the Sea of Cortés. Many gringos trade old, used clothing in return for their ironwood carvings

The marina, San Carlos Bay.

(the local wood is so named because it is so hard) and cheat them terribly.

Off Kino Bay is **Tiburón** (Shark) **Island**, a wildlife and game preserve. You can rent a boat for fishing (you need a permit but there's no hassle about getting it) in most of the resort towns. Boats come complete with tackle, crew and cold beer. Prices vary greatly; ask around. If you go out, don't forget to wear a hat and take suntan lotion – the sun can be your undoing.

Winter nights can get chilly along the coast of Sonora in winter and although it will be sunny during the day, the water will be too cold for a swim. When it does warm up, however, the Pacific coast seldom gets muggy like the Gulf coast, thanks to ocean breezes. The ocean can get rough; there may be big waves and an undertow, except in protected bays, so be careful when you go swimming.

Though the coast offers great beaches, good fishing, and delicious seafood, it has almost no colonial architecture, nor interesting archaeological sites. And most of the handmade craft for sale is produced elsewhere in Mexico. The tourist season from mid-December through the Easter week brings the biggest crowds. During the Christmas and Easter seasons you must have confirmed reservations at the hotels, unless you plan to camp under a palm tree or sleep on the beach. During the rest of the year you can usually drift into a resort town and find accommodations.

Though many people call **Guaymas** a beach resort, it is not. Nearby San Carlos is the beach resort; Guaymas is a port and sport fishing hub. A ferry to Santa Rosalía in Baja California also leaves from here three times a week. The hours and days change often, so don't plan your trip too closely. It used to be dirt cheap, but is now priced fairly. While you won't save any money taking the ferry rather than driving to Baja, you will save a lot of time. The cost per passenger is still very reasonable.

San Carlos is a gringo oasis and many retired Americans and Canadians live here. There are dozens of hotels and restaurants in all price ranges. It also has

Fishing harbour at sunrise, Guayamas.

one of Mexico's largest marinas, where you will see sailing vessels from all around the world. The 1970 movie *Catch 22* was shot nearby.

There were about 30,000 Yaqui Indians when the Spanish conquistadors landed. Today there are half as many, mostly clustered around the Yaqui river in Sonora. While this is one of the most productive agricultural regions of Mexico, thanks to the "Green Revolution" of modern farming methods financed by the Rockefellers to feed the world, the Yaquis have not benefited. They were given the north side of the Yaqui river, which has very little water, as a homeland by President Lázaro Cárdenas in the 1930s, but without sufficient capital were unable to take advantage of the modern farming methods practiced on the south side. The tribe fiercely independent even today and can be summed up in a quote from an unnamed laborer in the book *The Tall Candle: The Personal Chronicle of a Yaqui Indian*: "There will always be a Yaqui tribe. The Yaquis are not like the Mayos or the Pimas, who have all become Mexicans."

Hunting terrain: Soon you pass through **Cuidad Obregón**, an agricultural center and a base for deer and duck hunters. **Navojoa**, south of Ciudad Obregón, is the center of a major cotton-producing area and the home of the Maya Indians. A detour from Navojoa takes you to the old mining town of **Alamos** in the foothills of the Sierras. This was a rich mining center in the 18th century, with dozens of fabulous residences built along its cobblestone streets. When the mines were exhausted, it was practically abandoned until the 1940s, when wealthy Americans rediscovered it, buying up many of the old houses and restoring them. These are the best examples of colonial architecture on the West Coast.

The entire town has been declared a national monument and to visit it is like stepping back in time. The baroque facade of the main church of **Nuestra Senóra de la Concepción** dates back to 1784. The town is also the home of the Mexican jumping bean (whose restlessness is due to a small larva growing inside it). As you drive south, you'll pass some of the richest farmland in Mexico. Tomatoes, peppers and flowers are some of the crops you'll see.

From Alamos-Navojoa, the main highway continues to **Los Mochis**, a pleasant town with wide streets and friendly people. There are hotels in all categories and RV parks here.

Most people spend a day or two here while waiting for the Copper Canyon train, which traverses the rugged Sierra Madres to Chihuahua. Offering one of the most spectacular train rides in the world, it leaves early in the morning and arrives in Chihuahua in the early evening. Thanks to irrigation, Los Mochis has become a boom town, producing rice, cotton, winter vegetables, sugar cane, and marigolds. What you may not know is that when marigolds are fed to chickens, it makes the yolks of their eggs bright yellow.

South of Los Mochis is **Topolbampo**, where the ferry from Santa Rosalía on the Baja Peninsula docks. There are quarrelsome game fish in the ocean; goose and duck-hunting on the land. The rocky island of **Farallon** (sometimes called Animas Island) is a breeding ground for sea lions and attracts flocks of seabirds. The underwater marine life around the island is colorful.

From Los Mochis, you can take a side-trip to **El Fuerte**, through rich, irrigated farmland. You can fish for catfish and carp in the artificial lake in the back of **Hidalgo Dam**, one of the best bass fishing lakes in the country, or hunt for game-birds in the hills.

From Los Mochis to Mazatlán, the highway cuts through **Culiacán**, capital of the state of Sinaloa, known for its bumper crops of tomatoes and opium, both destined for the US. (The opium is legally exported; it is used for medicinal purposes.) In the complex landscape of the Sierra Madre Occidental, marijuana is grown amongst the hemp plantations. Despite support from the US in the fight against the activities of the drug barons, Culiacán remains the center of the Mexican drugs trade, and visitors must be warned against both using and dealing. The Mexican anti-drugs laws are strict.

The most expensive leg of the toll road is from Culiacán to Mazatlán. The toll road saves about 1½ hours on the drive and traffic on the old free route is congested, but the road surface is usually in good shape. About halfway between Culiacán and Mazatlán is **Cosalá**, another old mining town with hot springs just before the entrance to town. While there is some evidence of a desire for tourism here, for the most part the town is not particularly friendly to outsiders.

Mazatlán (the name means "Place of the Deer") is now the most important port on Mexico's west coast and is the home base for the country's largest shrimp fleet. Fishermen take something like 9,000 marlin and sailfish a year off Mazatlán. Because there is such a great demand for shrimp in the US, most native shrimp go north by cold trucks and are sold in the American market. The few that remain at home tend to fetch a premium price (so don't order shrimp if you are budgeting). Stick to fish, which is prepared in many mouth-watering ways. Restaurants on the beach or in beach hotels usually have the best-quality seafood, but it tends to be the most expensive: the farther you are from the beach, the lower the prices.

Mazatlán's central plaza is typically Mexican. It is not unusual here to see herbal medicine neatly laid out for sale. The cathedral, a mosaic of styles, is graced by a fine and unusual facade with intricate carving of volcanic rock. Most tourists spend their time in the so-called Golden Zone, the long stretch of hotels, restaurants and shops on the north side of the bay about 3 km (2 miles) from downtown. Here, close to the biggest hotels, is the well-stocked **Mazatlán Arts and Crafts Center**, where there are frequent performances by a group of Papantla Flyers – an Indian quartet who perform some colorful but rather tame acrobatics swinging from a pole. Shoppers should also try the **Indio Gift Shop**. On Calle Laguna, Marlin Tours organizes city and jungle tours, and there are also boat trips around the harbor and to Mazatlán's nearby islands.

For a panoramic view of town and

The Plaza, Alamos.

ocean, climb the hill to the lighthouse, **El Faro**. In pre-Spanish times, the Indians of the area produced fine polychrome pottery. During colonial times pirates were a menace. A lookout was built on what is now called **Cerro de Nevería** (Icebox Hill) to look out for sea marauders. The port became important after docks and harbor works were constructed, and roads and railways were opened to the rest of the country.

Winter is the most popular season here, though any time of the year is pleasant. Summer is the "rainy" season, but unless there is a hurricane nearby it will not greatly inconvenience you. Hurricane season is from June to October. Like any beach resort, it will be jam-packed between Christmas and New Year, at Easter (the week before) and around Mother's Day (three days before). During these times reservations are essential. Any other time, you will find hotels in all price ranges. The ocean-front boulevard, which has most of the hotels, changes names several times along its length, so don't become con-fused. Mazatlán has a small bullring and the aquarium, which has over 200 species of fish, is definitely worth seeing.

While shopping here, you will see items from all over the Republic. Of particular note is the beaded artwork and weavings of the Huichol Indians. Like most Indians, they are not always paid a fair price for what they produce. It's more hepful to them – and more interesting for you – to drive about 3 hours south to **Santiago Ixcuintla** (turn off Highway 15 at Kilometer 55, 5 km/ 3 miles south of Heroico Batalion de San Blas, at the sign to Los Corchos). Here there is a hospital and Huichol Center for Cultural Survival. You can watch Huichol families engaged in crafts, and any money you spend goes directly to the tribe. Much of it is used in the little hospital. Because of tuberculosis, malnutrition and other ailments Huichol children suffer a 50 percent infant mortality rate.

The next resort along the coastal highway south is San Blas. On the way, a slight detour just north of the San Blas

Mazatlán, the West Coast's biggest shipping port.

turnoff and then a short boat ride brings you to **Mexicaltitán**, an island which likes to be called the "Venice of Mexico," perhaps because during heavy rains the streets are flooded and you have to pole your way around in a canoe.

More and more of the streets have been filled in, so its waterlogged days are probably limited. Mexicaltitán's principal fame is derived from being the original home of the Aztecs and the place where they first had the vision of the eagle and the serpent, which they eventually found in what is now Mexico City. The seafood here is excellent, but don't look for luxury hotels; the town is a bit rundown.

A few kilometers south on Highway 15 is the **San Blas** turnoff. This coastal resort is famous for the ferocity of its gnats, known as *jejenes*, so be sure to stock up on insect repellent – *Deet*, citronella oil, or even Avon's Soft Skin Lotion. The insects are at their worst early in the morning, in the evenings and during the full moon.

A popular pastime is to take the jungle boat-ride up the San Cristóbal estuary to La Tovara springs. You ride through a green tunnel of vegetation; you can swim in crystal-clear springs, picnic, or eat at various restaurants.

Also in San Blas you can visit the old "fort," actually a counting house built in 1768. The customs house harks back to the port's importance in colonial times. Once a ship-building center it was the point of departure for exploring the Pacific Northwest. Father Junipero Serra's ship *La Concepción* was built here and the Good Father made missionary trips in it to California. Ships were built here for the Philippines' trade and at one time warships hid out in Matanchén bay, on the lookout for pirates.

To continue south from San Blas you have to backtrack and go past **Tepic**, where there's a pleasant Zócalo, flanked by a cathedral with Gothic towers. While you are here you can also visit the fine regional museum, which houses a collection of pre-Columbian ceramics and buy Huichol handicrafts far cheaper than in the resort boutiques.

The "Venice" of Mexico, Mexicaltitán.

BAJA CALIFORNIA

For many Americans, Baja is the best fish story ever written. Author Zane Grey fished the Gulf around the turn of the century and ever since both writing and non-writing fishermen have found it a place where fish stories come true. There are at least 650 species of fish in the waters off Baja and at least as many species of fishermen, who trek here from all over the world.

Highway 1, the 1,690-km (1,050-mile) road that traverses the peninsula from Tijuana to Los Cabos, didn't even exist until 20 years ago and although there are half a dozen much shorter subsidiary routes, hundreds of miles of Baja's coastline and almost the entire interior can be comfortably reached only with four wheeled drive vehicles. While some people deplore this inaccessibility, the majority of Baja fans rejoice in their knowledge of a land that – though neighbor to California with its teeming millions – remains largely unexplored.

The peninsula was opened, Christianized and depopulated by the Spaniards. An early Jesuit missionary wrote of idle Indians, each supported by a number of complacent wives. However, the good life for them didn't last long. The Church gathered them in. Small pox and syphilis wiped them out. Of the 40,000 indigenous inhabitants of Baja, there are less than 500 left. Those few survivors live in the north.

In the south all that is left of the Indians' ancestors are some cave paintings to show they existed. There are some 400 known cave sites, which are 500 to 1,000 years old. Erle Stanley Gardner, prolific author of detective books, did some investigative work himself and discovered some of the caves.

Cortés, hearing that some of the Aztec gold came from the north, sent out ships to explore. It was a catastrophic mission during which 22 crew members were slain by Indians on landing at what is now La Paz. The survivors returned with a lot of harrowing tales, including one about maidens clad only in strands

of pearls, a tale that must have titillated Cortés who visited La Paz himself and set up a short-lived colony there. For years, the Spaniards forgot about Baja until the pirates operating out of its sheltered bays intercepted too many treasure-laden Spanish galleons.

The saving of souls: In the 17th century the Order of Jesuits persuaded the Spanish Crown to let them tame this barren land which, even if it had no wealth, at least abounded in Indian souls to be saved. Father Eusebio Kino was the first of these missionaries, soon to be followed by Father Salvatierra, who founded the first mission at Loreto in 1697. For 70 years, the Jesuits built churches and taught (and sometimes fought) the Indians. When the Jesuits were expelled from Mexico in 1767, the Franciscans were given the monopoly on soul-saving. Six years later the Dominicans took over. Some 30 missions in all were founded in Baja, but they were abandoned by the 1850s. There simply weren't enough Indians left to make it worthwhile. According to one

Preceding pages: the Bahía de Los Angeles. Left, paper flower vendor, Tijuana. Right, promoting Tecate.

report, there were 50,000 Indians in Baja in the 17th century, of whom only 3,700 remained by 1842.

During the 1846–48 Mexican War, the US Navy invaded the main ports of Baja, but although this and later attempts – William Walker, who sacked La Paz in 1853, wanted to incorporate Baja into the Union as a slave state – aimed at US domination, this was not to be. As late as 1911, when some Mexican revolutionaries, teaming up with an incongruous group of American anarchists and land developers, tried to take over Baja, the Mexican government sent in troops to quell their ambitions.

Yankees quickly realized the potential of the irrigated regions of northern Baja, however, in particular the Colorado River Land Company which farmed near Mexicali. In 1946 the Mexican government bought the land company out. Baja's population and its economy are both concentrated in the north. Bumper crops are produced in the irrigated lands around Mexicali: cotton, alfalfa, wheat, tomatoes, grapes. Workers in northern Baja get the highest minimum wage in Mexico.

There are three major crossings into Baja at the California border – Tijuana, Tecate and Mexicali – all connected by Highway 2. Most of those crossings at Mexicali are heading 193 km (120 miles) down Highway 5 for the seaside town of San Felipe on the Gulf coast; Tecate (site of a famous brewery) marks the start of Highway 3, which runs 106 km (66 miles) across the mountains to Ensenada; **Tijuana**, once a rip-roaring, anything-goes border town, and now one of Mexico's busiest and most prosperous cities, claims to be the most-visited border city in the world, with almost 50 million tourists to date.

A shopper's paradise: Because Tijuana is a duty-free zone, imported goods can be surprisingly cheap and there are bargains to be found in Russian caviar, Spanish leather, French perfume, Italian and even Cuban cigars. The city's main drag, **Avenida Revolución**, is lined with popular bars, nightclubs, craft stores and clothing and jewelry shops mixed

Mercado Artesianas, Tijuana.

among the sarapes (blankets) and sandals, but shoppers will find even more variety in the **Plaza Rio Tijuana** shopping mall (open until 9pm) near the river, whose 100 stores make it the largest shopping center in northwestern Mexico. For a massive selection of footwear, head for the **Plaza del Zapato** (within the Plaza Fiesta), which has no less than 20 shoe shops.

Tijuana has a large number of excellent, reasonably priced restaurants. Good Mexican cuisine is served at the **Hacienda el Abajeño**, **Uruapan**, **La Fonda Roberto** and the **Hacienda las Torres** in the Hotel Fiesta Americana. A casual meal can be had in Tia Juana **Tilly's**, while **Reno's**, which serves excellent fish dishes, is chic. Further recommendations for lovers of seafood are Pedrin's and La Costa.

The distinctive red Tijuana Trolley runs continuously between the city's main sightseeing attractions between 10am and 5pm every day, but it's a pleasant stroll back northwards along Via Poniente adjoining the river. It will bring you to an older, funkier shopping center, **Puebla Amigo**, which comes alive at night when crowds arrive to dine at the yellow and green **Señor Frog's** and numerous other restaurants. There's also a disco, a theater/concert hall and an ingenious mural.

Things to see: Topped with a glass pinnate visible from the pedestrian bridge, is **Mexitlan** (10 am–6 pm daily, closed Monday), an intriguing $23 million theme park containing enormous relief maps of all Mexico with 150 of its major landmarks reproduced to scale.

Behind the Plaza Revolución is the **Wax Museum**, whose eclectic subjects range from Madonna, Gandhi and the Pope, to Mexican Revolutionary heroes and a grey-haired lady known as Tia Juana ("Aunt Jane"), the legendary *cantina* owner around whom the city was founded.

Adjoining a building that resembles a giant golfball – housing the concert hall and the 26-meter (85-ft) high **Omnitheater** (a film about Mexico's history and culture is shown at 2pm daily) – is

Surfboards to rent or buy.

the ultra-modern **Tijuana Cultural Center**, with its comprehensive survey of Mexican history. The famous old **Agua Caliente Racetrack**, with its marble floors, ornate decoration, mirrored elevators and lobby filled with sculptured *charros* (cowboys), caged birds and an incongruous pair of playful anteaters, hosts greyhound racing every night except Tuesday plus Monday and Wednesday afternoons. There are nightly contests at the **Jai Alai Fronton** (Tuesday–Thursday, at 7:30pm).

The highway west of Tijuana leads to the **Monumental Bullring**, 10-km (6-miles) away beside the sea. Bullfights take place on various Sundays during the season, which runs from May–September. The season is split between the oceanside bullring and the older one on the Boulevard Agua Caliente downtown. Tickets are on sale at the bullrings but can also be obtained through tourist agencies. There are inexpensive motels along the seashore road and stalls selling coconut drinks and seafood.

The expensive *Cuota* toll road to Ensenada includes stretches of fine ocean scenery. The *libre* (free) road, which parallels the *cuota* as far as Rosarito (20 km/13 miles from Tijuana), then dips inland.

Heading south: About 27 km (17 miles) south of the border is **Rosarito**, an over-commercialized beach town which gained celebrity after 1927, when the newly-opened Rosarito Beach Hotel began to attract the movie crowd as well as other celebrities and even heads of state. The hotel features glorious indoor murals by Matias Santoyo and a large swimming pool and bar area above the gray, sandy beach. Lobster is a favorite in the town's numerous restaurants and there is even a so-called "Lobster Village" – **Puerto Nuevo**, 10 km (6 miles) to the south, where this dish is widely available and uniformly overpriced.

About 31 km (23 miles) south of the border, a free road curves inland off the toll road to head up through the tiny village of **La Misíon**, where there are the fenced-off crumbling ruins of the San Miguel mission. A cross marks the

San Francisco mission, Central Baja.

old boundary between the Dominican missions of Baja and the Franciscan missions in Upper California.

As you enter the big city of **Ensenada** (population 230,000) almost 113 km (70 miles) south of the border, turn right off Highway 1 and drive up Avenida Aleman into the Chapultepec Hills, a high-rent district which offers a magnificent view of the city set around Todos Santos Bay. A busy port, Ensenada is a regular stop for cruise ships and the furthest south that the vast majority of tourists penetrate. It stages bike rides, regattas and, in November, a noted off-road race. Popular with fishermen, it tags itself "the yellowtail capital of the world," with surf fishing along the rocky shoreline and organized trips from the sport-fishing piers off Boulevard Lazaro Cardenas. Charter boats are reasonably priced and first-rate. They will take you out for half a day, a whole day, or for a week-long trip to the tip of Baja Peninsula and around into the Sea of Cortés for some of the finest fishing to be had anywhere in the world. In winter whale-

Whale watching.

watching trips are also popular. Robert Louis Stevenson wrote part of *Treasure Island* while he was relaxing in the port of Ensenada.

The fish market, open until noon, is just to the right after the immigration office as you enter town. Men wearing garlands of garlic bulbs circulate between cars at stop lights. There are winery tours every day except Monday at the **Bodegas de Santo Tomas** (Miramar and 6th streets) and occasional bullfights during the summer months.

The main tourist shopping zone is along **Avenida Lopez Mateos**, a few blocks from the bay, but prices are lower in the "non-tourist" part of town around Avenida Ruiz and 11th Street, where every second store or bar seems to bear the name Hussong ("the bar that built a city"). The venerable original *cantina*, with its sawdust floor and old pictures, is a funky drinking place, long popular with tourists from all over the world who have been pinning samples of their currency to the walls for a century. Among the other restaurants around

here, the most pleasant is the upstairs terrace in – where else? – Hussong Plaza. On Lopez Mateos between Ruiz and Gastelum, Las Briusas and Los Amigas restaurants share an open patio.

When it's time for dinner, you're in luck. Sample the first-rate abalone at La Cueva de los Tigres restaurant or the fabulous Mexican fare at the Hotel Mision Santa Isabel's La Ermita restaurant. And El Rey Sol, a French/Mexican restaurant, is widely considered to be the best in Baja.

South of town take the turnoff to La Bufadora, where incoming waves are forced into narrow clefts and up the hillside, amusingly spraying spectators. Incoming tides are best, of course, sometimes spouting some 18 meters (60 ft) into the air. (Consult the *Baja Sun* for the tide timetable.)

South of Colonet at **San Telmo de Abajo** a reasonably good road (in the dry season) heads east to the sprawling **Meling Ranch**, at which you can stay in comfortable quarters, swim in the pool and ride horses into the San Pedro Martir Mountains, a national park where an observatory has been built near the top of the highest peak, **Picacho del Diablo** (3,094 meters/10,154 ft). It was sited here because Baja – along with the west coasts of Africa and Chile – has some of the clearest skies in the world.

Productive agricultural land surrounds **San Quintin**, as might be guessed from the numerous men and boys seen on horseback. To reach the best place for an overnight stop, turn right off the highway just south of the military camp at Lazaro Cardenas and drive 5 km (3 miles) along the unpaved road to the **Old Mill Motel**, where only the antics of early-rising fisherfolk disturb the tranquility. Hundreds of swaggering seagulls gather to watch the catch being eviscerated at sunset.

Both the Old Mill and the Old Pier Hotel further down the lagoon are reminders that this area was once colonized by an English land company, which tried unsuccessfully to harvest crops and grind corn but went bankrupt for lack of rain. The names of these

Oranges in San Quintin.

almost forgotten pioneers are recorded on a group of lonely graves by the shore.

To reach the outer bay (good for clam digging) take the road west from Lazaro Cardenas. San Quintin itself is strung out along both sides of the highway for about 2 km. Try the restaurant Costa Azul near the Pemex station for seafood and get questions answered at the Motel Chavez at the south end of town.

Camping on Bahia de San Quintin's wild peninsula, fishing and digging for "chocolate-tipped" clams is a favorite pastime of the cognoscenti.

South of San Quintin you will begin to see the spidery *cirio* trees (*Idria columnaris*) which bear tiny yellow flowers and are sometimes referred to as boojum trees after the mythical species described by Lewis Carroll in *The Hunting of the Snark.*

Near the south end of the boojum area, a paved side road leads to **Bahía de Los Angeles** on the Gulf's calm waters, protected by the aptly-named **Isla del Angel de la Guardia** (Guardian Angel Island). The facilities are few (small motel, trailer park and small store, which has gas most of the time). On the other hand, the fishing and shelling are great and the view is splendid. A tiny island, **Isla la Raza**, is a wildlife refuge.

Gigantic boulders, many of them irresistible to graffiti pests, carpet the landscape and at **Catavina** – an unexpected oasis with a Pemex station – they serve as the rear walls of several makeshift homes. Heading southeast, the road climbs over the 820-meter (2,690-ft) summit of Sierra Columbia, then drops into the arid bed of **Laguna Chapala**. Ahead are the windswept wastes of the **Vizcaíno Desert** where, surprisingly, as many as 80 species of plants turn out to be edible despite the fact that it's lucky to get 25 cm (10 inches) of rain a year – in years when it rains at all. It is only 20 years since **Highway 1**, running all the way from north to southern Baja, was completed and at San Ignacio the two crews working on the road met. A small marker celebrates the meeting.

Back on the main road, going south, you reach the **28th Parallel**, where a

Saltworks, Guerrero Negro.

looming metal sculpture marks the boundary between Baja California Norte and Baja California Sur. Just south of this border, **Guerrero Negro** offers hotels, restaurants, stores and gas. Only in the whaling season is it of much interest to tourists although acres of shallow saltwater ponds produce 5 million tons of salt a month for export each year, one-third of the world's supply.

The town is better known however for **Scammon's Lagoon**, at the end of a dirt road several kilometers south of town past the salt-evaporating ponds. For centuries whales have come here from the chilly Bering Sea to breed in the warm, shallow bay. About 1,800 gray whales now gather off the Baja coast, about the same number as at their peak in 1850, shortly before the infamous Captain Charles Scammon began a slaughter emulated by a succession of other black-hearted whalers. Expensive whale-watching tours take place here between early January and mid-March, but you can also watch (for free) from the shore.

From Guerrero Negro, the highway cuts across the peninsula to the Gulf. A mandatory stop should be made at tiny **San Ignacio**, whose square lined with shady laurel trees is dominated by **San Ignacio mission**, erected in 1786 by Dominican Padre Gomez out of lava rock with 1.2-meter (4-ft) thick walls and arched ceiling, replacing an earlier (1728) Jesuit mission. The church, with its perfect symmetry and baroque facade, is a charming example of what is left of colonial architecture in Baja. An oasis of almost 100,000 date palms, sustained by an underground spring which surfaces here, has become the basis of the town's economy. On the square are two mini-markets, one also selling clothing, but not much else.

Baja never had enough precious metal to make mining worthwhile but there was a little silver mining in colonial times and a small-scale gold rush in the late 19th-century. In 1887 the French opened a copper mine, called El Boleo, in **Santa Rosalía**. In 1953 it was taken over by the Mexican government. Don't miss Santa Rosalía's **Eiffel**

Fruits of the sea.

church, built by the same French engineer responsible for the famous tower which bears his name. A prefabricated metal structure, it won second prize at the 1889 Uni-versal Exposition in Paris and was then packed in crates, in preparation for shipment to Africa. Declined by its original buyer, it was eventually acquired by the El Boleo company and put together here. From Santa Rosalía, an overnight ferry goes to **Guaymas** on the Sonora coast.

The road south from Rosalía follows the dry Gulf coast to **Mulegé**, from which, in 1847, threatening US warships were frightened away by a subterfuge. In July and August the town is stifling hot, but usually the palm trees and plantings along the Santa Rosalía river make Mulegé a pleasant oasis. There's a wonderfully situated 1766 mission church on the outskirts of town, good fishing and comfortable hotels, notably the Hotel Serenidad owned by Don Johnson, a US consular official.

South of Mulegé the highway skirts the shore, offering tantalizing glimpses of delightful coves and bays virtually inaccessible without a car. Framed to the east by a northward-pointing peninsula, the 40-km (25-mile) long **Bahía Concepción** is famous for its enticing camping beaches, all with at least a few facilities such as toilets, trash cans and sheltering *palapas*. Most of the rocks between beaches are occupied by morose pelicans gazing silently at the sea. The pelican rookeries in the rocky coves of the gulf have fared better than their cousins on the Pacific Coast, where survival is apparently more hazardous, but many birds are regular commuters over the intervening mountains. Needless to say, fishermen at sea are avid followers of the hovering pelican.

Loreto, about 136 km (85 mile) south, was the site of the first mission and for 130 years the capital of Baja. After it was leveled by a storm in 1828 the capital was moved to the pearling center at La Paz. The twin towers on the restored mission were replaced with money that its padre won in the national lottery. The town's main street is named

The Bahía Concepción.

after the multilingual, multi-talented Jesuit Padre Juan Maria Salvatierra who ran the mission here for 20 years. The government-planned tourist complex at **Nopolo,** 25 km (15 miles) south of Loreto, expects to attract 8,000 boats to its marina by the end of the decade.

Thirty-seven kilometers (23 miles) southwest, along a steep, mountain road which takes almost two hours by taxi (an expensive ride) is the beautifully preserved **San Xavier mission,** originally built in 1699 by Salvatierra's assistant, Padre Francisco Piccolo.

The scenery south of Loreto is spectacular; lovely beaches and reddish-brown slopes of the Sierra de la Giganta sometimes distract attention from dangerous curves and steep switchbacks on the coastal highway. Then comes a wide valley and a major agricultural region.

At Ciudad Constitución, Highway 22 heads 57 km (36 miles) west to the port of **San Carlos,** a small town overlooking mango-fringed Bahía Magdalena, which shelters a commercial fishing fleet (and sometimes, whales).

Ciudad Constitución is a fast-growing, busy agricultural center (population 45,000) – with some of the ambience of the old American West. It produces lots of cotton, wheat, and vegetables. Almost all of its water supply comes from wells. It is not a tourist town although it does have hotels, trailer parks, a supermarket and an interesting public market. The best place to find overnight accommodation is the Hotel Maribel (on the highway), with its restaurant Sancho Panza.

Just south of town is an unpaved road leading 50 km (31 miles) southeast to an oasis in the desert housing the **San Luis Gonzaga mission,** recently repaired by the National Institute of Anthropology and History. The mission, built of bright rose-colored stone, stands beside a lagoon bordered with date palms.

Early this century there were steamboat connections from **La Paz** to other Baja ports; now there are daily ferries to Mazatlán and Topolobampo on the Sonora coast. It's a pleasant city with a population of about 180,000, its streets shaded by coconut palms and laurel trees. In the spring blossoming jacaranda, acacia and flame trees add to the splendor. Apart from its celebrated sports fishing, it is also famous for its sunsets (best viewed from the terrace café of the popular Hotel Perla). The tourist office, also on the Malecon, is a block away.

Take a look at the old paintings and photographs in the **Biblioteca** on the Zócalo and also the **Museum of Anthropology,** Altamirano and 5 de Mayo.

Northwards out of La Paz, the road goes up the Magote peninsula, past the ferry terminal at Pichilingue (bus every hour) to lovely bays and beaches at **Balandra** and **Tecolote** at the end of the peninsula. Eight kilometers (5 miles) offshore in the gulf is the 22-km (14-mile) long island of **Espiritu Santo,** with its 600-meter (2,000-ft) high mesa, once known as the "isla de perlas" after Cortés harvested black pearls here in the 16th century. The French tried unsuccessfully to revive this industry in the 19th century, but it is now uninhabited. Although pearls may now be in **At the Museum of Anthropology, La Paz.**

short supply in the Bahia de la Paz, shark and shrimp fishing are popular.

The highway continues on down to the tip of Baja at **Cabo San Lucas**, a former supply station for the Spanish treasure galleons from Manila and now a bustling tourist center. There are dozens of luxury hotels, some with private beaches and their own landing strips for small aircraft.

Baja, which broke off from mainland Mexico millions of years ago, is twice as long, but much skinnier than Florida, and its tip, now Cabo San Lucas, was located between Mazatlán and Puerto Vallarta. A great crack in the San Andreas fault created the Gulf of California and the Pacific Ocean rushed in. The water is 3,290 meters (1,800 fathoms) deep off La Paz.

The Gulf narrows as it moves north; the tides are powerful and tricky, and the wind is strong. This means it's hard to handle a small boat and it can be very dangerous. If you are not an experienced boatman, you should rent a boat with an experienced local crew. The marina is the place for this and also to take glass-bottomed boat trips to **Los Arcos**, the famous stone arch at the southernmost point.

Much less glitzy is the typically tranquil town of **San José del Cabo**, at the eastern end of the "corridor" between the two towns. The 32-km (20-mile) strip of highway is filling up with resorts, golf courses and all the impedimenta of a developing tourist region, but San José itself remains unspoiled. Rent a bicycle or car, or walk to **La Playita** beach where you can dine on freshly caught seafood, go fishing in a *panga* or just admire the estuary, home to thousands of birds.

From the town of Cabo San Lucas you can make your way back to La Paz along the west coast on a good but partially unpaved road which follows the Pacific and deserted beaches to **Todos Santos**, cutting back across the peninsula. Or, from a new dock at Cabo San Lucas, you can ferry yourself, family, car, trailer and Baja memories to Puerto Vallarta on the mainland.

Cacti along the Santa Gertrudis road.

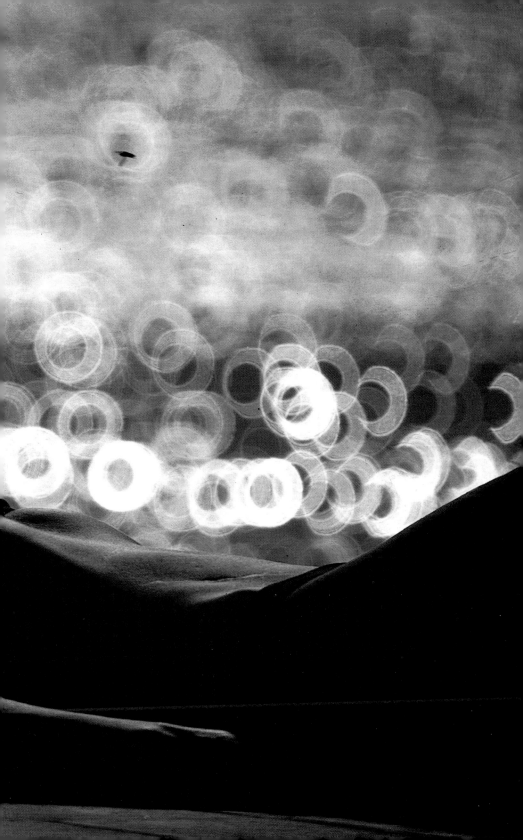

THE GLAMOR COAST

When a Basque sailor, Muguel Lopes de Legazpi, retook the Philippines in the name of Spain in 1564 and founded Manila, the treasure-filled galleons needed a way-station on their route to and from Europe. So for the next 250 years Acapulco became the port from which they sailed. Something like 200 million *pesos* worth of silver was shipped out of Acapulco to exchange for the silk, porcelain, spices and ivory of the Orient. The goods were transferred by mule train to the Gulf coast port of Veracruz, from where they were shipped to Spain.

Naturally, the rich shipments attracted pirates, freebooters and the enemies of Spain. British men-of-war fell upon Spanish shipping with great regularity, a special target being the Manila galleon on its way to Acapulco. Sir Francis Drake himself captured the cargo-filled *Nuestra Señora de la Concepción* as it sailed out of Acapulco. The English geographer, Richard Hakluyt, wrote: "We found a ship with a cargo of linen and plates of fine white earth (bone china) and a great quantity of silks, all of which we took [along with] a gold falcon and a great emerald."

In colonial times Acapulco was a sleepy town that came alive only when a Manila galleon approached. When the galleon stopped briefly at La Navidad, on the Jalisco coast, on its way south, a messenger would ride hell-for-leather to Mexico City with the news, which was greeted in the capital with church bells and a special Mass. The merchants would then assemble mule trains and set out for Acapulco to be there when the treasure ship tied up to an old ceiba tree.

Bags of gold and silver were set out on the beach and the merchants implored officials to finish their work quickly. Their reward came when the ship's cargo was unloaded: fine porcelain from China and Japan, made-to-order drapes and hangings for churches, furniture, fine silks and metalwork.

Developing coastline: Acapulco, with its dramatic mountains sweeping down to the Pacific, was the first to achieve international fame as a mecca for the "beautiful people." Then, many years later, when the government of Mexico realized the value of tourism as a major industry, Ixtapa was developed about 257 km (160 miles) northwest. But gradually this whole glamorous coast achieved fame.

Puerto Vallarta, for example, owes its name to Hollywood. It leaped to fame with the 1964 filming of *Night of the Iguana* on **Mismaloya beach** just outside town. Many other forgettable movies have been filmed here since, including Arnold Schwarzenegger's 1987 *Predator*. The jungle, which can be explored on horseback, nourished the steamy romance of Richard Burton and Elizabeth Taylor who bought a home in what is now called "Gringo Gulch."

Vallarta lines the shore of spacious **Bahía de Banderas**, sometimes known as Humpback Bay because of the migrating whales that gather here each spring. There are different Vallartas: the relatively unspoiled old town astride

Preceding pages: soaking up the sun on the Pacific Coast. **Left**, diving off La Quebrada. **Right**, local glamor.

the **Cuale river** has tiled roofs, donkey traffic, and the church of Guadalupe, topped by an imposing crown – a replica of that worn by the short-lived Empress Carlotta. Charming bridges lead to the art galleries, restaurants and museum on an island in the river.

Zona Hotelera to the north, where luxury hotels line the beach, terminates at **Marina Vallarta**, a 178-hectare (440-acre) upscale resort area with even more luxurious hotels, condos and a large golf course. Both sides of town offer parasailing, an easy and spectacular parachute ride behind a speedboat.

Among the excursions you can take by boat or catamaran from Los Muertos Pier are trips to the tiny communities of **Las Animas** with its inexpensive hotels, to idyllic **Yelapa**, and its northern neighbor **Quimixto**, where movie director John Huston built a house, and which is popular with divers. At Yelapa you can rent a *palapa*, or stay in a small hotel. You can go horseback riding, or ride a *burro* up a mountain to a waterfall or fish for marlin, dorado and tuna.

Those seeking a peaceful vacation off the beaten track might enjoy a visit to **Mar de Jade**, at the charming fishing village of Chacalla between the jungle and sea two hours' drive north of Puerto Vallarta. Here Dr Laura del Valle runs a community where you can relax, explore the jungle, take Spanish lessons, and volunteer some of your time to help in the medical clinic or other community-based projects.

From Puerto Vallarta the road runs, mainly inland, 272 km (170 miles) to the next resort, Barra de Navidad. Near Vallarta, the road snakes in and out of a jungle-covered canyon, lined with waterfalls (above one waterfall is the restaurant **Chico's Paradise**). The highway goes past fishing villages which will probably awaken only when someone decides to put up yet another hotel. The final 96 km (60 miles), known as Costalegre, has been designated an "Ecological Tourism Corridor" and is filled with delightful bays that have changed little, if at all, since the Spanish galleons sailed these waters 400 years ago.

Taking the back roads above Puerto Vallarta.

About 140 km (87 miles) from Vallarta you pass **Playa Blanca**, a Club Med facility. **Pueblo Nuevo**, farther along, is a budding American-style resort community. Then comes **Barra de Navidad**, a sleepy beach aimed mainly at vacationers from Guadalajara. Barra de Navidad was once a piece of history. In 1564, Miguel López Lagazpi sailed off from here to conquer the Philippines. In April or May, the Green Roller comes to call. He is not a dice-player, but a monster of a wave, almost tidal-wave-size (10 meters/33 ft in height), which periodically comes rumbling in at **Cuyutlán**.

Manzanillo, in Colima state and but a hop away, is a busy railhead and port, with traffic-choked, narrow streets. There are a few good hotels, in and out of town, and for the affluent there is the top-of-the-line **Las Hadas** ("The Fairies") complex. Built by the Patiño Bolivian tin-magnate family, Las Hadas is a development mixing pseudo-Moorish, Mediterranean and Disney. Now owned by Monterrey's Alfa Group, the rococo complex offers classy comfort.

Manzanillo, which used to be Guadalajara's port to the Orient, is still a thriving harbor town, and claims to be "the sailfish capital of the world." Not far inland is the capital city of **Colima**, a short ride through the lemon groves. Colima is dominated by the **Nevado de Colima**, an often snowcapped and still rumbly volcano. At the **Museum of Western Mexican Cultures** there are exhibits covering the anthropological history of the area and exquisite pre-Columbian pottery. Another museum here houses 350 antique cars.

Twin resorts: Flying into the airport destination of Ixtapa/Zihuatanejo (pronounced *ees-tapa* and *see-wa-tan-ay-ho*) gives no clue to the wildly different characters of these towns, once miles apart, but whose boundaries have now almost blended. **Ixtapa**, the newer of the two resorts, is (like Cancún and Huatulco) the result of Mexican government-planned tourism. It came into existence about 20 years ago, but now attracts almost 400,000 visitors each year, three-quarters of whom are Mexi-

A rococo beetle.

can. The community (it can hardly be called a town) is strung out along a stretch of hilly terrain where looms the handsome **Westin Hotel**, an Aztec-inspired construction. Beyond the road finally settles down to the flat stretch that accommodates a dozen or so high-rise hotels located along or close to a dramatic beach. These hotels include many of Mexico's finest – like the **Krystal**, part of a small family-owned chain. In keeping with its sister hotels, the Krystal has an outstanding restaurant, Bogart's (designed in stunning Casablanca-style and with pictures of its namesake sprinkled liberally about the bar), and a lively disco (Christine's).

Across a beautifully manicured roadway that runs past the hotels is a cleverly constructed mall that has the feel of a village rather than a strip shopping center. There are byways with restaurants and juice shops interspersed with stores offering necessities in addition to fripperies. Trendy boutiques like Ralph Lauren/Polo, Aca Joe and Calvin Klein are represented, too, and an outstanding silver shop (Plateria Roberto's) carries a stunning selection of contemporary jewelry along with traditional designs. Shopping is a major activity in these twin resorts, with more than 1,000 stores including three handicraft markets.

In addition to its hotel zone and an island which is a wildlife refuge, Ixtapa has beautiful condominiums and two golf courses (one designed by Robert Trent Jones) and a sheltered marina. **Beccofino**, a dead ringer for any *ristorante* in Portofino (down to waiters dressed in striped jerseys) is just across from the marina and, along with authentic Italian fare – emphasizing local seafood – provides a romantic spot to enjoy a drink while watching the sunset, as well as a full meal. The "smart set" doesn't start to arrive until 9:30pm.

Less touristy: On the other hand **Zihuatanejo** – or Ziwa as it's known to anyone who has been there more than a few hours – is a real town with real people engaged in real activities, rather than merely catering to tourists. Getting around in either place or from one to the other is fairly easy. The hotels know what the prices for cabs should be, and the drivers rarely take advantage of the tourists. Occasionally, particularly late at night or if it is raining really hard, the prices escalate, but usually a compromise can be negotiated.

Fishing is important in Zihuatanejo, providing food for the locals and visitors, in contrast to the sport fishing that occurs in the waters off Ixtapa. The small boats used by the fisherman leave from the beach in the center of town. Sometimes you can strike a deal with one of the fishermen and tag along for the ride. If you have the time and can stand to be in the sun for several hours, this trip is obviously a lot more fun than just hiring a boat by the hour to tool around the bay. Sometimes lunch comes with the package.

Ziwa is full of little restaurants of all kinds. **La Bocana**, just across from the Main Beach, has been around for years and is still a favorite with the locals for its *sopa de mariscos* and grilled fish. Then, at Ejido 24, **El Meson del Cabrito** is a typical local restaurant (with table- **Keeping a beady eye.**

282

cloths in the evening) that serves roasted kid goat. And, in an unprepossessing small eatery called **La Marina**, on Calle 5 de Mayo, across from the little handicraft market, Paul, the Swiss owner-chef, makes culinary magic in a tiny open kitchen, producing dishes such as herb-scented chanterelles and sautéed quail.

Facing the sea, in the heart of "downtown," on Paseo del Pescador y Plaza Olof Palme, is the small **Museo Arqueologico de la Costa Grande**, whose contents offer an insight into the very early lifestyle of the people of the area, including evidence of a fertility cult. Most of the hotels in Ziwa qualify as "budget," with two notable exceptions: **La Casa Que Canta**, a stunning building that cascades down the hill overlooking La Ropa beach; and, just a little way beyond, the older, but beautifully maintained and exquisitely landscaped **Villa del Sol**. Among the interesting low-cost hotels are **Villas Miramar**, a small and charming all-suite hotel, with garden or ocean views; **Bungalows Pacificos**,

Sand-carrying mules.

which are not actually separate bungalows, but tiny apartments in the large hillside home of Anita Hahnew Chimalpopoca, who seems to knows just about everything about Ziwa and where to find it. (Indeed, many of the artifacts at the Archaeological Museum came from her personal collection.)

For a change of pace, outside Zihuatenejo and Ixtapa, but still in the same vicinity, there's the inexpensive and fairly primitive **Casa de La Tortuga**. This secluded hideaway is in the tiny village of Troncones (co-owner Dewey McMillan provides transportation from "his beach" and "his jungle" to and from either Ziwa or Ixtapa).

Acapulco is changing rapidly and expanding south. It's going that way primarily to take advantage of the new 263-km (164-mile) toll road from Cuernavaca that discharges its passengers just a few miles south of the city, in an area not too far from the airport where most visitors land before flocking into the city and to the beaches. The initial high tolls on the highway may

eventually be reduced if the 15-year concession granted to its operators can be extended. Nowadays the custom of spending the hours before noon on Acapulco's "morning beach" (to escape the fiercest rays of the sun) and then going to the "afternoon beach" is pretty much obsolete. People are now more used to the effects of tropical sun and use better sunscreens, so they sunbathe and swim wherever they stay, regardless of location and time of day.

Nevertheless, traditional Acapulco, as the older part of the town is known, is still vital, and attracts tourists to sites like **La Quebrada**, where several times a day and into the evening young men execute dazzling dives from dramatic cliffs, timing their dives to the waves so that they don't get dashed on the jagged rocks below.

Then, also in the old town, there's the area's most historic landmark, **Fort San Diego**, built in 1616 to protect Acapulco from pirates. The fort contains a small but interesting museum and it is occasionally used for open-air receptions.

The fort was leveled by an earthquake in 1776, but was rebuilt and stands today as a historical monument to Acapulco's colorful past. The Mexican War of Independence brought an end to the galleon trade. Father José Maria Morelos, the priest-warrior, captured Fort San Diego from its Spanish defenders. Thereafter the town was forgotten for a long time until a few wealthy Mexicans and some Americans discovered it as a resort in the 1930s. Some of the older hotels built at about this time are still in operation and the hotels clustered around Caleta beach and the Mirador hotel, overlooking the cliffs of La Quebrada, are reliable, although not as luxurious as the newer "superstar" hotels.

The **Zócalo**, in the heart of town, is a reminder that this is Mexico and not just a resortland. There are parks, benches and shade, a cathedral built in the 1930s with a mosque-type dome, open-air cafés, inexpensive restaurants and plenty of shops. Across the Costera are the docks where the deep-sea fishing vessels moor. While new hotels and restau- **Acapulco Bay**.

284

rants may be opening to the south, traditional Acapulco still boasts the largest artisan market, where hard bargaining is not only expected, but required.

There are also small, authentic eateries like **Mi Amigo Miguel** and **Pipo's** that cater mostly to locals and Mexican tourists, but nevertheless welcome others. They serve up wonderful fish every day of the week. Thursday is *pozole* day in certain restaurants throughout this state of Guerrero. Every week certain restaurants cook the regional specialty, a thick hominy soup that comes in red, green and more or less clear versions, depending on the seasonings used. Signs outside restaurants may advertise *pozole* and newspapers will also tell you which places feature it.

Leaving the warren of streets in traditional Acapulco, and heading south along the water, there's the 11-km (7-mile) **Costera Miguel Aleman**, a broad boulevard that stretches along Acapulco Bay and the area most people remember best about Acapulco. The Costera is lined with high-rise hotels and restaurants and little thatched-roof bars advertising "3 x 1" (three drinks for the price of one) at *feliz hora* (happy hour). Most of the hotels also feature *feliz hora*, but the drinks are usually two for the price of one, and may or may not have the open-air view of the beach and the Pacific. These lively bars are situated along "the strip" between the reliable **Hotel Continental** and the better than reliable **Condessa Fiesta Americana**.

Shops and shopping malls abound, mostly across the street from the beach, but there are also some attached to hotels – in fact wherever there's enough space to accommodate them. There are also art galleries galore, as well as restaurants of every nationality in every price range. Health food eateries back up to sophisticated purveyors of Continental cuisine, such as **El Real** (which is both an art gallery and a restaurant), and staples like **Carlos 'n' Charlie's**.

After night falls, Acapulco takes on an entirely different cast and people head for discos such as **Extravaganza** and **Fantasy** (with startling light shows

inside and magnificent views of Acapulco Bay from their ceiling-to-floor windows), to the newer disco known as **Palladium**, or to **Baby 'O'**, a favorite among the younger set. A brand-new club, **Salon Q**, opens at midnight and keeps at it until dawn. For more sedate types there are "Mexican Fiesta" nights at the Convention Center and in some of the hotels. These fiestas feature dancing from various parts of the country, a buffet of toned-down Mexican food and (usually) *margaritas* or tequila sunrises. Several nights a week the Convention Center features performances by the Voladores, the astounding Flying Indians from Papantla.

The **Cici Recreation Center** on the Costera is great fun for kids, offering a wave-pool with slides, a large aquarium and a dolphin show. It has room for 5,000 visitors. A further attraction is the Papagayo Park in the center, with its Manila galleon and cable car.

Acapulco offers a lot of sunshine. Even in the rainy season, from June to October, it's sunny most mornings, with the showers generally occurring only in the afternoon. Hotel prices vary with the season. Mid-December through Easter is the "in" time: the best weather, the highest prices. It's necessary to make reservations well ahead of time, particularly at Christmas and Easter, when affluent Mexicans stream in. The jet-set favors February, while smart people come in November and early December, when the weather is ideal but the prices haven't yet popped.

For people who want to go big-game fishing, there are sailfish, marlin and tuna in the local waters (the best fishing months are November–May). There is also small-game fishing for dolphin, barracuda, yellowtail, bonita, pompano and red snapper. Boats may be chartered through the various hotels or directly at the downtown **Malecon** for $200 a day or more (less off-season). These trips require an early start. Rise and shine at 6am for 7am departures. For water-sports enthusiasts, there's also waterskiing and parasailing (easier than it looks). It's occasionally possible to

rent a sailboat for a jaunt around the bay. Snorkeling is best in the shallow waters near **Roqueta Island**. Heading away from town to the southeast and toward the airport, there's **El Cano**, a delightfully refurbished hotel in a splendid setting, and **Las Brisas**, whose location offers startling views of the entire town. There is also a **Camino Real Hotel** located at the bottom of a villa-studded hill, enjoying a view of its own small bay. A few kilometers south of town is **Acapulco Diamante**.

Along the road, the so-called "gateway" to Diamante is marked by a stunning metal sculpture by the renowned metalsmith and jeweler Pal Kepenyes. Landmark hotels in this Diamante area are the **Princess** and **Pierre Marques** hotels, located right next to each other. They are on the way to the airport, which is 24 km (15 miles) from downtown Acapulco. Built to resemble a pre-Columbian pyramid, the **Princess** is, architecturally, the more striking of the two, with all its terraces awash with tropical flowers. The posh **Pierre Marques** was built by the late John Paul Getty and is under the same management as its neighbor. Aside from their isolated splendor, the attractions of the two hotels include two golf courses, a score of tennis courts, plus swimming pools, restaurants, nightclubs and bars.

A short way beyond the Princess there's a spectacular new hotel complex known as the **Vidafel Mayan Palace**. Several of its dramatic buildings are topped with Mayan-style thatches, interspersed with glass-roofed pavilions and reflecting pools strung out along a series of canals. The development has a variety of bars and restaurants and is planning a multiplex underground movie theater. The complex includes several buildings of time-share suites, spreading out over 4½ hectares (11 acres), in which can be found a dozen sheltered tennis courts with a variety of surfaces.

Puerto Marqués, a village on a bay south of the town, has a hotel and seafood restaurants, along with sailing craft for rent.

With completion of the *cuota* (toll road), there's even more interest in a formerly remote fishing village known as **La Barra Vieja** that is locally famous for a delicious specialty known as *pescado a la talla*. The daily catch goes directly to one or more of the several primitive beachfront restaurants (try **Beto Godoy** or **Cira La Morena**), where the fish is slathered in a time-honored secret mixture of different chilies and grilled over an open fire.

Getting around from one of these areas to another isn't as difficult as it sounds. Taxis are pretty reasonable, and most hotels list the prices for the most common destinations.

Eight kilometers (5 miles) north of town is **Pie de la Cuesta**, a fishing village with open beachfront and restaurants. It is the best place to watch the sunset but not a good place to swim – there's a vicious undertow. A long sandbar peninsula sheltering **Coyuca Lagoon** (abounding in catfish, snook and mullet) is gradually filling up with villas and hotels, one of which, **La Hacienda**, has a nude beach. The lagoon is popular for waterskiing and fishing trips.

Folk dancing at the busy Centro Acapulco.

OAXACA

Oaxaca is Indian country *par excellence*. Though the Zapotec and Mixtec Indians, the founders of the ancient civilization of the area, still dominate the state, there are 16 other groups living here as well, each linguistically and culturally different from the others. No other Mexican state can lay claim to such diversity.

There's so much to see in this wild and wonderful state: major archaeological sites, tiny rural villages where people actually produce many of the country's best handicrafts, and increasingly, the remote, exquisite seashore that lies over the mountains from the high valley where Oaxaca, the capital, and most of the other major attractions lie at an altitude of about 1,500 meters (4,920 ft).

Spaniards founded the city of Villa de Antequera de Guaxaca, now called simply **Oaxaca**. Its climate is splendid; never too hot nor too cold. In the 17th century, the English friar Thomas Gage remarked that "there was no place I so much desired to live in while I was in these parts as in Oaxaca."

Mountain vistas: Oaxaca city is 548 km (341 miles) from Mexico City and you can fly, take a train or go by road. All roads pass through mountain scenery of great beauty, whether you go by way of Cuernavaca, Cuautla or Izúcar de Matamoros. Or you can begin with Puebla, go south to Izúcar and then pick up the Pan American Highway. Another route from Puebla takes you through Tehuacán, famed for its mineral waters and hot baths. If you drive through Puebla, go to Izúcar and see the town of Atlixco, known for its bandstand and tiled benches. In September a dance festival is held there. Izúcar is a center for ceramics, including the "tree of life" candelabrum. Farther down the road is Acatlán, also famous for ceramics.

The state of Oaxaca was the birthplace of two of Mexico's most prominent leaders: Benito Juárez (the country's first elected president, who was born in the village of San Pablo Gelatao,

high in the hills about 65 km (40 miles) north of Oaxaca; and Porfirio Díaz, who seized the presidency in a coup in 1877 and remained in power until the Mexican Revolution in 1910.

Before the Spanish arrived, the Aztecs had conquered parts of what is now Oaxaca and set up a colony. As a result of the varied cultures that inhabited this area and left their mark, there are more than 4,000 archaeological sites, but only about 800 have been surveyed to any extent. In fact, there is so much in the area that someone once suggested putting a roof over the whole of Oaxaca and calling it a museum.

However, the city of Oaxaca is not the Mexico that most people conjure up in their minds when they are considering a vacation: there are no beaches in the city or nearby and relatively few palm trees.

Indian strains: What reigns in Oaxaca, a city of nearly 500,000 inhabitants, is the strong Zapotec and Mixtec influence in a real city where real people live and earn their living in a unique culture, a culture that still bears the stamp of its

Preceding pages: a group of Tzeltal officials. **Left,** Atzompa pottery. **Right,** check that your vehicle is in good order.

early Indian inhabitants. There is also superb colonial architecture, magnificent archaeological riches, and interesting food. *Chapulines* (fried grasshoppers) are sold every day in the central markets and routinely used as a condiment in many homes.

With its high, dry atmosphere and pleasant climate, Oaxaca is an ideal base for rest and contemplation as well as exploration of the city itself with its fine museums, striking churches, excellent restaurants, varied shopping (both in markets and boutiques) and music of many kinds. The city is easy to get around on foot. Otherwise, taxis are cheap and plentiful and willing to shave their prices by at least a *peso* or two from quoted rates.

Oaxaca is also justly famous for its markets. The **Mercado de Abastos**, or Saturday Market, is extraordinary chiefly for its size and the opportunities it offers for people-watching as the locals come to do their weekly or monthly shop. This buying frenzy takes place on a huge plot of ground adjacent to the second-class bus station on the *Periferico* (the city bypass) south of town. The sections that sell fruit, vegetables and pottery are most interesting (and the extensive displays provide wonderful opportunities for photographers). Otherwise, there's a hodgepodge of furniture, clothing and not-too-unusual kitchen equipment.

On the other hand, the **Benito Juárez market** and its adjacent **Mercado 20 de Noviembre**, both open daily, are more varied and attractive. Located at Flores Magon and Magon in two permanent buildings, just a few blocks south of the main square, they offer crafts (many of which are found in stalls on the street outside the market), souvenirs of all sorts, flowers and food, both raw and prepared (although many people enjoy the sights and smells, they tend to shy away from eating unfamiliar dishes prepared from unfamiliar ingredients). Photographers and cooks will find it particularly interesting for its huge mounds of dried peppers in a range of subtle colors and not-so-subtle flavors. And, yes, the Agriculture Department allows them to be taken into the United States.

Observe the action: For yet another sort of pleasure, it's possible to choose a bench in the beautifully planted **Zócalo** or to sit at a table in one of the many restaurants under the arcades and watch the local population carrying on their various pursuits: families at play, couples holding hands, vendors selling balloons, Chiclets chewing gum and, occasionally, some of the local crafts.

It is delightful to linger over a cappuccino at **Terranova**, or to sip one of the many excellent Mexican beers at **El Jardin**, where there's lively action of one sort or another all day and into the night. Or book a table overlooking the entire scene for lunch or dinner at **El Asador Vasco**, a consistently excellent second-floor Basque/seafood specialty restaurant, across from the central bandstand where concerts are performed nearly every evening. **El Asador Vasco** is a good option for dinner, when a strolling group of *mariachis* serenade the guests, and the resident piano player continues to provide live music after

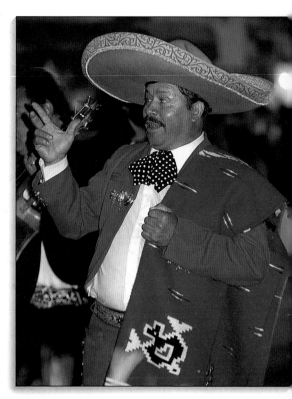

A *mariachi* singer performs.

the itinerant musicians have moved on.

In addition to its superb vantage point overlooking the bandstand, the location of Asador Vasco provides an opportunity to observe whatever *huelga* (strike or demonstration) is taking place outside the imposing **Palacio de Gobierno**. These are usually pretty peaceful, although spirited, and the action gives great insight into the way the local people comport themselves under duress.

The busy **cathedral**, with its baroque facade, is on another corner of the Zócalo. In addition to its regular masses, the building is often used for concerts, both inside and on the plaza. Notices for the concerts are posted at the **tourist office** at 200 Cinco de Mayo at Morelos.

Oaxaca offers inveterate museum fanciers two particularly interesting museums: the **Museo Regional del Estado**, housed in a handsome convent adjoining the 16th-century church of **Santo Domingo**; and the **Museo Rufino Tamayo**, which contains the artist's personal pre-Columbian collection, which he presented to the city of his birth.

Oaxaca's baroque church of Santo Domingo.

Assembled by Tamayo for their aesthetic, rather than historical significance, the figures were installed under the supervision of the artist.

Ancient artifacts: Oaxaca's **regional museum** is most noted for its spectacular collection of gold, turquoise, obsidian and glass that was found in tomb 7 at nearby Monte Albán, when it was uncovered in 1932. Although the sophisticated, intricate artifacts date from approximately AD 500, their jewelry designs are frequently faithfully copied by the local jewelers in gold or gold-washed silver, and sold in several of the better shops in the city. The museum, which houses superb displays of textiles, clothing and household implements of Oaxaca's earlier settlers, is a short five-block walk from the Zócalo along the **Alcalá**, a pedestrian walkway lined with excellent shops and beautifully maintained colonial buildings.

The **Dominican church** is remarkable for its magnificent golden interior work and its two handsome belltowers.

The **Basilica de la Soledad**, on

Avenida Independencia, is renowned chiefly for its statue of the the Virgin, Oaxaca's patron saint, wearing a superb jewel-studded black velvet robe. The statue, which is believed to possess miraculous healing powers, is displayed in an ornate golden shrine.

Also along the Alcalá pedestrian mall is the **Instituto de Artes Graficas de Oaxaca**, a small but important collection of lithographs, aquatints and silk screen prints located in the elegantly arcaded former home of artist Francisco Toledo. The collection includes works by such internationally famous artists as Picasso, Matisse and Rouault, as well as the prominent Mexican muralists Rivera and Orozco.

In addition to the galleries and churches along the Alcalá, there are a number of outstanding shops for crafts and jewelry, either on the same walkway, or a short distance away on adjoining streets. One of the most versatile and important is **La Mano Magico**, whose owner has a fine eye for authentic folk art. Her husband is a weaver of some note. **Yalalag de Oaxaca** also carries a large selection of gifts, some qualifying as folk art and some as crafts. The woven place mats, tablecloths and napkins in contemporary colors are particularly appealing. **Artisanías Chimalli** on Garcia Vigil has authentic folk art and is reliable for shipping purchases.

Other stops of interest in the area are the **Biblioteca Circulante de Oaxaca**, a library with a fine selection of books in English. Although this is a private library costing $10 to join, librarian Ruth Gonzalez is an invaluable source of information and helpful to people who just drop in to read a magazine or two.

Hosteria de Alcala, a restaurant in a beautiful old building next door to the first of Oaxaca's modern shopping centers, features a jazz duo on some evenings. Things tend to be a bit pricey in the shops but there's a good selection of *à la mode* clothing. And if, after all this shopping and sightseeing, people feel the need of a little something to appease their hunger, there's **3 T's** just off the Zócalo that specializes in *tortas*, *tortillas* and *tacos*.

Oaxaca, in short, is a superb shopping town, where one can also buy handicrafts directly from the Indians, who come to town to sell their wares, chiefly handwoven rugs or sarapes. Don't be afraid to bargain; it's expected. Prices don't come down as easily as formerly, but there is usually room for some maneuvering if you are politely insistent. It's helpful to at least know numbers in Spanish or have a pad of paper at the ready on which to write your offers.

For many people, the primary magnet of Oaxaca is the proximity of its archaeological wonders: Monte Albán, a grand Zapotec center and necropolis with its fascinating carvings; and Mitla, much more intimate in feeling and size and with quintessential abstract mosaic work adorning its reconstructed buildings. In recent years, Yagul (just off the Pan American Highway, not far from Mitla) has been excavated. It is less extensive than the two venerated "giants" of Monte Alban and Mitla, but, nevertheless impressive in its own right, commanding a stunning view of the **Oaxaca's Indians.**

valley and its plantings. For those interested in seeing a dig in progress, there's **Cerro de Atzompa**, in the early stages of excavation, near Atzompa, a few kilometers north of Oaxaca.

Each site is magnificent in its own way. Early morning is the best time to see the structures and tombs at **Monte Albán**, about 10 km (6 miles) from the city on a sheared-off mountain top. There are few sculptures at Monte Alban, except for the famous low-relief Dancers, which have sometimes been construed to be medical specimens, deformed persons or even dead prisoners of war. Many archaeologists will admit to being baffled by their meaning. At tomb 104 there is a fine figure of Cocijo, the rain god; tomb 105 has a fresco which seems to represent the deities. A climb to the top of one of the pyramids (they are called the north and south platforms) at either end of the plaza provides a compelling view of the valley.

Mitla (about 40 km/25 miles from the city) and **Yagul** (about 31 km/19 miles from Oaxaca en route to Mitla) can be combined in one expedition, along with a stop at the astounding Tule tree, an enormous specimen 50 meters (164 ft) in diameter, whose age is said to exceed 2,000 years. Just outside the entrance to Mitla, there is an extensive craft market with some excellent buys on the locally-woven lacy white shawls. There's also a handsome church just a short stroll away. **Santa Maria de Tule**, where the tree is located, also has a small craft market and a charming little village church that is worth a peek.

There is a small entrance fee to each of the ruins, except on Sundays, when admission is free. Mitla, unlike most ceremonial centers, was not abandoned after the Spanish conquest. It remained inhabited well into the 16th century. The buildings, with their carefully fitted stones, resemble the geometric frieze of Greek buildings of antiquity. Even the catacombs where the priests are buried are worth a visit. Another site worth visiting is the church next to the site – it is built of stones taken from the original Indian ceremonial center. Just off the

Monte Albán, Oaxaca

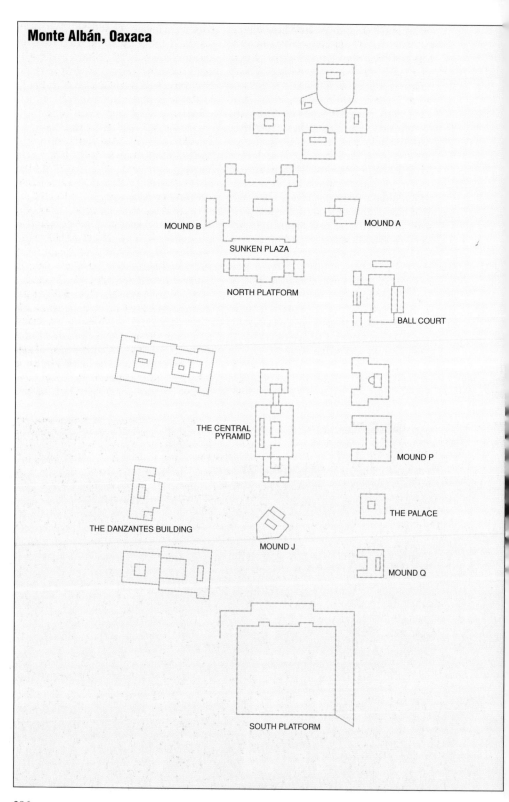

MOUND B

MOUND A

SUNKEN PLAZA

NORTH PLATFORM

BALL COURT

THE CENTRAL
PYRAMID

MOUND P

THE DANZANTES BUILDING

THE PALACE

MOUND J

MOUND Q

SOUTH PLATFORM

plaza is the **Frissell Museum**, which has artifacts on display and handicrafts for sale. The museum is a research center for the University of the Americas.

Several tour companies run minibuses with English-speaking guides to the various archaeological sites. The one to Monte Alban operates from the Meson del Angel hotel and to Mitla from the Stauffer Presidente, Victoria and Marques del Valle hotels. People who would prefer to explore on their own can drive, negotiate an hourly rate with a taxi driver, or take a local bus that goes near but not directly to the sites. Wear sturdy shoes. Many city bookshops and hotel gift boutiques carry specific guidebooks providing background and directions to the more established locations.

Taxis an option: The price of car rentals is so high these days that it's actually more economical to rent a taxi for several hours, establishing a fair price first, than to rent a car and drive yourself. Mexican history buffs might enjoy a jaunt to **Guelato**, Benito Juárez's birthplace, high in the hills overlooking Oaxaca. It is is about an hour from downtown by local bus to the Juarez *monumento* on the Pan American Highway and then by *collectivo* (shared taxi) over torturous roads that wind through spectacular scenery.

For the adventurous – and those in good physical condition – Oaxaca offers some fascinating sidetrips into nearby mountainous areas where many Indian groups live in relative isolation. From the city of Oaxaca you can take second- (lower-) class buses to villages several jolting hours away. You will ride squeezed betwixt local animals and people, but the grand vistas en route are worth the discomfort. Oaxaca is one of the poorest states of Mexico. Erosion is devastating. There is not enough land to go around and plots, often small to begin with, diminish with each succeeding generation, as they are divided among the heirs.

To supplement what they earn from farming, many Oaxacans have become artisans and craftsmen. They sell their pottery, weaving and leatherwork in the

The mountain top site of Monte Alban.

marketplace. The craft villages in the area surrounding Oaxaca offer opportunities to see artisans at work. Don't really count on paying a whole lot less here than at the city market stalls, though. **Teotitlán del Valle**, a couple of kilometers off the main road, is one of the best villages to visit. Stores are often in the front of the house and sometimes the weavers can be seen creating the designs from wool woven and dyed by the women of the household. Motifs range from traditional geometric shapes to portraits of Che Guevara, copies of pre-Columbian sculpture or even of paintings by Picasso or Miró. Best buys tend to come on orders of multiple pieces.

The village has a standing restaurant, **Tlamanalli**, featuring updated versions of traditional Zapotec food. Unless there's a bus tour in place, the cheerful owner, Abigail Ruiz, will make you welcome without a reservation (there's no phone). Take a chance. At nearby **Tlacolula** is a 16th-century church and also the best of the Sunday markets in the region. The town (and surrounding region) is a mezcal center. It's one of the best places to get top-quality *mezcal de pechuga*. Not only does it contain the usual cactus base, but also fruit and chicken. Some types of mezcal are flavored with herbs and occasionally include a worm that lives in the mezcal cactus plant. The coveted worm is often presented to an honored guest.

Other craft centers are:

● **San Bartolo Coyotepec**, known for its black pottery, is also the home of the late Dona Rosa who fashioned some of the more interesting and intricate designs which are now widely copied.

● **San Martin Tilcajete** is the center for fancy, carved wooden *animalitos*. Some of the pieces by better artists here bring big prices both locally and in craft shops in the US. Lesser versions can be found in city boutiques and on the street near the Stauffer Presidente Hotel.

● **Ocotlan de Morelos**, the home of many renowned pottery artists, namely the Aguilar family, who draw aficionados of their colorful work, but ship most of it to craft shops out of the country. Friday is market day and occasionally

it's possible to find outstanding baskets.

● **Santa Tomas Jalieza** is the center of backstrap weavings in the form of belts, bags, placemats and napkins.

● **Santa Maria Atzompa** is a pottery center famous for intricate renditions of the Virgin de Soledad and other raw clay figures. Much of the pottery here is glazed with a green finish, and because of its lead content is unsafe for cooking.

Cuilapan is worth visiting for its early colonial church and convent. The building was never completed but there is a series of arches curving to support the roof that was never built. The walls, however, are interesting since they house the tomb of the last Indian nobles of the region. Once this town was a center for the production of cochineal, a scarlet dye made from dried female insects that feed on cactus. Used as a base for magenta hues in Europe and even in the red coats of the British Army, this dye was so highly prized that under the Spanish its export was strictly controlled.

The beaches: Oaxaca has 480 km (298 miles) of Pacific coastline with excellent beaches, quiet lagoons and good surfing. The highway from Acapulco in Guerrero state to Salina Cruz in Oaxaca has been resurfaced, although it is still rough in many places. Puerto Escondido, Puerto Angel and now Huatulco are the three major destinations.

Puerto Escondido has been in the business of tourism perhaps the longest, although much of its revenue still comes from fishing as an industry. The fishing boats that are seen from the town beach ply the waters on a daily basis and the catch turns up on the table in local restaurants and in the marketplace.

There are different aspects to Puerto Escondido. First there is the town itself, which is on a hill above the beach and is of slight interest to the tourists, unless they need a pharmacy or shoe repair or some other non-tourist-oriented service. The main tourist area stretches from the main beach, **Playa Principal**, and the swimming beach, **Playa Marinero**, around the bend to **Playa Zicatela**, where the "Mexican Pipeline" of waves is a magnet for surfers. Most tourist facilities are on or near the beach.

The pedestrian walkway that parallels the beach through the tourist part of town is lined with shops including silver shops with jewelry that ranges from inexpensive junk to sophisticated and well-designed pieces. Prices are usually fair. There are simple but excellent fish/seafood restaurants, such as **La Perla Flamante** and **Nautilus**, as well as bars that have live jazz and dance music starting at about 10pm.

The most outstanding hotel in Puerto Escondido is the **Santa Fe**, at the point where the surf beach and the swimming beach converge. It has a pool of its own as well as charming architecture, beautifully planted grounds and comfortable rooms. Its excellent dining room is primarily vegetarian with fish and chicken also on the menu. There's a charming new hotel on the hill at the other end of town. **El Aldea del Bazar** is handsomely designed, but a taxi is needed to get to or from anywhere else.

Puerto Angel is a resort for people who mostly want to do nothing except relax. The most exciting thing to do in town is to watch the sea spray up through a blow hole.

Huatulco, on the other hand, is poised to become a trendy destination. The beautifully planned area stretches along several bays that are being developed as a mega-resort, complete with golf courses, scuba diving and horse-riding stables. Beaches sprawl over 35 km (22 miles) of coastline. Several hotels, including the Sheraton, Holiday Inn Crowne Plaza and the Omni, plus Club Med and the Royal Maeva complexes, have been completed, and more are on the drawing-board. Eventually there will be 30,000 rooms available. Mexicana and Aeromexico fly into the airport, 20 km (12 miles) to the northeast.

For people who prefer a glimpse of Mexican life away from the strictly resort venues, a good place to visit is a tiny new town, **La Crucecita**, which is complete with a delightful central plaza, a range of restaurants, a couple of inexpensive hotels that ferry their patrons to one of the beaches and a perfect gem of a marketplace.

Puerto Escondido.

TABASCO AND CHIAPAS

Tabasco's original capital was founded on the Gulf coast by Cortés in 1519, but pirate raids forced its removal inland. Now called **Villahermosa**, it has endured an oil boom in recent years and is now an urban center of more than a quarter of a million people.

The city can be reached overnight on the bus from Mexico City. It is a good place to rent a car for exploring neighboring Chiapas. There is a spartan but clean hotel right across from the bus station and cars can be rented at the Hotel Maya Tabasco one block away.

Villahermosa's major attraction is the immense **La Venta Museum Park**, set beside the charmingly named Lagoon of Illusions just to the west of town. It was to here that the 15-ton giant stone heads and other artifacts of the Olmec civilization (1200 BC–AD 400) were brought from an island 130 km (80 miles) to the west after the 1925 excavations by archaeologist Franz Blom were threatened by oil drilling.

The most fascinating site is that of **Comalcalco**, 62 km (39 miles) to the northwest, not least because it is set in lush greenery in a tranquil grove that sees relatively few visitors. Here the Mayas built pyramids of baked brick (because of abundant clay but lack of stone) between AD 800 and the time when the site was abandoned 500 years later. The road to Comalcalco passes through Cárdenas, where an enormous plant processes most of the cacao grown in the region, for distribution to chocolate manufacturers throughout the world.

Tabasco benefits not only from oil but also from a successful agricultural industry, which includes livestock farming, enormous acreages of bananas, and the cultivation of cacao, pineapples, honey, plantains and citrus. All contribute to the state's prosperity.

The neighboring state of **Chiapas** was a meeting ground of the Olmec and Mayan pre-Hispanic cultures. With the break-up of the classic Mayan culture, the Chiapan Indians conquered other Mayan tribes and came to dominate the area. During their relatively short-lived control of central Mexico the Aztecs conquered parts of Chiapas and after their defeat Cortés was obliged to send in armed forces to subjugate the area. For its three centuries of colonial history the region was controlled at times by Mexico, sometimes by Guatemala. Soconusco, the agriculturally rich southeastern part of the state which even then specialized in the production of cocoa, was administered directly by the Spanish Crown but depended on Guatemala for judicial procedure.

The Catholic Church in Chiapas was run mainly by Dominicans from 1544, and beautiful baroque churches were built, especially in San Cristóbal. The Indians, compelled to do heavy labor and pay tribute, frequently rebelled. They were defended by Father Bartolomé de las Casas, a slave-owner himself who nevertheless won their love – as well as the hate of the Spanish. Because of the padre's devotion, the name of the old capital was changed from Ciudad Real to San Cristóbal de las Casas.

At first, Chiapas decided to side with Mexico and its first emperor, Iturbide. But when he was eased from power (and later executed) the state withdrew from the Mexican federation, as did Guatemala and the rest of Central America. After a few years of confusion the Chiapans decided by plebiscite to go back into the Mexican union. Porfirio Díaz crushed any rebellion that might have flared in Chiapas. He tried to open up the country to foreign capital and interests, and encouraged Germans from Guatemala to settle and grow coffee. A railroad was pushed through along the coast, and this opened up marketing possibilities. The capital was moved from San Cristóbal to Tuxtla in 1892 because the residents failed to support Díaz in one of his elections.

When revolution put Madero in power, fighting erupted between the San Cristóbal and Tuxtla factions, which ended in victory for the latter. It was not until the regime of Lázaro Cárdenas that agrarian reform came to pass in Chiapas, with large estates being broken up and

Left, Tzeltals gathering for a religious festival outside their church at Tenejapa, Chiapas.

land handed to the peasants who had worked it for generations. Turmoil that erupted in 1994 was largely due to the fact that this process has never been completed. Vast tracts of land – even entire communities – remain in the grip of old-time *caciques*, or political bosses, and there is widespread poverty and exploitation. A quarter of the Indian population has no formal income and with almost one-third of the state's 3.2 million inhabitants having no access to health care, 15,000 die of curable diseases each year.

Chiapas is spectacularly beautiful but its steep, switchback roads are not for the faint-hearted. There is a constant panorama of mountains, rivers, and waterfalls. The two main roads into Chiapas both start in the Tehuantepec peninsula at Tapachula and run in roughly an east–west direction. One follows the Pacific coast and the other the Pan American Highway. The Pan American Highway climbs to the state capital of Tuxtla Gutiérrez, then runs east to San Cristóbal de las Casas before dropping down to the Guatemalan border. Chiapas is a land of many climates. In some areas there is almost continuous rain throughout the year. The rain, in the main, begins in May and ends in October. July and August are the wettest months.

Your adventure in Chiapas will probably begin at the state capital **Tuxtla Gutiérrez** ("Place of the Rabbits"), a city with few major attractions apart from the anthropology museum in **Madero Park** and the municipal **zoo**, which has animals indigenous to Chiapas, such as tapirs and jaguars, in natural settings along a wooded trail. One popular attraction of the town is the cathedral's German-style glockenspiel that features musical movements by the 12 apostles every hour. There's a display of weaving and other crafts in the **Bazar Ishcanal**, next to the cathedral.

It's worth exploring the environs of Tuxtla, especially **Sumidero Canyon**, either from a lookout point along cliffs over the dramatic 1,000-meter (3,280-ft) deep gorge of the **Grijalva river** or on a boat trip through the canyon itself.

Celebrants at the fiesta of San Sebastian in Chiapa de Corzo.

Volkeswagen minibuses called *combis* leave Madero Park whenever they fill up and take you up the highway to clifftop lookout points. Boats set off for the 2–2½-hour motorboat roundtrip through the canyon from **Chiapa de Corzo**, a 15-minute ride from Tuxtla and site of the first Spanish settlement in Chiapas, later abandoned because of the heat. The town's principal attraction is a 16th-century Moorish-style structure over the public fountain. Nearby is the huge, 16th-century **Santo Domingo** church. Chiapa de Corzo has a lacquerware museum, and crafts (mainly embroidered clothing) are for sale in shops along the plaza.

Take a hat and suntan lotion for the canyon trip and bring a wide-angle lens if you are a photographer. As you go through, the walls become steeper, sometimes rising to 1,000 meters (3,280 ft). The water is calm, the once-fierce rapids having been tamed by the dam.

Just west of Tuxtla there is a turnoff on the Pan-Am to **Chicoasén**, some 40 km (25 miles) away on a well-paved road. The dam was completed late in 1981 and is one of Mexico's largest. Just after you reach a tunnel and come out above the dam, there's a turnoff marked *Mirador* (lookout). A couple of kilometers along here takes you to a spectacular viewpoint. On one side you can see the imposing canyon of the **Grijalva** (the Sumidero is farther back at the top of the cliffs); on the other side is the top of the dam, with an artificial lake in between. There are buses from Tuxtla to Chicoasén. Hydroelectricity is big business in Chiapas and most of it is generated by the massive dams along the Grijalva river.

If you want to see the state to its best advantage, rent a car in Tuxtla. Much of the highway between the capital and Villahermosa to the north, and eastwards between Tuxtla and San Cristóbal runs through gorgeous mountains, with fabulous views and incessant hairpin bends. Northeast of Ocosingo and in the mountains beyond Palenque some villagers – modern highwaymen – have a disconcerting habit of stretching a rope

Canyon on the Grijalva river.

across the road and demanding "toll" from passing motorists. Unless they appear to be armed it is best to drive right through their rope at high speed. This small-time guerrilla activity predated – and in some ways predicted – the subsequent uprising.

The drive northwards, along the Gulf coast is disappointing. Despite some interesting stretches, roads are badly signposted and confusing and **Ciudad del Carmen**, despite its location, is a drab, commercial town which offers almost no access to its waterfront. Once beyond Carmen, however, it is a pleasant drive to the lovely city of Campeche.

South of Tuxtla is Arriaga and **Tonalá**, supposedly the hottest place in Chiapas. From here you can drive to **Paredón** on the Dead Sea, which is really a lagoon with excellent fishing, and calm water for year-round swimming. There are no hotels but plenty of seafood restaurants. An alternative to Tonalá is a quick 19-km (12-mile) drive to **Puerto Arista**, where the well-to-do of Chiapas have weekend homes. Again, there are no hotels but plenty of restaurants. It is possible to rent a hammock for a modest sum. In winter, bring a light blanket. The seafood is great and inexpensive.

Tapachula, near the Guatemalan border, the "Pearl of the Soconusco," is the center of the region's banana, cotton, cacao and coffee plantations, operated by people of German origin who moved into Chiapas from Guatemala during the Díaz administration. Planting large tracts of virgin land at elevations of 650–1,500 meters (2,130–4,900 ft), the settlers gave the economy a strong push. When they were interned during World War II, coffee production dropped drastically. Of course many are now Mexican citizens and the names of the plantations have been localized. Still there is the town of Nueva Alemania (New Germany) in the coffee-growing district near Tapachula. The Soconusco area of Chiapas is one of Mexico's chief sources of coffee, which is the major agricultural export (only Colombia and Brazil grow more). Cotton is also grown, with corn, wheat, fruit and sugar cane: the cane is used mainly to produce alcohol.

From Tapachula, the route backtracks to **Huixtla**, begins an incredible climb, then drops along Highway 190 which follows the Guatemalan border to the crossing point at Ciudad Cuauhtémoc. It's worth the drive for the scenery alone, but don't try it at night. There are checkpoints along the way where customs officials stop travelers. They are looking for contraband drugs, arms and illegal Guatemalan immigrants. Because of political instability in Guatemala, Mexico has had to deal with increasing numbers of illegal immigrants.

Shortly after you enter the mountainous region, you'll reach **Ciudad Cuauhtémoc** (no hotels). If you plan on going to Guatemala have your visa ready. Cross before 1pm, or between 4pm and 6pm. Most problems, however, can be resolved by the payment of an extra "fee."

Ciudad Cuauhtémoc is at the end of the Mexican part of the Pan American Highway, which begins at Ciudad Juárez, just over the Texas border. If you follow the Pan-Am going west, you will climb to the Chiapas central highlands and, across a broad valley, you will see Guatemala's imposing mountains looking hazy in the distance. Before reaching the town of **Comitán**, there's a turnoff to the **Montebello Lakes** and the archaeological site of **Chinkultic**.

The most popular destination after Tuxtla is 80 km (50 miles) to the east: **San Cristóbal de las Casas,** at an elevation of 2,300 meters (7,550 ft) and believed by many aficionados to be the most agreeable town in Mexico. There are many clean, inexpensive hotels and good food at reasonable prices. Almost every other storefront along Calle Madero, off the Zócalo, houses a different restaurant.

San Cristóbal, a place of immense colonial charm, has a leisurely atmosphere; it is cool and healthy and is full of Indians wearing traditional dress. The town was founded in 1528 and churches dominate the architectural scene. The best is **Santo Domingo**, begun in 1547. Its baroque facade is intricately beautiful. The interior is filled with excellent religious paintings. Outside dozens of

Indians squat doing embroidery and selling an amazing variety of brightly colored clothing and other woven items. There are similar sidewalk markets outside some of the other churches. Get an idea of comparable prices in one of the downtown shops or at the cooperative in the former convent beside Santo Domingo church, and be prepared to bargain. Pottery and leather goods are specialties of the area but there are also woolen and cotton clothing and also amber items (fossilized pine resin).

People-watching is the most interesting thing to do in San Cristóbal. Chamula Indians wear long white woolen tunics; their civic leaders wear black tunics. Male Zinacantecs wear reddish-pink tunics and hats with colorful ribbons. If a man is married, he ties the ribbons down tight. If he is single he lets the ribbon wave in the breeze announcing that he's available. Be sure to have lunch or dinner, if not stay at **Casa Bolon**, the institute set up by the late anthropologists Gertrude Blom and her husband, Franz – the excavator of La Venta – in a large house with flower-filled patios and beautifully furnished rooms with log fires. A student and friend for half a century to many Indian tribes (whose languages she spoke), Trudi died aged 92 in 1993.

San Juan Chamula, 9.5 km (6 miles) from San Cristóbal on a paved road, is the best known and most accessible of the Indian centers. Upon arrival, report to the local visitors office in the municipal building. Upon payment of a small fee, you will be issued a permit to photograph the church and an escort will be assigned to make certain you don't take photos inside the building. The church is filled with saints with mirrors around their necks, apparently to show how they see the world.

To photograph people in the streets of San Cristóbal, you should either catch them with a long telescopic lens or politely ask and offer to pay. They are justified in asking for a small fee. After all, *they* are the main attraction in town, but the profits are made by the airlines, hotels, restaurants and tour operators.

The nearby village of **Zinacantán** is

The church of Santo Domingo in San Cristóbal.

Palenque, Chiapas

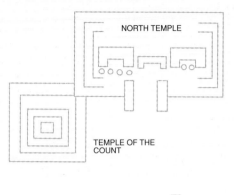

NORTH TEMPLE

TEMPLE OF THE COUNT

BALL COURT

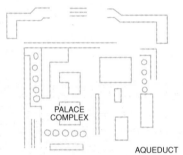

PALACE COMPLEX

AQUEDUCT

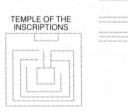

TEMPLE OF THE INSCRIPTIONS

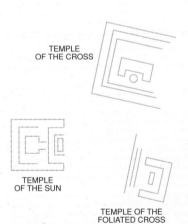

TEMPLE OF THE CROSS

TEMPLE OF THE SUN

HOUSE OF THE JAGUAR

TEMPLE OF THE FOLIATED CROSS

reached by taking the same paved road that goes to San Juan Chamula, then branching off to the left. Market day is Sunday when colorful services take place in the church. (No photos allowed.)

If you want more spectacular scenery, you can drive or take a bus to **Tenajapa**, some 29 km (18 miles) away. There's excellent weaving, embroidery, and brocaded crafts in Tenajapa, especially at the Sunday market.

Out of San Cristóbal the Pan American Highway running toward the Guatemalan border passes the **Amatenango del Valle** where the Tzeltal women specialize in making beautiful unglazed pottery fired in the pre-Columbian way. They do not use a baking oven; they simply light a pyre around sun-dried clay vessels. These natural colors will not fade, but the pottery is not as hard as pottery which has been fired in high-temperature kilns.

Farther down the road, you come to **Comitán**, known for fiery liquor, steep streets, and ears of corn that measure almost half a meter long. There is a

pleasant plaza and good hotels. Stay overnight, or push on to the more pristine if rudimentary accommodations around the lakes of **Montebello**.

From Comitán it's an easy hour's drive to the lakes, of which there are some 60. All are located in peaceful settings. A path takes you to a limestone arch, the **Arco de San José**. A few kilometers back on the paved highway, there's a dirt road which leads to more lakes, including the **Tziscao**. You can stay at a dormitory-style hotel here. A bit farther back on the highway, there's a turnoff to the archaeological site of **Chinkultic**, where a pyramid looms high over the valley.

Palenque, probably the largest and most impressive of the Mayan sites, can be reached by frequent VW bus service from the lively town, whose action centers around the Zócalo and the busy main street leading up to it. On this are numerous hotels (best is Chan Kah), restaurants and an amazingly well-stocked supermarket/general store. All the hotels near the site – and none are

really near – are exorbitantly expensive. There are also tours (about $10) from town to **Agua Azul**, waterfalls to the northeast (however, as there's nothing else there it's hardly worth making a three-hour round trip).

At the archaeological site, just outside town, are some of the most exquisite sculptures of the Mayan civilization, some in stone; most in stucco. Take, for example, the **Temple of the Inscriptions**, a pyramid. In 1949 the Mexican archaeologist Alberto Ruz Lhullier discovered that the stone on top of the structure was a sort of cap, and was meant to be lifted. Underneath he found a rubble-filled passageway. About 1.5 meters (5 ft) under the base of the pyramid he found a royal tomb, covered by a stone lid weighing 4½ tons. Using truck jacks, Ruz and his crewmen lifted the massive stone and found a skeleton – probably that of a priest-ruler, who wore a mosaic jade mask. Certain pop archaeologists have put forward the theory that the bas-relief figure on this heavy stone lid is that of an astronaut who visited this site in ancient times. On one side of the temple is the **Temple of the Folliated Cross**.

Next to the Temple of the Inscriptions is the **Palace**, which features a unique four-story tower which may have been used as an observatory. Its walls are embellished with detailed stucco panels, and its courtyards have low walls decorated with mysterious stone sculptures and hieroglyphics, many of which have never been deciphered.

The other two important Mayan sites, **Yaxchilán** and **Bonampak**, are in the heart of the rain forest near the river Usumacinta, which marks the border with Guatemala. Yaxchilán is famous for its intricate stucco roof decorations; Bonampak for its lively-colored Mayan paintings. During the dry season only, you can reach Bonampak by truck from Palenque. Yaxchilán is accessible only by plane or boat. To visit either you'll need a strong spirit of adventure or to be a fervent archaeology buff.

Right, masked performers at the fiesta of San Sebastian.

308

VERACRUZ

Veracruz (the very tropical state that extends along the Gulf of Mexico) is an area of mega-contrasts. Its coastal cities (among them, the well-known port of Veracruz) are hot, humid and, until recently, unknown to international tourism. While several of the interior towns played an important commercial role in early colonial times, only a few hardy souls interested in the ancient Indian culture traveled through this largely uncharted territory.

History buffs, however, will certainly take pleasure in realizing that it was very near the modern city of Veracruz that Cortés and his men took possession of the area in the name of Spain. The central part of the country was exploited for its mineral treasure; the hot and malarial Gulf coast was neglected, except for the port of Veracruz.

Historical conflicts: At the beginning of the 10-year struggle for Mexican independence, there was a short-lived conspiracy in Veracruz, led by a 17-year-old boy, Evaristo Molino, who was quickly captured and shot. The Spanish clung to the Fort of San Juan de Ulua until 1825, four years after Mexican independence had been won. In 1838 the French blockaded Veracruz and in 1847 American forces landed troops in Veracruz and marched inland during the Mexican War. The US Navy took the coast town of Frontera and bombarded San Juan de Tabasco, now Villahermosa. In 1864 Maximilian landed at Veracruz and under the protection of French troops imposed himself on Mexico as emperor. Eventually, the French had to leave (through Veracruz, of course). In 1914 US troops occupied Veracruz for two months.

Southern Veracruz produces almost all of Mexico's sulfur and has proved a rich source of oil. Still, Veracruz, with a population of 6 million including 350,000 Indians, remains essentially an agricultural state. It tops all other Mexican states in growing sugar cane, potatoes, beans, chilis, pineapples and oranges. It comes second in the production of coffee, corn and cocoa.

The area is full of drama. For example, the Olmec Indians of this area have left glorious relics of their sophisticated early civilization and the Totonacs, in the northern part of the state, still conduct their religious rites for the enjoyment of locals and tourists. Even the changes in the landscape are remarkable – extinct volcanoes and coffee plantations, rolling mountains, extensive banana and pineapple plantations, and endless fields of sugar cane.

Heading east: From Mexico City the best route to Veracruz is via the main highway east through Puebla and the city of Orizaba, home of the famous Monctezuma brewery where Dos Equis, Tres Equis and Superior brands of beer are brewed. Nearby is **Tuxpango Falls**.

Out of Orizaba you pass **Fortín de las Flores**, with its quaint plaza, and, of course, flowers. Then on to **Córdoba**, one of the centers of Mexico's coffee industry, from where you can take a side trip to a coffee plantation. From Córdoba

Left, southern Veracruz is rich in oil. **Right**, a welcome smile.

it's a gradual 1,000-meter (3,280-ft) drop to the tropical port of **Veracruz**.

In the city: While the ocean water is warm, and leisurely waves roll in from the Gulf of Mexico, the beaches on this coast are really no match for the white expanses of sand on the west coast or the Carribean. Gulf waters are pretty shallow and not terribly conducive to serious swimming, but some of the newer hotels such as the attractive **Torremar**, in the fashionable Mocambo suburb, about 8 km (5 miles) from the heart of the city, locate their pools so that guests can watch the sea while they enjoy the advantages of pool swimming.

The sprawling **Hotel Mocambo** nearby, the only hotel in the area for most of its 60 or so years in existence, is evocative of the more gracious way of life that prevailed when it was built. Places to stay in the downtown area are less like resort hotels and more business-oriented, with the exception of the small and cheerful **Hotel Hawaii**, across from the so-called "craft market" (if T-shirts can be classified as "crafts").

Downtown Veracruz has the liveliest main square in the country, the **Plaza de Armas**. In additional to the usual parade of hawkers of toys and souvenirs, stalls here offer cigars, both local and Cuban, singly and by the box. Amber jewelry is also for sale and carvings from neighboring Chiapas (items should be examined carefully in case they are plastic). Eat the locally caught seafood – *huachinango à la Veracruzana* (red snapper in a thick tomato sauce), or oysters on the half-shell and exotic shrimp soup. Do try the local tropical fruit and treat yourself to a strong coffee and a cigar. Maybe you'd even like to play a game of dominos in a café or listen to marimba combos. Stroll around admiring the wood and stucco buildings with their overhanging balconies, as well as the old **La Parroquia** church and the arcades of the **Municipal Palace**. Take the waterfront walk along the **Malecon** down to the port and the sailors' bars.

Musical city: There is organized music several nights a week, and casual

The port of Veracruz.

marimba groups and a few *mariachi* bands ply their trade at the various restaurants in the surrounding area. More often than not people will get in the mood and start dancing in the street to the irresistible rhythms. The show goes on late into the night while people are eating and drinking endless cups of the wonderful coffee that comes from other parts of the state. The **Gran Cafe de la Parroquia** (with two locations, one directly on the Plaza and a newer, larger branch close to the port) is the traditional location for "serious" coffee drinking, both by the men who grow and roast it and congregate here early in the day to discuss business, and by the women who gather strictly for recreation.

Veracruz has a talent for merriment, which is at its height at the time of Carnaval, held during the week before Ash Wednesday (i.e. the first day of Lent). People stream into town from all over the country and more and more foreign tourists have begun to observe and participate in the colorful proceedings. (Mexico City dwellers have used it as a quick getaway destination for years.)

Unlucky fortress: Traditional sightseeing in Veracruz is somewhat limited. There is, however, the charming small **Museo de la Ciudad**, with artifacts and displays of early culture, and the forbidding **Fuerte de San Juan de Ulúa**, which guards the mouth of the harbor. It's worth a taxi-ride to visit its grim confines that were used as a prison after it outlived its usefulness as a fortress. In spite of the building's strategic location Veracruz was overrun on several occasions by foreign invaders, beginning with Sir Francis Drake and Dutch pirates who attacked it from the early 16th century until 1846, when it fell to US troops. There is a fine new **aquarium** on the waterfront – well worth a visit for the beautifully crafted tanks full of fish from southern waters.

As might be suspected, the location of Veracruz directly on the waters of the Gulf of Mexico with its abundance of fish, makes it a center for seafood of all descriptions. **Restaurant Imperial**, in the arcade next to the Plaza, has mag-

Veracruz is one of the best places to eat fish.

nificent, huge grilled shrimp and **Villa Marina**, on the waterfront boulevard, prepares sophisticated dishes for people to enjoy along with the sea views.

As a change from fish, however, there's **El Meson de los Coras** for *barbacoa* (barbeque) on Saturday and Sunday; **Pozolver** for *pozole* (hominy soup with pork or chicken); and **La Mansion** for excellent steaks.

Serious seafood lovers should make it their business to head for **Boca del Rio**, a fishing village about 10 km (6 miles) from downtown Vera Cruz, where the river and sea come together and provide the catch for the several lunch-only restaurants there (actually open until about 6 pm). Topnotch is **Las Brisas del Mar**, large, open and airy, with the (deserved) reputation for buying only the best and preparing it to perfection. Also worth trying is the well-established **Pardino's**, which also has a branch in the city.

From Veracruz, head for Alvarado and Tlacotalpan. It's only a few kilometers up the **Papaloapan river** to **Alvarado**, where the **Port Authority**

Café serves scrumptious seafood at budget prices. **Tlacotalpan** was founded by the wealthy of Veracruz who wanted to escape the reach of pirates. It's a charming town, full of pastel colors and graceful arches. People are friendly; room and board is inexpensive. Its riverside location is an added bonus – bring your camera or your watercolors.

North of the city: It's almost necessary to rent a car for excursions out of Veracruz, except for point-to-point bus transportation to the larger cities like **Jalapa** (spelled Xalapa locally). Jalapa is the state capital and home of the University of Veracruz, with its superb anthropological museum, **El Museo de Antropología de Jalapa**. The museum is located in the northern suburbs at the corner of Avenida Xalapa and Avenida 1 of Mayo. Without an automobile, visitors are dependent on infrequent and inconvenient buses or taxis – it is, however, worth the journey.

The museum has among its treasures several colossal Olmec heads and examples of "laughing children" ceram-

Geared up and ready to go.

ics, which are unusual both for their subject matter and their impressive state of preservation. Be warned, however, that the official guidebook (1912 edition) is printed only in Spanish.

Jalapa is built on hills and although it's often drizzling – locals call the rain *chipichipi* – on clear days you will get a spectacular view of snowcapped **Pico de Orizaba**, Mexico's highest mountain (5,654 meters/18,551 ft). It is the third highest peak in North America, after Mount McKinley in Alaska and Mount Logan in the Yukon Territory. Some call Orizaba by its pre-Hispanic name, *Citlaltepetl* (Star Mountain). It is said that the first climbers to scale the mountain were American soldiers in 1848, who were part of General Winfield Scott's invading army. If you intend to try the climb, it is well to have had experience in mountain climbing and even then you need a guide.

Lodgings in Jalapa are, with the exception of the new and lovely **Fiesta Inn**, pretty dispiriting. However, in the neighboring town of **Coatepec**, widely known for the fine coffee grown in the region, there is a charming converted hacienda, the **Posada de Coatepec**. The *posada* is delightful, not only for its individually decorated rooms and tranquil atmosphere but also for its central location, perfect for exploring this pretty little city on foot. In addition to the dining room at the hotel, a local restaurant, **El Tio YeYo**, is well worth a stop for a meal of mountain trout.

Xico, a small, graceful town, is a short side-trip, reached after a beautiful ride through plantations where coffee is grown under the shade of banana trees. The fine mist (called *chipi-chipi*) that prevails so frequently in this mountainous area is credited with maintaining the balance necessary for the cultivation of excellent coffee. There are coffee-roasting establishments throughout Coatepec and the price per kilo is extremely reasonable. Xico is the site of the **Texolo Waterfall** (La Cascada de Texolo) where *Romancing the Stone* was filmed in 1984.

Still further to the north along moun-

Pico de Orizba.

tainous country roads (or via the coast road which requires some backtracking) is **Papantla**, best known for its Totonac Indians who perform a startling religious feat from a 30-meter (100-ft) pole that has resulted in their being known as "The Flying Indians."

Another reason for making the trip to Papantla is the proximity of the exquisite archaeological site known as **El Tajín**. This site is remarkable for its artwork and the state of preservation of its numerous handsome buildings, the most famous of which is known as the **Temple of the Niches**. There is some controversy about the actual significance of the niches, but absolutely none about the aesthetic appeal of the structure.

A local lawyer/historian, Leonardo Zaleta, has written a guidebook to El Tajin and one about the origin and symbolism of the "Dance of the Voladores" (better known as "The Flying Indians"). At the present time they are available only in Spanish but plans are underway for translations into English.

An announcement early in 1994 about the archaeological site of **El Pital**, 65 km (40 miles) from El Tajín, suggests that El Pital may have been an even more important place than the El Tajin. Researchers have discovered that it may have supported a population of 20,000 from AD 100–600. The city's demise may have been due to the climatic phenomenon known as El Nino. The city was later reclaimed by the jungle.

There are two routes to Papantla: – either up the coast or inland via the mountain road. Not far out of Veracruz on the former route is **Zempoala** (also spelled Cempoala), an archaeological site of secondary importance and the first town Cortés saw in Mexico when he landed in 1519. It then had 30,000 inhabitants and conducted the grim ritual of human sacrifice. Near the ruins of Zempoala is the town of **Antigua**, the first Spanish settlement in New Spain. The townspeople will show you an old house, said to have belonged to Cortés, and a church, the foundation of which, it is claimed, is the oldest in Mexico.

High up (2,300 meters/7,545-ft) be-

El Tajin's Pyramid of the Niches.

tween Veracruz and Papantla on the inland route is **Tezuitlán**. Cool off here in the handsome plaza; look at the colonial architecture and the homes of the influential, carved out of the mountain.

The Tuxtlas: South of the city of Veracruz the terrain changes and the main road (Highway 180) passes through cattle ranches and pineapple farms and then into the hills. **Santiago Tuxtla** is the first small town of any interest with its charming Zócalo and small museum.

Lake Catemaco, a few minutes out of Santiago, is a a 16-km (10-mile) long volcanic crater lake guarded by two 920-meter (3,000-ft) extinct volcanoes, both called San Martin. The lake's islands house a colony of about 500 rhesus monkeys, the result of three specimens (one old male and two young females) being left behind by a Mexico City film company about 15 years ago. There is an extensive nature preserve in the magnificent rain forest on the lake, not far from the **Playa Azul Hotel**, which is spearheading a new eco-tourism industry in the area with a spectacu-

lar new nature preserve of flora and fauna. The Playa Azul, covering several lakeside acres, is in the process of a much-needed rehabilitation.

There is also the newer but relatively cheerless **Hotel Lafinca** located right on the highway. The local lake fish, *mojarra,* is outstanding and is cooked to perfection at a lakeside restaurant, **Los Sauces**.

You can ride in a boat to **Teotapan Falls** and to the **Coyame springs**. If you are of an adventurous bent, try *chango-con*, a dish of monkey meat.

Next comes **San Andres Tuxtla**, a center for cigar production and known for its local culture of male *brujas* (witches). Outsiders are not welcome at the annual *bruja* festival but witch souvenirs of all sorts are widely available for sale. The **Hotel del Parque** on the main square in the center of town is pleasant and lively with above-average food. Its verandah is a constantly changing scene of the local denizens, who congregate for morning cappuccino and evening espresso.

A bite to eat.

THE YUCATÁN

Mexico, bordering the Gulf, is shaped like a fishhook and the Yucatán Peninsula is the bait which has lured many a voyager. Today's tourists are charmed by the Caribbean beaches and ancient Mayan cities.

Ruled from Spain: The Yucatán was not governed through the viceroys in distant Mexico City but directly from Spain and over nearly 300 years of the colonial period developed its own particular syncretism of the Mayan and Spanish cultures. Isolated from the center of Mexican power, it took little part in the independence movement.

If one word could serve to sum up the colonial history of the Yucatán, the word would be "strife." There were constant wars with the Mayas, attacks by pirates, friction between the Franciscan monks, the civil authorities and the clergy. Often drought struck and hunger ravaged the land. The Mayas were treated shamefully by the Spanish. Their lands were taken away; they were humiliated and despised. As result of mistreatment and epidemics, their population plummeted.

The Yucatán always preferred to handle its own problems and for that reason it favored the form of federal government which governed least. When the centralists won the power struggle in Mexico, the Yucatán reacted by declaring its independence. During the ensuing contretemps with the central government, Santiago Iman, a local patriot, armed the Mayas and induced them to fight the federal troops. Thousands of Indians volunteered. They overran Valadolid and expelled federal troops from Campeche. This was the start of the War of the Castes.

The built-up outrage of the Indians was explosive and directed against every white person. Some Mayas were armed with rifles, but most preferred to do their work with a machete. The Indians killed even the priests, who often earned as much as 14,000 *pesos* a year through parish fees while Indian laborers made between 12 and 36.

What eventually stopped the Indian rampage was the appearance of winged ants whose arrival presaged the rainy season. The Indians, farmers not soldiers, returned home to plant corn, for they knew that unless the seeds were in the ground before the rains came, they would later starve.

When the Mayas left, the whites recovered their strength and retaliated. From Cuba, came rifles and artillery. The federal government in Mexico City sent troops and supplies. Some 1,000 mercenaries came from the US.

To help regain their nerve, the Mayas revived the image of the Talking Cross, a pre-Columbian symbol representing the gods of the four cardinal directions: north, east, south and west. In Mayan belief when one of the crosses "spoke," they listened (the voice was actually that of a ventriloquist). Faith in the cross welded the Mayas together and they built a community headquarters called the Chana Santa Cruz (Small Holy Cross), complete with a High Priest and a Master Spy.

In 1857 the Talking Cross gave the word: it was time to attack. The Mayas knew the time was ripe: there was rivalry between Mérida and Campeche and squabbling among the whites. The followers of the Talking Cross marched against town after town and in three years had captured or killed 4,000 whites.

The Yucatán didn't come under the control of central government until Porfirio Díaz took power in 1876. He had the Talking Cross destroyed and exiled dissidents to eastern Yucatán. Once the Indians had been quelled, the economy picked up, thanks to henequen, a fibrous plant used to make rope. Between 1879 and 1916 production of henequen increased 10-fold.

The Yucatán today, with oil, sulfur and tourism, is hopeful. As in southern Veracruz and Tabasco, Campeche is filled with men drilling for oil which has changed the way of life.

Exploring the Yucatán: From **Ciudad del Carmen**, an uninteresting island that was once a pirate stronghold, the barely signposted and not very reliable coastal road proceeds to **Champotón**. It was there, in 1517, that Spanish blood was shed for the first time in Mexico, when an expedition under the command of Francisco Hernández de Córdoba fought the Mayas. Córdoba was wounded and died a short while afterwards in Havana.

An easy 62-km (40-mile) drive along the coast brings you to **Campeche** (population: 183,400), which has retained much of its colonial character. As the city developed, it proved to be an attractive target for pirates and after a particularly devastating attack in 1663, when the buccaneers of several nations joined forces in a ferocious onslaught, the Spanish authorities ringed the city with 2.5-meter (8-ft) thick walls – originally 2,536 meters (8,320 ft) long – turning it into a hexagonal stronghold guarded by eight towers. In 1717 an attack led by Alonso Felipe de Aranda against the pirates on Isla del Carmen finally wiped them out.

In the decades after Mexico's Independence in 1821, when shipping to Spain was reduced to a trickle, Campeche was little more than a backwater, and fishing became its main source of income. Its walls saved it yet again in the mid-1800s during the War of the Castes, when Maya insurgents took every town and city in the peninsula except Campeche and Mérida. However, the Indians' siege of Campeche would have undoubtedly ended in their victory had they not suddenly abandoned the attack when a plague of winged ants signaled that it was time for the Mayas to sow their crops.

By the end of the 19th century, the *Campechanos* decided they no longer needed bulwarks against attacks, and they began to dismantle them. They also wanted to install trolley lines to areas outside the fortifications However, the Sea Gate, razed in the 19th century, was rebuilt when its value as a tourist attraction was realized in the 1950s.

The **Santiago bulwark** is now the site of a botanical garden and the **Baluarte Soledad** houses some Mayan stelae covered with hieroglyphs which have been of key importance in the

Left, fine facade, Campeche. **Below**, on the bastions.

decipherment of the ancient language. Adjoining the **San Carlos bulwark**, and housing the city museum, is the **Congreso del Estado** (State Congress building: Campeche is a state capital), whose curious shape, reminiscent of a shelled oyster, has earned it the local nicknames UFO, the flying saucer, and the sandwich. The **San Juan bulwark** is still connected to a stretch of fortification containing the **Puerta de Tierra** (Land Gate), the former entrance of the city for travelers coming overland. You can walk along the top of the wall here. Nearby is the **Museo Regional de Arqueología** (Regional Archaeological Museum), which exhibits an extensive collection of Mayan pieces, scale models, clay figures and even the wooden contraption used by the Mayas to reshape the heads of their children in order to achieve the sharply sloping forehead which they considered a mark of beauty. There's a good overall view of the city from the **San Miguel fort**.

The old colonial plaza or **Parque Principal** is bound by Calles 8 and 10, running roughly parallel to the coast, and Calles 55 and 57 which are perpendicular to it. As in other Mexican towns, this plaza is the center of city life, where people congregate to enjoy the shade of the trees, listen to concerts and attend mass in the **Cathedral Concepción**, whose plain facade and tall twin towers are typical of the earliest churches on the peninsula. Its dome has curious flying buttresses. Note also the old **Los Portales** building, with its graceful facade and arcade.

One of the most dramatic buildings in the city is the former **Carvajal mansion**, at Calles 10 and 53, a luxurious design with undulating Moorish arches, striking black and white checked floors and sweeping staircase – attesting to the wealth that once flowed through the city. It now houses stores, offices and the **Museo de la Canción y del Compositor Campechano** (Museum of Campechan Song and Composers).

The oil boom of the 1970s brought new life to the city and the entire region, and the Mexican oil industry is still a major source of income. Famous both for its hospitality and its seafood, Campeche is a good place to shop for Panama hats, cattle horn jewelry that looks rather like tortoiseshell, and objects with nautical themes, such as ships in bottles.

Uxmal means "thrice built" in the Mayan language, but, in fact, archaeologists have found as many as five different construction periods represented at Uxmal. Building began in the classical period, in the 6th and 7th centuries. Some of the sapodilla-tree lintels from this period have endured through the years and are still in place (sapodilla wood is extremely tough and the climate is relatively dry).

The first building encountered after entering via the Visitors' Center is the almost oval-shaped **Pyramid of the Magician** or **Dwarf**. Its name is derived from the legend that it was built in a single night by the son of a witch, who had hatched him from an egg. In reality, the building consists of five superimposed pyramids built over a period of centuries. If you are fit enough, you can

Cathedral niche.

Uxmal, Yucatán

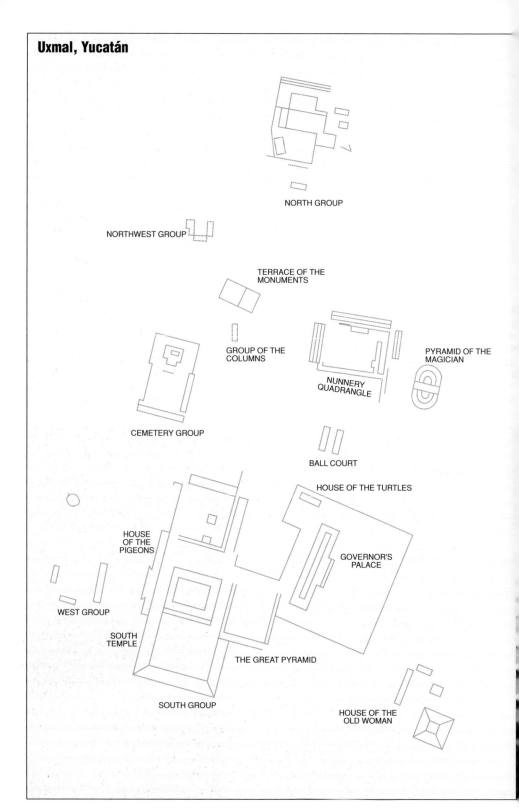

NORTH GROUP

NORTHWEST GROUP

TERRACE OF THE
MONUMENTS

GROUP OF THE
COLUMNS

PYRAMID OF THE
MAGICIAN

NUNNERY
QUADRANGLE

CEMETERY GROUP

BALL COURT

HOUSE OF THE TURTLES

HOUSE
OF THE
PIGEONS

GOVERNOR'S
PALACE

WEST GROUP

SOUTH
TEMPLE

THE GREAT PYRAMID

SOUTH GROUP

HOUSE OF THE
OLD WOMAN

go to the top of the pyramid, up very steep narrow steps which have a chain at the side for holding onto.

There are other points at Uxmal where you can get a sweeping sight of the ruins. Around the back of the pyramid a plaza formed by four buildings has been known since the 1600s as the **Nunnery Quadrangle** because it reminded its discoverer, Friar Diego López de Cogolludo, of the cloister of a Spanish convent. The use of these buildings isn't known but its 74 chambers suggest some sort of residence or school.

Inspired architect: Mexico's best known architect, Pedro Ramírez Vázquez, was inspired by this quadrangle when he designed the Museum of Anthropology in Mexico City. The entire complex is built on an elevated, man-made platform and typifies the characteristics of the Puuc architectural style, which is based on the Mayan hut, the *na*, with its smooth walls and high-peaked thatched roof. Notice the complexity of the stonework, which was created piece by piece following a master plan and then interlocked like a three-dimensional jigsaw puzzle. Note, too, the scores of Chaac masks, often artfully placed on corners, where the god's curved nose can be seen to best advantage silhouetted against the sky, seeming to pierce the clouds to bring life-giving rain.

It's no accident that the rain god has been given such a prominent place, since this part of the peninsula not only has no rivers but even *cenotes* (sinkholes), found just a few kilometers farther north, are absent. Here rain water was collected and stored in *chaltunes*, bottle-shaped cisterns carved out of stone and lined with thick coats of plaster.

On the way to the **Governor's Palace** you'll pass the remains of an unrestored ball court, with a stone ring still embedded in one wall, and will note a building on the right with a series of perforated triangular roof crests. This been dubbed the Dovecote but it may have been designed for astronomical sightings. The Palace, on a high platform which provides a panoramic view, is considered one of the masterpieces of all Mayan

An overview of Uxmal, featuring the Nunnery Quadrangle and the Pyramid of the Magician.

architecture, with its corbelled arches, delicate proportions and light and shadow created by its sculptured decoration, many doors, corbelled arches and gentle recesses. Its name may not be so far off, since the building certainly befits a ruler. The facade of the palace has some 20,000 hand-carved stones fitted in geometric friezes. The Mayan expert Sylvanus Morley called this palace "the most magnificent, the most spectacular single building in all pre-Columbian America."

Many of the tours visiting Uxmal also take in Kabáh, Sayil (noted for its 9th-century palace) and Labná.

At **Kabáh** you can view the Temple of the Masks, whose facade is covered with inlaid stonework representing masks or deities. The Arch of Kabáh, which has been compared to a Roman triumphal arch, once marked the start of a processional route leading to the ceremonial center of Uxmal. Not far away are the villages of **Ticul**, which has hats, footwear, ceramics and jewelry for sale, and **Mani**, with its huge church and convent, where Bishop Landa burned hundreds of priceless Mayan writings, denouncing them as "lies of the devil."

Mérida once liked to think of itself as the "Paris of the New World." At the turn of the century, profits from the sale of henequen prompted the city to claim more millionaires per capita than any other place. They built fabulous homes in Mérida but spent much of their time in Paris or New York.

Throughout the colonial period, Mérida was by far the most important city in the province. As the seat of civil and religious authority, it boasted a fine cathedral, a monastery and civic buildings. The Spaniards lived in the center of town, while the Indians and *mestizos* lived in the segregated areas outside. It was the most aristocratic of towns, proud of its pure Spanish blood.

Once enclosed by walls, Mérida's downtown area is compact, its narrow streets and closely packed buildings defined by the limited space available within the fortifications. Two Moorish-style gates, **La Ermita** and **Arco de San Juan**, remain out of 13 such gates erected in the 17th century. It is an excellent town for a self-guided walking tour; many sights are near to each other and the streets are laid out on a grid plan (even-numbered streets run north–south, odd-numbered east–west).

Horse and buggy: You might prefer to sightsee in one of the horse-drawn carriages called *calesas*, which can be hired downtown; be sure to agree on a route and price with the driver before setting off. A popular ride to take is along the chic, shaded **Paseo de Montejo** to see some of the old mansions, noting the monuments along the way. One of these commemorates Felipe Carrillo Puerto, called the Red Governor, who was assassinated by his political enemies not for falling scandalously in love with an American journalist (which he also did) but because of social reforms he tried to introduce in the 1920s to improve the lives of Indians. Tour buses along the Paseo stop at the **Monumento a la Patria** (Monument to the Nation) created by Colombian sculptor Romulo

Nunnery Quadrange.

Rozo in 1946 and imaginatively depicting the history of Mexico.

The laurel-shaded **Plaza de Independencia** or Zócalo was the site of a great Mayan temple and pyramid whose remains contributed to the Franciscan **Church of the Tercera Orden**. Inside this church a panoramic painting depicts a formal visit made by Tutul Xiu, the Mayan ruler of Mani, to the conquistador Montejo. The tall twin towers are topped by a shingle design that coils under the crosses. One local guide maintains this embellishment was introduced by the Indian stonemasons and is intended to symbolize the Mayan god Kukulcán, the plumed serpent. If that is so, the god occupies the place of honor he might have held in a temple at the summit of a pyramid.

The **Casa de Montejo** on the Zócalo was built in the mid 1500s by Francisco de Montejo el Mozo and was the home of successive generations of his family until the 1980s when it was taken over by Banamex. The elaborate facade depicts two conquistadors symbolically standing on the heads of the defeated Indians. Each window bears the coat of arms of a branch of the Montejo family.

In the **Palacio del Gobierno** (government building) are impressive paintings by Fernando Castro Pachecho depicting the history of Yucatán, while historic photographs can be inspected in the **Museo de la Ciudad**, housed in the former church of San Juan de Dios at the corner of Calle 58.

There's lots of good shopping in Mérida: *guayabera* shorts for men, embroidered *huipil* blouses for women, panama hats, footwear and hammocks. The latter are most reasonably-priced at the **Mercado Municipal**, the city market. Check out the FONART store, on Calle 63, for well-made arts and crafts.

Before leaving Mérida for Chichén-Itzá and points east, take a quick trip north if you can. The port of **Progreso** lies a few kilometers away. Just off the road is the site of **Dzibilchaltún**, one of the oldest continuously occupied settlements in the Americas. People have lived here since 1500 BC. The best

Mexican fast food.

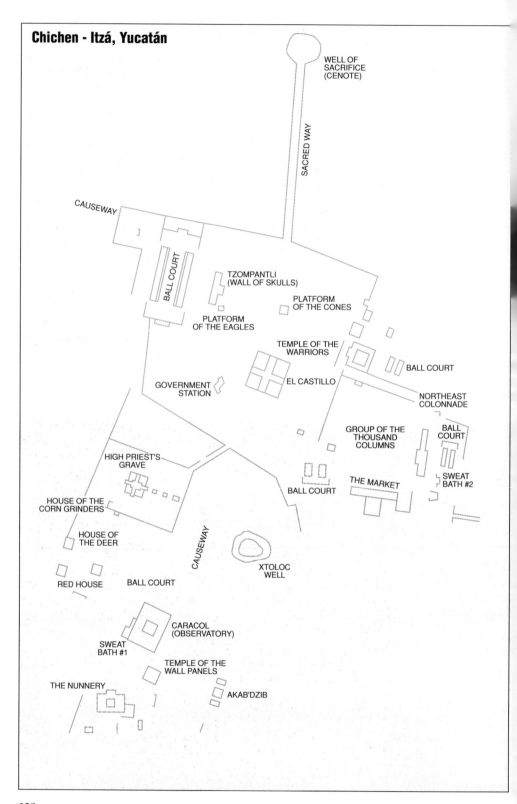

Chichen - Itzá, Yucatán

WELL OF SACRIFICE (CENOTE)

SACRED WAY

CAUSEWAY

BALL COURT

TZOMPANTLI (WALL OF SKULLS)

PLATFORM OF THE CONES

PLATFORM OF THE EAGLES

TEMPLE OF THE WARRIORS

GOVERNMENT STATION

EL CASTILLO

BALL COURT

NORTHEAST COLONNADE

GROUP OF THE THOUSAND COLUMNS

BALL COURT

HIGH PRIEST'S GRAVE

HOUSE OF THE CORN GRINDERS

BALL COURT

THE MARKET

SWEAT BATH #2

HOUSE OF THE DEER

CAUSEWAY

RED HOUSE

BALL COURT

XTOLOC WELL

CARACOL (OBSERVATORY)

SWEAT BATH #1

TEMPLE OF THE WALL PANELS

THE NUNNERY

AKAB'DZIB

known structure is the **Temple of the Seven Dolls**, named for the figurines found there. Some of the buildings have elaborate facade ornamentation. You can also have a look at (and then take a dip in) the big **Xlaca cenote** (ceremonial well), from which thousands of art objects have been retrieved.

Chichén-Itzá is located 120 km (75 miles) – less than two hours' drive – east of Mérida. One of Mexico's chief sights, it's a place that should be seen. Try to get there early although if you're on a tour you won't have much choice. There are several hotels within walking distance of the site: the Hotel Mayaland, close to the eastern entrance (near the Observatory), is the oldest and most gracious; **Hotel Hacienda Chichén** was formerly the *hacienda* purchased by Edward H. Thompson, the American consul who excavated the Chichén-Itzá *cenote*; and the Hotel Villa Arqueológica, where you can enjoy the usual Club Med amenities. Staying overnight has advantages, the main one being that you can then visit the ruins early in the morning or late in the afternoon, avoiding the midday heat and tourist rush.

Built by Toltecs: Chichén-Itzá is built on a grand scale. There is little evidence of classical Mayan refinements, for the architects were Toltecs who arrived in the Yucatán in the late 10th century. They left behind their version of warriors, eagles and plumed serpents and they introduced the worship of Quetzalcóatl (called Kukulkán in Mayan). Chichén-Itzá was their capital.

Dominating the site is the pyramid the Spaniards called **El Castillo**, which was actually the Temple to Kukulcán. The pyramid incorporates key measurements of time in its structure: its four staircases have 91 steps each and, including the platform at the top, total 365, the number of days in a year; each side has 52 panels, representing the 52-year cosmic cycle, the point at which their two calendars, the religious and the secular, coincided and when, they believed, time ended and began anew.

At the spring equinox (March 21) thousands come to Chichén-Itzá to wit-

Chichén-Itzá's main pyramid.

ness the astonishing play of sunlight on the ballustrade of the northern staircase. The effect created is that of a living serpent creeping down to the foot of the pyramid, where it slithers into the ground. The Mayan priests claimed this phenomenon was Kukulcán's signal that it was time for the citizens to sow the crops. In contrast, at the fall equinox (September 21) the "snake" appears to ascend the pyramid, indicating the time for the crops to be harvested.

Next to the pyramid is the **Temple of the Warriors**. Hundreds of columns representing plumed warriors were used to hold up the roof. On top of the stairway, between two massive stone snakes, reclines what may be the most photographed statue in the Americas. He is the *chacmool* (the word comes from the Mayan words for "claw" and "red"); his lap once held a receptacle for receiving the hearts of sacrificial victims.

The *cenote* is a short walk away. Bones of children under the age of 12 have been recovered from the well. Its dark waters were first investigated between 1903–07, by US consul Edward Thompson, under the sponsorship of Harvard University's Peabody Museum. He found skeletons and precious objects of jade and gold, obviously brought here from a great distance, since neither gold nor jade was found in the peninsula. These natural sinkholes, which dot the landscape of the northern Yucatán lowlands, were the only source of water, and some, such as this one, were used for ritual purposes, with human sacrifices thrown to the rain god Chaac.

The Mayans were great observers of the heavens and the **Observatory**, in the older (southern) part of the city, is particularly fascinating because of its resemblance to modern observatories (the main difference being that there were no telescopes here but painstaking calculations, based on exact observations over a long period of time).

One of the most intriguing structures here is the restored **Ball Court**, the largest and best preserved anywhere in Mesoamerica. The ritual game played here, on a court longer than a football

The Ball Court.

field, is still somewhat mysterious. What is known for sure is that two well-padded teams propelled a heavy rubber ball around without using their hands or feet, bouncing it off their hips and shoulders and through one of the rings on each side. The reliefs at the end of the field, which include a headless kneeling figure with writhing snakes symbolizing blood coming out of his neck, have led some experts to suppose that the losing team was decapitated.

East of Chichén-Itzá is **Valladolid** which, in the middle of the 19th century, before it was nearly wiped out by the Indian insurgents in the War of the Castes, had almost the same population as Mérida. Because of its proximity to Chichén-Itzá and the lower prices that generally prevail, some people prefer to stay here than in Chichén-Itzá. The town's main architectural sights are the **Cathedral de San Servacio**, the **San Bernardino de Siena convent** and the **Palacio Municipal**. Check out the **Zací cenote** if you are interested in seeing a sinkhole which has a cave tucked into its steep sides (Calle 36 between Calles 37 and 39).

Pink flamingos: North of Valladolid, on the coast on Highway 295, is **Río Lagartos**. The town's chief attractions are the thousands of pink flamingos that gather here. There is an inexpensive hotel in town and good tarpon fishing close by.

From Valladolid, most travelers head for the beaches of Quintana Roo. Following Highway 180, you reach the Caribbean coast at **Puerto Juárez**, close to Cancún. From near Puerto Juárez, you can take a ferry 13 km (8 miles) across the water to **Isla Mujeres**, so called because many female figurines were found there by the Spaniards (*mujer* is Spanish for woman). Two roads run the length of the 8-km (5-mile) long island, which is less than 1 km (½ mile) wide in some places. You can hire a boat to visit the turtle pens or to take you to an underwater coral garden called **El Garrafon** (the Jug) and to **El Dormitorio** (the Dormitory), a pirate ship graveyard under 10 meters (30 ft) of

Head for the beach from Valladolid.

clear water. A little farther along is **Contoy island**, a bird sanctuary.

Virtually every current architectural concept of high-rise luxury can be found among the 50 or so hotels lining the 23-km (14-mile) long hotel zone of **Cancún**, from the verdant lobby of the Meliá Cancún, with its lush tropical atmosphere, to the cosmopolitan ambience of the Ritz Carlton and everything in between: domed Mexican neo-colonial complexes and a number of buildings clearly inspired by the sloping walls of Mayan pyramids. Luxury is at your beck and call: gourmet meals, bright nightlife, drinks on the beach while lazing under the shade of a thatched *palapa* shelter. Protected from crashing waves by coral reefs, Cancún's turquoise sea and powdery white beaches (that never get unbearably hot) are legendary. In fact, Cancún is the Mayan word for "pot of gold."

Computer chosen city: It was during the administration of President Luis Echeverría (1968–76) that construction began in Cancún after a computer study

determined that the best site in the nation for creating a new, world-class resort was this narrow sandstrip enclosing a brackish lagoon on the Yucatán Peninsula. Unlike the port city of Acapulco, the reigning resort at the time but which had extensive poor areas, Cancún was created with complete infrastructure for everyone, including modern housing for personnel providing services in the hotel zone, from managers to maids. The population is now around 350,000. The first hotels opened in 1972 and the building boom has gone on ever since, with 200,000 rooms planned by the end of the 1990s.

For getting around Cancún, you can drive, take a tour, rent a car, take a taxi (be sure to agree on the price before setting out) or go by local bus (look for those with signs saying *Hoteles* or *Turismo*). There are shops and restaurants in the business section of downtown Cancún, bisected by **Avenida Tulúm** running north–south between Monumento Historía del Mexico and Monumento Dialago Norte-Sur. Most

Having fun at Cancún.

of the malls, however, are in the hotel zone along **Boulevard Kukulcán**. Plaza Caracol has 200 shops, restaurants, cafés; while upscale Plaza Kukulcán, adorned with a frieze inspired by Mayan hieroglyphs, is the newest mall offering 350 possibilities for buying goods. For Mexican arts and crafts, check out Plaza La Fiesta and Plaza Mayfair; for shopping in a setting with a Mayan flavor, go to Plaza Flamingo.

Be sure to take a tour of the impressive **Centro de Convenciones** (Convention Center), where the **museum** has Mayan artifacts, including examples of deformed Mayan skulls.

The coastal highway running south has been tagged "the Cancun-Tulum corridor." It runs past newly developed beach resorts almost all the way to Chetumal, beginning with **Puerto Morelos**, from which the car ferry runs to Cozumel, and then, 32 km (20 miles) farther, at the end of a unpaved road running through a banana grove, idyllic **Puerta Bete**.

From **Playa del Carmen** you can take the passenger ferry to **Cozumel**, 19 km (12 miles) offshore. Cozumel, the "Island of the Swallows," was a sacred place to the Mayas, who came to pay tribute to the moon goddess, Ixchel. Women would travel here seeking her divine intervention in matters of love and fertility. Later, it was an important trading port and a haunt of pirates. It boasts some of the clearest water in the world, with visibility often reaching some 70 meters (200 ft) deep. **Palancar reef**, where Jacques Costeau filmed in the 1960s, is a mecca for divers. The island's tiny capital, **San Miguel**, has an attractive museum and a score of modest places to stay, although many visitors just come for the day.

About 8 km (5 miles) south of town is the **Chankanab National Park**, where you can admire reproductions of Mayan buildings set in a botanical garden and observe the marine life in the lagoon.

Back on the mainland the coastal highway heads past **Xcaret**, a privately owned eco-archaeological park where you can don a mask and fins to explore

Mayan remains at Cancún.

an underground river system; **Akumal**, famous for its turtle sanctuary; and **Xel-Ha** whose lagoon is like a big, natural aquarium (also popular with divers).

More Mayan ruins can be seen at **Tulúm**, one of the few enclosed settlements the Mayans built and virtually the only one with such an extensive boundary still standing. Dating from after 900 AD, when the main Mayan ceremonial/urban centers were abandoned, it was a sort of provincial outpost, considered by some to have been a fortress protecting sea trade routes, one in a series of coastal strongholds and undoubtedly a port from which to channel goods inland. At its height prior to the Spanish Conquest, it is estimated to have had a population of around 600, possibly with the priestly and noble classes resident within its walls and the rest of the population outside.

Lantern beams: It has been suggested that **El Castillo** (the Castle), the most imposing building and the tallest in the complex, might have been a lighthouse. Michael Creamer, funded by the National Geographic Society to study its function, came to the conclusion that it was a navigational station. "We placed a lantern on shelves behind each of two windows located high on the face of the Castillo. At sea where the two beams can be seen at the same time, there's a natural opening in the reef." If this is so, then it was still a functioning beacon when the Spanish arrived, since some conquistadors wrote that they could clearly see the light of a flame coming from the building as they sailed by.

Extending over 6 hectares (16 acres), several buildings merit special attention. The **Temple of Frescoes** is a two-story structure with columns on the bottom level and a much smaller room on top. Look between the columns to see the painting full of human figures in the style of the distant highlands and probably due to Toltec influence, after they took over Chichén-Itzá. Note the masks extending around the corners of the facade, perhaps representing the rain god Chaac. The **Temple of the Descending God** is decorated with a relief which

A two-headed turtle.

may have represented the Mayan bee god Ab Muxen Cab.

Forty kilometers (25 miles) away is **Cobá**, hub of the Mayans' system of roads *(sacbeob* in Mayan). The longest of these roads ran over 100 km (60 miles) straight through the jungle and swamp to Yaxuná near Chichén-Itzá. Cobá was once a trade settlements with 50,000 inhabitants. There is a pyramid and a ball court. The city was set in a five-lake area with sacred causeways connecting it to outlying settlements.

Near the entrance, between two lakes is the 24-meter (80-ft) **Iglesia Pyramid**, which has nine terraces with rounded corners topped by a Toltec-looking temple. Depending on your stamina, you might want to climb to the top for a view of the site or wait until you reach the taller **El Castillo Pyramid** in the Nohoch Mul group, 2½ km (1½ miles) east on the path.

Eric Thompson, who was among the archaeologists that first mapped out Cobá in the 1920s, had this to say about the route to Yaxuná: "[The road] aver-

Shooting the wildlife.

ages thirty-two feet in width. For the greater part of its length it is a little over two feet high, but in crossing swampy depressions, its height increases, in one case slightly more than eight feet. Walls of roughly dressed stones form the sides; large boulders topped with smaller stones laid in cement compose the bed, and the surface, now badly disintegrated, was of cement and stucco." This *sacbé* was wider than the Great Wall of China, which was designed to permit several horsemen to ride abreast."

Footpaths lead through the jungle connecting the 6,000 structures that have been identified in Cobá. They extend over 77 sq. km (30 sq. miles), although few have been restored. They're marked, but as the dense vegetation cuts off the view from one group of buildings to another at ground level and distances between them are long, you'll need patience and a map to explore.

South of Tulúm the vast **Sian Ka'an Biosphere Reserve** sprawling along the coast protects hundreds of species of animal life under the auspices of UNESCO, which is dedicated to saving the region from development as well as providing work for local people. At the fishing village of **Punta Allen**, on the tip of a slender peninsula, you can sleep in a hammock on the beach.

After passing through **Felipe Carillo Puerto**, Highway 307 skirts the length of lovely **Laguna Bacalar** (the lakeside town has an 18th-century fortress), beyond which is the turnoff east to **Chetumal** (pop: 120,000), an ancient port which is the jumping off point for visitors to Belize. From here, Highway 186 heads west across the peninsula through thick jungle to **Escarcega**, where Highway 261 heads north to Champotón and Campeche. On the way are some notable Mayan ruins, notably at **Kohunlich** (on a side road out of Francisco Villa), then at **Becan** and **Xpuhil** north of the highway and **Chicanna** and **Rio Bec** to the south. Although interest in these jungle sites is growing they are still unspoiled, but gas stations and other facilities are in short supply. There is a small hotel and several cafes at Escarcega.

INSIGHT GUIDES
TRAVEL TIPS

So, you're getting away from it all.

Just make sure you can get back.

AT&T Access Numbers
Dial the number of the country you're in to reach AT&T.

ANGUILLA	1-800-872-2881	**CHILE**	**00◇-0312**	HONDURAS†	123
ANTIGUA (Public Card Phones)	#1	**COLOMBIA**	**980-11-0010**	JAMAICA††	0-800-872-2881
ARGENTINA◆	001-800-200-1111	*COSTA RICA	114	MEXICO◇◇◇	95-800-462-4240
BAHAMAS	**1-800-872-2881**	**CURACAO**	**001-800-872-2881**	MONTSERRAT†	1-800-872-2881
BARBADOS†	1-800-872-2881	DOMINICA	1-800-872-2881	**NICARAGUA**	**174**
BELIZE◆	555	DOMINICAN REP.††	11-22	PANAMA	109
BERMUDA†	1-800-872-2881	ECUADOR†	119	PARAGUAY†	0081-800
*BOLIVIA	0-800-1112	*EL SALVADOR	190	ST. KITTS/NEVIS	1-800-872-2881
BONAIRE	**001-800-872-2881**	GRENADA†	1-800-872-2881	**ST. MAARTEN**	**001-800-872-2881**
BRAZIL	**000-8010**	*GUATEMALA	190	**SURINAME**	**156**
BRITISH V. I.	1-800-872-2881	***GUYANA††**	**165**	URUGUAY	00-0410
CAYMAN ISLANDS	1-800-872-2881	HAITI†	001-800-972-2883	*VENEZUELA	80-011-120

Countries in bold face permit country-to-country calling in addition to calls to the U.S. **World Connect**℠ prices consist of **USADirect**° rates plus an additional charge based on the country you are calling. Collect calling available to the U.S. only. *Public phones require deposit of coin or phone card. ◇ Await second dial tone. †May not be available from every phone. ††Collect calling only. ◆ Not available from public phones. ◇◇◇ When calling from public phones, use phones marked "Ladatel" ©1994 AT&T.

Here's a travel tip that will make it easy to call back to the States. Dial the access number for the country you're in to get English-speaking AT&T operators or voice prompts. Minimize hotel telephone surcharges too.

If all the countries you're visiting aren't listed above, call **1 800 241-5555** for a free wallet card with all AT&T access numbers. Easy international calling from AT&T. **TrueWorld Connections.**

AT&T

TRAVEL TIPS

GETTING ACQUAINTED

THE PLACE

Time Zones

Most of Mexico is on Central Standard Time year-round. The northern Pacific coast states of Sonora, Sinaloa and Nayarit, along with Baja California Sur, are on Mountain Standard Time year-round. Baja California Norte is on Pacific Standard Time, with a seasonal change to Daylight Savings Time – the same as the state of California north of the border.

Central Standard Time = GMT –6 hours
Mountain Standard Time = GMT –7 hours
Pacific Standard Time = GMT –8 hours.

Climate

Mexico City, Guadalajara and many other cities of Mexico lie in the central plateau where the climate is temperate year-round. High altitude (1,545 meters/5,069 feet for Guadalajara, and 2,240 meters/7,349 feet for Mexico City) keeps these cities from becoming really hot, even at midsummer.

In an average year, **Mexico City**'s highest temperature will be around 31°C (88°F); **Guadalajara**'s around 35°C (95°F). In Mexico City, expect temperatures in the upper 20s°C (low 80s°F) in April and May, in the low 20s°C (70s°F) in the summer and fall, and in the upper 10s°C (60s°F) to low 20s°C (70s°F) in the winter. Summer is the rainy season – in July and August, Mexico City has rain nearly every day – but usually the rain lasts only for a couple of afternoon hours. It is cool at night: in winter the temperature may fall as low as 0°C (32°F) in early morning and at night.

In southern Mexico and the **Yucatán** peninsula, the climate varies: some areas are dry, others have nearly 5 meters (about 16 feet) of rainfall a year. In **Oaxaca** which is over 1,500 meters (about 5,000 feet) high the nighttime temperature in winter can fall to below 0°C (32°F) but in summer, at midday, it can rise to nearly 38°C (100°F). On the peninsula, **Merida**'s temperature can rise as high as 42.2°C (108°F); **Cozumel**'s maximum is scarcely above 32°C (90°F), because it is on the coast. Anywhere in the peninsula, expect daily temperatures in the upper 20s°C (low 80s°F) year-round; nighttime temperatures seldom go below 16°C (60 °F).

Acapulco has daily highs of 27°C (80°F)–32°C (90°F) year-round, seldom falling much below 21°C

(70°F) at night. As in most of Mexico, the rainy season is summer and early fall; there is little rain in the winter. Pacific breezes keep things comfortable. Further north along the Pacific coast, the temperature is somewhat cooler at night, but otherwise similar. In an average year, the maximum temperature experienced by **Mazatlan** or **Puerto Vallarta** will be in the mid-30s°C (mid-90s°F). North of Mazatlan, the coast becomes a desert, and summer weather is hotter. In **Guaymas,** the maximum temperature in an average year is 44°C (112°F). Typical summer temperatures would be in the upper 20s°C (80s°F)–30s°C (90s°F). The winter is temperate, usually in the 20s°C (70s°F) in the daytime.

Baja has very low annual rainfall, with what rain there is falling in the late fall and winter months. Temperatures are more comfortable where the land is cooled by sea breezes, on the southern tip of the peninsula and along the Pacific coast. In an average year Ensenada's temperature will not rise above 35°C (95°F); but San Felipe, on the Gulf of California, may go up to 48°C (118°F). The desert is cold at night.

Northern Mexico is largely desert. The days are very hot in summer – well over 38°C (100°F) – except up in the mountains. It is cold in winter, when the temperature may drop below freezing at night. As you go east toward Monterrey, the climate is more moderate and less dry, but still very hot in summer.

The People

*M*ost travelers like to leave a good impression on the country they are visiting. One way is to be polite. Asking for directions in the street, for example, might be prefaced by a simple *buenas tardes* or *por favor*. You can improve the impression you make by trying to speak Spanish and shaking hands frequently. Mexicans shake hands not only when first introduced, but whenever they meet again, and when they take leave of one another.

A few warnings about the Mexican version of politeness: Mexicans believe it is less rude to accept an unwanted invitation, and fail to appear, than to refuse it. Don't be too offended by being stood up in this way. Most travelers needn't be warned that Mexicans are not always punctual. As in any country, some remarks are strictly for politeness and should not be taken literally. When you ask a Mexican where he is from, he will often give the name of the town or the address, followed by "*donde tiene su casa*" ("where your home is"), implying that "my home is your home." Don't take him up on this; he is only being polite. Unless, of course, he specifically invites you over.

A Wise Man Never Thinks How Far He's Come. He Thinks How Far He Can Still Travel.

REMY **XO** BECAUSE LIFE IS WHAT YOU MAKE IT

FOR THOSE
WITH MORE THAN
A PASSING INTEREST
IN TIME...

Before you put your name down for a Patek Philippe watch *fig. 1*, there are a few basic things you might like to know, without knowing exactly whom to ask. In addressing such issues as accuracy, reliability and value for money, we would like to demonstrate why the watch we will make for you will be quite unlike any other watch currently produced.

"Punctuality", Louis XVIII was fond of saying, "is the politeness of kings."

We believe that in the matter of punctuality, we can rise to the occasion by making you a mechanical timepiece that will keep its rendezvous with the Gregorian calendar at the end of every century, omitting the leap-years in 2100, 2200 and 2300 and recording them in 2000 and 2400 *fig. 2*. Nevertheless, such a watch does need the occasional adjustment. Every 3333 years and 122 days you should remember to set it forward one day to the true time of the celestial clock. We suspect, however, that you are simply content to observe the politeness of kings. Be assured, therefore, that when you order your watch, we will be exploring for you the physical—if not the metaphysical— limits of precision.

Does everything have to depend on how much?

Consider, if you will, the motives of collectors who set record prices at auction to acquire a Patek Philippe. They may be paying for rarity, for looks or for micromechanical ingenuity. But we believe that behind each $500,000-plus

bid is the conviction that a Patek Philippe, even if 50 years old or older, can be expected to work perfectly for future generations.

In case your ambitions to own a Patek Philippe are somewhat discouraged by the scale of the sacrifice involved, may we hasten to point out that the watch we will make for you today will certainly be a technical improvement on the Pateks bought at auction? In keeping with our tradition of inventing new mechanical solutions for greater reliability and better time-keeping, we will bring to your watch innovations *fig. 3* inconceivable to our watchmakers who created the supreme wristwatches of 50 years ago *fig. 4*. At the same time, we will of course do our utmost to avoid placing undue strain on your financial resources.

Can it really be mine?

May we turn your thoughts to the day you take delivery of your watch? Sealed within its case is your watchmaker's tribute to the mysterious process of time. He has decorated each wheel with a chamfer carved into its hub and polished into a shining circle. Delicate ribbing flows over the plates and bridges of gold and rare alloys. Millimetric surfaces are bevelled and burnished to exactitudes measured in microns. Rubies are transformed into jewels that triumph over friction. And after many months—or even years—of work, your watchmaker stamps a small badge into the mainbridge of your watch. The Geneva Seal—the highest possible attestation of fine watchmaking *fig. 5*.

Looks that speak of inner grace *fig. 6.*

When you order your watch, you will no doubt like its outward appearance to reflect the harmony and elegance of the movement within. You may therefore find it helpful to know that we are uniquely able to cater for any special decorative needs you might like to express. For example, our engravers will delight in conjuring a subtle play of light and shadow on the gold case-back of one of our rare pocket-watches *fig. 7*. If you bring us your favourite picture, our enamellers will reproduce it in a brilliant miniature of hair-breadth detail *fig. 8*. The perfect execution of a double hobnail pattern on the bezel of a wristwatch is the pride of our casemakers and the satisfaction of our designers, while our chainsmiths will weave for you a rich brocade in gold *figs. 9 & 10*. May we also recommend the artistry of our goldsmiths and the experience of our lapidaries in the selection and setting of the finest gemstones? *figs. 11 & 12*.

How to enjoy your watch before you own it.

As you will appreciate, the very nature of our watches imposes a limit on the number we can make available. (The four Calibre 89 time-pieces we are now making will take up to nine years to complete). We cannot therefore promise instant gratification, but while you look forward to the day on which you take delivery of your Patek Philippe *fig. 13*, you will have the pleasure of reflecting that time is a universal and everlasting commodity, freely available to be enjoyed by all.

Should you require information on any particular Patek Philippe watch, or even on watchmaking in general, we would be delighted to reply to your letter of enquiry. And if you send u

fig. 1: *The classic face of Patek Philippe.*

fig. 4: *Complicated wristwatches circa 1930 (left) and 1990. The golden age of watchmaking will always be with us.*

fig. 6: *Your pleasure in owning a Patek Philippe is the purpose of those who made it for you.*

fig. 9: *Harmony of design is executed in a work of simplicity and perfection in a lady's Calatrava wristwatch.*

fig. 10: *The chainsmith's hands impart strength and delicacy to a tracery of gold.*

fig. 5: *The Geneva Seal is awarded only to watches which achieve the standards of horological purity laid down in the laws of Geneva. These rules define the supreme quality of watchmaking.*

fig. 7: *Arabesques come to life on a gold case-back.*

fig. 11: *Circles in gold: symbols of perfection in the making.*

fig. 2: *One of the 33 complications of the Calibre 89 astronomical clock-watch is a satellite wheel that completes one revolution every 400 years.*

fig. 8: *An artist working six hours a day takes about four months to complete a miniature in enamel on the case of a pocket-watch.*

fig. 12: *The test of a master lapidary is his ability to express the splendour of precious gemstones.*

fig. 3: *Recognized as the most advanced mechanical regulating device to date, Patek Philippe's Gyromax balance wheel demonstrates the equivalence of simplicity and precision.*

PATEK PHILIPPE
GENEVE
fig. 13: *The discreet sign of those who value their time.*

your card marked "book catalogue" we shall post you a catalogue of our publications. Patek Philippe, 41 rue du Rhône, 1204 Geneva, Switzerland, Tel. +41 22/310 03 66.

Swatch. The others just watch.

seahorse/fall winter 94-95

shockproof
splashproof
priceproof
boreproof
swiss made

swatch+
SCUBA 200

PLANNING THE TRIP

Clothing

A trip to Mexico requires clothing appropriate to the climate and social environment. Styles of acceptable dress differ in the city, in the country and in resort areas. Mexico's climate is diverse, and you should be at least minimally prepared for the weather of every area you pass through (see *Climate*). Keep in mind the time of year, and the activities planned: you may be absolutely certain that it is always hot in Baja, but if you go camping there in mid-winter you will discover that the nights are quite cold. Even visitors not camping out should take a woollen sweater to mountain and desert areas. May–October is the rainy season in much of Mexico, and though you can work around it – plan indoor activities for the afternoon when the rain usually comes – you should bring a folding umbrella and perhaps a lightweight raincoat.

In cities, except the resorts, dress tends to be rather formal. It's a good idea for a man to bring at least one jacket and tie; the more elegant restaurants won't admit you without them. For Mexico City vacations, depending on your choice of activities, you may want to bring a suit, a sports-jacket with a couple of pairs of slacks, and a tie or two. If you never go anywhere at home in a suit, don't bring one to Mexico, but do bring slacks and sports shirts. The same principle holds for women. Elegant restaurants will expect you to dress rather formally; but if you won't be going to such places you needn't bring fancy clothes. Mexican women in cities tend to dress up more than women in the US and some other countries, but you don't have to imitate them. Pants worn by women are perfectly acceptable. Permanent-press or knit dresses and skirts are comfortable in hot weather and easy to pack. Women traveling alone should keep in mind that many Mexican men have unreasonable expectations about foreign women (i.e. that they are likely to be sexually promiscuous). Of course, you have the right to wear what you like, but if you compromise by trying to avoid clothing that might be taken to be sexually provocative, you will save yourself many annoyances.

The same standards of decency are applied by Mexicans in the country and in provincial towns. Shorts and very casual clothes are fairly widely seen; but going to public places shirtless or in bathing suits is frowned upon and should be avoided, as well as, in the case of women, wearing outrageously provocative apparel. You are not very likely to require formal dress, but you still need something in your wardrobe besides jeans. Baggy khakis are cooler than jeans, and easier to hike in. Long-sleeved shirts help prevent mosquito bites and sunburn, though you'll also need insect repellent and sunscreen. A hat will also help keep off the sun. A decade ago, any woman traveling in Mexico needed a hat or scarf (or at least a handkerchief) to cover her head when visiting churches; now this is considered unnecessary. However, your best approach will always be to observe what the people around you are wearing. Remote areas are often conservative, and conservative people often feel most comfortable with people who are not too conspicuous. Appearing bizarre to the local people will gain you nothing, except perhaps the suspicions of the police and put you and your country in a bad light in the eyes of the local people.

Standards are quite different in resort areas: Acapulco, Ixtapa/Zihuatanejo, Puerto Vallarta, Mazatlan, Cozumel, Cancún, and the beach towns of Baja frequented by Californian surfers. Shorts and bathing suits are acceptable on the street in these areas, even in restaurants (except the more formal ones). Dress tends to be high style in many resorts. Rarely will a man feel the need for a suit and tie; bring or buy a *guayabera* shirt, which you can wear over slacks to look more dressed up while staying cool and comfortable. Women often choose long, loose, embroidered dresses which are also cool and comfortable. No matter where you plan to travel in Mexico, bring a pair of comfortable walking shoes that are already broken in.

Electricity

Sixty-cycle alternating current is standard in Mexico, as in the US. There are occasional power shortages, and the current may be weak or fluctuating, especially in remote areas. Any electric appliance you bring should have an extension cord as well so that you will be able to use it conveniently. It would be wise to carry a small flashlight for those occasions when there is a blackout. This will also come in handy when you are visiting some of the archaeological sites.

Photography

Each traveler is permitted to bring into Mexico one ordinary camera and one portable movie camera, with 12 rolls of film for each. These restrictions are intended to prevent people from importing cameras or film for resale; both cameras and film are expensive in Mexico. As long as the quantity of film you are bringing in is not unreasonable, and there is no evidence that you intend to resell it, you will probably be allowed to bring in as much as you will need. Film, as well as batteries for your camera, are especially expensive in hotel and resort shops. Note that tripods and flashes are not permitted in museums, archaeological zones, or colonial monuments without a special permit.

You can have any type of film processed in Mexico. It's best to have your films developed in Mexico City or one of the larger cities. If you take it there yourself, processing takes a few days; if it is sent from elsewhere in Mexico, it can take over 10 days. There are places where you can have films developed in just a few hours. Unless you are spending a lot of time in the country, or just can't wait to see your shots, and you're in Mexico City or one of the larger cities, take your film home to have it processed. Meanwhile, try to keep it cool. Cars get very hot, and the glove compartment is an especially bad place for film. Also beware of airport X-ray inspections: one passage through the machine may not ruin your film; but several inspections might do so. Ask to have your camera and film inspected by hand.

Photographing Indians can be difficult. You can offer to pay them, but chances are that your shots will look posed. If you have a telephoto lens, you may be able to get good pictures without offending anyone. You can also try using a wide-angle lens, shooting from waist level without looking through the viewfinder. However, none of these strategies will get you the great photographs you want. The best way is to spend time with the people until you and your camera become part of the scenery. Remember to be friendly, polite and respectful.

MAPS

Maps are not sold in gas stations in Mexico; but some of the bigger supermarkets, like Sumesa, as well as Sanborn's, now stock good roadmaps (*Guiá Roji*). Try a map specialty store, if you live in a big city, or write to one or more of the following, asking for a price list of maps covering the area of your intended trip:

Mexican Government Tourism Office, 405 Park Avenue, New York, NY 10022.
Guiá Roji, SA, Gob. José Morán No. 31, San Miguel Chapultepec, Mexico City 1, Mexico. (Publishers of a road atlas, the *Atlas Turístico de Carreteras*, and an extremely detailed map of Mexico City.)
American Map Company, 1926 Broadway, New York, NY 10023. US distributors for the *Patria* series of maps which are also available from Librería Patria, SA, at Cinco de Mayo No. 43, Mexico City, Mexico.

Patria maps are available for each state, and they are excellent driving maps; but their Mexico City map is not as easy for foreign travelers to understand as either the *Guía Roji* or the DETENAL map.

If you lack the time or inclination to attempt mail-order, bookstores in large Mexican cities carry these maps. American gas stations and bookstores near the border should also have Mexican maps. Members of the Automobile Association of Southern California can ask for free maps.

VISAS & PASSPORTS

Most travelers will need a valid passport with visa, smallpox vaccination certificate, and a tourist card to enter Mexico. British subjects do not require a visa. Canadian citizens and US citizens need only the tourist card, or FMT in Spanish.

There are three exceptions:
1. Naturalized US citizens, who must have either naturalization papers or a US passport
2. Those traveling on business, who need a business visa
3. Children under 15 who are included on the tourist card or visa of one of their parents (*see below*).

US citizens can visit Mexican border towns (and in Baja California, as far south as Ensenada) for up to 72 hours without even a tourist card.

A visa can be obtained from any Mexican embassy or consulate. Tourist cards are free and valid for a maximum of 180 days. They can be acquired in advance from Mexican embassies, consulates and National Tourist Council Offices (see *Tourist Information* for lists), Mexican border crossing-points, travel agents and airline companies. To order the card by mail, write to Oficina de Migración, *Av.* Chapultepec 284, Col. Roma, 06700 Mexico, DF. Ask for the *tarjeta de turista* and enclose a self-addressed, stamped envelope. Allow plenty of time, and be aware that if you don't enter Mexico within 90 days of the issue date, the card becomes invalid.

To obtain a tourist card, you must present proof of citizenship: a US passport, a US birth certificate, or US voter registration, plus a photo ID, such as a driver's licence. The licence alone is not enough. You may obtain a 180-day multiple-entry tourist card if you present proof of sufficient funds. If you want a multiple-entry tourist card, you must obtain it from a Mexican consulate; three passport-type photographs will be required. Otherwise, only proof of citizenship is needed; send a photocopy of your birth certificate, passport or voter registration.

Most travelers from the US obtain tourist cards from immigration officials at the border. Even if you already have the card, you must sign it in the presence of the border official, who then stamps it. You will need to present proof of US citizenship (birth certificate, passport, voter registration or military ID – *not* a driver's licence). If you fly into Mexico, you'll go through this procedure on landing. Don't forget to bring three passport-type photographs if you need a multiple-entry card: for example, if you're on a sailboat or cruise ship with several Mexican ports of call.

When you first enter Mexico, the immigration official who stamps your tourist card will decide how long you can stay: 30, 60, 90 or 180 days. Since getting an extension is a chore, ask for more time than you think you will need. It is impossible to predict, however, whether the border official will give you what you want. His decision is based in part on how you look.

Once you're in the country, if you feel you have an insufficient amount of time on your tourist card you can have it renewed. This is a time-consuming procedure, so begin at least a week before the expiry date. Go to the Mexican Immigration service (Dirección General de Servicios Migratorios) of the Immigration Department; there is one in most major towns. In Mexico City, the office is at the address given above (tel: 626-7200). You must fill out a form, then take it to another office where they will want to see how much money you have. They will count only traveler's checks in your name, *not cash*. Approval takes five working days, after which you can pick up the card or have it mailed to you anywhere in Mexico. Another option, if you are near a border, is to cross into the United States or Guatemala, then renew your tourist card on re-entry into Mexico.

Keep your tourist card (and the pink slip) with you at all times, even though you may never have to show it except at the checkpoints south of the border. You will have to return the card to Immigration on departure. If you lose the card, report the loss immediately to the nearest Mexican Tourism Office. These offices are in the state capitals (see *Tourist Information*). In Mexico City, you can get help from the Immigration Department (*as above*) or from the Secretaría de Turismo (central National Tourism Office) at Masaryk No. 172, Colonia Polanco, tel: 250-0123. English is spoken.

Children over 15 years of age must have their own proof of citizenship and tourist card. Those under 15 may be included on the tourist card of one parent. Children under 18 years of age traveling with one parent must have written, notarized consent from the other parent to travel or, if applicable, carry a decree of sole custody for the accompanying parent or a death certificate for the other parent. A child traveling alone or in someone else's custody must have notarized consent from both parents to travel or, if applicable, notarized consent from a single parent plus documentation that the parent is the only custodial parent.

Unless you are flying into Mexico, try not to enter the country at night. Waiting for a border official to wake up is a waste of your time, and, having been inconveniently disturbed, he is not likely to accommodate your request for a 180-day tourist card.

CUSTOMS

Tips for Travelers to Mexico is a helpful pamphlet issued by the US Department of State Bureau of Consular Affairs. It contains much useful information as well as Embassy, Consulate and Consular Agent addresses and phone numbers. It can be ordered at US$1 a copy from the Superintendent of Documents, US Government Printing Office, Washington, DC 20402, tel: (202) 783-3238.

On entering Mexico, remember that the following items are exempt from duties and import permits. Correspondingly, anything not on the list may be subject to duty, or, in some cases, detainment by Customs officials. For business travelers – who need a business visa – note that portable computers are not on the list and require special permits. Penalties for smuggling in such items is a high percentage of their cost.

Exempt from duty are:

1. Personal articles such as clothing, footwear, and toilet articles, in reasonable amounts.
2. A photo, movie or video-recording camera, including its power source, excepting professional equipment. You can also bring up to 12 rolls of unexposed film or videocassettes and printed or filmed photographic material.
3. Up to 20 different books or magazines.
4. One used sports article, or individual sporting equipment, provided it can be carried by one person.
5. Up to 20 packages of cigarettes, or 50 cigars or 250 grams of tobacco.
6. Up to 3 liters of wine or liquor (if the person is of legal age).
7. Medicine (with a prescription from your doctor if appropriate).
8. One pair of binoculars and one photo camera in addition to what's allowed in No. 2.
9. One portable television.
10. One portable radio or radio/recorder.
11. Up to 20 records or tapes.
12. One musical instrument, provided it can be carried by one person.
13. One tent and camping equipment.
14. Up to five toys if visitor is a minor. (If you are bringing toys in as gifts, it's advisable to remove the price tag and packaging.)
15. One set of fishing tackle, one pair of skis, and one tennis racquet.
16. One boat without motor, less than 5.5 meters long, or a surfboard with or without sail. These are allowed if you enter Mexico in a privately registered mobile home, airplane or yacht.
17. One videocassette recorder.
18. One bicycle with or without motor.
19. Household linens.
20. Kitchen, sitting-room, and/or bedroom utensils and furniture.
21. Pets may enter Mexico along with you only if you have a certificate of good health, signed by a veterinarian, and a certificate of rabies vaccination, dated within the last six months. Both must be stamped by a Mexican Consul. Before going to all this trouble, consider that few hotels will accept your pet; airlines and trains will require it to travel in a kennel in the baggage compartment; and it will not be permitted on first class buses. Only if you are driving and plan to camp out nearly all the time does it make sense to bring a pet.

When leaving Mexico, don't try to take with you narcotics or pre-Columbian artifacts. Travelers from the US are permitted to bring home some 2,700 different items duty-free from Mexico, under the General System of Preferences. The brochure *GSP and the Traveler* is available at the border or by mail from the US Customs Service, Dept of the Treasury, Washington, DC 20229. Another useful brochure is *Know Before You Go: Customs Hints for Returning US Residents* available at the border and by mail from the Superintendent of Documents, US Government Printing Office, Washington, DC 20402. If you order the brochures by mail, send a self-addressed stamped envelope.

The long list of items that American visitors to Mexico can take home duty-free includes the majority of the items that most travelers want to bring back: pottery, folk art, handmade clothing, etc. For items not on the GSP list, each traveler may bring back up to US$400 worth of purchases duty-free, as long as they are not expressly limited or prohibited from entering the US. Be sure to keep your receipts, to substantiate the value of your purchases. Family members may pool their exemptions.

If you want to take plants from Mexico into the US, write for information to the Import and Permit Section, Plant Quarantine Division, 209 River Street, Hoboken, NJ 07030. Or, check in your phone book for the nearest office of the US Department of Agriculture, Animal and Plant Health Inspection Service, Plant Protection and Quarantine or call the central office at (301) 436-8645.

HEALTH

Medical Advice

Take it easy for the first few days. Many travelers arrive in Mexico City jet-lagged, then begin walking for miles, eating and drinking heavily and immersing themselves in unfamiliar customs – all of this in the low-oxygen environment of a smoggy, high-altitude city. Any ability to resist infection takes a plunge, and the result is the infamous Montezuma's revenge (stomach disorder). Besides keeping yourself in shape, avoid exposure to sources of unfamiliar bacteria.

Malaria is present in remote areas, and travelers to such regions should take a course of anti-malaria pills. It is also advisable to be inoculated against polio, tetanus and hepatitis, and to ask your doctor whether you should have a typhoid booster shot. Aids is widespread, and rabies is prevalent.

Drinking Water

Water in Mexico may be contaminated. All hotels and restaurants catering for foreigners provide purified water although make sure you are not paying for a bottle of commercial water (unless, of course, that's what you want). In restaurants, ask for *agua purificada*. If you are in any doubt about the purity of the *agua purificada* ask for *agua mineral*

(mineral water), *un Tehuacán* (by brand name), or drink beer, soft drinks, or fruit juice. Be aware of the difference between fruit juice (*jugo*) and fruit drink (*agua fresca*) which is made with water – probably not purified. Brush your teeth with the same water you drink. Wash fruits and vegetables with purified water, or peel them. If you are camping out or traveling in remote areas, be prepared to purify water yourself: either boil it for 20 minutes or more (depending on altitude), or use halazone tablets. One final reminder: it does no good to obtain pure beverages if they are served with impure ice, or in glasses which have not been washed in hot water with detergent (or in purified water). This is a good reason to stick with bottled beverages, drunk out of the bottle or, when eating in restaurants, to ask for no ice, *sin hielo*.

Useful Drugs

There are plenty of pharmacies (*farmacias*) in Mexico but it is a good idea to bring with you basic items. For Montezuma's revenge, Kaomycin is frequently recommended. Symptoms may be relieved by Kaopectate (Kaomycin without the antibiotic), Lomotil (anti-diarrhoea), or Paregoric (fights both diarrhoea and stomach cramps, but is an opiate). Never self-prescribe or use antibiotics or Lomotil without a physician's or nurse's recommendation; take Kaopectate or Pepto Bismol as a first treatment. Whether or not you take a drug, rest and drink lots of fluids.

An alternative treatment is recommended by the US Center for Disease Control (CDC). You'll need two clean glasses, a cup of fruit juice (8 fluid ounces, about a quarter of a liter), half a teaspoon of honey, a pinch of salt, a quarter teaspoon of baking soda and a cup of boiled or carbonated water. In one glass, mix the water and baking soda; in the other glass, mix the fruit juice, honey and salt. Sip from one glass, then the other. Believe it or not, this relieves the diarrhoea (as well as dehydration). The CDC suggests avoiding antibiotics unless you have a high fever or are passing blood, and does not recommend the old standby drugs, Lomotil and Paregoric.

In Mexico, avoid going barefoot in areas where many other people do so; foot infections are sometimes common. Bring along a good insect repellent and use it, because many diseases are carried by mosquitos and other insects. Check the labels before you buy: the repellent with the highest percentage of N-Diethyltoluamide is the strongest (and strongest-smelling) one. Bring with you aspirin or its equivalent; something for treating minor wounds (rubbing alcohol, hydrogen peroxide, iodine); Band-aids; halazone tablets to purify water; any prescription drugs you need, along with their prescriptions; and a good sunscreen lotion. Tiger Balm is a useful all-purpose ointment.

Hikers should also bring an ice bandage, gauze bandages and adhesive tape. If you'll be traveling

INSIGHT *POCKET* GUIDES

EXISTING & FORTHCOMING TITLES:

North America	Corsica	Middle East and Africa
Atlanta	Costa Blanca	Istanbul
Boston	Costa Brava	Kenya
British Coumbia	Cote d'Azur	Maldives
Florida	Crete	Morocco
Florida Keys	Denmark	Seychelles
Hawaii	Florence	Tunisia
Miami	Gran Canaria	Turkish Coast
Montreal	Hungary	**Asia/Pacific**
New York City	Ibiza	Bali
North California	Ireland	Bali Birdwalks
Quebec	Lisbon	Bangkok
San Francisco	Loire Valley	Beijing
South California	London	Bhutan
Toronto	Madrid	Canton
Latin America and	Mallorca	Chiang Mai
The Caribbean	Malta	Fiji
Bahamas	Marbella	Hong Kong
Baja	Milan	Jakarta
Belize	Moscow	Kathmandu,
Bermuda	Munich	Bikes & Hikes
Jamaica	Oslo/Bergen	Kuala Lumpur
Mexico City	Paris	Macau
Puerto Rico	Prague	Malacca
US Virgin Islands	Provence	Nepal
Yucatan Peninsula	Rhodes	New Delhi
Europe	Rome	New Zealand
Aegean Islands	Sardinia	Penang
Algarve	Scotland	Phuket
Alsace	Seville	Sabah
Athens	Sicily	Sikkim
Barcelona	Southeast England	Singapore
Bavaria	St Petersburg	Sri Lanka
Berlin	Tenerife	Sydney
Brittany	Tuscany	Thailand
Brussels	Venice	Tibet
Budapest	Vienna	Yogyakarta

• •

United States: **Houghton Mifflin Company, Boston MA 02108**
Tel: (800) 2253362 Fax: (800) 4589501

Canada: **Thomas Allen & Son, 390 Steelcase Road East**
Markham, Ontario L3R 1G2
Tel: (416) 4759126 Fax: (416) 4756747

Great Britain: **GeoCenter UK, Hampshire RG22 4BJ**
Tel: (256) 817987 Fax: (256) 817988

Worldwide: **Höfer Communications Singapore 2262**
Tel: (65) 8612755 Fax: (65) 8616438

66 I was first drawn to the Insight Guides by the excellent "Nepal" volume. I can think of no book which so effectively captures the essence of a country. Out of these pages leaped the Nepal I know – the captivating charm of a people and their culture. I've since discovered and enjoyed the entire Insight Guide Series. Each volume deals with a country or city in the same sensitive depth, which is nowhere more evident than in the superb photography. 99

Sir Edmund Hillary

American Express offers Travelers Cheques built for two.

Cheques *for Two*ᴿᴹ from American Express are the Travelers Cheques that allow either of you to use them because both of you have signed them. And only one of you needs to be present to purchase them.

Cheques *for Two* are accepted anywhere regular American Express Travelers Cheques are, which is just about everywhere. So stop by your bank, AAA* or any American Express Travel Service Office and ask for Cheques *for Two*.

through cactus country, bring a pair of tweezers and a candle. When you encounter the kind of cactus spines that are too fine to tweeze out, light your candle. Pour melted but slightly cooled wax over the afflicted part. When the wax solidifies, pull it off. The tiny spines will come out, embedded in the wax.

Sunburn Protection

Burning yourself to a lobster hue in your first two days will not lead to a quick bronze tan. It is better to build up your exposure time gradually, avoiding the midday sun (11am–2pm) and using a good sunscreen lotion with PABA. Sunscreens have numbers listing their Sun Protection Factor (SPF). Most people will find an SPF between 5 and 10 to be sufficient protection for tanning without burning. SPF 15 lotion is a sunblock. Only a few brands specify on the label that the sunscreen will stay on your skin during and after your swim. A small tube of lip sunscreen is also a good idea.

MONEY MATTERS

The Mexican currency is the *nuevo* – or new – *peso*, which is divided into 100 centavos. Bills are issued in 10, 20, 50, 100, 500, 1,000, 5,000 and 10,000 peso denominations. Coins are 5, 10, 20 and 50 centavos, and 1, 2, 5, 20 and 10 pesos. The same sign, $, is used for pesos as for US dollars, except that it is written N$. If you see a menu item listed at, say, $25,000, it invariably means that the restaurant has not yet converted to the new peso. Simply deduct the last three zeros.

In border towns patronized by large numbers of US day trippers, many visitors use American currency instead of changing money. Stores here often have price tags in both pesos and dollars but you will still be better off changing your money in advance, since the stores are unlikely to give you the best rate of exchange. Those going further into Mexico, or staying more than a day, will certainly want to trade their money into pesos; and those coming from other countries must do so. The best place to change your money is a bank – or a bank-run exchange counter (labelled *Cambio*) in an international airport. You can also change money at a hotel, or at a money-changer.

The currency switch to the *nuevo peso* (new peso) in 1993 was mainly to do away with all the zeros in the old devalued peso (the computers couldn't handle the enormous figures!). Both the old peso, simply called "peso" and running into the thousands, and the new peso are in use side by side. Bills and coins look alike, except that the new peso says "*nuevos pesos*" before the amount. Be sure to check, before paying, that you're giving the correct amount. It might be helpful to acquire a new peso chart, which shows the old and new currency side by side for easy translation. And try to obtain a current money conversion table, available from travel agents, hotels and department stores.

The safest way to travel is to bring traveler's checks of a well-known issuer, in fairly large denominations, and cash them in banks. If you have multitudes of US$20 checks, you will tend to cash them as you go – rarely at the best rate of exchange – because the trip to the bank may not seem worthwhile for less than US$100. On the other hand, don't carry large amounts of cash; Mexican pickpockets are efficient.

Major credit cards are widely accepted in tourist areas but away from the big cities, you may find only the largest hotels, restaurants and stores accept them.

PUBLIC HOLIDAYS

January 1	New Year's Day
February 5	Constitution Day
February	Flag Day
March 21	Birthday of Benito Juarez
(date varies)	Easter
May 1	Labor Day
May 5	Battle of Puebla
May 10	Mother's Day
September 1	President's State of the Union Message
September 16	Independence Day
October 12	*Dia de la Raza* (Columbus Day)
November 20	Revolution Day
December 25	Christmas

GETTING THERE

By Air

Mexico City can be reached by direct flights from many US cities, as well as major cities in Europe, Canada, and Central and South America. The American airlines, most of which serve several Mexican cities in addition to Mexico City, include American, Continental, Delta, Alaska Airlines, America West, and North West, United. European carriers include Air France, Aeroflot, Alitalia, British Airways, Iberia, KLM, Lufthansa and Swissair. Mexico City is also served by Air Canada and Canadian Airlines International, El Al, Japan Airlines and Singapore Airlines. Some of these carriers fly to other Mexican cities, particularly Acapulco and Guadalajara. If you cannot fly direct to your destination, connections can be made with Aeromexico, Mexicana or TAESA, which have numerous domestic flights. All three national airlines also fly to the United States.

There is a proliferation of discount air fares at different times of the year. It would be wise to ask your travel agent to check in their Computer Reservations System the availability of the most advantageous air-fares, and also the domestic air-fares within Mexico. In addition to scheduled airline services, there are also some reduced-rate charter air-fares from the US and Canada.

By Sea

Round-the-world cruise ships frequently include Acapulco and other Pacific ports of call on their voyages as well as Mexico's Caribbean resorts. From the US, a selection of one- to three-week cruises is available. Caribbean cruises departing from New Orleans, Tampa, Miami and Fort Lauderdale may stop at Cancún and Cozumel. Numerous cruises along the west coast of Mexico start from Los Angeles; some of these ships can be boarded in San Francisco, Portland, Seattle and Vancouver, British Columbia. These west coast voyages may stop at Acapulco, Ixtapa/Zihuatanejo, Manzanillo, Puerto Vallarta, Mazatlán, and in Baja, at Cabo San Lucas and Ensenada. Cruises are a leisurely, comfortable and value-for-money way to get to Mexico, but they leave little time for travel within the country.

Traveling to Mexico in your own boat requires clearance papers, obtained at a Mexican Consulate or through a marine customs broker before you leave home. You must present them at your ports of entry and departure; sanitary inspection will also be made at the port of entry. In addition, each passenger and crew member needs a multiple entry tourist card (see *Immigration*). The boat and all passengers and crew must leave Mexico at the same time.

By Rail

Railroads can be a good way of traveling within Mexico, but are not recommended as a means of getting to the country. If you travel by rail from the United States or Central America, you must transfer at the border to the Mexican national railroad system. This can be inconvenient and time-consuming, and it is difficult to arrange reservations and buy tickets before arriving at the railroad station in Mexico. Few travel agents handle reservations on Mexican trains because they are run by the Mexican government which pays no commissions to travel agents. (See *Getting Around* section about rail travel within Mexico.) The only sure way to secure train seats before you arrive in Mexico, or before you arrive in an area served by the railroad line you want to travel on, is to have a friend in the appropriate place who will go to the station and buy tickets on your behalf.

Once you are in Mexico, you can make reservations by going to the train station a few days in advance (much earlier if you plan to travel during holiday periods). It is also possible to make your reservations from another train station, provided it is on the same railroad line as your journey. Many trains have inadequate or no catering facilities so it is highly advisable to take something to eat and drink with you.

If you want to make stop-overs and can be definite about the amount of time at each intermediate destination, buy the whole set of tickets together. Be sure to check the dates on each ticket, as well as the type of accommodation.

By Bus

Bus travel within Mexico has many advantages, and those travelers coming from the US have the option of making their entire journey by bus. However, unless you live near the border or have more time than money, flying to the area you want to visit and then using buses is a better bet. Bus tours are available through Greyhound Lines. For more information about bus travel refer to the *Getting Around* section.

By Car

Many Americans, particularly those living in the border states, drive to Mexico. To take your car into Mexico you must obtain a permit from the Mexican Tourist Office or any branch of the Automobile Association. For a fee, the AAA will complete the documentation for a temporary automobile permit. You will need the following:

1. Vehicle Title. (Registration is often accepted). Owner is considered the NAME on title only. For example, a wife cannot take the car if the title is only in her husband's name. You must have the original or state-issued documents only. Photocopies are not accepted.
2. Birth certificate, passport or notarized affidavit of citizenship. (voter's registration card *may* be accepted with photo ID.)
3. Visa, MasterCard, or American Express card with the same name as on the title. (There is an US$11 fee for your car permit – payable by credit card only.)
4. Valid driver's license (with same name as on title).
5. Notarized letter of permission from the Bank or lienholder is required on leased or company cars. This must be on the letterhead of company or bank.
6. Copies of the above, provided they are made by Mexican Customs, are valid. No borrowed cars or borrowed credit cards are accepted. Mexico requires that the vehicle permit be canceled in person on your last trip out of Mexico. Mexican officials must see the car and remove the window sticker personally.
7. You must sign an affidavit of promise to return the vehicle back to the US.
8. It is very important to note that the person named on the car permit document must be in the vehicle whenever it is driven. If you lend your car to anyone else, it could be confiscated and there is nothing you can do about it.
9. You must have Mexican auto insurance. US insurance is not valid in Mexico. If you have an accident without insurance you face imprisonment until all damages are paid. Those who wish to be completely safe should purchase a legal assistance insurance package from their Mexican insurance carrier. Many of these policies, however, are limited to $500 of coverage and have few lawyers backing them. The only company that has unlimited coverage and guarantees to resolve cases for

you is ASSET SA, who have reputable lawyers on call throughout Mexico. They work with Sanborn's Mexico Insurance Services. Sanborn's has offices in Texas, Arizona and California, at every major border crossing except Tijuana. They also include a parts shipping service with their legal policy. If you need a part for your car, they will clear Customs for you and ship it by bus.

Sanborn's Mexico Insurance Services also offer an annual policy that is cheaper than 40 days of daily coverage, plus a free *Travelog*, a mile-by-mile guidebook custom-made for your route. Their US office is: PO Box 310, McAllen, TX 78505-0310, tel: 1-800-222-0158. Sanborn's Mexico Club membership also has a medical air evacuation policy which will locate an English-speaking doctor, arrange transfers of money from your bank and relatives to coordinate payment of medical bills and if doctors agree you need to be evacuated, arrange and pay for a air ambulance to repatriate you to your own country.

The American Automobile Association, with offices throughout the US, is also reputable. Their insurance is good, they have US adjusters and they give members a small guidebook. Their hotel listings usually concentrate on upmarket places.

For Baja, Oscar Padilla offers insurance only, no guidebooks or other services, but he provides a map and drive-thru service. If you are going only to Ensenada or crossing for a single day, he's as good as any. If you are driving over the whole of Baja, for the same price you can get much more from Sanborn's or AAA.

If you fail to obtain a policy before crossing the border, there are kiosks at the border crossings. Some will settle your claim only in Mexico. This is not ideal, but is better than nothing. No matter where you buy your insurance, please be aware that driving at night is foolhardy; there are animals and people on every road at all hours. You can't see a boy on a bike in the dark. Cows don't wear taillights. Potholes cannot be avoided. There are fewer shoulders for disabled vehicles to pull on to. So don't drive at night.

USEFUL ADDRESSES

Tourist Information
Before arriving in Mexico, write for information to the Mexican National Tourist Council. Its main office is at Mariano Escobedo 726, Mexico, DF, tel: 211-0099.

There are offices in some other countries, including several in the US. The regional offices for North America are at:
New York: 405 Park Avenue, Suite 1002, NY 10022, tel: (212) 755-7261.
Miami: 128 Aracon Ave, FL 33134, tel: (305) 443-9160.
Los Angeles: 10100 Santa Monica Blvd, CA 90067, tel: (310) 203-8191.

Washington DC: 1911 Pennsylvania Ave, 20006, tel: (202) 728-1754.
Houston: 2707 N. Loop W., TX, tel: (713) 880-5153.
Chicago: 70 East Lake St, IL 60601, tel: (312) 565-2766.

There are two offices in Canada:
Toronto: 181 University Av, tel: (416) 364-2255.
Montreal: 1 Place Ville Marie, Quebec, tel: (514) 871-1052.

Office in Europe include:
London: 60 Trafalgar Square, London WC2N 5DS, tel: 171 734 1058.
Paris: 4 Rue Notre Dame des Bictoires 75002, tel: (33) 1 40200734 or 720-6911.
Frankfurt: Neisenhuettenplatz 26, D6000, Frankfurt An Main 1, tel: 253413.
Madrid: Calle Valazquez 126, tel: 261 3120.
Rome: Via Barbereni 3, 00187, tel: (396) 487 2182.

PRACTICAL TIPS

EMERGENCIES

Security and Crime
Always lock your car, and take valuables with you or lock them away safely and out of sight. Do not pick up hitchhikers, not even fellow countrymen, to avoid not only possible robbery but also the unwitting transport of narcotics.

If you are traveling long distances by bus (occasionally subject to bandits) it is safest to travel on buses that head to their destinations without stopping.

One sure way to get arrested is to buy marijuana from strangers (or smoke it in public). Marijuana has a different history in Mexico than in the US; until recently, most Mexicans associated it almost exclusively with criminals. Near the Guatemalan border, and in remote areas elsewhere in Mexico, you can expect to have police descend on your car for a search. Don't forget: Mexico has some pretty stringent rules regarding drugs, and they're definitely not limited to marijuana alone.

Medical Services
If you need a doctor, ask your hotel for a list of local English-speaking physicians (or dentists). In Mexico City, you can call the embassy of your home country. In other cities, ask at the government tourism office. If you are in a remote area you will have to depend

345

upon a hotel manager or other appropriate individual to give you a referral. Both Mexico City and Guadalajara have hospitals that cater for the English-speaking foreigner.

In Mexico City:

Hospital Ingles – ABC (American British Cowdray Hospital), Calle Sur 136, No. 201 (at the corner of Observatorio), Colonia Americas, Mexico 18, DF 01120, tel: 272-8500.

In Guadalajara:

Hospital Mexico-Americano, Colomos 2110, 44610 Guadalajara, Jalisco, tel: 41-3141.

WEIGHTS & MEASURES

In Mexico, weights and measures follow the metric system. To calculate imperial equivalents, use the following formulae:

To convert	Multiply by
Centimeters to inches	0.393701
Meters to feet	3.2808
Meters to yards	1.09361
Kilometers to miles	0.621371
Sq. centimeters to sq. inches	0.155000
Sq. feet to sq. meters	0.0929030
Sq. meters to sq. yards	1.19599
Sq. kilometers to sq. miles	0.386103
Hectares to acres	2.47101
Gallons to liters	4.546
Grams to ounces	0.035274
Grams to pounds	0.00220462
Kilograms to pounds	2.20462
Kilograms to tons	0.0009842

BUSINESS HOURS

If you need to have money transferred to you while you are in Mexico, or to transfer money to someone who is in Mexico, ask your home bank which bank in the relevant Mexican city they have dealings with, and have the funds transferred there.

Banks are open 9am–1.30pm, Monday–Friday. The main offices of some banks are open Saturday mornings until noon. Offices are generally open 9am–2pm, then close for dinner and siesta, reopening from 4pm–6pm. Men of importance, whether in government or the private sector, are seldom available before 10am. Stores open at 9am or 10am and stay open until early evening, perhaps 7pm or 8pm; some close from 2pm–4pm.

TIPPING

In restaurants, the usual tip is 15 percent before tax; no tip is expected in inexpensive eating places that do not cater for tourists. Porters and bellhops are tipped one peso per suitcase. The same is appropriate for a taxi driver who helps with your luggage; otherwise, there is no need to tip taxidrivers. Gas station attendants are usually given a small tip, even if they don't wash your windshield or check your oil

(you must ask for these services). Many Mexicans, for example, ask for N\$4.50 worth of gas, then give the attendant five. Boys who guard your car when you park on the street may be given one–two pesos; be sure to remember what the boy looks like or you may feel compelled to tip the whole group surrounding the car on your return. Parking lot attendants are tipped two pesos. In barber shops and beauty salons the usual tip is about 20 percent of the bill before IVA (Value Added Tax). Tour guides are tipped according to the amount on the bill and the quality of their performance, but the usual is a minimum of US\$1 for the day. Keep in mind that many people in Mexico depend almost exclusively on tips for their livelihood.

MEDIA

Newspapers & Magazines

Mexico fares well for daily newspapers, both national and regional, although with certain exceptions the press is not as independent as it might be. If you read Spanish, compare *El Excelsior* (information-packed, if cumbersome), *UNO mas UNO* and *La Jornada* (both left-leaning) and *El Financiero* (business-oriented). *Tiempo Libre,* on Thursdays, lists the week's cultural activities in Mexico City. *El Excelsior*'s weekly magazine *Insight* covers mainly business matters. In English, *The News* is a right-leaning daily aimed at English-speaking foreigners and dominated by wire service stories. The (free) *Mexico Daily Bulletin* (which always carries a downtown map) is an institution and can usually be found at Sanborn's and many hotels. *Time* and *Newsweek* are readily available, as well as other US magazines. Foreign-language publications, such as *Der Spiegel* and *L'Express* are also often found. Many newsstands carry some foreign-language publications; but you can always count on a Sanborn's, or the hotel shops, to have a good selection.

Radio & Television

Mexico has numerous radio stations, both FM and AM, ranging from *mariachi* music to rock 'n' roll. All broadcast in Spanish, with the exception of two English language stations in Mexico City. Radio VIP (AM 1560) is a CBS affiliate; Stereo Best (FM 105) is an NBC affiliate. ABC news is heard over Radio NRM (AM 590).

All television broadcasts are in Spanish except late-night movies in English and Cable TV. Bigger hotels feature cablevision with programs from America: ABC, CBS, NBC and CNN. Many homes, especially in Mexico City and the larger cities, subscribe to one of the cable television networks. If you want to watch sports events originating in the US, your best bet is to go to one of the big hotels, or you can listen for the English narration beneath the louder narration of the Mexican sportscasters. Some American serials are shown, either with Spanish dubbed in or with subtitles.

Post offices are usually open 9am–7pm Monday–Friday, and 9am–1pm Saturday. Some close for lunch from 1pm–3pm. In smaller towns the hours vary: most will be closed on Saturday afternoons. Registered mail (*carta certificada*) must be picked up before 5pm on weekdays, before noon on Saturday.

Mark all your correspondence *Correo Aereo*; surface mail is very slow. You can mail out packages of up to 20 kilos (44 lbs) but it involves a lot of paperwork. Go to the central post office of a large town, and have the package registered.

MEXPOST is similar to Federal Express or United Parcel Service and will pick up your packages for shipping on request, tel: (525) 682-1716 or you can visit their office at Calle Georgia 120B, Col. Napoles, Mexico DF 03810. You may find It easier to ask the store to mail your purchases home. Most large stores are experienced at this and are reliable. Over the Christmas period, however, expect delays and some losses.

The surest way to receive mail in Mexico is to have it sent to a hotel at which you have a reservation, marked "Please hold for arrival." You can receive mail at post offices if it is addressed to *Lista de Correos*, with your last name in capital letters and underlined. When you go to the post office where you are expecting mail, ask for the *Lista*. The postal clerk will need your name, the date of the list and the number next to your name on the list, plus some identification. Mail addressed to *Lista de Correos* will be held for 10 days before being returned to the sender. If you leave town before receiving mail that you know is en route, fill out a change-of-address form at the post office. Packages sent to Mexico are subject to Customs duty, which can be substantial.

TELECOMS

Telephone

Trying to make a call from a public telephone in Mexico can be frustrating. Assuming you find a phone that works, you may need to operate it (a) a big old peso; (b) a small new peso; (c) a tiny new 20 centavo coin; (d) a Ladatel telephone card; or (e) nothing. Ever since the 1985 earthquakes, calls made from some public telephones have been free. Good luck. The only long-distance calling possible on these phones is collect calling (dial 09 for the long-distance operator).

For directory information in Mexico City, dial 04 and prepare your Spanish; for the long-distance operator for calls within Mexico, dial 02; for the international long distance operator, dial 09. The international long-distance operators (*Operador Internacional*) speak English. Be patient; the operators do eventually answer.

The least expensive way to make long-distance calls is at the *Larga Distancia* office; there's one in almost every town. Write out the area code and

number, the city and country. If the call is to be person-to-person, write the name clearly. Specify *persona a persona*; station-to-station is called a *quien contesta* (literally, "to whoever answers"). When the operator puts your call through, your name will be called and you will be assigned to one of the phone booths: "*Señor Mueller, cabina dos!*"

When making a collect call (*por cobrar*), be aware that if the answering party refuses to accept the call you will be charged for a one-minute call. The operator in your hotel will place long-distance calls for you, but usually a hefty surcharge will be added to the bill.

Long-distance calls can be dialed direct from Mexico to the US and most other countries, but only from private telephones. If you want to know the cost of the call so you can repay the friends whose telephone you are using, you will need the services of an operator and will not, therefore, get the cheaper direct-dial rates.

For those who are in a position to dial direct, the prefix for calls within Mexico is **91** (followed by the area code and number); **95** for the US and Canada; and **98** (plus country code) for the rest of the world. Normally, a 39 percent tax is added to the cost of all outgoing calls, so if possible arrange for your family, friends or business associates telephone you rather than vice-versa.

Telegraph/Fax

You must go to a telegraph office, *Oficina de Telegrafos*, to send a telegram; you can't telephone it in from your hotel. You can send a telegram from a private phone. Telegraph offices are usually open from 9am until early evening on weekdays, possibly closing for siesta, and will be open at least in the morning if not all day Saturday. If you require rapid delivery to your destination, ask for urgent service *(urgente)*; regular service (*ordinario*) is less expensive. Write out your message and the address of the recipient clearly to minimize errors. For international telegrams, dial 709-8625.

To receive a telegram in Mexico, if you are not staying at a hotel or home where it can be sent, have it addressed to you at *Lista de Correos* (to receive it at the post office) or at *Lista de Telegrafos* (to receive it at the telegraph office).

Western Union Financial Services have introduced a money-transfer service, *Dinero en Minutos* (Money in Minutes), which money can be sent from any Western Union office in the US and picked up in pesos at any of the 300 furniture-and-electronic stores in the Elektra SA de CV chain throughout Mexico.

Fax bureaus are not common, although they can be found in certain parts of central Mexico City. Some luxury hotels have fax machines, and you could inquire whether it is possible to use their facilities. Do note, however, that fax services can be very expensive, and faxes will not necessarily be sent as soon as you would hope.

CULTURAL DIFFERENCES

Mexicans take nudity very seriously. Avoid any public exposure that might offend people. Shorts are considered indecent by many Mexicans, and the same goes for shirtless men. If you are caught in the nude by someone who seems upset about it, don't try to laugh it off – apologize and put some clothes on. The alternative could be arrest.

Women Traveling Alone

One of the most common sources of misunderstanding in Mexico is the disparity between Mexican and foreign women in their dress and behavior. A respectable American, European or Asian woman wears clothing on the street which, in Mexico, might signify sexual availability although in Mexico City, Acapulco and other large, more progressive cities attitudes are changing. Mexican men simply adore women, and are lavish with their "politically incorrect" admiring glances and comments. However, since many Mexican men still believe that foreign women are in fact sexually available (Mexican women seldom being available outside marriage), the misunderstandings which arise can be unpleasant for the woman traveler, especially if she is traveling alone, or with another woman. Groups of three or more are less likely to be bothered, and women with men are unlikely to receive more than whistles.

Even if you enjoy the attention and flattering comments known as *piropos*, be careful not to respond to any overtures unless you mean to follow through. If you don't enjoy the attention, you can minimize your discomfort by following these rules: don't make eye contact; don't respond to compliments by strangers on the street – don't smile, don't say thanks, don't glare or make nasty remarks. Just walk on. Go with groups whenever possible. If you want to take a long walk and you're traveling alone, try to recruit congenial fellow-travelers to come along. Observe the wide differences between respectable Mexican women and hookers, and adjust dress and behavior accordingly.

Women traveling in Mexico, with or without men, should also be aware that some Mexican drinking establishments admit only men. Bars in hotels and restaurants, cocktail lounges and many other bars admit women, but true *cantinas* do not. *Pulquerias* not only don't admit women, they usually don't take too well to men who are strangers.

If you see two Mexican men hugging one another, keep in mind that the hug, *abrazo*, is normal behavior between good friends. In the same way, girls will walk with their arms around one another's waists; nothing is implied except friendship. Incidentally, homosexuality between consenting adults is not illegal in Mexico, although it can lead to blackmail and other forms of persecution. Pornography is illegal, but prostitution is not, provided the girl is not a minor.

TOURIST OFFICES

In Mexico, each state capital has an office of the Secretariat of Tourism (*Secretaria de Turismo*). In Mexico City, the main office is at Av Presidente Masaryk No. 172, 11587 Mexico, DF. This office has three useful telephone numbers. For standard information (for example, directions, dates, times and prices of special events) call 250-0123, with 24-hour hotline service. For other assistance, call 254-1954 or 545-4613.

There is also a tourist information office (*Oficina de Informacion Turistica Nacional*) at Mexico City Airport, section "A," where the domestic flights are located. They can be contacted on tel: 571-1663, 762-6773, or 762-6763. They're very pleasant and helpful, and can handle at least three languages: English, Spanish and French. There are plans to have another office at the airport, in the new International terminal which, as this goes to print, is under construction.

In Mexico, tourist offices are at:

Aguascalientes: Ecuador 811, Fracc. Sta. Elena Col. Centro, 20000 Aguascalientes, AGS, tel: (491) 5-1155.

Baja California Norte: Blvd Díaz Ordaz, Edif. Plaza Patria, 3er Piso Zona K, 22440 Tijuana, BC, tel: (66) 11-5266.

Baja California Sur: Fraccionamiento Fidepaz, AP 419 23090 La Paz, BCS, tel: (682) 2-1190.

Campeche: Av. Ruíz Cortinez, Plaza Mouch Couch, 24000 Campeche, Camp, tel: (981) 66-0687.

Chiapas: Blvd Belisario Doming 950, 4to Piso, Colonia Xamaipak, 29060 Tuxtla Gutiérrez, Chiapas, tel: (961) 2-4535.

Coahuila: Carretera 55 Km 6.5, Centro de Convenciones, Piso 2, 25280 Saltillo, Coahuila, tel: (84) 30-0783.

Colimá: Hidalgo 75, Colonia Centro, 28000 Colima, tel: (331) 2360.

Chihuáhua: Libertad y Calle 13, Piso 1, No. 1300, 1000 Chihuahua, tel: (14) 16-2436.

Durango: Hidalgo 408 Sur, Col. Centro, 4000 Durango, tel: (181) 1-2139.

Estado de Mexico: Edificio Plaza Toluca Piso 1, Puerta 307, Colonia Centro, 50000 Toluca, Estado de México, tel: (72) 14-1342.

Guanajuato: Plaza de la Paz 14, Col. Centro, 36000 Guanajuato, tel: (473) 2-1574.

Guerrero: Centro de Convenciones de Acapulco, 33359 Acapulco, tel: (74) 84-3149.

Hidalgo: Blvd Felipe Angeles, Colonia Centro, 32000 Pachuca, tel: (771) 1-4237.

Jalisco: Morelos 102, Plaza Tapatía, 44100 Guadalajara, tel: (3) 614-0123.

Michoacan: Nigromante 79, Palacio Clavijero, 58000 Morelia, tel: (43) 12-5244.

Morelos: Av. Morelos Sur 802, Colonia Las Palmas, 62050 Cuernavaca, tel: (73) 14-3860.

Nayarit: Av. México 34 Sur, Colonia Centro, 63000 Tepic, tel: (321) 2546.

Nuevo Leon: Zaragoza Sur 1300, Edif. Kalos, Desp. 137, Nivel A-1, Colonia Centro, 64000 Monterrey, tel: (83) 44-1169.

Oaxaca: 5 de Mayo 200, Esq. Morelos, Colonia Centro, 68000 Oaxaca, tel: (951) 6-0670.

Puebla: 11 Oriente 2224, Piso 3, Colonia Centro, 72000 Puebla, tel: (22) 34-1239.

Queretaro: Av. Constituyentes 102, Colonia Quinea Márquez, 76000 Querétaro, tel: (12) 13-9802.

Quintana Roo: Palacio de Gobierno, Piso 2, Colonia Centro, 77000 Chetuma, tel: (983) 2-0855.

San Luis Potosi: Av. Venustiano Carranza 325, Colonia Centro, 78000 San Luis Potosí, tel: (48) 12-9939.

Sinaloa: Paseo Olas Altas 1300, Col. Centro, Piso 1, Edificio Banco de México, 82000 Mazatlán, tel (69) 85-1847.

Sonora: Comonfort & Tehuantepec, Palacio Administrativo PB, 83150 Hermosillo, tel: (62) 17-1941.

Tabasco: Paseo Tabasco 1504, Centro Administrativo, Col. Tabasco 2000, 86030 Villahermosa, tel: (931) 5-2575.

Tamaulipás: 16 Rosales 272, Colonia Centro, 87000 Ciudad Victoria, tel: (131) 2-1057.

Tlaxcalá: Juárez 18, Colonia Centro, 90000 Tlaxcala, tel: (246) 2-0027.

Veracruz: Av. Avila Camacho 191, Colonia Centro, 91000 Jalapa, tel: (281) 8-7202.

Yucatán: Calle 59 No. 514, entre 62 y 64, Colonia Centro, 97000 Mérida, tel:(99) 24-8013.

Zacátecás: Explanada del Ferrocarril, Colonia Centro, 98000 Zacatecas, tel: (492) 4-0393.

Distrito Federál: Zona Metropolitana, Presidente Mazaryk 172, 6o Piso Colonia Polanco, 11587 México DF, tel: (5) 250-0123.

EMBASSIES & CONSULATES

All these are located in Mexico City:

Albania: Calle Solón 337, Polanco, tel: 520-1065.

Argentina: Blvd Avila Camacho 1, Piso 7, Lomas de Chapultepec, tel: 520-9430.

Australia: Jaime Balmes 11, Piso 10, Polanco, tel: 395-9888.

Austria: Campos Elíseos 305, Polanco, tel: 280-6919.

Belgium: Musset 41, Polanco, tel: 280-0758.

Belize: Thiers 152-B, Anzures, tel: 203-5642.

Bolivia: Felipe de los Angeles 9, Huizachal, tel: 584-1386.

Brasil: Lope de Armendáriz 130, Lomas Virreyes, tel: 202-7500.

Bulgaria: Reforma 1990, Lomas de Chapultepec, tel: 596-3283.

Canada: Schiller 529, Polanco, tel: 724-7900.

Chile: Montes Urales 460, Lomas de Chapultepec, tel: 520-0081.

China: Av. Río Magdalena 172, Tizapan (San Angel), tel: 550-0823.

Colombia: Reforma 1620, Lomas de Chapultepec, tel: 202-7299.

Costa Rica: Río Po 113, Cuauhtémoc, tel: 525-7764.

Cuba: Presidente Masaryk 554, Palmitas, tel: 280-8039.

Czechoslovakia: Cuvier 22, Anzures, tel: 531-2544.

Denmark: Tres Picos 43, Bosques de Chapultepec, tel: 255-3405.

Dominican Republic: Insurgentes Sur 216-301, Roma Sur, tel: 533-0215, 207-9700.

Ecuador: Tennyson 217, Polanco, tel: 545-3531.

Egypt: Alejandro Dumas 131, Polanco, tel: 281-0698.

El Salvador: Paseo de las Palmas 1930, Lomas de Chapultepec, tel: 596-3390.

Ethiopia: M. de Cervantes Saavedra 465, Irrigación, tel: 557-2238.

Federation of Independent States (formerly USSR): José Vasconcelos 204, Hipódromo Condesa, tel: 273-1305.

Finland: Monte Pelvoux 111, Piso 4, Lomas de Chapultepec, tel: 540-6036.

France: Havre 15, Juárez, tel: 533-1360.

Germany: Lord Byron 737, Polanco, tel: 280-5409.

Greece: Paseo de las Palmas 2060, Lomas Reforma, tel: 596-6333.

Guatemala: Av. Explanada 1025, Lomas de Chapultepec, tel: 540-7520.

Haiti: Taine 229, Piso 4, Polanco, tel: 250-7918.

Honduras: Alfonso Reyes 220, Hipódromo Condesa, tel: 211-5250.

Hungary: Paseo de las Palmas 2005, Lomas de Chapultepec, tel: 596-1822.

Iceland: Blvd M. Avila Camacho 80, Piso 3, tel: 557-7644.

India: Musset 325, Polanco, tel: 531-1050.

Indonesia: Julio Verne 27, Polanco, tel: 280-5748.

Iran: Reforma 2350, Lomas Altas, tel: 596-5399.

Iraq: Reforma 1875, Lomas Reforma, tel: 596-0254.

Ireland (Honorary Consulate): Av. San Jerónimo 790-A, tel: 595-3333.

Israel: Sierra Madre 215, Lomas de Chapultepec, tel: 540-6340.

Italy: Paseo de las Palmas 1994, Lomas de Chapultepec, tel: 596-3655.

Jamaica: Euken 32, Anzures, tel: 250-0011.

Japan: Reforma 395, Cuauhtémoc, tel: 211-0028.

Korea: Lope de Armendáriz 110, Lomas Virreyes, tel: 202-7160.

Lebanon: Julio Verne 8, Polanco, tel: 280-6794.

Malaysia: Paseo de la Reforma 325 (Ma. Isabel Sheraton), Cuauhtémoc tel: 207-3933.

Morocco: Paseo de la Reforma 635, Los Morales, tel: 292-8921.

Netherlands: Montes Urales Sur 635, Piso 2, Lomas de Chapultepec, tel: 202-8267.

New Zealand: Tres Picos 50, PH-3, Bosques de Chapultepec, tel: 250-5914.

Nicaragua: Payo de Rivera 120, Lomas de Chapultepec, tel: 520-2449.

Norway: Av. Virreyes 1460, Lomas de Chapultepec, tel: 540-3486.

Pakistan: Hegel 512, Polanco, tel: 203-3636.

Panama: Campos Elíseos 111-1, Polanco, tel: 250-4229.

Paraguay: Homero 415-3, Polanco, tel: 545-0403.

Peru: Paseo de las Palmas 2601, Lomas Reforma, tel: 570-5509.
Philippines: Calderón de la Barca 240, Polanco, tel: 254-8230.
Poland: Cracovia 40, San Angel, tel: 550-4700.
Portugal: Alejandro Dumas 311, Polanco, tel: 545-6213.
Romania: Sófocles 311, Los Morales, tel: 520-9847.
Senegal: Montes Urales Sur 760, Lomas de Chapultepec, tel: 202-0680.
Spain: Parque Vía Reforma 2105, Lomas Reforma, tel: 596-2562.
Sweden: Blvd M. Avila Camacho 1, Piso 6, Lomas de Chapultepec, tel: 540-6393.
Switzerland: Hamburgo 66, Piso 4, Juárez, tel: 533-0735.
Thailand: Sierra Vertientes 1030, Lomas de Chapultepec, tel: 596-1290.
Turkey: Paseo de las Palmas 1525, Lomas Reforma, tel: 520-2344.
United Kingdom: Río Lerma 71, Cuauhtémoc, tel: 207-2089.
United States of America: Reforma 305, Cuauhtémoc, tel: 211-0042.
Uruguay: Hegel 149 Piso 1, Polanco, tel: 531-0880.
Venezuela: Schiller 326, Polanco, tel: 203-4233.
Vietnam: Sierra Ventana 255, Lomas de Chapultepec, tel: 540-1612.
Yugoslavia: Av. Montañas Rocallosas Ote 515, Lomas de Chapultepec, tel: 520-6823.

GETTING AROUND

BY AIR

For domestic flights there are three major airlines, Aeromexico, Mexicana, and TAESA. They have reservations offices in a number of cities; not all are listed here. Telephone numbers may be changed, so check at your hotel if necessary.

Airfares are generally the same whether you fly Mexicana or Aeromexico on routes served by both. TAESA fares tend to be lower. On domestic flights, each passenger is permitted to check in two bags, with neither weighing more than 32 kg (70 lbs) and with total weight not exceeding 50 kg (110 lbs). You are also permitted one carry-on bag, small enough to fit under a seat, and a garment bag.

For an **Aeromexico** timetable write to their office at Reforma 445, Col. Cuauhtemoc, 06500 Mexico, DF. For **Mexicana**, write to Blvd Xola 535, Col.

Del Valle, 03100 Mexico, DF, Mexico. Write to TAESA at Zona de Hangares "C" No. 27, 15620 Mexico, DF.

In Mexico, domestic airline tickets and information are available at the ticket desks in airports, at travel desks in many hotels, and through travel agents.

Domestic Airline Offices

AEROMEXICO
Acapulco: Av. Costera M. Aleman 286, tel: 85-1525.
Aguascalientes: Calle Madero 474, tel: 7-0252.
Campeche: Aeropuerto Intl de Campeche, tel: 6-6656.
Cancún: Av. Coba 80 Supermanzana 03, tel: 84-1097.
Chihuahua: Victoria 106, tel: 15-6303.
Cd. Juarez: Av. Lincoln 759, tel: 13-8089.
Cd. Obregon: No Reeleccion 509 Ote, tel: 3-2190.
Culiacan: A. Rosales 77 Pte, tel: 5-3772.
Durango: Juarez 201-B Sur, tel: 1-2813.
Guadalajara: Av. Corona 196, tel: 14-5400.
Guaymas: Aquiles Serdan 236, tel: 2-0266.
Hermosillo: Boulevard Navarrete 165, tel: 6-8206.
Huatulco: Apto. Int. de Bahias de Huatulco, tel: 4-0328.
La Paz, BC: Hidalgo y Morelos, tel: 2-7636.
León: Madero 410, tel: 6-6226.
Los Mochis: Gabriel Leyva 168 Nte, tel: 5-2570.
Manzanillo: Centro Comercial "Carrillo Puerto" Local 107, tel: 2-1267.
Matamoros: Alvaro Obregon 21, tel: 3-0701.
Mazatlan: Av. Camaron Sabalo 310, tel: 4-1111.
Mérida: Av. Paseo Montejo 460, tel: 27-9000.
Mexico City: Reforma 76, tel: 207-8233. Information, arrivals and departures, tel: 762-4022.
Monterrey: Av. Lazaro Cardenas 2499, tel: 40-0617.
Oaxaca: Av. Hidalgo 513 Centro, tel: 6-3765.
Puebla: Av. Juarez 1514-A, tel: 32-0013.
Puerto Vallarta: Juarez 255, tel: 2-1910.
Reynosa: Guerrero 1510, tel: 2-1115.
San Jose del Cabo/Los Cabos: Zaragoza e Hidalgo s/n, tel: 2-0398.
Tapachula: 2a Av. Norte 6, tel: 6-2050.
Tijuana: Av. Revolución 1236, tel: 85-2230.
Torreon: Blvd Independencia 565 Ote, tel: 13-6477.
Villahermosa: Periferico Carlos Pelicer, tel: 2-6991.
Zihuatanejo: Calle Juan N. Alvarez 34, tel: 4-2018.

MEXICANA
Acapulco: Cost. M. Aleman 1252, tel: 84-8192.
Cancun: Av. Coba No. 39, tel: 87-4444.
Cd. Carmen: 22 x 37 Edificio "Jaber", tel: 2-1171.
Coatacoalcos: Corregidora No. 401, tel: 2-6559.
Cozumel: Av. Gral. Rafael E. Melgar Sur 17, tel: 2-2945.
Cuernavaca: Hidalgo 26, tel: 12-3681/91.
Guadalajara: Mariano Otero 2353, tel: 47-1731.
Hermosillo: Rosales 35 Esq., tel: 7-1103.
Huatulco: Hotel Posada Binniguenda Hab. 116, tel: 4-0077.
La Paz: Av. Alvaro Obregón 340, tel: 2-4999.
León: Blvd A. Lopez Mateos No. 401 Ote, tel: 4-9500.

Manzanillo: Av. Mexico No. 382, tel: 2-1972.
Mazatlan: Paseo Claussen 101-B, tel: 2-7722.
Mérida: Calle 58 No. 500, tel: 24-6633.
Mexicali: Av. Fco. I. Madero 832, tel: 53-5401.
Mexico City: Reforma y Amberes, tel: 660-4444. Information, arrivals and departures, tel: 571-8888.
Minatitlan: Av. Hidalgo 117-Bis, tel: 4-0026.
Monterrey: Hidalgo 922 Pte, tel: 44-1122.

TAESA
Av. Aviacion General, Zona de Hangares "C" No.27, Col. Federal 15620 Mexico, DF, tel: 227-0727.

Offices also in Acapulco, Cancún, Cozumel, Guadalajara, Hermosillo and Mexicali.

BY BOAT

Ferries run between Baja California and the mainland, and between the Caribbean islands of Cozumel and Isla Mujeres, and the Yucatán peninsula. The latter are mainly passenger ferries, traveling short distances. The Baja ferries make long journeys across the deep Gulf of California, which gives the traveler the chance to appreciate both the peninsula and the mainland without making the extremely long and hot drive around the Gulf.

For the long-distance ferries, make sure you have the latest timetable as boats don't leave every day. They are run by SEMATUR, Paseo de la Reforma 509, 4 Piso (4th floor), tel: 553-7957. Write for reservations not more than two months in advance but not less than two days ahead at the address in Mexico City, or at their offices in La Paz, Mazatlan, Topolobambo, Santa Rosalia, Pichiringue, or Guaymas. Or ask at your hotel for ferry information, preferably a few days before you want to leave. If you are coming from the US, ask your travel agent or the insurance agent at the border for an up-to-date schedule.

Telephone numbers for local ferry offices are:
Mazatlan: (69) 81-7020.
Guaymas: (622) 2-3390.
Santa Rosalia: (685) 2-0013.
La Paz: (682) 5-3833.
Pichiringue: (682) 2-9485.
Topolobampo: (686) 2-0141.

There are cabins on the ferries running from Topolobampo to La Paz and from Guaymas to Santa Rosalia, as well as a public (not very comfortable) saloon area. Food and drink are available on the ferries but you might prefer to take fruit and sandwiches. The northernmost route connects Santa Rosalia with Guaymas, leaving Santa Rosalia at 8am arriving in Guaymas at 3pm, then leaving Guaymas at 8am with arrival in Santa Rosalia at 3pm. A similar but not identical schedule applies between Mazatlan and La Paz. Double-check schedule information as boats are sometimes delayed.

Reservations and schedules are not a problem for the frequent, short-distance ferry-trips from the Yucatán peninsula to offshore islands. The passengers-only ferry to Cozumel departs from Playa del Carmen three times a day; if you are driving, there is a parking lot near the ferry landing. If you want to take your car on to the island – not a bad idea, for Cozumel is fairly large – the departure point is Puerto Morelos, further north. This ferry goes in each direction once a day.

For the shorter trip to Isla Mujeres, you can take a car-ferry from Punta Sam or a passengers-only ferry for Puerto Juarez. The latter runs several times a day; again, parking is available if you are leaving your car on the mainland. Alternatively you can drive right on to Cancún over a causeway. There are no ferries to Isla Contoy, a bird refuge popular with fishermen and snorkelers as well as bird-watchers; but you can charter a boat.

BY SCHEDULED TOUR

The government tourist agency SECTUR maintains a 24-hour hotline to provide information of all kinds: tel: 250-0123 or toll free (from outside Mexico City) 91-800-90-392.

American Express, Paseo de la Reforma 234, tel: 533-0380 and **Viajes Americanos,** Reforma 87, tel: 566-7711, both in the Zona Roja, are two big agencies which can arrange tours and sightseeing throughout Mexico. For information about **limousine rentals** call 208-1817. If you speak Spanish it might be worthwhile visiting one of the Mexican tourist agencies where prices are sometimes lower than those on offer to foreign visitors. **Turissste,** Reforma 19, tel: 592-7755, for example, operates relatively inexpensive tours to almost all Mexican resorts and tourist sites.

Excursions from Mexico City
Grey Line operates trips to all tourist sites accessible from the capital, including Teotihuacán (taking in the Shrine of Guadalupe and, on Tuesdays, the market in Chiconcuac), and one-day excursions to places such as Tula and Tenayuca.

Their office is at Londres 166 in the Zona Rosa. Tel: 208-1163 for reservations and free hotel pickup. Between 8pm and 7am call 208-2838. (You can get to Teotihuacán on your own by taking the Metro to the Terminal Central del Norte and catching a bus onwards from there.)

Reservations for spa resorts in **Tequisquiapan** (188 kms/117 miles from Mexico City via federal Highway 57 and then Highway 120) can be made in Mexico City at 533-3550. The Hacienda Jurica is located on the Mexico–San Luis Potosi Highway at Km 229 (tel: 207-0562).

Reaching the **Hotel Ixtapán** (described as the "Shangri-la of America" since its mineral waters are said to be rejuvenating) is easy as you can be picked up in Mexico City and driven there and back by phoning 264-2613. They charge for this service. Accommodation is expensive but includes good meals. There are less expensive resorts nearby and buses offering second-class service leave the Terminal Central Poniente every 10 or 20 minutes between 5 or 6am and 9pm.

A number of US companies organize packaged camping tours, among them **Adventure Vacations** in Boulder, Colorado (tel: 1-800-444-0099) specializing in hiking trips through Copper Canyon; **Trek America** of Blairstown, NJ (tel: 1-800-221-0596) with two- to six-week excursions covering both northern and eastern Mexico; **Wilderness: Alaska/Mexico** of Fairbanks, Alaska (tel: 907-479-8203) also offering both sea kayaking and rafting trips; and **Baja Expeditions** (tel: 1-800-843-6967) whose specialty is the 1,609 km (1,000-mile) peninsula. **Club de Exploraciones de Mexico** offers guides for hiking through the urban jungle that is Mexico City (call 5-740-8032).

PUBLIC TRANSPORTATION

Trains

For those who want to see the countryside, trains are more comfortable than buses. Although they don't go everywhere, as the buses do, there are some 24,140 kms (15,000 miles) of track in Mexico. You can get to any district, and then take a short bus-ride to your ultimate destination. In general, the scenery will be better than along the highways; and some of the most spectacular landscape in North America — the Barranca del Cobre, or Copper

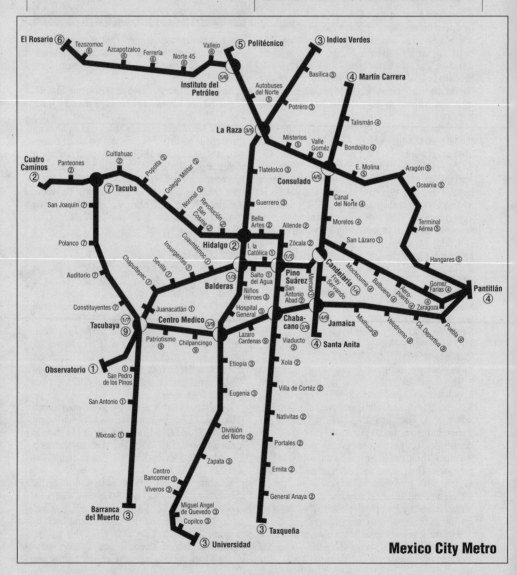

Mexico City Metro

352

Canyon, in the state of Chihuahua – is accessible only by rail.

Prices are low, due to government subsidy. As with buses, second-class trains are not a good choice for most foreign travelers: they will be very hot or very cold, the seats uncomfortable, the bathrooms inadequate. On main routes, it is advisable to go for the higher priced ride. For example, to travel from Mexico City to Guadalajara overnight, you can take the regular train or, for about US$50, *El Tapatio*, where you'll have a tiny bunk-sized room to yourself with toilet and washbasin and an airline-type dinner served right to your door. Considering that you save the cost of a hotel, prices are low.

Pullman cars are retired from US railroads and are fairly well-maintained, though don't expect everything in your compartment to work. On some trains there are also dormitory cars (*dormitorios*) with curtained-off beds that are less expensive than the Pullman compartments. When you make your reservation you can choose an upper or a lower bunk or berth (*cama alta* or *cama baja*). Some trains have inadequate or no catering facilities so take something to eat and drink with you.

Reservations are advisable and at vacation times, especially Christmas and Easter, they are essential. Since the railroads are government-owned and pay no commissions to travel agents, obtaining reservations before you arrive in Mexico can be difficult. If you are already in Mexico, you should go directly to the station for your tickets (*billetes*). Or, before coming to Mexico, you can try writing for information, schedules and fares to:
Ferrocarriles Nacionales de Mexico, Departamento de Trafico de Pasajeros, Estación Central de Buenavista, Insurgentes Norte, Mexico 3, DF, tel: 547-1084.

As this is a busy office you may not get a very prompt answer. If you receive the information you need, send a certified check or cashier's check to purchase the tickets. Specify whether you want them sent to you (be sure there is sufficient time) or held for you to pick up. If some of your tickets are for children, make the appropriate adjustments: children between five and 12 travel for half-fare, those under five travel free.

Reserved seats on the *Constitucional*, a railway coach car to Queretaro leaving every morning at 7am and returning every afternoon at 5.30pm, can be booked at Buenavista Station on Av Insurgentes North, tel: 547-1097. This must be done in person at least a day ahead.

Subways

Mexico City has an excellent subway system, operated by STC (Sistema de Transporte Colectivo, tel: 709-1133). A free map of the network (too small for easy reading) is available at most stations. Stay away from the Metro at rush hour and don't plan on using it for a trip to the airport or bus station with all your luggage, or for coming home after a successful shopping trip: no package larger than one briefcase per rider is permitted.

Line 1 runs east-west through downtown and past Chapultepec Park; it gets you to the airport and two bus stations, the Central Camionera de Oriente and the Central Camionera Poniente.

Line 2 runs from Cuatro Caminos, near the bull ring, to downtown and then south to Taxqueña, near the Central Camionera Sur.

Line 3 runs from Indios Verdes south to the University.

Line 4 also runs north-south also, but further east.

Line 5 runs from Pantitlan in the east, where it meets Line 1, northwest past the airport and the Central Camionera del Norte.

Line 6 runs east-west in the northern part of the city.

Line 7 runs north-south in the western part of the city, past the Auditorio Nacional (a good place to start seeing the museums and Chapultepec Park), to Barranca del Muerto.

Subway tickets are very cheap; buy a strip of five at a time.

Buses

In Mexico City, green private buses run up and down main boulevards such as Insurgentes and the Paseo de la Reforma. The fare is inexpensive; tell the driver where you plan to get off and he will charge accordingly.

One can go virtually anywhere in Mexico by bus. Hundreds of bus companies criss-cross the country, their vehicles ranging from the very clean, modern and fast to the opposite extreme. Most foreign travelers will prefer the first-class buses, which are air-conditioned and have a toilet in the back. First-class buses stop only at major centers, while others stop whenever someone flags them down. If you are going to a remote area you will need to take a second- or third-class bus, but use a first-class bus to reach the general district more quickly. The trip from Mexico City to Guadalajara, for example, takes about nine hours even on a first-class bus, but is relatively inexpensive. On long hauls, drivers usually stop at meal-times (especially around 2pm).

Another advantage of first-class buses is that seats are assigned. The best view is from near the front; the center provides the smoothest ride, the back the bumpiest. For night travel a seat on the right side is preferable, away from the glare of headlights. An afternoon trip in hot country is more comfortable if you're on the side away from the sun. You can usually purchase the right to use the seat next to yours for your bags or to stretch your legs, and pay the charge for excess luggage. There have been holdups of buses so it's safer, if you're going a long way, to travel on buses that head to their destination without stopping. ADO, for example, travels overnight non-stop between Mexico City and Villahermosa, showing a movie, providing blankets, pillows, free sodas and coffee, and offers seats that recline to about 45 degrees. The cost is higher than first-class but you may consider it worth it.

Reservations are a bit of a problem. You cannot reserve a seat by telephone. You cannot buy a round-trip ticket, nor can you buy a ticket to your ultimate destination with stop-over privileges. At busy times of the year, make reservations well ahead. Especially around Christmas and Easter, buses are very crowded and you should reserve your seat at least two weeks in advance. If you make several stops, buy your seat for the next stage of your trip as soon as you arrive – otherwise, you may have to stay a day or two longer than you intended.

If you are traveling from the US, **Greyhound** will arrange your reservations from the border as far as Mexico City. In Mexico City, Greyhound has an office at Reforma 27, tel: 535-4200 or can be contacted through Wagons Lits Mexico, tel: 325-0921, ext. 260. **Mexicorama** near downtown Mexico City, Londres 161, in the Zona Rosa, tel: 533-2047, will also help you with bus tickets. They speak English.

Otherwise, reservations must be made and tickets purchased at the bus stations. In most cities, the bus station is conveniently located. In Mexico City, you must go to one of four stations – all are well away from downtown to avoid traffic problems.

Buses for the northern part of the country – beyond Manzanillo on the Pacific side, or beyond Poza Rica on the Gulf side – use the **Terminal de Autobuses del Norte** (Metro station with same name) at Av. de los Cien Metros 4907. **Terminal del Autobuses del Sur** (Tasquena Metro station) at Av. Tasquena 1320, handles buses for points south and southwest of Mexico City, such as Cuernavaca, Taxco, Acapulco and Zihuatanejo. Other buses westward use the **Terminal de Autobuses del Occidente** (Metro Observatorio), at Avenida Sur 122, in Colonia Tacubaya. Buses to the east and southeast, including the Yucatán Peninsula, use the Terminal de **Autobuses de Pasajeros de Oriente,** TAPO (Metro San Lazaro) at Zaragoza 200, near the airport.

Since the bus stations are in outlying areas, you may want to take a taxi; the taxi-driver can probably tell you which of the many bus companies at that terminal will take you to your destination.

There are a number of deluxe-class buses which travel from Mexico City to Queretaro. Primera Plus buses operated by **Flecha Amarilla** leave every two hours for Queretaro from the Terminal Central del Norte. **Tres Estrellas de Oro** (tel: 567-8444) and **Transportes del Norte** (tel: 587-5511) also operate buses to the north and northwest from this station, as does ADO (tel: 567-8455) with buses heading northeast to such towns as Pachuca, Tuxpan and Matamoros. Heading east and south to such destinations as Puebla, Veracruz, Tehuantepec and Tuxtla Guittierez are **Omnibus Cristobal Colón** (tel: 542-7263) and ADO (tel: 592-3600) operating from the TAPO bus station. **Estrella Roja** (tel: 522-0269)

offers deluxe-class services to Puebla also from the TAPO terminal. Many bus lines offer deluxe trips to Toluca from the Terminal Central Poniente (Metro station Observatorio). **Enlaces Terrestres Nacionales** leaves every hour and TNT buses leave every five minutes. Buses for the southwest, including Acapulco, are operated by **Estrella de Oro** (tel: 549-8520) from the terminal Central del Sur.

Baggage is limited to 25 kg (55 lb) on first-class buses, but the limit is not usually enforced. On second-class buses there is virtually no limit, although you may have to load it yourself. Live baggage is also permitted on second-class buses: this includes pigs and chickens on their final journeys, as well as your pet parrot or poodle.

City buses are often convenient for the traveler without a car, and in Mexico City – where driving is a nightmare for the visitor – they are highly recommended. The fare is quite low, less than a peso. There are also inexpensive mini-buses or *microbuses*, which often give you a ride at break-neck speed. In addition to the regular city buses, Mexico City has special Ruta 100 (Route 100) buses which run only on the system of *Ejes Viales* or main thoroughfares. This makes them more efficient; they are also more comfortable and more clearly labeled.

Taxis

Mexico has a bewildering variety of taxis. Fares are generally low, but if you are going some distance you should tell the driver your destination and ask the fare: *Cuanto cuesta*? For an idea of what is reasonable, ask the desk clerk at your hotel. The easiest Mexico City taxis for the non-Spanish speaking traveler to use are those waiting outside hotels. Drivers often speak English but their fares are very expensive by Mexican standards, roughly comparable to those of taxis in the US.

Somewhat less expensive than hotel cabs are the *sitio* taxis, which work out of cab-stands, usually found on street corners. You can telephone them to pick you up, but you will need to speak some Spanish to do so. Some *sitio* stands accept advance reservations; and some even offer 24-hour service, like *Sitio 154* "Cuautemoc," tel: 282-1830.

Many cruising taxis are Volkswagen Beetles which charge about half as much as hotel cabs. The green ones (usually cleaner and in better condition) are environment-friendly, and use unleaded gas. Always check that the driver has turned on the meter or you will find yourself paying what he guess-timates is the right amount. It is virtually impossible to hail a cruising cab if it is raining, or during rush hours (7–10am, 4–9pm).

The cheapest cabs are collective taxis, *colectivos*. Those called *peseros* travel only on set routes, using the main thoroughfares. They are large American cars with a green stripe painted down the side. The driver will take two passengers in front, four in the back – sometimes more. You will be charged according to the length of your ride. Special *colectivos* carry passengers leaving the Mexico City bus stations. Tickets are sold in the bus stations for rides in these taxis. The first passenger to get in determines the direction the cab will take; the driver will then wait for a full load before leaving. During holiday periods, there is a mad rush for each taxi as it pulls in to the loading zone; you may find it faster to pay for a private cab.

If your Spanish is good and you want to do some touring in Mexico City, try to settle on an hourly rate with a taxi driver. You could try to hire a street cab for less, but be sure to ask, negotiate and agree a price before starting out.

Leaving the airport, porters will shuttle you over to the taxi stand. Buy your ticket or coupon according to the city zone to which you're going. The coupon is valid for four people and the luggage that fits in the trunk. The fares from the airport are fixed according to zones. Ask somebody what the usual rate is.

PRIVATE TRANSPORTATION

Exploring Mexico by car is a popular option and for the necessary documents see *Getting There*.

Before you drive, buy special comprehensive Mexican auto insurance. Get coverage for liability, property damage and theft, at a minimum. Your regular insurance does not cover you in Mexico, but your home agent may be able to arrange the policy for your through a Mexican company. Mexican auto insurance is easily purchased in any border town. Buy a policy for the longest period you might stay; if you leave the country sooner, you can arrange for a pro-rated partial refund.

Special insurance is vital because Mexican law is based on the Napoleonic Code – guilty until proven innocent – and if you have an accident, you could be jailed until fault is established. With the insurance, damages will be paid regardless of fault. However, keep in mind that motor vehicle insurance is invalid in Mexico if the driver is found to be under the influence of alcohol or drugs. When you buy the policy, get the names and addresses of the company's adjustors in the areas you intend to visit, and contact the adjustor immediately if you are involved in an accident of any kind.

It is recommended you leave the scene of the accident as quickly as practical, however much it may offend your sense of decency; likewise, it is advised that you do not stop to help if you witness an accident. Instead, notify the nearest Green Angel patrol you see, or – if there are injuries and no Green Angels in sight – notify the police. This is to avoid medical malpractice suits that may result from well-intentioned first-aid.

The Green Angels are Mexican tourism employees in green-and-white radio-equipped vehicles patroling major highways. They are ready to offer first-aid, minor repairs to your vehicle, or an emergency supply of gas and oil. You pay only for the parts used and for gas and oil. The Green Angels operate daily 8am–9pm except Tuesdays, when they start at noon. Most speak some English. In time of need, just raise your hood and wait.

If you don't drive into Mexico, you may want to rent a car for your stay. There are agencies in most cities and resorts. You'll need a major credit card as well as a valid driver's license. During busy vacation periods, advance reservations are necessary. Costs vary according to location and type of car but are not cheap and it is costly to drop off the car in any place other than where it was rented. If you drive your own car into Mexico, you must also leave with it. This is to prevent you from selling it – at a handsome profit, since import taxes keep auto prices high. To leave without your car in an emergency, you can post a bond with Mexican Customs officials or leave the car with them at the airport; a storage fee will be charged. The car may also be left at the Registro Federal de Automoviles, Calzada de Tlalpan 2775, Mexico 21, DF.

Always carry water for the radiator, a jack and spare tire (or two, in rugged and remote areas of the country), fuses and any other spare parts that might need replacement – even if you're not prepared to do the repair yourself. You can count on the Green Angels for mechanical know-how but not for the fan belt or other parts specific to your make and model (and remember, away from the main roads you may well be on your own).

Fill up on gasoline every chance you get. Have your car tuned up and checked before you leave for Mexico. Fortunately, if problems do arise, Mexican mechanics are familiar with American-made autos and some foreign-made cars, especially Renaults and Volkswagens. Mechanics are to be found in nearly any village, and at the ubiquitous Pemex gas stations.

The Pemex stations are a government monopoly. Leaded and non-leaded (*magna sin*) gasoline and diesel fuel are sold. Some attendants are reputed to overcharge customers by failing to set the pump at zero first, and sometimes then neglect to replace the gas tank cover, so be alert. Gas stations don't accept credit cards.

Major highways in Mexico are generally very good, but it is wise to exercise caution. Don't drive at night in Mexico. Animals seem to have suicidal urges that lead them to sleep on highways at night, and there are many other hazards your headlights reveal when it is too late to avoid them. In some mountainous regions – Chiapas is one – there is a growing tendency for remote villages to set up impromptu "toll booths" by stretching a rope across the road. If you encounter such a blockage and the outlaws do not seem to be armed, it is best to slow down and then suddenly accelerate and drive straight through, then report the incident to the nearest Federal police.

Road Signs

Many road signs are of the international variety, easy to guess at. Others assume a knowledge of Spanish. If you don't understand a highway sign, slow down and be prepared to stop. Here are some key words:

Alto	Stop
Despacio	Slow
Peligro	Danger
Precaución	Warning
Ceda el paso	Yield right of way
Puente angosto	Narrow bridge
Curva	Curve
Transito Circulacion	One way usually on an arrow.
Estacionamiento	Parking; also abbreviated E, with E meaning no parking.
Vado	Dip; in wet weather, a ford.
Conserve su derecha	Keep right
Altura maxima	Vertical clearance (in meters)
Ancho libre	Horizontal clearance (in meters)
Maneje despacio neblina	Drive slow, fog (seen on toll booths – lights up when the warning applies).
Una hora, Dos horas	One hour, two hours (parking time limits, printed beneath a large circled E).

If you encounter a policeman directing traffic, and he is facing toward you or away from you, **stop**; if he is sideways to you, **go**.

If you park illegally you may return to find your license plates missing. Usually the policeman will be nearby and you can retrieve them by offering him some money. The same technique is effective if you commit a minor traffic violation. Try to think of it as an on-the-spot fine, rather than as a *mordida* (bribe). The same goes for the tow-truck if you're lucky enough to see them when they are about to drive off with your car. If you drive to Mexico City, your best chance of avoiding parking violations is to leave your car in the garage of your hotel. You will want to do this because, bad as parking is in Mexico City, driving is even worse. You can rent a car and driver or take taxis, buses or the subway.

Car Rentals

In the US the toll free numbers (1-800) for the major car rental companies (all of which have subsidiaries in Mexico) are:

Hertz, tel: 564-3131
Avis, tel: 331-2112
Budget, tel: 527-0700
National, tel: 328-4567.

In Mexico they are listed in local phone books and contactable through the concierge in the lobby of almost any major hotel.

In Baja California:

AMCA Rental de Autos, Calle Madero 1715, La Paz, tel: 3-0335 with offices also at Cabo San Lucas and San Jose del Cabo. For toll free reservations in the US, tel: 1-800-832-9529.

Principal Mexican Road Signs

Doble Circulacion
Two Way Traffic

Glorieta
Rotary Intersection

Transicion
Transition

Tramo Angosto
Road Narrows

Puente Angosto
Narrow Bridge

Stop

Yield
Right of Way

Inspection

Speed Limit
(km)

One Way
Traffic

Altura Maxima
Vertical Clearance (m)

Camino Derrapante
Slippery Road

Pendiente
Hill

Vado
Dip

Cruce Ferrocarriles
Railroad Crossing

No
Pedestrians

Keep
Right

No
U Turn

Horizontal
Clearance (m)

No Left Turn

Trabajadores
Workmen

Escuela
School Zone

Zona de Derrumbes
Slide Area
(Watch for Falling Rocks)

Semaforo
Traffic Light

Ganado
Cattle

Do Not Pass

Do Not Enter

One Hour
Parking

Parking Limit

No Parking

WHERE TO STAY

HOTELS & RV PARKS

Hotels in Mexico number in the thousands, and range from luxurious suites in some of the world's most opulent hostelries to small rooms costing as little as 30 or 40 pesos per night. These are fine for those with a tight budget and plenty of time, but they do not pay commission to travel agents and so it is difficult or impossible to make reservations in advance. Mexico's trailer-park industry has experienced a boom. Almost every city has a trailer-park or motel with amenities including modern hook-ups, laundries, cafeterias, showers, small grocery stores, and even gas stations. Many National Parks (*Parques Nacionales*) have at least parking areas for RVs or tents and parking, plus 24-hour vigilance. They charge very modest fees for overnighting. There are several good sources of information for campers, whether you have a trailer or a tent. The *Rand McNally Campground and Trailer Park Guide*, available in bookstores, lists many Mexican campgrounds. You can also order campground directories from KOA (PO Box 30558, Billings, MT 59114); from Climatic Data Press (PO Box 413, Lemont, PA 16851); and from *Margarita* (Apartado Postal 5-599, Mexico 5, DF). Write well in advance for a price list, specifying that your interest is in Mexico. You may want to seek information from the AAA, from the company from which you buy your Mexican auto insurance, and from offices of the Mexican National Tourist Council. Keep in mind that campgrounds, like hotels, can be very crowded at peak tourist season.

A guide to room rates is given below. Rates are based on a double room:

$$$ = US$100 and above
$$ = US$50–100
$ = under US$50.

ACAPULCO – GUERRERO

Acapulco Malibu, Av. Costera Miguel Aleman 20, tel: (74) 84-1070. Small, old beach hotel but still comfortable. Pool, restaurant. $$
Acapulco Princess, Playa Revolcadero, Acapulco Diamante, tel: (74) 84-3100, US tel: 1-800-223-1818. Largest hotel in Acapulco. Two 18-hole golf courses, 11 tennis courts, five pools. Modified American plan in high season. $$$

Bali Hai, Av. Costera Miguel Aleman 186, tel: 85-6622. Indoor and outdoor pools. $$
Camino Real, Carretera Escenica Km 14, Baja Catita, tel: (74) 81-2010, US tel: 1-800-228-3000. New member of the prestigious Camino Real chain on its own small bay. $$$
Pierre Marques, Playa Revolcadero, Acapulco Diamante, tel: (74) 84-2000. Sister hotel to the Acapulco Princess – more relaxed. Princess's facilities available via shuttle bus every 10 minutes. $$$
Ritz, Av. Costera Miguel Aleman 159, tel: 85-7544. Older hotel on beach with some nice Art Deco finishings. Pool, restaurants. $$$
Vidafel Mayan Palace, Geranios 22, Fracc. Copacabana 39000, tel: (74) 62-0020. Stunning Mayan architecture, thatched roofs and glass pavillions. Large complex with canals connecting facilities. $$$
Ukae Kim, Pie de la Cuesta, US tel: (619) 451-8838. A few miles north of town on the beach. Comfortable. $$
Villa Vera, Lomas del Mar 35, tel: (74) 84-0333, US tel: 1-800-223-6510. Some villas have private pools. Only 80 rooms. Book well in advance. $$$

AGUASCALIENTES – AGUASCALIENTES

Fiesta Americana, Paseo de los Laureles, tel: 18-5059. Near San Marcos park and convention center. 200 rooms, air conditioning, pool, restaurant, gym. Very obliging staff. $$$
Francia, Av. Madero & Plaza Patria. 87 stately units on main square. $$
Hotel Senorial, Plaza Principal, tel: (491) 15-1630. Some rooms overlook the plaza. $
La Vid, Blvd José Ma. Chávez, tel: 16-0150. 68 units, restaurant, pool. $
Las Trojes, Blvd Campestre & Blvd Zacatecas, tel: 14-0468. In own grounds north of town. Restaurant, pool, tennis courts. $$
Quinta Real, Av. Aguascalientes Sur, tel: 18-1842. This is as luxurious as Aguascalientes gets. 81 suites, restaurant, pool. $$$

AJIJIC – JALISCO

Danza del Sol, Zaragoza 165, tel: 6-0630. 40 suites with 1–3 bedrooms, pool, restaurant. $$
Laguna Bed 'n' Brunch, Zaragoza 29, tel: 6-1174. Four comfortable units with private baths. $
La Nueva Posada, Donato Guerra 9, tel: 6-1333. 12 charming suites, pool, fine restaurant. $$

BAHIA DE LOS ANGELES – BAJA CALIFORNIA

Villa Vita Motel, Reservations: 509 Ross Drive, Escondido, CA 92025, tel: (619) 298-4958. Central, opposite beach. Pool, restaurant, bar. $

BATOPILAS – CHIHUAHUA

Hacienda Batopilas (Riverside Lodge), tel: 14-1505. 15 rooms. Feather beds, Oriental rugs, fans, meals and tours. Reservations in Chihuahua, tel: 14-1582. $$$

Palmera. Best economy hotel in town. Clean, with restaurant. $

RV Parks

Paradaor de la Montana, tel: 6-0075. In connection with hotel. Accepts RVs in secured parking area. No hookups but owner will let you use facilities if not full. English spoken.

Pension Creel, tel: 6-0071. In connection with hotel. Tours available. English and French spoken.

CABO SAN LUCAS – BAJA CALIFORNIA

Hotel Cabo San Lucas, PO Box 48088, Los Angeles CA 90048, tel: 1-800-SEE-CABO. Outside town. Fountains and statuary dot the tropical gardens, private beach and airstrip. $$$

Los Cabos Inn, 16 de Septiembre & Abasolo, tel: 3-0510. Tiny motel just west of town. $

Mar de Cortez, Calles Guerreo & Cardenas, tel: (684) 3-0032. Downtown near marina. Pool, restaurant, bar. $

CAMPECHE – CAMPECHE

Hotel América, Calle 10 No. 252, tel: (981) 6-4588. Converted colonial home, rooms around a patio, good budget choice for downtown location. $

Hotel Baluartes, Av. Ruiz Cortines 61, tel: (981) 6-3911. On the waterfront. Pool, restaurant. $$

Ramada Inn, Av. Ruiz Cortines 51, tel: 6-2233. Newly refurbished, city's luxury hotel, on the waterfront. Pool, restaurant. $$

CANCÚN – QUINTANA ROO

There are 20,000 hotel rooms in Cancún and all the international chains are represented. The following list is necessarily a brief sample of available accommodation, ranging from five-star luxury to a budget youth hostel:

Club Med, Punta Nizuc, Blvd Kukulkán Km 22, tel: (988) 5-2409. Secluded location with view of hotel row, all Club Med amenities, casual atmosphere. $$$

Hotel America and Beach Club, Av. Tulúm and Brisa, Cancún city, tel: (988) 4-7500. Pleasant large rooms, beach club on Cancún island for ocean access. $$

Hotel Camino Real Cancún, Blvd Kukulkán, Punta Cancún, tel: (988) 3-0100. Surrounded by the sea on three sides, truly private balconies, architectural drama. $$$

Hotel Meliá Cancún, Blvd Kukulkán 23, Zona Hotelera, tel: 51-1160. Tropical modern luxury, one of the most dramatic and pleasing atriums anywhere. All amenities. $$$

Hotel Oasis Cancún, Paseo Kukulkán Km 18.5, tel: (988) 5-0752. Set in 12 hectares (30 acres) of manicured grounds, with on-site nine-hole golf course and one of largest pool expanses in Latin America. $$$

Hotel Randall, Av. Tulum 49 at Cobá, Cancún city, tel: (988) 4-1122. Pleasant, low-rise, lots of cool marble surfaces for the budget-minded. $$

Hotel Tankah, Av. Tankah 69, Cancún city, tel: 4-4446. Simple lodgings downtown for a modest price. $

The Ritz-Carlton Cancún, Retorno del Rey 36, Zona Hotelera, US tel: 1-800-241-3333. Traditional Ritz-Carlton continental elegance and refinement, with an introspective air. $$$

Villa Deportiva Juvenil (Youth Hostel), Blvd Kukulkán Km 3.2 Zona Hotelera, tel: 3-1337. Economical lodgings in exclusive Hotel Zone, in communal dorms divided by gender. $

CATEMAC – VERACRUZ

Motel Playa Azul, Carretera Sontecomapan Km 2, tel: (294) 3-0001. Resort on gorgeous Lake Catemaco. Being gradually renovated. $$

CELAYA – GUANAJUATO

Hotel Celaya Plaza, Blvd López Mateos Pte, tel: (461) 4-6677. Restaurant, pool, tennis. $$

CHAPALÁ – JALISCO

Villas Buenaventura, Km 13.5 Chapala–Jocotepec highway, tel: 3-0505. 15-unit hotel. Spa. $$

CHICHÉN-ITZÁ – YUCATÁN

Hotel Dolores Alba, Km 122 Carretera Valladolid-Chichén-Itzá. No phone. For reservations, contact its sister hotel the **Hotel Dolores Alba** in Mérida, tel: (992) 8-5650, clearly specifying a room at the Chichén-Itzá establishment. Modest, clean rooms, restaurant with moderately priced meals, 2 km (1 mile) from ruins. $

Hotel Hacienda Chichén-Itzá, Zona Arquelógica, tel: (985) 24-2150. Stay at one of the bungalows once the home of a famous archaeologist. $$

Hotel Mayaland, Zona Arqueológica, tel and fax: (985) 6-2777. Dignified old hotel, pool, three restaurants, 53 rooms plus 12 Mayan villas. $$

Hotel Villa Arqueológica, Zona Arqeológica tel: 6-2830. Club Med amenities. Library. Excellent French and Yucatecan food. Attractive rooms, near to ruins. $$

CHIHUAHUA – CHIHUAHUA

Apolo, Carranza 102, tel: (14) 16-1100. 44 rooms, restaurant, bar. $

Avenida, corner of Juarez and Carranza, downtown, tel: 15-2891. 56-rooms, air conditioning, restaurant, bar. $

Casa Grande, Tecnologico 4702 off Highway 45, tel: 19-6633. Air-conditioned motel with restaurant, pool, tennis. Toll free (in Mexico) tel: 91-800-14-222, US tel: 1-800-343-6344. $$$

Castel Sicomoro, Periferico Ortiz Mena 411, tel: 13-5445. 130 rooms, air conditioning, restaurant, cafeteria, video bar, pool, washeteria. Toll free (in Mexico) tel: 91-800-14-567, US tel: 1-800-448-6970. $$$

El Capitán, Tecnologico 2300, tel: 13-0824. Air-conditioned motel, 22 units. $

Mirador, Universidad 1309, tel: 13-2205. Spotless 87-room motel, restaurant, bar, pool. $$

Nieves, Tecnologico and Ahuehuete, tel: 13-2516. 62-room, air-conditioned motel, restaurant, bar, pool. $$$

Palacio del Sol, Niños Heroes at Independencia 500, tel: 16-6531. 176-rooms, air conditioning, two restaurants, bars. Toll-free (in Mexico) 91-800-14-007, US tel: 1-800-852-4049. $$$

San Francisco, Av. Victoria 409, tel: 16-7550, US tel: (713) 449-4900. Air conditioning, 140-rooms, two restaurants. $$$

Victoria, Juarez & Colón, tel: 10-0547. Older, colonial-style 120-room air-conditioned hotel with attractive lobby, restaurant, bar, disco, pool. $$$

Villa Suites, Escudero 702 at Ortiz de Campos, tel: 14-3350. Fully equipped kitchens in suites, pool, Jacuzzi, steam bath, tennis, laundry. $$$

CIUDAD JUAREZ – CHIHUAHUA

Calinda Juarez, Av. Hnos. Escobar 3515, tel: 16-3421. Three kilometres (2 miles) south of border. Restaurant, pool. $$

Colonial Las Fuentes, Av. de las Américas 1355, tel: (16) 13-5050. Large 230-room motel. Swimming pool, nearby restaurant. $$

CIUDAD VALLES – CHIHUAHUA

Hotel Valles, Blvd Mexico-Laredo 36 Norte, tel: (138) 2-0050. Restaurant. Pool, children's play area in attractive grounds. $$

COATEPEC – VERACRUZ

Posada Coatepec, Hidalgo 9, tel: (281) 6-0544. Charming conversion of a 19th-century *hacienda*. $$$

COZUMEL – QUINTANA ROO

Hotel Casa del Mar, Costera Sur Km 3, tel: (987) 2-1900. Great swim-up bar, on-site dive-shop for top diving facilities and pier. $$

Hotel Flamingo, Calle 6 Norte 81, San Miguel, tel: (987) 2-1264. Attractive, quiet rooms a short distance from main plaza at budget prices. $

Hotel Holiday Inn Cozumel Reef, Carretera a Chankanaab Km 7.5, tel: (987) 2-2622. Luxury right at fabulous Palancar reef, fabled international diving destination. $$$

Hotel Meliá Mayan Plaza, Carretera Santa Pilar Km 3.5, tel: (987) 2-0072. Secluded setting on a very long beach, luxurious lobby and rooms, all with an ocean view. $$$

Hotel Safari Inn, Av. Rafael Melgar and Calle 5 Sur, San Miguel, tel: (987) 2-0101. A prime budget choice for a pleasant room, adjoining dive-shop premises and offering diving packages. $$

Sol Cabañas del Caribe, Carretera Santa Pilar Km 4.5, tel: (987) 2-0017. Smaller hotel, with all the amenities of the Spanish chain, a favorite with divers. $$$

CREEL – CHIHUAHUA

Cascada Inn, tel: 6-0151. 32 rooms. Indoor heated pool. $$

Copper Canyon Lodge, 20 km (12 miles) south of town, tel: (14) 12-8893, US tel: 1-800-776-3942. 29 rooms. Rustic accommodation with restaurant. Reservations (groups only) advised through travel agent in Chihuahua. $$$

Hotel Divisadero Barrancas, PO Box 661, 31328 Chihuaha, tel: (14) 10-3330. On rim of the canyon. American plan only with meals. $$$

Korachi, S. Categorta, tel: 6-0207. 12 rooms. $

Margaritas, tel: 6-0245 Seventeen *cabanas*. With breakfast and dinner. $

Margaritas Casa Mexicana, Calle Chapultepec, tel: 6-0045. Guest house (Casa de Huespedes). With breakfast and dinner. $

Parador de la Montana, Av. López Mateos 44, tel: 6-0075. 40 rooms. Restaurant, bar, tours. The casts of *Altered States* and *Wolf Lake* were given rooms here when the movies were filmed nearby. Reservations in Chihuahua, tel: (14) 12-4580. $$$

Pension Creel, Av. López Mateos 61, tel: 6-0071. B&B. Large cabins with and kitchen. Laundry. RV Parking. English and French spoken. Reasonable tours. Day-trips with transportation and overnight camping. $$

RV Parks

Parque Deportiva, just off Av. Tecnologico at university stadium. Dry camping only.

CUERNAVACA – MORELOS

Hotel Casino de la Selva, Av. Vicente Guerrero, tel: 12-4700. Suites and rooms overlook a lovely garden. Pool, restaurant, disco. $$$

Hotel Colonial, León 104 at Aragón, tel: 18-6414. Small, a couple of blocks from the Jardín. Rooms arranged around interior patio. $

Hotel del Prado, Nardo 58, tel: 17-4000. In residential area with lovely garden. Pool, restaurant, coffee shop. $$$

Hotel Las Mananitas, Ricardo Linares 107, tel: (73) 14-1446. Garden has pool, fountains, peacocks. $$$

Hotel Papagayo, Motolinia 13, tel: 14-1711. Three long blocks below the cathedral but bargain-priced and with twin pools. $

Camino Real Sumiya, tel: (72) 20-9199. Woolworth's heiress Barbara Hutton's former estate is the setting for the city's new lavish hotel. It has 163 rooms in a cluster of four-story modules connected by roofed corridors. Fully equipped business center in acres of gardens. The house was constructed with materials imported from Japan and contains Hutton's prized collection of oriental art and furniture.

DIVISADEROS – CHIHUAHUA

Hotel Divisaderos Barrancas, PO Box 661, 31328 Chihuaha, tel: (14) 10-3330. On rim of the canyon. American-plan only with meals. $$$

La Mansion Tarahumara, Areponapuichic, tel: (14) 16-2672 in Chihuahua. Fifteen cabins. Restaurant, bar. Owner Maria Barriga is very friendly and knowledgeable. RVs can park here. $$$

Mision, Cerocahui, about 5 km (3 miles) past the *Cabanas*, tel: 681-57046, (in Chihuahua tel: (14) 16-5950). Thirty rooms: Restaurant. $$$

Posada Barrancas del Cobre, tel: 681-57046, (in Chihuaha tel: (14) 16-5950). Thrity-five rooms. View of Canyon. $$

DURANGO – DURANGO
Gobernador, 20 de Noviembre 257, tel: (181) 3-1919. Restaurant, pool. $$$

ENSENADA – BAJA CALIFORNIA
Bahia Resort Hotel, López Mateos & Alvarado, tel: (667) 8-2101. Midtown. Pool, ocean views, outdoor dining plus La Tortuga restaurant. $$

Hotel Paraiso Las Palmas, Blvd Sagines 206, tel: (526) 177-1701. Pool, Jacuzzi, ocean-view rooms. $$$

Motel Sahara, Calle Espinoza 174, tel: 6-0207. Simple, clean, opposite the post office. $

GUADALAJARA – JALISCO
Camino Real, Av. Vallarta 5005, tel: 647-8000. Sprawling air-conditioned 205-unit resort, five pools, tennis, restaurant. 20-minute ride from downtown. $$$

De Mendoza, Venustiano Carranza 16, tel: 613-4646. Centrally located. 110-units, pool, restaurant. $$

Fiesta Americana, Aurelio Aceves 225, tel: 625-3434. Modern, centrally located, 391-unit, air-conditioning, pool, tennis, restaurants. $$$

Francia, Maestranza 35, tel: 613-1190. Excellent downtown location but staff can be sullen. 60 units in a colonial building designated a national monument. Decent restaurant. $$

Quinta Real, Av. Mexico 2727, tel: 615-0000. Very luxurious. 53 suites (all with fireplaces), pool, restaurant. $$$

Vista Aranzazú, Av. Revolución & Degollado, tel: 613-3232. Commercial hotel with friendly staff. 500 decent units, popular nightclub and restaurant. $$

GUANAJUATO – GUANAJUATO
La Casa de Espíritus Alegres, Ex-Hacienda de la Trinidad, tel: 3-1013. An artist couple converted an 18th-century mansion into a charming B&B. $$

Las Embajadoras, Parque Embajadoras, tel: 2-0081. Somewhat hidden, 27 units around a patio. Good restaurant. $

Real de Minas, Nejayote 17, tel: 2-1460. Guanájuato's largest, with 175 units, pool, restaurant, nightclub, 10 minutes from downtown. $$$

San Diego, Jardín de la Unión 1, tel: 2-1499. 43 rooms, centrally located. Originally a 17th-century convent. $$

GUAYMAS – SONORA
Armida, Blvd García López, tel: 4-3035. 125-unit air-conditioned hotel on Highway 15 in town shaded by 200-year-old Yucateco trees. Restaurant, bar, pool. $$

Flamingos, North Highway 15, tel: 1-0961. Surprisingly nice 55-unit motel with some air-conditioned rooms. Restaurant, bar, pool. $

Las Playitas, Carr. Varadero Nacional Km 6 by the naval base, tel: 2-2727. Thirty air-conditioned cottages on Las Playitas Peninsula in conjunction with RV facility of same name. Popular restaurant. Boat ramp. $$$

Leo's Inn, Bacochibampo Bay, tel: 1-0104. Beachfront inn in Colonia Miramar. 15 air-conditioned rooms. Attractive grounds. $

Playa de Cortes, Bacochibampo Bay, tel: 1-0142. Famous hotel, originally built by Southern-Pacific Railroad. Three elegant dining rooms. Pool, tennis, boat ramp. RV park. $$$

RV Parks
Bahia, on Playitas Peninsula, tel: 1-5030. Boat ramp, 80 space park. All hookups.

Las Playitas, on road to naval base around Guaymas Bay 2 kms (1 mile) or so beyond La Bahia, tel: 1-5227. 100 space park. All hookups. Restaurant, pool, friendly owner Josephina Borboa is English-speaking. Apartments/motel.

Playas de Cortes, Bacochibampo Bay, tel: 1-0142. Beside hotel with same name. 55 spaces, all hookups. Use of hotel facilities. Pool.

GUERRERO NEGRO – BAJA CALIFORNIA
El Morro Motel, Blvd Zapata, tel: (685) 7-0414. Just before town, restaurant. $

Las Dunas Motel, Blvd Zapata. Adjoining market, no phone. Simple, rockbottom cheap. $

HERMOSILLO – SONORA
Calinda Hermosillo, Rosales y Morelia 86, tel: (62) 17-2430. Restaurant, pool. $$

Pitic Valle Grande, Blvd Kino y Ramón Corral, tel: 14-4570. Restaurant, pool. $$$

IRAPUATO – GUANAJUATO
Hotel Flamingo, Blvd Diaz Ordaz 72, tel: 6-3646. Small pleasant motel, just north of town. Restaurant, pool. $

Hotel Real De Minas, Portal Carrilo Puerto 5, tel: (462) 6-2380. A block from the main plaza. Restaurant. $$

ISLA MUJERES – QUINTANA ROO
Hotel Martínez, Madero 14, tel: (988) 7-0154. Fan-cooled, simple rooms, in smaller and older-style hotel. $

Hotel Na-Balam, Zazil-Ha 118, tel: (988) 7-0279. Quiet location for 12 junior suites with ocean views. $$

Hotel Roca del Mar, Av. Norte Bravo 1, tel: (988) 7-0101. Some rooms have great sea views and all are cooled by natural cross-ventilation. $$

Poc-Na, Matamoros & Carlos Lazo, tel: (988) 7-0090. Pleasant, well-run youth hostel, or very cheap stay in communal dormitories. $

Ixtapa/Zihuatanejo – Guerrero

Ixtapa Sheraton, Paseo de Ixtapa, Zona Hotelera, tel: (753) 3-1858, US tel: 1-800-325-3535. Soaring lobby atrium with glass elevators. Walking distance from Palma Real golf course. $$$

Krystal Ixtapa, Paseo de Ixtapa, Zona Hotelera, tel: (753) 3-0333, US tel: 1-800-231-9860. Lively in evenings at Bogart's restaurant and Christine's disco. $$$

La Casa Que Canta, Camino Escenico a la Playa La Ropa, Zihuatanejo, tel: (753) 4-2722. Eighteen suites, two pools. No children under 14. $$$

Villa del Lago, adjoins golf course, tel: (753) 3-1482. B&B in a luxurious colonial-style villa with pool. $$

Villa del Sol, Playa La Ropa, Zihuatanejo, tel: (753) 4-2239, US tel: 1-800-223-6510. One- and two-bedroom suites. Rates include breakfast and dinner. Member of Relais et Chateaux. $$$

Villas Miramar, Playa La Ropa, Zihuatanejo, tel: (753) 4-2106. Small colonial style hotel. Popular with seasoned travelers; book well in advance. $$

Westin Resort Ixtapa, Playa Vista Hermosa, tel: (753) 3-1685, US tel: 1-800-228-3000. On secluded Vista Hermosa Beach. All rooms with private balconies, some with private pools. $$$

Ixtapan de la Sal – Mexico

Hotel Ixtapan, Plaza San Gaspar, tel: 3-0125. Immense spa in landscaped grounds with mineral baths, health club, pools, tennis, restaurant. $$$

Hotel Kiss, Blvd San Román & Av. Juárez, tel: (724) 3-0349. Restaurant, pool, Jacuzzi, laundry. $$

Kino Bay – Sonora

Kino Bay, tel: (62) 14-1492 in Hermosillo. Two-story 18-unit, air-conditioned motel at north end. Small restaurant, eight kitchenettes. $

Posada del Mar, tel: 2-0155 or (62) 14-4193 in Hermosillo. Good value. 48-unit, two-story air-conditioned motel across from beach. Restaurant, pool. $$

Posada Santa Gemma, tel: 2-0001. Pricey 14-unit air-conditioned apartment motel. Two-bedroom split-level units with bath, kitchen, and fireplace. $$$

Saro. Simple but very neat 16-roomer on beach. Laundry. Saro speaks English, Italian and Spanish. $$

RV Parks

Caverna del Seri, tel: (62) 14-7134 in Hermosillo. Thirty spaces on beach at far north end on paved road. All hookups.

El Cactus, tel: 6-1643. 33-space park 1km (œ mile) off main street on sand road. All hookups.

Kino Bay, tel: (62) 12-0216 in Hermosillo. 200-spaces. All hookups. Dump station. Bungalows.

Kunkaak, tel: 2-0209, tel: (62) 17-0682 in Hermosillo. 54 large spaces with patio and all hookups.

Parador Bella Vista, PO Box NR 27, tel: 2-0139. 18 spaces. All hookups. Two furnished bungalows.

Posada Santa Gemma, tel: 2-0026. Small 14-space park next to motel. All hookups.

RV Park & Cabins Islandia Marina, tel: 2-0081. 73 spaces and eight cabins on beach. All hookups. Eight kitchenettes.

Saro, tel: 2-0007. Seven spaces. All hookups.

La Paz – Baja California

Hotel Perla, Paseo Obregón 1570, tel: (682) 2-0777. Irresistibly friendly place on the Malecón. Popular restaurant, pool. $$

Hotel Purisma, 16 de Septiembre 408, tel: (682) 2-3444. Four floors of plain rooms overlooking busy downtown street. $

La Posada de Engelbert, Av. Reforma & Playa Sur (10 minutes along road to airport), tel: (682) 2-4011. Owner Engelbert Humperdinck rarely being there, Mlle. Jacqueline presides over beachside suites and a fine restaurant. $$$

León – Guanajuato

La Estancia de León, Blvd López Mateos 1311 Ote, tel: 16-3939. Restaurants, pools, Jacuzzi. $$$

Los Mochis – Sinaloa

Hotel Colinas, Carr. Internacional No. 15 & Blvd M. Gaxiola, tel: 2-0101. Restaurant, pools, playground. $$

Santa Anita, Leyva & Hidalgo, tel: (681) 5-7046. Same owners as Posada Barrancas on rim of canyon. Restaurant. $$

Loreto – Baja California

Hotel Misión de Loreto, Blvd Mateos 1, tel: (683) 3-0048. On the Malecon. Attractive neo-Colonial style with bar, restaurant, pool. $$$

Hotel Oasis, Blvd Mateos, tel: (683) 3-0211. In tropical garden with pool, tennis court, meals included. $$$

Hotel Plaza, Hidalgo 2, tel: (683) 5-0280. One block from mission. Attractive rooms around small patio. Bar/restaurant, pool. $$

Manzanillo – Colima

Club Maeva, PO Box 442, Manzanillo, tel: (333) 3-0141. Four pools, fitness center, tennis, beach games, disco. $$$

Las Hadas Resort, Av. de los Riscos & Vista Hermosa, tel: 3-0000. Gorgeous location overlooking sea. Restaurants, pools, tennis, golf. $$$

Mazatlán – Sinaloa

Facilities are air-conditioned unless otherwise noted. Budget hotels tend to be located near the bus station, between the beach and downtown, and near the ferry terminal.

Ammaczatán, Sábalo Cerritos 576, tel: 14-1219. Three-story, 40-condo complex on beach at north end. $$

Aqua Marina, Av. del Mar 110, tel: 81-7080. Two-story with 100 units. $$

Azteca Inn, Av. Rodolfo T. Loaiza 307, tel: 13-4655. Three-story motel with 74 rooms. Jacuzzi. $$

Balboa Towers, Camarón Sábalo next to Balboa Club, tel: 13-7784. Delightful 52-unit hotel with 30 rooms, suites. $$$
Bella Vista Beach Club, La Mojarra 1412, Sábalo Country Club, tel: 14-2122. All rooms with view. $$$
Belnar, Olas Altas 166, tel: 85-1111. Inexpensive 200-room, old-time hotel near downtown. Some rooms have magnificent views. $
Beltran, Aquiles Serdan 2509 Nte, tel: 82-4654. Backpacker hotel. 28 rooms, all with ceiling fans. $
Bungalows de Rueda, tel: 82-5278. Sandy, six-apartment layout on north end. $
Bungalows Mar-Sol, Av. Camarón Sábalo 1001, tel: 84-0108. Kitchenettes. Just beyond Posada la Misión. $$
Camino Real, tel 13-1111, US tel: 1-800-228-3000. Four-story hotel, on north end up on knoll. Disco, masseuse. $$$
Caravelle Beach Club, Camarón Sábalo, tel: 13-0200. Seven-story, 128-room, beachfront hotel. $$$
Costa Brava, Camarón Sábalo Cerritos, tel 83-6444. 164-condo complex. $$$
Costa de Oro, Camarón Sábalo, tel: 13-5444. Toll free (In Mexico) tel: 91-800-69-666, US tel: 1-800-342-2431. Four-story, 292 room motel on beach. $$$
Damy's Bungalows, Av. del Mar 1200 at Camáron Glorieta, tel: 83-4722. Three-story, 28-unit motel. 19 kitchenettes, some air-conditioned. $$
De Cima, Av. del Mar, tel: 82-7855. Four-story, 150-room hotel with tunnel from hotel to beach. $$
Del Sol, Av. del Mar 800, tel: 85-1103. 20 rooms, 12 kitchenettes. $
El Cid, Av. Camarón Sábalo, tel: 13-3333, US tel: 1-800-525-1925. Expensive 960-room hotel on beach. Discos, gambling. 18-hole golf course, squash, sauna. $$$
El Dorado, Av. del Mar 117, tel: 81-3046. Four-story, 41-rooms, condo-hotel across from beach. $$
El Rancho, Sábalo Cerritos 3000, tel: 88-0099. Luxurious private club with 28 villas. $$$
Hacienda, Av. del Mar & Flamingos, tel: 82-7000. Nine-story, 95-rooms, air-conditioned hotel with sauna and Jacuzzi. $$
Holiday Inn, Camarón Sábalo 696, tel: 13-2222. Toll free (in Mexico) tel: 91-800-00-999, US tel: 1-800-465-4329. $$$
Islas del Sol, Camarón Sábalo, tel: 13-0088. Nineteen-story, 75-unit condo-hotel tower with use of adjoining Holiday Inn facilities. $$$
Jacarandas, Av del Mar, tel: 84-1177. Ocean view. 160 rooms, kitchenettes. $$
La Casa Contenta, Playa Gaviotas just north of Playa Mazatlan, tel: 13-4976. Eight one-bedroom kitchenettes, five air-conditioned units. Pool.
La Marina Yacht Club, Av. Sábalos Cerritos, tel: 83-0000. 103 rooms, kitchenettes. $$
Las Brisas, Av. del Mar 900, tel: 83-5976. Seven-story hotel, 53-rooms, across from beach. $$$
Las Palmas, Camarón Sábalo north of Camarón Glorieta, tel: 13-4255. Two-story eight-room hotel. Restaurant, bar, pool. $

Marley, Playa Las Gaviotas, tel: 13-5533. Two-story 16-kitchenette beachfront motel with pool. $
Milan, J.M. Canizales Pte 717, tel: 81-3588. A popular backpacker's place. 24 rooms, some with air conditioning. $
Paraiso Mazatlan, Calle del Calamar & Atún, tel: 83-8786. Suites and houses plus a penthouse. Pool, tennis, recreation hall. $$
Posada de la Mision, Camarón Sábalo, tel:13-2444. Two-story, 96-unit hotel across from beach. Restaurant, bar, pool. $$
Suites Las Flores, near arts-and-crafts center on Loaiza, tel: 13-5100, US tel: 1-800-452-0627. 12-story hotel with pool, tennis. $$
Suites Tecali, Gabriel Ruiz 3 (in El Dorado subdivision), tel: 14-7754. Budget three-story, 14-kitchenette complex with pool. $
Villa del Mar, A. Serdan 1506 Nte 26, tel: 81-3426. Budget hotel with ceiling-fans in rooms and rocking chairs in lobby. $

RV Parks

El Camarón. Eight space park at Camarón Circle directly in front of statue Bedide. All hookups. Restaurant/disco and motel.
Holiday RV Park, tel: 83-2578. Tropical, 232-space park out on far north end beyond Camino Real. 195 spaces with hookups.
Las Palmas, tel: 13-6424. 66-space park on beach, 11 kms (7 miles) north at Camarón Sábalo 333. All hookups. Pool. Apartments.
Mar Rosa, tel: 83-6187. 65 small spaces at north end next to Holiday Inn on beach. All hookups.
Maravilla. 26-space park on secluded beach at far north end of town on Cerritos beach beside DIF. All hookups.
San Bartolo, tel: 12-1278. North end park off Camarón Sabalo across from beach with 48 spaces. All hookups.

MÉRIDA – YUCATÁN

Casa del Balam, Calle 60 No. 48, tel: 99/24-8844. Upscale colonial decor on lively Calle 60. $$$
Hotel Caribe, Calle 59 No. 500 & Calle 60, tel: (992) 4-9022. Lovely historic building on attractive plaza downtown. $$
Hotel Holiday Inn, Av. Colón 498 & Calle 60, tel: 25-6877. Good service in slick setting, catering to business market. $$$
Montejo Palace, Paseo de Montejo 483-C, tel: (992) 4-7644. Modern highrise on beautiful boulevard. $$

MEXICO CITY – INSURGENTES SUR

Hotel Roosevelt, Insurgentes Sur 287, tel: 208-6813. Low-key, budget-priced place about 2 km (1 mile) from the Zona Rosa. $
Westin Galeria Plaza, Hamburgo 195, tel: 211-0014. In Zona Rosa. Three restaurants, rooftop pool. $$$

MEXICO CITY – DOWNTOWN AREA

Casa de los Amigos, Ignacio Mariscal 132, tel: 705-0646. Friendly hostel near Revolution Monument.

Low-budget hideaway ideal for students, writers, academics. $

Hotel Bamer, Av. Juarez 52, tel: 521-9060. Very central, very reasonable. Restaurant. $

Hotel de Cortés, Av. Hidalgo 85, behind the Alameda, tel: 518-2182. Former 18th-century hospice has colonial charm with modern comfort. Patio restaurant. $$$

Hotel Galicia, Calle Honduras 11, just beyond Plaza Garibaldi, tel: 529-7791. Interesting location in musical area; adjoins Guadalajara night club. $

Hotel Majestic, Av. Madero 73, tel: 521-8600. On the Zócalo with a terrace restaurant offering a terrific overview. $$$

Hotel Sevilla Palace, Reforma 105, near Cristobal Colon statue, tel: 566-8877. Pool, sauna, restaurants. $$$

Howard Johnson Gran Hotel, 16 Septiembre 82, tel: 512-9275. Just off the Zócalo in splendid old shell of an ornate former department store complete with gilded elevators and awesome ceiling. $$$

MEXICO CITY – ZONA ROSA & CHAPULTEPEC

Calinda Geneve, Londres 130, tel: 211-0071. Colonial, traditional, comfortable. $$

Century, Liverpool 152, tel: 227-7272. Highrise anchoring the southern side of the Zona Rosa. $$$

Hotel Aristos, Reforma 276, tel: 211-0112. Pool, sauna, coffeeshop. $$

Hotel Camino Real, Mariano Escobedo 700, tel: 203-2121. Huge, modern complex with many restaurants, pool and dramatic whirlpool, just across from Chapultepec Park. $$$

Hotel Nikko Mexico, Campos Eliseos 204, near Chapultepec, tel: 280-1111. Pool, sauna, tennis courts, restaurants. $$$

Maria Christina, Rio Lerma 31, tel: 546-9880. Classy mansion-style hotel with garden. Restaurant, bar. $$

Marquis Reforma, Reforma 465, tel: 211-3600. High-class accommodation in distinctive building. Health club, sauna. $$$

Westin Galeria Plaza, Hamburgo 195, tel: 211-0014. In Zona Rosa. Three restaurants, rooftop pool. $$$

MEXICALI – BAJA CALIFORNIA

Holiday Inn, Juarez 2220, tel: (657) 66-1300. One mile south of town. Pool, restaurant. $$$

Hotel de Norte, Melgar & Madero, tel: 52-8101. Nearest hotel to the border. Bar, restaurant, air conditioning. $

Hotel Plaza, Av. Madero 366, tel: (62) 52-9757. Downtown, restaurant, air conditioning. $

MONTERREY – NUEVO LEÓN

All Monterrey hotels are expensive, except on weekends when most offer discounts and some will pay your highway tolls.

Alamo, José Esponceda 100, tel: 52-0045. 40 air-conditioned units, on North Highway 85 in Colonia Anahuac at far north end. Restaurant, pool. $.

Ambassador Camino Real, Av. Hidalgo 310 Ote & Emilio Carranza, tel: 42-2040. Top-flight, 11-story, 242-room downtown hotel. Well-equipped fitness center with weights, Jacuzzi, steam room, pool, tennis. $$$

Ancira Inter-Continental, Ocampo 440 Ote, tel: 45-1060. Distinguished, five-story, 269 rooms. Restaurants, lobby bar, pool. Monterrey's most famous landmark hotel. Pancho Villa stabled his horse in the lobby in 1913. $$$

Bahia Escondida, south of town on Highway 85 near Horsetail Falls, tel: (828) 5-1112. Beautiful 100-suite resort hotel, overlooking lake. Huge pool, waterslide, tennis, basketball, skating rink, gym, steam room, picnic area. $$$

Colonial, Hidalgo 475, tel: 43-6791. Six-story, 85-room downtown hotel across from Ancira. Reasonably priced but sometimes a bit noisy. $$

Dorado, Carr. A. Laredo 901 Nte, tel: 52-4050. At far north end of Highway 85, a 34-unit air-conditioned motel with pool. $$

El Paso Autel, Zaragoza 130 Nte, tel: 46-6090. Good air-conditioned three-story, 64-room drive-in hotel. Conveniently situated 10 blocks north of business district. $$

Fiesta Americana, Vasconcelos 800, tel: 63-3030, US tel: 1-800-FIESTA-1. Hotel with 228 rooms in San Agustín. Restaurant, coffee shop, bars, pool, tennis, gym. $$$

Granada, on Topo Chico Hill, 13 km (8 miles) southwest of bypass just west of Highway 85 at far north end of town, tel: 76-7384. Three-story, 165 air-conditioned rooms, bar, pool, tennis. $$$

Holiday Inn Express, Av. Eugenio Garza Sada 3680 Sur, Col. Contry, south side of town on Highway 85, tel: 29-6000. Four-story 141-room hotel. Outdoor pool. $$$

Monterrey Clarion, Zaragoza & Morelos 574, tel: 43-5120. Good downtown Best Western with 200 air-conditioned rooms, some with excellent views. $$$

Royal Courts, Av. Alfonso Reyes 314, tel: 76-2710. Pleasant 74-unit air-conditioned motel on North Highway 85 (across from Holiday Inn). Restaurant, cafeteria, pool. $$$

Santa Rosa Suites, Escobedo 930 Sur, tel: 42-4200. Beautiful, elegant suites with refrigerator, sofas etc. $$$

Son Mar, Av. Alfonso Reyes 1211 Nte CP 64490, tel: 75-4400. Air-conditioned 90-room, five-story economy hotel on North Highway 85, near central bus depot. Restaurant, bar. $$

RV Parks

Bahia Escondida, tel: (828) 5-1112 or 5-1373. Will allow RV parking. It's supposed to be for members, but if they are not full, you can use the spaces. 12 spaces. All hookups. Very nice.

Nueva Castilla, tel: 84-1502. 26-space RV facility at north end of town on Highway 85 (2 km/1 mile south Saltillo bypass at Km 15.5) in conjunction with hotel. 110- and 20-volt electrical hookups and water available.

MORELIÁ – MICHOACAN

Hotel de la Soledad, Zaragoza 90, tel: 12-1888. Two short blocks from the main square. 60 rooms in converted monastery. Good dining room. $$
Posada Vista Bella, Santa Maria, tel: 14-0284. Motel with 16 apartments and 42 rooms, pool, restaurant and a great view. $
Villa Montaña, Patzimba, tel: 14-0231. On the outskirts of town. 40 units, all uniquely decorated. Private patios, pool, outstanding view. $$$
Virrey de Mendoza, Portal de Matamoros 16, tel: 12-0633. The first floor dates from the 16th century (the second and third were added later). Perfect location on the main square. 52 units, restaurant. $$

MULEGE – BAJA CALIFORNIA

Hotel Las Casitas, Madero 50, tel (685) 3-0019. Comfortable rooms around patio with plants, fountains and attractive restaurant. $
Hotel Serenidad, Apdo Postal 9, Mulege, tel: (685) 30-1111. Where the river meets the sea. Comfortable, attractive with bar, restaurant and pool. $$$

NUEVO LAREDO – TAMAULIPAS

Hotel El Presidente, 5 de Mayo 300, tel: 6-0611. Situated in a former convent. $$$
Hotel Meson del Rey, Guerrero 718, tel: 2-6360. Centrally located on the main plaza. $
Hacienda Motor Hotel, Prol. Av. Reforma 5530, tel: (871) 4-4666 On Highway 85, 3 km (2 miles) south of International Bridge. Restaurant, pool. $$
Motel Don Antonio, Gonzalez 2437, tel: 2-1149. $

OCOSINGO – CHIAPAS

Hotel Central, on the plaza, tel: 3-0024. A dozen simple rooms with bath, sidewalk restaurant. $

OAXACA – OAXACA

Hotel Senorial, Portal de Flores 5, tel: 6-3933. Simple hotel with a pool, facing Zócalo. $
Stouffer Presidente-Oaxaca, between Murguia & Abasolo streets, north of Zócalo, tel: 6-0611. Formerly a 16th-century convent ith cloisters and courtyard. Deposit required. $$$
Hotel Victoria, Lomas del Fortin 1, tel: 5-2633. Bungalows and rooms overlook the city and the valley. $$

PALENQUE – CHIAPAS

Hotel Chan-Kah. On the Zócalo, tel: 5-0318. Small and comfortable hotel with balconied rooms. Restaurant. $
There is another **Chan-Kah** (same phone number) nearer the ruins. Attractive cottages adjoining pool and outdoor restaurant. $$
Los Leones, Carr. Palenque-Ruinas Km 2.5, tel: 5-1110. Hotel, restaurant. Trailer park in large grounds 3 km (2 miles) from ruins. Travel agency. $$$
Plaza Palenque, Blvd Pakal, tel: (934) 5-0555. Modern, comfortable hotel at entrance to town. Restaurant, pool. $$

PAPANTLA – VERACRUZ

Hotel Premier, Enriquez 103, tel: (784) 2-0080. On the Zócalo. Best in town. $$
Hotel Tajín, Nunez y Dominguez, tel: (784) 2-0644. One block from Zócalo. Spacious rooms. $$

PÁTZCUARO – MICHOACÁN

Mesón del Gallo, Dr José María Coss 20, tel: 2-1474. 25 small, well-maintained rooms, restaurant, pool. $
Misión de San Manuel, Portal Aldama 12, tel: 2-1050. Small, 35-unit downtown hotel on a quiet square. Restaurant. $
Posada de Don Vasco, Calzada de las Américas 450, tel: 2-0227. 103 rooms in a colonial setting at the entrance to the city. Restaurant, pool. $$

PUEBLA – PUEBLA

Hotel Colonial, Calle 4 Sur 105, tel: 46-4199. Attractively renovated former monastery. Restaurant, cafeteria, bar. $
Hotel del Portal, Avila Camacho 205, tel: (22) 46-0211. On the Zócalo. restaurant, bar. $
Hotel Mesón del Angel, Av. Hermanos Serdán 807, tel: 48-2100. Three km (2 miles) from town. Restaurants, bars, two pools, tennis. $$$

PUERTO VALLARTÁ – JALISCO

Casa Helga and other luxurious villas, mostly on the hillside above Banderas Bay. Booking through Hegla Farrill, Fairfield, Ct., fax: (203) 579-9133.
Fontana del Mar, Manuel M. Dequez 171, tel: 2-1712. On beach five minutes from town center. Pool, terrace restaurant, bar. $$
Hotel Pelicanos, Carr. Aeropuerto Km 2.5, tel: 4-1010. Beachfront rooms and villas, restaurant, pools. $$
Hyatt Coral Grand, Carr. a Barra de Navidad Km 8.5, tel: 2-5196. In landscaped, beachfront grounds. Restaurant, gym, tennis, pool. $$$
Las Palmas, Paseo de las Palmas, tel: (322) 4-0650. Pool, restaurant, *palapa* bar on the beach. $$
Molino de Agua, Ignacio L. Vallarta 130, tel: 2-1957. In attractive beachside gardens near center of town. Pool, restaurant. $$

QUERÉTARO – QUERÉTARO

Antigua Hacienda Galindo, Carretera Amealco Km 5, tel: 5-0250 (San Juan del Río). Sprawling yet charming resort. 166 rooms and suites, restaurants, tennis, horses. $$$
Hacienda Jurica, Carretera a San Luis Potosí Km 229, tel: 18-0022. 178 rooms and suites, 14 hectares (35 acres) of garden. Pool, tennis, restaurant, golf, riding. $$$
Impala, Ignacio Zaragoza & Colón, tel: 12-2570. Decent downtown hotel. 102 rooms, restaurant. $
Mesón de Santa Rosa, Pasteur Sur 17, tel: 14-5781. Centrally located in colonial mansion. 20 intimate suites around three patios. Pool, restaurant. $$$

ROSARITO – BAJA CALIFORNIA

Baja Village Motel, Juarez & Via de las Olas 228, tel: (661) 2-0050. On main street, easy access to adjoining beach. $

Calafia, Km 35.5 Free Road Tijuana-Ensenada, tel: (661) 2-1581. Vast amusingly designed complex of terrace restaurants, bars and bric-a-brac. Pool, 24-hour coffee shop. $$

La Fonda, Km 59 Carretera Tijuana–Ensenada Highway where Libre and Cuota highways meet. Write for reservations to PO Box 430268, San Ysidro, CA 92143 (no telephone). Charming oceanfront *hacienda*, bar and restaurant on tropical patio. Four-person studios with kitchens. $$

Rosarito Beach Hotel, PO Box 430145, San Diego, CA 92143, tel: (661) 2-1106. Legendary resort on highway in town, with pools, tennis, shopping arcade etc. $$$

SALTILLO – COAHUILA

Camino Real, Blvd Los Fundadores 2000, tel: 15-2525. Very good, 144-room motor inn atop knoll on Highway 57 southeast of town. Pool, disco, tennis, putting green. $$$

Centenario, Luis Echeverria 1932, tel: 15-2418. 37 rooms. Restaurant. $$

Central, Luis Echeverria 231, across from bus depot, tel: 17-0004. Fifty-eight rooms. $

El Morillo, Prolongación Obregón & Echeverria, tel: 17-4078. Popular guest ranch 3 km (2 miles) southwest of town. Beautifully landscaped grounds around old *hacienda*. Pool, tennis, horses. $$

El Paso, V. Carranza Blvd 3101, tel: 17-4078. 34 room motel on Highway 40–54 at east edge of town. Restaurant, pool, parking. $$

Eurotel Plaza, Blvd V. Carranza 4100, tel: 15-1000. 156 rooms. Pool, laundry. $$

Huizache, V. Carranza Blvd 1746, tel: 16-1000. 66 room motel east of Periferico junction of highways 40–57–54. 14 kitchenettes. Restaurant next door. Pool. $$

La Fuente, Blvd Los Fundadores Km 3, tel: 30-1719. 52 room motel on Highway 57 southeast of town. Disco. Tennis, pool. $$

Saade, Aldama 397 Pte, tel: 12-9120. Seventy-two rooms. Restaurant. $$$

Urdinola, Victoria 211, tel: 14-0993. Cozy, older 46-room downtown hotel. English spoken. $$

RV Parks

Centro de Convenciones. 10km (6 miles) south of town with helpful tourism office on second floor. Several spaces with no hookups. Restrooms and shower facilities indoors. Nice management.

Imperial del Norte, V. Carranza Blvd 3747, tel: 15-0011. 30 space facility in conjunction with motel. Eight spaces with hookups. Showers, restrooms, friendly. Completely remodeled in 1993 with concrete pads and other amenities.

La Fuente, Blvd Los Fundadores Km 3, tel: 15-2599. Parking only. No use of facilities. On Mexico City Highway 57.

SAN BLAS – OAXACA

Las Brisas, Paredes, tel: 5-0112 S/N. The nicest place in town! 42-rooms, some air-conditioned, some ceiling fans. Pool. Breakfast included. English, French, German spoken. $$$

Misión San Blas, Cuauhtemoc 197 Sur, tel: 5-0023. 20 unit beachfront motel. *Palapa* restaurant, bar, pool. $$

Suites San Blas, Fracc. Palmar De Los Cocos, tel: 5-0047. 5km (3 miles) south of town. Three-story, 23-unit hotel. Ceiling fans only. Pool, playground, disco. $$

RV Parks

Los Cocos. 100-space park off main stem near beach, tel: 5-0055. All hookups. Pets OK. Nice place

Playa Amor. Between San Blas & Santa Cruz. Highly recommended! 40-space facility on beach. 25 with all hookups. 15 with electricty (30 amps) and water.

SAN CARLOS – SONORA

Apartamentos Ferrer, tel: 6-0467. Six apartments, kitchen, also rents a house. $$

Creston, tel: 6-0020. Excellent 24-unit air-conditioned motel on beach. Pool. $$

Fiesta San Carlos, Carr. San Carlos Km 8, tel: 6-0229. Three story, 33-unit, air-conditioned motor hotel right on beach. Mayan temple style. Circular pool. $$

Hacienda Teta Kawi, (Best Western), tel: 6-0220. 22 rooms, four suites with refrigerator. Pool. $$$.

Howard Johnson's, Playas Los Algodones, tel: 6-0777. Toll free (in Mexico) tel: 91-800-6-4368, US tel: 800-854-2320. Highrise with 173 rooms. Pool, Jacuzzi, health center. $$$

Loma Bonita, at entrance to country club and shopping center, tel: 6-0713. Great place for families. Two-bedroom apartments, pool, water slides, Jacuzzi, tennis. $$$

Posada de San Carlos, Carr. San Carlos, tel: 6-0122. Part hotel, part condo. 146-room air-conditioned beachfront complex. $$$

Suites Mar Rosa, on left just before country club going into town, tel: 6-0250. $$

RV Parks

Teta Kawi, across street from the largest San Carlos Beach, tel: 6-0220. 132-space facility. All hookups. Jacuzzi. Four furnished apartments.

Totonaka, adjoins Teta-Kawi 1, tel:6-0323. All hookups. 40 spaces. Twenty-five furnished apartments, some with kitchens.

SAN CRISTÓBAL DE LAS CASAS – CHIAPAS

Hotel Ciudad Real, Diagonal Centenario 32, tel: (967) 8-1886. Charming, colonial building with patio restaurant, comfortable rooms. $$$

Hotel Flamboyant Espanol, Calle 1 de Marzo 15, tel: 8-0726. Colonial building, with restaurant, and interior patios filled with pottery and greenery. $$$

Hotel Real del Valle, Real de Guadalupe 14, tel 8-0680. Center of town. Comfortable and with English-speaking owner. $

SAN FELIPE – BAJA CALIFORNIA
El Cortéz, Reservations: PO Box 1227, Calexico, CA 92231, tel: (526) 561-8324. Right by the sea, wide-screen TV. $$

SAN JOSÉ DEL CABO – BAJA CALIFORNIA
El Delfin Blanco, La Playita road near lighthouse, tel: 2-1199. Cabanas and trailer park very close to beach. $$

Hotel Posada Terranova, Degollado & Zaragoza, tel: 2-0534. Restaurant and bar. $

Howard Johnson's, Paseo Finisterra off highway 1, tel: 2-0999. Distinctive architecture; pool in tropical gardens. $$$

Posada Real, Paseo Malecón, on the beach, tel: 2-0793. Comfortable, pleasant resort hotel with pool and restaurant. $$$

Tropicana Inn, Blvd Mijares 30, tel: 5-2684. Pool, fountain, resident parrot, charming patio restaurant. $$

SAN LUIS POTOSÍ – SAN LUIS POTOSÍ
Hostal de Quijote, Carretera 57, Km 426, tel: 18-1312. 211 rooms and suites in a garden setting outside town. Restaurant, tennis, pool. $$

Panorama, Carranza 315, tel: 12-1777. Commercial-style hotel in downtown location. 137 units, restaurant, pool. $$

Quinta Real, Real de Lomas 1000, tel: 25-0125. 121 suites exquisitely decorated with antiques, Mexican handicrafts and original works of art. Pool, gym, restaurant. $$$

SAN MIGUEL DE ALLENDE – GUANAJUATO
Aristos, Calle del Cardo 2, tel: 2-0149. Next door to the Instituto Allende, San Miguel's famous art school. 60 units set in a lovely garden. Pool, tennis, restaurant. $$

Casa Sierra Nevada, Hospicio 35, tel (485) 2-0415. 18 exquisitely furnished units divided among five adjoining colonial mansions, refined, friendly service, fine restaurant, pool and spa. Three blocks from the main square. $$$

La Puertacita Boutique'otel, Santo Domingo 75, tel: (465) 2-5311/2-5505. Charming, small hilltop hotel, exquisitely furnished, wonderful views. 10 minutes from downtown. 12 suites (two with Jacuzzi). Pool, gardens, good restaurant, music room. $$$

Rancho El Atascadero, Prolongación Santo Domingo, tel: 2-0206. 51 units, extensive grounds, about 2 km (1 mile) east of town. Popular with families. $

Villa Santa Monica, Parque Benito Juárez, tel: 2-0427. Facing a tranquil park, eight large suites (ask for one that does not open onto the main patio-bar-restaurant). $$$

SAN IGNACIO – BAJA CALIFORNIA
Hotel La Posada, Av. Carranza 22, tel: (685) 13. Spartan but clean. Has much-needed fans. $

SAN QUINTIN – BAJA CALIFORNIA
Old Mill Hotel, Reservations: 223 Via de San Ysidro, San Ysidro, CA 92173, tel: (619) 428-2779. Century-old converted mill with excellent restaurant. $$

SANTA ROSALIA – BAJA CALIFORNIA
Hotel del Real, Av. Manuel F. Montoya at Malecon, tel: (685) 2-0068. Attractive wooden building with terrace. Restaurant and long distance phone. $

Hotel Francis, Calle 11 de Julio, tel: 2-0829. Dominates hill near mining office, north end of town. $$

Hotel Olvera, Calle Playa 14, tel: (685) 2-0057. Plain and simple. $

SONORA – SONORA
Hotel Elba, Santa Ana, tel: (632) 4-0361. Restaurant has good food. $$

Howard Johnson Plaza Hotel & Resort, Apdo Postal 441, San Carols. Toll free (in Mexico) tel: (91) 662-6-0777. Five-star hotel in a cove where mountains meet the ocean. $$$

Motel San Francisco, Santa Ana, tel: (632) 4-0322. $$
RV Park
Punta Vista RV Park is 2 km (1 mile) south of the junction with Highway 2.

TECATE – BAJA CALIFORNIA
Hotel El Conquistador, Blvd Agua Caliente 1777, tel: 81-7955. Where the bull-fighters stay. $$

Hotel Nelson, Av. Revolución 100, tel: 85-4302. $

TIJUANA – BAJA CALIFORNIA
Hotel Lucerna, Av. Rodriguez & Paseo de los Heroes, near the river, tel: (66) 84-2000. Away from the crowd. Restaurant, attractive coffee shop, pool, tennis. $$

Paraiso Radisson, Blvd Aguacaliente, tel: 81-7200. Adjoins country club with golf course. Pool, excercise room, restaurant. $$

TAMPICO – TAMAULIPAS
Camino Real, Hidalgo 2000, tel: 13-8811. Expensive, 100-unit, air-conditioned motor inn on highways 80–180 through town. $$$

Colonial, Madero 210, tel: 12-7676. 150-room air-conditioned hotel Restaurant. $$

Impala, Diaz Miron 220 Pte, tel: 12-0990. Four-story, 80-unit air-conditioned downtown hotel a couple of blocks below main plaza. $$

Imperial, López de Lara Sur 101, tel: 14-1361. Passable 100-room air-conditioned downtown hotel with dining room. $

Inglaterra, Diaz Mirón 116 Ote, tel: 12-5678. Very nice 126-room, two-story air-conditioned downtown hotel across from plaza. $

Posada de Tampico, north end on highways 180–80, tel:5-3050. Good, but pricey. 130-room air-conditioned motor inn. $$$

Posada del Rey, Madero 218 Ote, tel:14-1024. Oldest hotel in town, but has been renovated. Downtown 60 rooms with ceiling fans and air-conditioning. No elevator. Inner rooms quiet. $$$
Tampico, Carranza 513 Ote, tel: 12-4970. Pleasant, budget-priced former "grand hotel" type with 80 units downtown. $

RV Park
Airport. Expensive overnight parking welcomed in parking lot. Ask at front gate. **Posada Tampico** allows parking in their lot if you eat at the restaurant.

TAXCO – GUERRERO
Hotel Agua Escondido, Plaza Borda 4, tel: (732) 2-0726. Very central with rooftop terrace above the noise. $$
Hotel de la Borda, Cerro del Pedregal 2, tel: 2-0225. International restaurant, garden pool. $$$
Hotel Loma Linda, Av. Kennedy 52, tel: 2-0206. On the edge of town with pool, terrific views. $
Hotel Posada de la Misión, Cerro de la Misión 32, tel: 2-0063. Famous O'Gorman mural, pool. $$$
Posada de las Palmas, Exastro 4, near the post office, tel: 2-3177. Sprawled on sloping hillside – flowers, lawn and pool. $

TEHUACÁN – PUEBLA
Hotel México, Reforma Nte & Independencia Pte, tel: (238) 2-0019. Restaurant, garden, pool. $$

TOLUCA – MEXICO
Del Rey Inn, Km 63.5 Carr. México-Toluca, tel: (72) 12-2122. Restaurant, pools, sauna. $$$
Hotel Plaza Las Fuentes, Km 57.7 Carr. México-Toluca, tel: 16-0010. Restaurant, pool, playground. $$$

TUXPÁN AND POZA RICA – VERACRUZ
El Tajín, Km 2.5 Highway to Cobos, tel: (725) 4-2312. 163 air-conditioned rooms, with great views and beautiful grounds. $$$
Florida, Juarez 23, tel 4-0650. Old but serviceable. Mostly air-conditioned, but look first. Resembles a ship, with wrap-around balconies overlooking the river. $
Plaza, Juarez 39, tel: 4-0738. 57-room hotel all air-conditioned. Vintage photographs of Tuxpan give it atmosphere. $$
Plaza Palms, on bypass. 110 air-conditioned rooms. Restaurant-bar, pool, tennis. $$$
Poza Rica Inn. Very nice 50 room motel close to the ruins. Pool. $$$
Riviera, Blvd Reyes Heroles 17, tel: 4-5349. Faces river. 30 rooms. $
Sara, Garizurieta 44, tel: (783) 4-0010. New, with huge air-conditioned rooms and pool. $$$

RV Parks
There are two choices: There is an **agricultural fairground** by the river on the western edge of town or the **lighthouse** on the beach. Neither have hookups, but both are safe.

TUXTLA GUTIÉRREZ – CHIAPAS
Bonampak Tuxtla, Blvd Belisario Domínguez 180, tel: (961) 3-2050. Pool, restaurants, tennis. $
Hotel Flamboyant, Belisario Dominguez Km 1081, tel: 5-0888. 3 km (2 miles) west of town. Rich and exotic decor. Restaurants, bar, disco, tennis, car rental. $$
Safari, Seguna Nte Oriente 635, tel: 2-7459. Restaurant, bar, pool. Base for taxis. $

UXMAL – YUCATÁN
Hotel Hacienda Uxmal, Km 80 Carretera Mérida-Uxmal, tel: (992) 4-7142. Uxmal's oldest and most traditional. $$$
Hotel Misión Park Inn Uxmal, Km 78 Carretera Mérida-Uxmal, tel and fax: (992) 4-7308. Very modern, with sweeping view of Uxmal. $$
Villa Arqeológica, Ruinas Uxmal, tel: (992) 4-7053. Club Med amenities, smack by ruins. $$

VALLADOLID – YUCATÁN
Hotel El Mesón del Marqués, Calle 39 No. 203, tel: 6-2073. On the main plaza
Hotel San Clemente, Calle 41 No. 206, tel (985) 6-2208. On the main plaza.

VERACRUZ – VERACRUZ
Hawaii Hotel, Insurgentes 458, tel: (293) 1-0327. Small modern hotel located between the harbor and the Zócalo. $$
Hotel Emporio, Malecón y Xicotencatl, tel: (293) 2-0020. Downtown on the harbor. Most rooms have balconies with splendid views. $$$
Hotel Mocambo, Carretera Mocambo, tel: (293) 7-1710. Grand old tourist hotel on Mocambo Beach. Ten-minute taxi-ride to the Zócalo. $$$
Hotel Veracruz, Independencia y Miguel Lerdo, tel: (293) 1-2233. A bit old-fashioned, but comfortable. Next to the Zócalo. $$$
Torremar Resort, Blvd A. Ruiz Cortines, tel: (292) 1-3466. New facility, popular with Mexican tourists. Near Hotel Mocambo. $$$

VILLAHERMOSA – TABASCO
Holiday Inn Tabasco Plaza, Paseo Tabasco 1407, tel: (931) 13-4400. Luxurious. Pool, restaurants, bars. $$$
Hotel Miraflores, Reforma 304, tel: 12-0022. Restaurant, car rental. $
Hyatt Villahermosa, Av. Juarez 106, Zona Hotelera, tel: 13-4444. Restaurants, disco, pool, tennis. $$$
Maya Tabasco, Blvd Ruiz Cortines 907, tel: 12-1111. Pool, garden, restaurants, car rental. $$

ZACATECAS – ZACATECAS
Gallery Best Western, López Mateos & Cjon, tel: (492) 2-3311. Central. Restaurant, cafeteria, squash court, nearby golf and tennis. $$$
Mision del Real, Blvd López Portillo 12, tel: 3-4008. At entrance to town. Bar, restaurant, airport bus. $$

EATING OUT

Mexican Food

In spite of misconceptions to the contrary, eating in Mexico is one of the country's chief pleasures. The indigenous Indians had their own cuisine, principally dependent on locally grown ingredients. Then along came the Spanish Conquistadors, who found much of what they ate in this land thoroughly distasteful because it was so different from their own.

Eventually, hankering for familiar flavors, the Spaniards began to transport to their new territory many of their own native foodstuffs. As trade expanded throughout Mexico, both Spanish and Indian ingredients were carried from one area to another and over the years the blending of different foods and styles of cooking became accepted as Mexico's own cuisine.

Mexican cooking is thus amazingly rich and varied, a great blend with a distinct personality. Like so many other things in Mexico, the food is the result of centuries of encounters and mixings of cultures and peoples.

To this culinary feast, the Indians brought tropical fruits – papaya and pineapple – as well as avocados, pumpkins, herbs, hot chili, cacao, and those two essential staples: corn and beans, the soul of Mexican food. The Spaniards brought meat and poultry, cheese and wheat, oil and wine, contributing a solid and substantial Mediterranean style, not nearly as subtle as French, Italian or even Turkish cooking, but certainly meant to appease the appetite. Cattle and other livestock also arrived on Spanish ships and were immediately adopted by the local people whose mainstay had previously been the native turkeys. Turkey is still prized in Mexico and is frequently converted into a rich, unctuous festival dish by the addition of one of a number of regional *moles*. *Mole* is a seasoning paste made of two dozen or more ingredients according to local taste. The most famous are the *moles* of Puebla and Oaxaca, the former being usually more subtle and the latter spicier and more robust.

Africa sent along the blessing of coffee. Spices and the sensual mango came aboard ships from China and the Philippines. So the great blend that turned out to be Mexican cuisine is better than either Indian or Spanish food, though it may not be as healthy as the mainly vegetarian diet of the Indians nor as devastatingly nutritious as the food from Spain. Mexican food is horribly fattening and has a strong personality, but at its most exquisite it has great refinement and subtlety.

The prestige of Mexican *haute cuisine* is based on sophisticated recipes, but that does not mean plain cooking cannot be tasty. Simple cooking anywhere – fresh food, simply prepared – is delicious. A good *taco*, for instance, made with a hot, fresh, white and soft *tortilla*. Beans are good, too, no matter how you prepare them, whether the simple, boiled *frijoles de la olla* or the multi-fried and spiced *frijoles refritos* (refried), traditionally the last dish before dessert and coffee in any Mexican meal worth its chili.

Some wonderful authentic cookbooks have been written by Mexican writers such as Patricia Quintana and Susanna Palazuelos, but it is the American writer Dianna Kennedy, who fell in love with Mexico and stayed on there, who has been most instrumental in spreading the flavors of her adopted country to the rest of the world.

In recent years, women chefs from two acclaimed restaurants (**Flamanalli** in the weaving village of Teotitlán del Valle and **Nuu-Luu**, in San Filipe del Agua, a suburb of Oaxaca) have become well-known for their role in creating contemporary, yet authentic, renditions of their ancient Zapotec and Mixtec dishes.

Visitors to Mexico who observe the basic rules of hygiene, and eat only purified, peeled and cooked ingredients, will enjoy one of the world's great cuisines without fear of intestinal repercussions.

Widely available dishes

Ceviche: Fish marinated in lime juice until it is "cooked." Seasoned with chilis and served with raw chopped vegetables and avocado. (Take care to eat this only in good restaurants where all vegetables have been "purified".) The same dish made with sea scallops is called *Caya de Acho.*

Chiles Rellenos: Mild (usually) large green chili peppers stuffed with cheese or a mixture of ground meat and spices, dipped in egg batter, fried and served with a tomato sauce.

Chilaquiles: *Tortillas* cooked in a more or less spicy sauce and served with grated cheese (and sometimes cream).

Cochinita Pibil: Suckling pig, seasoned with Yucatán spices and cooked in banana leaves.

Enchiladas: *Tortillas* rolled around meat, cheese or fish, covered in sauce. *Enchiladas Suizas* are always served with a cheese-based sauce.

Tortillas: Thin pancakes made of cornmeal or flour. Some regional variations, but a staple in Mexican food and used as a form of bread with just about everything.

Guacamole: Chopped avocados mixed with onions, lime juice, chilis (and, sometimes, tomatoes). Served as an appetizer or side dish.

Mole: Seasoning pastes in several varieties, most frequently in the style of Puebla or Oaxaca and usually used to season chicken or pork. *Moles* come in green (made principally from pumpkin seeds and chilis), dark (chocolate and with chilis), and a milder variation known as *coloradito*.

Pozole: Hominy stew seasoned with chilis and prepared with pork or chicken.

Quesadillas: *Tortillas* folded around cheese (or other fillings) and deep-fried.

Tacos: *Tortillas* rolled around any sort of filling. *Tacos al Pastor* are a favorite Mexican snack, consisting of roasted meat on a spit (usually pork) rolled in a *tortilla* and served warm.

Tamales: Corn husks or banana leaves filled with a cornmeal mixture, then stuffed with any of a variety of highly seasoned mixtures of chicken or pork.

Tortas: Mexican sandwiches served on some form of roll. Usually including some form of mashed beans and avocado along with meat and/or cheese. Frequently served grilled or warm.

Ordering a meal

Restaurants that in English are called coffee shops, snack bars or cafés, in Mexico are labelled *café fonda*, *merendero*, *comedor* or *loncheria*. The *loncheria* may specialize in sandwiches, or *tortas*. In any of these eating places, however, the food will be inexpensive; in some, it will be very good indeed; in others, it will be contaminated. The safest course is to look carefully before ordering. Some travelers avoid eating in the marketplace, arguing that a regular restaurant is safer. However, the *fondas* in the market have the advantage that you can see the kitchen and the food before committing yourself. At these stalls, there is unlikely to be a menu.

Breakfast is sometimes the same as in North America but sometimes more exotic: *menudo* (tripe), *chilaquiles* (hot shredded *tortillas* with heavy cream and chili peppers), or *carne ranchera* (hot beef with beans), chocolate and sweet rolls.

Many a traveler who is adventurous at the midday and evening meals wants only the familiar for breakfast. For them, here is a list of breakfast staples, with the warning still to expect the unexpected:

eggs	*huevos*
omelet	*tortilla de huevos*
scrambled eggs	*huevos revueltos*
fried eggs	*huevos estrellados*
boiled eggs	*huevos hervidos*
bacon	*tocino*
ham	*jamón*
oatmeal	*avena*
toast	*pan tostado*
plain bread	*pan Bimbo*
not toasted	*sin tostar*
buns	*bolillos*
butter	*mantequilla*
biscuits	*bisquets*

Regional cooking

Think of *huitlacoche* when you think of exotic **Mexico City** dishes. It is a blackish fungus which grows on corn – *tacos* and *crêpes* are made with it. *Huitlacoche* is a distant throwback to the days when the Aztecs, confined to a tiny island in a lake, had to eat anything they could find. As heirs to Aztec cooking, the cooks in Mexico City utilize everything edible, including maguey worms which are eaten dead or alive, blanketed in a hot sauce and tucked into a *taco*. Another Mexico City favorite is a soup made of *flor de calabaza* (squash blossoms). *Capitalinos* also use *epazote*, a herb similar to parsley but stronger, which housewives use to flavor everything from soup to beans.

Among the great dishes of Mexico City are *romeritos*, akin to spinach, served during Christmas with dry shrimp and sauce; and *memelas*, a bizarre *torta* (sandwich) served with cream, mustard, chili peppers, tomato, onion, avocado, meat, chicken or sardines. Only a few places, such as Fonda del Refugio, San Angel Inn or Las Delicias in Mexico City offer the good old dishes – *manchamantel*, a pork dish (the word means "tablecloth stainer," because the bright red sauce which goes with the dish leaves a flaming mark on the tablecloth), *pepian* (sesame paste), *romeritos*, a stuffed spinach-like vegetable, or *sopa de lima*, a lemon soup.

To discuss regional cooking in Mexico you must make basic divisions. The **North** is the poorest region for cooking, with food that is nutritious but simple and unspiced. Its main assets are *tortillas de harina* (flour tortillas), grilled meat, black coffee and beer. But even the sparse northern cooking offers such delicacies as *caldo sudador* (sweating soup) from Sinaloa and Sonora, with its ingredients of shrimp, abalone and turtle; and in Chihuahua a cheese soup, resembling a Swiss fondue, to be eaten with clean-tasting flour *tortillas*. **Monterrey**'s specialty is *cabrito* (baby goat), grilled and greasy but very tasty, washed down with another local institution, cold Carta Blanca beer.

Highlands cooking includes many varieties of traditional dishes, such as *pozole*, *tamales* and *enchiladas*, also chicken cooked in various ways, regional sweets, and fruits, from standard papaya and guava to juicy cactus fruits such as *tunas* and *pitahayas*. Mexicans like to eat fruit with a bit of lemon – not the tame yellow lemon of North America, but the stronger and more acid green Mexican *limón*. Mexicans also favor the avocado in much of their cooking, either cooked with the food or as an accompaniment.

Puebla is the home of the *mole poblano*, the queen mother of Mexican recipes. The dish was invented by a colonial nun whose recipe contains variations upon spices and chili peppers and Mexican cooking chocolate. It is Mexico's celebration dish. Other regions may offer a *mole*, but Puebla's is unique. Similar to *mole*, but milder, is *pepián*, lighter in color and easier to digest. Both *mole* and *pepián* are eaten with plenty of *tortillas* and, preferably, washed down with a rich, dark beer. From Puebla, too, comes an Indian delicacy known only to discriminating eaters – *mixiotes*, a sort of barbecue, wrapped in maguey leaves and cooked in earthen ovens. The maguey leaf gives this a very particular taste.

Nayarit has splendid seafood. **Jalisco** is famous for its *pozole*, made with pork and hominy corn, garnished with onion, lettuce, radish, oregano, and chili sauce with a few subtle drops of lemon.

From **Michoacan** come *corundas* and *huchepos*, the local *tamales*, and the white fish from **Patzcuaro**, which has acquired national fame.

Veracruz cuisine is superb, with a strong Spanish influence. They make use of the local produce – such as the giant tropical *macho* banana (plantain), eaten fried. Their best-known dish is *huachinango a la Veracruzana* (red snapper Veracruz-style), a classic with tomato sauce, olives and capers. Veracruz boasts the most delicious fruit in Mexico, huge pineapples and aromatic mangoes. At one time a restaurant in Veracruz served only meals prepared with fruit. An odd feature to Veracruz cooking is black beans, refried several times. They are used in combo with magnificent *tamales*, made with *macho* bananas and stuffed with beans.

Oaxaca has a remarkable cuisine, with its famous dish *mole negro* an even more substantial variety than the Puebla version. Oaxaca *tamales*, wrapped in banana leaves, are bigger and more elaborate than the Highland kind. Many Mexicans associate Oaxaca with cheese. This is because Oaxacan cheese is an essential ingredient of *quesadilla*, a *taco* made of melted cheese, to which is added anything out of the cook's imagination: avocado, beans, potatoes.

The inspiration of **Yucatecan** cooking dates back through the centuries to the Maya. Oddly, in comparatively recent times another ingredient has been added to the old mix: Lebanese cooking. It came from Lebanese immigrants. Some of the best restaurants in **Mérida** offer both Yucatecan and Lebanese dishes.

Yucatecan cooking claims such outstanding dishes as *cochinita pibil*, a spiced pork dish, and *papadzules* (stuffed *tortillas*). There is a magnificent soup made with *limas*, a subtle Mexican fruit. Beer aficionados rate Yucatán's beer as the best in the country – both the light Montejo, and the dark and rich León Negro.

Another Yucateco-International dish is *queso relleno* or stuffed Dutch cheese (the red ball kind). It is somewhat like minced meat but with a full Maya flavor.

Venison is another Yucatán delicacy, though scarce and expensive. Other exotic dishes eaten in Mexico are baby shark, lizard, and dog – the almost extinct Mexican hairless breed, called the *itzcuintli* (Chihuahua). It once served as the *pièce de résistance* at many a pre-Columbian royal banquet.

The following restaurants have been given three price bands (per person, without wine):

$$$ = over US$25
$$ = US$10–25
$ = under US$25.

ACAPULCO – GUERREURO

Barbararoja, Av. Miguel Aleman at Condesa beach, tel: (74) 84-5932. Shrimps, fish and great steaks. $$$

Betos Traditional, Av. Miguel Aleman 99, tel: (74) 84-0473. Red snapper, lobster and a good view of Condesa beach. $$$

Carlos and Charlie's, Av. Miguel Aleman 999, tel: (74) 84-0039. Always a lively, noisy crowd as at all restaurants in this chain. Pleasant terrace. $$$

Casa Nova, Carretera Escenica 5256, tel: (74) 84-6819. Southern Italian cuisine. Homemade pasta. Reserve on weekends. $$$

El Amigo Miguel, Benito Juarez 31, tel: (74) 83-6981. Excellent seafood and fish. A favorite with the locals. $$

El Cabrito, Costera Miguel Aleman, tel: (74) 84-7711. Real Mexican food and ambience. *Cabrito* (baby goat) is a specialty. $

The Kooka Burra, Highway to Las Brisas 12, tel: (74) 84-1448. The bird is Australian but the food is American and the view magnificent. $$$

La Ceiba, in Hyatt Regency hotel, tel: (74) 84-2888. Open 24 hours. Claims to have best low-calorie food in town. $$

100% Natural, Av. Miguel Aleman 184, tel: (74) 85-3982. Open 24 hours. Vegetarian dishes, fondue, juices. $$

Maximilian's, Acapulco Plaza Hotel, tel: (74) 85-9050. Good French restaurant. Elegant, intimate, romance by candlelight. $$$

Mimi's Chili Saloon, Av. Miguel Aleman at Condesa, tel: 84-3498. Hamburgers, *burritos* and flavored margaritas. Open till 4am. $

Siroco, Av. Miguel Aleman at Carabali beach, tel: (74) 85-9490. Spanish food, especially *paella*. $$

BOCA DEL RIO – VERACRUZ

El Mesón de los Coras, Blvd A. Ruiz Cortinez 6, Boca del Rio. Local favorite serving grilled meats and *barbacoa*. $

Imperial, Miguel Lerdo 153, Veracruz, tel: (293) 1-1866. On the Zócalo, lively. Excellent shrimp and fish. Good flan. $$

La Mansión, Blvd Avila Camacho & A. Ruiz Cortinez, Boca del Rio, tel: (293) 7-1363. Argentine-type steak-house. Good wine-list. $$$

Las Brisas del Mar, Zamora y Juarez, Boca del Rio, tel: (297) 6-0080. Charming seafood restaurant open to the breezes (*Las Brisas*) on village harbor. Superb grilled shrimp. $$

CABO SAN LUCAS – BAJA CALIFORNIA

Restaurant Delfin, Playa Médano. On the beach. $$

Coconuts, Cascadas de Baja, East of town, tel: 3037. Tiled floors and graceful archways, it calls itself "the most romantic restaurant." $$

The Giggling Marlin, Matamoros at Marina, tel: 3-0606. Lively bar with lots of dancing, fun and games. $$

Señor Sushi's, Opposite Plaza Las Glorias, tel: 3-1323. Everything but sushi, includes lobster, steak ribs and chicken. $$

La Terraza, at the Marina. Wide selection, sushi to pizza. Eating outdoors. $

Pappi's, Zaragoza. A Mexican deli with burgers and ice cream. $

Kan Kun, Adjoining Hotel Marina. Casual place for big breakfasts to start the day. $

Pizza Oceano, Lázaro Cárdenas, tel: 3-0931. A favorite with locals. A variety of Italian food as well as pizza. $

CAMPECHE – CAMPECHE

Kalyope, Torres de Cristal, Av. Ruíz Cortines and Justo Sierra, next to Ah-Kim Pech plaza. Greek food and Campechano specialties, in modern office complex. $$

Ramada Inn, Av. Ruíz Cortínes 51, tel: 6-2233. Hotel dining, excellent food and service, pleasant atmosphere. $$

Restaurant Bar Marganza, Calle 8, No. 268, tel: 1-3898. Mexican food, hostesses in regional costumes, rather upscale favorite. $$

Restaurant La Parroquía, Calle 55, No. 9, tel: 6-8086. Open 24 hours, extensive menu, soak up local atmosphere in much-loved café. $

Restaurant Miramar, Calle 8, No. 293, near Calle 61, tel: 6-2883. Campeche's famous seafood and Mexican dishes. $$

CANCÚN – QUINTANA ROO

With a range of restaurants equaling that of any sophisticated city, Cancún offers the visitor a taste of just about every cuisine. Each hotel on Cancún Island has several dining rooms and there are scores of independent restaurants besides those mentioned here, so no vacation is long enough to try out the hundreds of possibilities.

HOTEL ZONE ON CANCÚN ISLAND

Casa Rolandi, Km 8, Plaza Caracol Shopping Center, tel: 3-1817. Italian and Mexican dishes in a lively atmosphere. $$

Grimond's Mansion, Pez Volador No. 8, near Casa Maya Hotel, tel: 83-0704. Service in evening only for elegant French. $$$

100% Natural, Plaza Terramar, tel: 83-1180. Delicious health food 24 hours a day in pleasant atmosphere. $$

Señor Frog's, Blvd Kukulkán Km 4.5, tel: 3-2931. Festive atmosphere, good food. $$

DOWNTOWN CANCÚN

Hong Kong, Av. Cobá 97, tel: 84-1998. Chinese, also offers take-out and delivery service. $$

Los Almendros, Av. Bonampak Sur (corner Sayil, front of bullring), tel: 4-0807. Color photo menu of house. Yucatecan dishes such as lime soup and *cochinita pibil*. $$

Perico's, Av. Yaxchilán 71 (between Cobá and Sunyaxchen), tel: 4-3152. Lively atmosphere and tasty Mexican seafood and steaks.

Tacolote, Av. Cobá 19, tel: 87-3045. Try famous *tacos al carbón* (charcoal grilled beef, chopped for easy eating in soft warm *tortillas*) among other varieties. Also at Hotel Zone: **Playa Linda Pier**.

Yamamoto, Uxmal 31, tel: 87-3366. Traditional Japanese cuisine. $$$

CATEMACO – VERACRUZ

Los Sauces, Paseo del Malecón, tel: (294) 3-0548. Fish restaurant on the lake front. Specialty: *mojarra* (perch from Lake Catemaco). $$$

CHICHÉN-ITZÁ – YUCATÁN

Hotel Hacienda Chichén-Itzá, just a few yards from southern entrance to site, tel: (985) 24-2150. Enjoy a meal where this century's first archaeological teams stayed, in a beautiful setting.

Hotel Mayaland, situated on old highway, just outside southern entrance to ruins, next to Hotel Hacienda Chichén, tel: 6-2777. A choice of three restaurants in hotel with dignified ambience. $$

Restaurant Carrousel, town of Pisté. For a tasty, economical meal under a *palapa* roof. $

CHIHUAHA – CHIHUAHA

Ben's, 20 de Noviembre y Voladores Ote. Ever-present soda fountain. Good, wholesome food, reasonable prices. $

Chihuaha Charlie's (Carlos Anderson chain), Av. Juarez 3329, tel: 15-7065. Live music on Sunday. Party-hearty atmosphere. Food OK. $$

Club de los Parados, 3901 Juarez Nte, tel: 10-5335. Excellent steak house in Western decor. Los Parados means "the stand-ups" and this is where men used to quaff their beer at a stand-up bar. $$$

El Bandido Pub, Av. de las Américas 1303, tel: 13-9492. Good steak house and seafood restaurant. $$

El Lenador, Tecnologico & Ahuehuete. Typical Western-style decor. $$

Futurama, Universidad at Pancho Villa Monument circle. Good semi-colonial air-conditioned restaurant specializing in steaks and seafood. $$

Galeon, Juarez 3312-B, tel: 10-1141. Elegant atmosphere, old ship style as befits the name. Seafood and shrimp only. $$$

La Bella Época, Pascual Orozco y Misioneros. Reasonable. European food and atmosphere. Meat, seafood, pastries. Open 7am–11pm. $$$

La Calesa, Juarez 3300, tel: 16-0222. Excellent steak-house, corner of Juarez and Colon at Juarez Monument. $$$

La Hacienda, Reforma & 20th, tel: 10-0200. Drive-in. Semi-fast food. $

Los Faisanes, Periferico Ortiz Mena & Maryland, tel: 15-7270. Cantonese and international. $$$

Los Parados de Tony Vega, Av. Juarez 3316, tel: 15-1333. Fabulous restaurant in old mansion. Steaks and seafood are specialties. $$$

Los Vitrales, Av. Juarez at Colón, tel: 15-0676. Beautiful mansion. Cantonese and international. Dressy. Reservations advisable. $$$

Mexico Español, Niños Heroes 314, tel: 12-8351. Very good Spanish-style restaurant near downtown. A bit of Mexico and Spain under one roof. Specialties include *paella*, baby lobster thermidor or garlic, shish-kebab, and char-broiled steaks. $$
Pelicans, 20 de Nov. & Apartado, tel: 12-8888. Seafood and meat dishes. $$$

COATEPEC – VERACRUZ

El Tio Vevo, Santos Degollado 4, tel: (281) 6-3645. Lively bar and restaurant serving local specialties. Excellent mountain trout. $$

COBÁ – QUINTANA ROO

El Bocadito, main street in village. Casual restaurant popular with tour groups. $
Villa Arquelógica, near entrance to ruins on Lake Cobá. Refined Gallic atmosphere and cuisine, plus Yucatecan dishes. $$$

COZUMEL – QUINTANA ROO

La Choza - The Grill, Carretera a Chankanaab Km 3.5, near Hotel Sol Caribe, tel: 2-4920. Great Mexican food, boasts best-restaurant rating by Food & Wine Magazine in 1992. $$
Las Palmeras, Av. Juárez and Av. Rafael Melgar, tel: 2-0532. Very popular spot downtown, for good eating and great people-watching. $$
Pepe's Grill, Av. Rafael Melgar 220, tel: 2-0213 (reservations advised). Mellow atmosphere for splurging. $$$

CREEL – CHIHUAHA

Copper Canyon Lodge and the **Parador** are both excellent restaurants with varied menus. $$$
La Estufa has a pleasant atmosphere and serves Mexican food. $
Lupita, across from the Parador, has excellent Mexican food and an old-fashioned jukebox. $

ENSENADA – BAJA CALIFORNIA

La Casa del Abulon, Blvd Costero, tel: 6-5785. Great seafood and ocean views. $$$
Las Cazuelas, Blvd Sangines 6, tel: 6-1044. Try the abalone with lobster sauce. $$$
China Land, Av. Riveroll 1149, tel: 8-8644. More than 100 Asian dishes offered in this delightful restaurant. $$
Señor Salud, 9th Espinoza Street, tel: 6-4415. Vegetarian dishes. $$
La Flor de Italia, Av. Ruiz 96, tel: 8-1220. As Italian as it sounds. $$

GUAYMAS – SONORA

Biblio Cafe, Av. Serdan between Calles 13 & 14. Mexican dishes and seafood. $
Del Mar, Av. Serdán & Calle 17, tel: 4-0225. Downtown restaurant with terrific seafood, wonderful clam and fish soups. Prime cuts from Sonora. Cocktails. $$$

El Oeste Steakhouse, next to Armida. Steaks. $$$
Helados Bing, on Serdán just east of 5th. Ice-cream parlour.
Jardines Xochimilco, Highway 15 just off Flamingos, tel: 2-7810. *Al fresco* dining. The adventurous can order the *paquete*, a package of assorted parts of cow - others should stick to ribs and steaks. $
Las Playitas, tel: 1-5227. Very good restaurant run in conjunction with RV park of same name on road to naval base around Guaymas Bay. Excellent seafood. $$$
Tio Juan, Serdán 394, at the Club Deportivo Miramar, near Playa de Cortés Hotel, tel: 2-5700. Mexican food.

HUATULCO – OAXACA

Crowne Plaza Beach Restaurant, Blvd Benito Juarez, Bahia Tangolunda, Huatulco, tel: (958) 1-0044. Fish specialties: excellent seafood soup and fish *alla talla* (grilled with special sauce). $$
Los Portales, Plaza Principal de La Crucesita, Huatulco, tel: (958) 7-0070. Simple and clean. Local cuisine. $

ISLA MUJERES – QUINTANA ROO

María's Kan Kin, Km 4 Carretera al Garrafón, tel: (987) 83-1420. French cuisine under a *palapa* overlooking sea. Live lobsters for your selection. $$
Miramar, unpretentious eatery with great view of dockside activity. $
Pizza Rolandi, Hidalgo between Abasolo and Madero. Lively atmosphere for other delicious Italian dishes besides pizza. $$
Roberts, Morelos on main plaza opposite church. Tasty Mexican fare. $

IXTAPA/ZIHUATANEJO – GUERRERO

Beccofino, Marina de Ixtapa, Ixtapa, tel: (753) 3-1770. Stunning Italian preparation of local ingredients specializing in fish and seafood. $$$
Bogart's, Paseo de Ixtapa, Ixtapa, tel: (753) 3-0333. Part of Hotel Krystal. Elegant restaurant in a Casablanca setting. Good wine-list. Reservations advisable. $$$
El Mesón del Cabrito, Ejido 24, Zihuatanejo. Grilled meats. Speciality is *cabrito* (baby goat). $$
La Bocana, Juan N. Alvarez 12, Zihuatanejo, tel: (753) 4-3545. Seafood. Favorite with the locals. $$
La Marina, Cinco de Mayo, Zihuatanejo, tel: (753) 4-2185. Swiss cuisine and seafood in a simple open-air restaurant. $

KINO (OLD) – SONORA

Dorita. In front of police station. Serves breakfast and lunch. Open 7am–3pm. $
Marlin Place. Clean, reasonably priced restaurant near Islandia Marina. Seafood specialties. Very good food and service plus George, a singing waiter. $$
Taqueria Prado. Great *tacos* on road into town across from park. Open late. $

KINO (NEW) – SONORA

El Pargo Rojo, Av. del Mar 1426, across from beach, tel: 2-0205. Pleasant seafood and steak restaurant. $$$

Kino Place, on the beach, tel: 2-0049. The only place for breakfast. Mexican food. Pleasant atmosphere. $$

Villas del Mar Nautilus Club. International cuisine and seafood. Closed Tuesday. $$$

LA PAZ – BAJA CALIFORNIA

Restaurant Dragon, 16 de Septiembre and Esquerro, tel: 2-1372. Upstairs, open late. Casual ambience. $$

Oasis, opposite tourist office on Obregón, tel: 5-7666. Dining between the trees. Vast menu, open late. $$

La Terraza, Obregón 1570, tel: 2-0777. Hotel Perla's sidewalk hang-out opposite the *malecón*. The best place to watch the sunset. $$

El Taste, *Melecón*, just past Los Arcos, tel: 2-8121. Famous for lobster. $$

Rosticceria California, Serdan and Bravo. Restaurant and take-away counter, sizzling roast chicken sold complete or by the piece. $

El Molino Steakhouse, Beside the marina, Bahía de la Paz, tel: 2-9896. Seafood as well as mouth watering steaks. $$

La Caleta, on the *malecón* north of Los Arcos. Beach restaurant and bar. $

LORETO – BAJA CALIFORNIA

Cesar's, Juárez at Zapata, tel: 3-0203. Loreto's oldest and probably best restaurant. Good food, occasional musical entertainment. $$$

El Nido, Salvatierra 154, opposite the bus station, tel: 3-0284. Atmosphere is fishnets, oak beams and open fireplace/grill. Good food, mostly steak and seafood. $$

Playa Blanca, Hidalgo and Davis. Bright, cheerful upstairs room overlooks the street. Varied menu. $$

Cafe Olé, Madero, tel: 3-0496. Just off the plaza. Perfect for breakfast and people-watching. $

Tiffany's Pizza, opposite Hotel Plaza on Hidalgo, tel: 3-0597. Italian-American owner who is very proud of his product. $

El Embarcadero, Blvd Mateos, opposite the fishing habor, tel: 3-1065. The owner operates the adjoining fishing tackle store so fresh fish is a speciality. $$

MAZATLÁN – SINALOA

Casa Loma, Las Gaviotas 104, tel:13-5398. Secluded dining room plus outside patio. International dishes. Reservations recommended. Open October–April. $$$

Doney, Av. Mariano Escobedo 610, tel: 81-2651. Downtown. Landmark restaurant since 1959. Mexican food including *cabrito*, seafood and steaks. $$$

Donk 'n Donas, Guillermo Nelson 171, at L. Valles. Donuts, coffee and *tortas* (sandwiches). $

Grill Larios, Rodolfo T. Loaiza 413, tel: 84-1767. Mexican food. Casual. $$

El Camarón, beachfront restaurant on Camarón Glorieta, tel: 83-5111. Specializes in seafood and steaks. Disco. $$

El Charro, 5 de Mayo & Morelos. Mexican food. *Menudo colorado*. Open 7 am–10pm. $

El Marinero, 5 de Mayo 530, across from Mexicana Airlines office, tel: 81-7682. Fresh seafood daily. *Mariachi* music. Open 12 noon–11pm. $

El Parador Español, Camarón Sábalo 714, next to El Cid, tel: 13-0767. Spanish restaurant whose specialty is *paella*. Open 7am–11pm. $$$

El Patio, Del Mar 30, near hospital overlooking bay, tel: 81-7301. Good, tropical-style restaurant. Lobster, steak, and Mexican specialties. Strolling musicians. $$$

Jade, Morelos 412. Cantonese food. Closed Monday. $$

Los Arcos, tropical open-air restaurant on Del Mar, tel: 13-9577. Seafood fresh from ocean. $

Mamuca's, Simón Bólivar 404, tel: 81-3490. Popular downtown seafood restaurant a block off waterfront. Features *parillada de mariscos* plus "seafood explosion," a variety tray, and other seafood. $$

Miyiko, Av. Del Mar 70, tel: 81-6590. Japanese food and drinks. *Sushi, teppan yaki, sake* and beer. $$$

Paraiso Tres Islas, Rodolfo T. Loaiza, on the beach, tel: 84-2812. Seafood. Casual. $$

Pedro's Fish & Chips, open-air restaurant on Camarón Sábalo next to Cavanderia. Mexican breakfast specials. $

Sr Frog, Del Mar 225, tel: 85-1110. Popular disco/ restaurant adjacent to Franky Oh! disco. Decent food. Usually a line to get in. $$

Shangri La, oriental restaurant on Loaiza near Playa Mazatla, tel: 83-6746. Cantonese and Mandarin specialties. $$$

Shrimp Bucket, well-known seafood restaurant at Olas Altas 11 in La Siesta, tel: 81-6350. The original restaurant of the Anderson chain. *Mariachi* and marimba band. $$$

Shrimp Factory, North Beach on east side of Playa Las Gaviotas, just north of Azteca Inn. Seafood only. $$$

Super Tacos La Carreta, Av. Gutierrez Najara 325, next to electrical store. Look for neon pig sign. $

Tony's Plaza, nice restaurant in Plaza Las Gaviotas, tel: 83-4233. Good international cuisine and excellent service. $$$

Tres Islas, good seafood restaurant on beach just north of Holiday Inn, tel: 83-5932. Disco. Open 1pm–2am. Very popular. $$

MELEGÉ – BAJA CALIFORNIA

Los Equipales, Moctezuma, near Zaragoza, tel: 3-0330. Cool airy terrace upstairs. Spotless and attractive with soft music. $$

El Nido, Calle Rubio, near the river, tel: 3-0221. Steaks, fish and chicken. $$

Pollo Salvate (The Wild Chicken), Zaragoza, just north of the square. Hole-in-the-wall snackery. $

El Almeja Restaurant, north side of the river. Lovely beachside restaurant with amicable owner. $

Las Casitas, Hotel Las Casitas, Callejón de los Estudiantes, tel: 3-0019. Seafood and Mexican *mariachi* band on Friday night. $$

La Jungla Bambu, south bank of river, œ mile from town, tel: 3-0200. Outdoor dining under the trees. Big-screen Monday night football. $

El Candil, Zaragoza. Down tiny passageway to tree-shaded patio. $$

MÉRIDA – YUCATÁN

Alberto's Continental Patio, Calle 64 and Calle 57, tel: 28-5367. International and Lebanese cuisine, for that elegant evening you've saved for. $$$

El Gatto Pardo, Paseo de Montejo 471 at Calle 35, tel: 27-3244. Pizza, pasta and other Italian goodies. $$

El Mesón, Parque Hidalgo (Calle 60), tel: 24-0022. For a long *al fresco* lunch in the corner of a charming plaza. $

La Bella Epoca, Calle 60 No. 497 between Calles 57 & 59, tel: 24-7844. Choose international or vegetarian dishes, soothed by the sound of a piano. $$

Leo, Paseo de Montejo 460-A between Calles 35 & 37, tel: 27-6514. Grilled steaks, *tacos* on trendy Paseo de Montejo. $$

Los Almendros, Calle 50 No. 493 between Calles 57 & 59, tel: 23-8135. The traditional choice for Yucatecan specialties.

MEXICALI – BAJA CALIFORNIA

La Casita de Patzcua, Blvd López Mateos, tel: 52-9707. Small, centrally located. $$

Sanborns, Calzada Independencia, tel: 57-5262. One of the old, familiar chain. $$

Chalet, Calzado Justo Sierra 889, tel: 68-2021. Tasty international cuisine. $$$

Mision Dragon, Blvd Lázaro Cárdenas, tel: 66-4375, 66-4400. Beautifully decorated Chinese restaurant. $$$

Rivoli, Blvd Benito Juárez 2151, tel: 66-1000. Good quality food, with plenty of choice. $$$

MEXICO CITY – DOWNTOWN AREA

Cafe de Tacuba, Tacuba 28, tel: 518-4950. Vaulted ceilings tiled wainscoting, large paintings and mural. Go for the atmosphere. $$

Casino Espanol, Isabel la Catolica, tel: 521-8894. Spanish food in a splendidly ornate decor.

Hotel del Cortés, Hidalgo 85, tel: 518-2181. Open-air patio delightful for lunch or drinks. Although downtown, a tranquil, soothing surprise. $$

Prendes, 16 de Septiembre 10-C, tel: 521-5404. One of the city's oldest restaurants, packed with photos of famous patrons ranging from Frida Kahlo to Walt Disney. Lunch only, 1.30–5.30pm. $$

Sanborn's Azulejos, Madero. Comfortably familiar dishes served in a dramatic patio. $$

MEXICO CITY – ZONA ROSA AREA

Beatriz, Londres 179, tel: 525-5857. Economical *tacos* and tasty soups at this perennially popular eating spot. $

Bellinghausen, Londres 179, tel: 207-4049. German specialties. Old-fashioned ambience and service. $$$

Bellini, Reforma 373 near Angel monument, tel: 207-8944. Upscale Italian, fine service. $$$

Chalet Suizo, Niza 37, tel: 208-7432. Knotty pine, check tablecloths, hearty food. $$

Fonda el Refugio, Liverpool 166, tel: 207-2732. Country-elegant, an institution for top-class Mexican cuisine. $$$

La Mansion, Hamburgo 77, tel: 514-3247. One of a chain of restaurants serving excellent Argentine-style steaks. $$

Luau, Niza 38, tel: 528-7474. Cantonese Chinese with elegant low lighting. $$

Paris 16, Reforma 368 near Varsovia, tel: 511-0119. Not visible from street. Yuppie hangout with changing art show. Crowded at lunchtime. $$

Raffaello, Londres 165, tel: 525-6585. Post-modern chalet for Italian cuisine. $$

Yug, Varsovia 3, tel: 533-3296. Vegetarian restaurant, a favorite with people from nearby offices. $

MEXICO CITY – INSURGENTES SUR

Benihana, Insurgentes Sur 640, tel: 523-3385. Famous Japanese steakhouse. $$

L'Italiano, Insurgentes Sur 729, tel: 523-3346. $$$

La Mansion, Insurgentes Sur 778, tel: 523-2000. The original Argentine steakhouse. Try the *chimichurri* sauce. $$

La Pergola, Insurgentes XXX, tel: 395-2692. Lots of pictures, dark. Italian food. $$

Mazurka, Nueva York 150, tel: 528-8811. Polish food in former private house. $$$

Suntory, Torres de Adalid 14, tel: 669-4676. Fine Japanese cuisine in stately dining rooms. $$$

MONTERREY – NUEVO LEÓN

Ben's. Above Farmacia Benavides and at 10 other sites. Reasonably priced fountain/restaurant. Breakfasts, burgers, banana splits. $

El Pastor, Madero Pte 1067 and at Madero Pte 3126, tel: 74-0480. Rather plain restaurant with the reputation for great *cabrito al pastor* (roast kid). Also good *carne al carbón* (charcoaled meat). $

El Rey de Cabrito, Constitución 817 at Calle Dr Coss, tel: 46-0291. Western Mexico decor with stuffed animals. They serve only tender *cabrito* and appetizers. Walking distance from downtown hotels. $$

El Tio, Hidalgo 1746 Pte & Mexico, Col. Obispado, tel: 46-0291. Pricey, noisy place, popular with young, affluent Mexicans. Charbroiled steak, *cabrito*, and Mexican food. A block north of Constitución Expressway. Open till midnight. $$$

Henry VIII, Hidalgo Pte 2726, tel: 48-5670. Expensive restaurant in Tudor-style mansion off Av. Constitución. Specialties include *lobster à la Enrique*, prime rib, steak, game, and seafood. Old English music. $$$

Gambrino's, Av. Gomez Morín 265 & Roble, tel: 78-9719. Spanish-style restaurant with well-prepared regional dishes. $$$

La Puntada, Hidalgo 123 Ote, tel: 40-9985. Good, cheap food. Popular for lunch. *Tacos, machacado con huevo* (shredded beef). $

Luisiana, Av. Hidalgo 530 Ote, tel: 43-1561. Old-time favorite on Hidalgo Plaza Mall near Ancira. Elegant modern decor. International cuisine: filets, game, seafood. Top-notch service. $$$

Regio, Regio Gonzalitos at Av. Gonzalitos and Insurgentes, tel: 46-8650; Regio Del Roble at Av. Alfonso Reyes Nte 200 at foot of overpass, tel: 76-5300; and Regio Apodaca, Av. Adolfo López Mateos 6255, tel: 53-6205. A chain of three good restaurants, open late and known for their charcoaled steaks and *cabrito*. $$

Sanborn's, Escobedo 920, tel: 42-1441. Downtown on Hidalgo Plaza with a wide variety of international and Mexican dishes, ice-cream sherbets, sundaes, malts, etc. Souvenirs, magazines, books, newspapers. $$$

Senor Frog's, Real de San Agustín 222, Local TA 102, tel: 63-2848. Part of a chain with outlets all over Mexico. Ribs, oyster soup with Pernod (booze in lots of dishes!) and beef. $$$

Senor Natural, vegetarian restaurant with three sites: Mitras, Centro, and Tecnológico, tel: 78-4815. Good assortment of healthy dishes including fruit salads, yogurt, granola, natural juices, and tasty soy dishes. $$

OAXACA CITY – OAXACA

Del Vitral, Av. V. Guerrero, tel: (951) 6-3124. Located in magnificent turn-of-the-century mansion. Good food – many dishes from old Oaxacan recipes. $$$

El Asador Vasco, Portal de Flores 11, tel: (951) 6-3124. Very popular restaurant located on the second floor facing the Zócalo, specializing in Basque and Oaxacan dishes. $$

Flamanalli, Av. Juarez 39, Teotitlan del Valle, tel: (956) 2-0255. Charming village restaurant serving Zapotec food and also selling attractive hand-woven rugs. $$

Hosteria de Alcala, Macedonio Alcala 307, tel: (951) 6-2093. In the interior court of an old colonial mansion. Music some evenings. $$

Las Tres "T", Col. Centro, tel: (951) 6-1483. Inexpensive establishment specializing in excellent *pozole* in addition to its three Ts: *tacos, tortas* and *tostados*. $

Nuu-Luu, Iturbe 100, San Felipe del Agua, tel: (951) 5-3187. In Oaxaca's northern suburb (10-minute cab ride from city center). Oaxacan specialties in a veranda dining room overlooking large garden of tropical fruit trees. $$

PUEBLA – PUEBLA

Fonda de Santa Clara, 3 Poniente. Traditional dishes such as *chiles en nogada* – green chilies (stuffed with meat, fruit and spices) and white walnut, cheese and cream sauce sprinkled with ruby red pomegrante seeds represent the Mexican flag.

PUERTO ESCONDIDO – OAXACA

Nautilus, Av. Pérez Gasca, Puerto Escondido. Palapa-covered terrace on second floor with great view of the bay. $$

Perla Flameante, Av. Pérez Gasca, Puerto Escondido. Tropical island ambiance, specializing in fish and seafood. $$

Santa Fe, Calle del Morro, Puerto Escondido, tel: (958) 2-0170. Restaurant of the Sante Fé Hotel with great view. No red meat, but good Mexican seafood, chicken and vegetarian dishes. $$$

SALTILLO – COAHUILA

Antonio's Pizza. Across the street from Unicorio. Good pizza. $$

Arcasa. Next to Hotel Colonial. Good Mexican food. $

Café Victoria, Padre Flores 221 down street across from market, tel 2-9131. Great *tacos*. $

Cafeteria Popular, Padre Flores 197. Good, cheap restaurant. $

Casa Vieja, Blvd V. Carranza at east end of town. Elegant restaurant housed in exquisite colonial mansion with adobe walls. International cuisine served from imaginative menu. $$$

El Tapanco, Allende Sur 225, tel: 14-4339. Superb downtown restaurant in converted 17th-century home. Excellent international cuisine and Mexican specialties. $$$

El Zaguan, in old Franciscan convent across from Los Cazadores. Intimate bar with live music on weekends. $$

La Canasta, Blvd V. Carranza 2485, tel: 13-8250. Good restaurant just east of university. Specialties include char-broiled steaks and seafood. Popular locally. $$

Los Cazadores, Padre Flores 155. Good, neat Mexican and seafood restaurant. $$

Tacos el Pastor, on Aldama by market. One of the great *taco* restaurants in Mexico. $

SAN BLAS – OAXACA

Bucanero, On main street. Specializes in seafood and Italian dishes. Open daily 8am–10pm. Seasonal. $$

La Familia, Batellon 18, tel: 5-0289. Attractive, authentic Mexican-style restaurant in restored colonial home in town. Host Domingo Gutierrez is a gracious man who once studied to be a vet. Hand-painted menus by his father, Rafael Gutierrez, whose paintings adorn the walls. $$$

La Hacienda, Calle Juarez 33, across street and down a few doors from bank. Charming decor. Wonderful *carnitas* (deep fried pork). $$

McDonald's, Calle Juarez 36 (no relation of the fast-food chain). Good restaurant a block west of main plaza. Mexican-style beef filets and fish, lobster, shrimp, *tacos*, and *enchiladas*. Inexpensive. Gathering place for local gringos. $$

Rosy's, on plaza, near church. Typical and clean family restaurant. Mexican food, including *enchiladas, tacos, tostadas*. $

Tony's Inn La Isla, Paredes Sur, tel: 5-0407. Decorated with nets and shells, serves excellent seafood. $$

Torino's. Largest restaurant in town, located downtown a block beyond plaza across from Bucanero, on main stem. $$$

SAN CARLOS – SONORA

Bejing, across from Country Club office, tel: 6-0550. Chinese food, seafood. $$

Caramba's Grill, Av. Serdán 664, tel: 2-9606. Next to supermarket. Good food and service. $$

Cesar's Burgers, across from Lanchas de Pesca de Ostion St. Great place for breakfast, lunch or early dinner. Good value. $

El Paradise, seafood restaurant (across from Creston) serving excellent selection of shellfish and other seafood. $$$

El Yate, tel: 6-0311. Good view of Yacht Club. More a sports bar with US events. Varied menu, seafood, steak and Mexican food. Bar. $$$

La Roca, seafood restaurant in front of El Paradise. Lovely view of ocean. Good selection of Sonoran fish. Dancing. $$$

Los Piratas, between Fiesta San Carlos & Creston. Excellent food and service. Popular with local American residents. $$

Norsa, off the main highway going into town, turn right across from Fiesta San Carlos. A family restaurant with good food. Clean, neat and friendly. $

Pappas Tappas, tel: 6-0707. Arizona decor. Beef and seafood. Bar. Weekly "all you can eat" buffet specials. $$

Rosa's Cantina, Carr. San Carlos. Casual place, popular with young people. *Cabrito*, steak, *enchiladas*. Bulletin-board for buying, selling, renting or local events. Open 7.30am–10.30pm daily. Good value. $$

San Carlos Grill, tel: 6-5009. Varied menu. Chicken, fish, steak, *crêpes*. Live music. Trendy. $$

Terraza, Carr. San Carlos Km 5, tel: 6-0039. Overlooking San Carlos Bay. Specializes in seafood and also serves Sonoran beef and chicken. $$$

SANTIAGO TUXTLA – VERACRUZ

El Trapiche de Ximagambazca, Km 114 Carretera Costera del Golfo, Popotepec. Charming roadside restaurant between Alvarado and Santiago Tuxtla. Smoked meats a specialty. $$

TAMPICO – TAMAULIPAS

Bone's Grill, Calle Francita y Cerro Azul in Col Petrolera, tel: 3-5576. Mexican and international restaurant. House specialties include seafood and steaks. $$

Cafe Mundo, corner D. Miron & L. de Lara, tel:14-1831. No-frills place where the tables are kept level by folded napkins and the waiters look as if they were born there. Cheap, fast and good Mexican food. Good coffee. Popular with students, downtown workers and budget travellers. $$

Diligencias, H. del Canoneros, corner C. de Lara one block off Plaza de Libertad, tel: 14-1279. Absolutely the best seafood in town, maybe the world. Reasonable prices. There's another branch at Ayuntamiento and Mayor, tel: 13-7642. $$$

Jardin Corona, Av. Hidalgo 1915. Don't let the funky exterior fool you. This is a marble-floored, white-tablecloth place, with prices to match. Seafood and beef, cappuccino and lots more. $$$

Le Bon Appetit, Av. Hidalgo, two or three blocks farther out from Camino Real. Clearly Tampico's premier restaurant with expensive couple reservation packages. $$$

Muraltas, across the street from Plaza de la Libertad at H. de Canoneros (also called Ribera) 7 Aduana. Sandwiches, *tacos*. Open 24 hours. $

Saloon Palacio, funky restaurant across from Plaza de al Libertad. Marble floors, some marble tabletops, interesting artwork and lots of character. Seafood, chicken, *milanesas* at decent prices. $$$

TIJUANA – BAJA CALIFORNIA

Alcazar del Rio, Paseo de los Héros, tel: 84-2672. International menu. $$$

Boccaccio, Blvd Agua Caliente, tel: 86-2266. Steaks and seafood. $$$

La Escondida, Las Palmas Av., tel: 81-4458. A local's favorite. Serves enormous margaritas. $$$

Hacienda del Abajeño, Sanchez Taboa and Antonio Caso, tel: 84-2791. Mexican folk music in a fountain-filled patio. $$$

Guadalajara Bar & Grill, Calle Orozco and Paseo de los Héroes. Mexican street scene setting. $$

Place de la Concorde, Fiesta Americana Hotel, Blvd Agua Caliente, tel: 81-7000. Tijuana's most elegant restaurant, with excellent French cuisine. $$$

La Placita, Av. Revolución 783, tel: 88-2704. Moderately priced, with music. $$

Tour de France, Gobernador Ibarra and Highway 1, tel: 81-7542. Patio, French food. $$

TULÚM – QUINTANA ROO

El Crucero Motel, on highway 307, 10-minute walk from ruins. Good food, lively atmosphere in restaurant. $$

TUXPÁN – VERACRUZ

Buffalo, Av. Hidalgo & the river, a few blocks west of plaza. Open-air hamburgers and *tacos*. Good. $$

Del Puerto, Juarez 44 at Humboldt, tel: (783) 4-4801. Good *tacos* and seafood. $$

UXMAL – YUCATÁN

Hotel Hacienda Uxmal, Carretera 261 Km 80, tel: (99) 24-7142. A choice of restaurants in beautiful 4-star hotel, former headquarters of archaeologists, just across from ruins. $$

Restaurant-Bar Yax Beh, Visitors' Center at ruins. Eat among other tired but elated travellers enjoying the air conditioning right on the site, at rather expensive prices. $$

Villa Arqueológica, entry road just by ruins parking lot, tel: (99) 24-7053. Club Med for French food, cultural setting. $$

VALLADOLID – YUCATÁN
El Bazar, Calles 40 and 39 at corner of Zócalo. A series of simple eateries, for a variety of tasty, economical dishes. $
Casa de los Arcos Restaurant, Calle 39 No. 200-A, tel: 6-2467. Enjoy delicious Yucatecan dishes in colonial ambience with helpful bilingual menu. $$
El Mesón del Marqués, Calle 39 No. 203, tel: 6-2073. Newly renovated, right on main plaza next to Hotel del Marqués for Mexican and Yucatecan dishes. $$
Hotel María de la Luz, Calle 42 No. 195, tel: 6-2070. Good Mexican/Yucatecan eating in a hotel setting, where you can look out on the street happenings. Very popular with the *Vallisoletanos*, the citizens of Valladolid. $

VERACRUZ CITY – VERACRUZ
Pozolver, Simón Bólivar 192, Veracruz. Simple *pozole* restaurant. Menu limited to local specialties. Try a *chelada* (beer with lime juice, hot sauce, salt and Worcestershire sauce). $
Villa Marina, Blvd Avila Camacho, Veracruz, tel: (293) 5-1034. Modern restaurant and bar cantilevered over the gulf. Continental cuisine. $$

DRINKING NOTES

Mexicans tend to drink copiously at fiestas and in times of great calamity or great good fortune. Otherwise, they are relatively sober folk. Beer is very popular as an accompaniment to the heavy *comida* in mid-afternoon, and you would be well advised to adopt this custom. Beer complements Mexican flavors and helps take the bite out of chili peppers. Mexican beers are excellent, as good as any in the world. Try drinking canned beer in the local fashion: squeeze lemon and sprinkle salt on the lid of the can. Wine is rarely drunk, although there are vineyards in some areas of Mexico. Some Mexican wines are good and others are not, but all tend to be rather expensive. Imported wines, especially French wines, are quite dear in Mexico.

Unless you go to bars that cater for foreigners, you may not be able to get your favorite cocktails prepared with the usual brands of liquors. Rather than become frustrated trying to obtain the familiar, try Mexico's own deservedly famous liquor, tequila. Besides beer and tequila, the drinks popular with middle-class and upper-middle-class Mexicans are *Cubas* (or *Cuba libres*), made with Coke and rum, and "highballs," made with whisky and soda. Poor people are more likely to drink grain alcohol made from sugar cane, often mixed with soft drinks.

You may also want to try some of the more esoteric Mexican beverages. There are other liquors, besides tequila, made from varieties of the maguey plant; the generic term is mescal. The most traditional of Mexican drinks is *pulque*. For better or worse, you will probably not have a chance to try it. Made from a type of maguey, *pulque* is not distilled as are tequila and other mescals. It must be drunk when freshly fermented, because it cannot be canned or bottled without being ruined. It is highly nutritious (unless diluted with contaminated water) and only mildly alcoholic, about the same as beer. In pre-Columbian Mexico, *pulque* was reserved for use in rituals and healing. It is still highly valued by Mexicans, although not expensive, and its popularity is why you will have trouble getting hold of some.

Another reason is that strangers are not generally welcome in *pulquerias*, the special bars (like informal men's clubs) where *pulque* is drunk. Make friends with a Mexican and ask him to invite you to a *pulqueria*; if you're lucky, he may ask you home to drink some special brew. Women, unfortunately, are virtually never allowed in *pulquerias*.

The *cantina* likewise does not welcome women. It is sometimes said that you can distinguish a real *cantina* from a bar that calls itself a *cantina* by observing whether women are admitted.

A wide variety of non-alcoholic beverages is available in Mexico. Soft drinks are called *refrescos*. You will see familiar and unfamiliar brands. If you want to avoid taking any risks with water but dislike soft drinks, order mineral water (*agua mineral*, often listed on menus by the brand name *Agua de Tehuacán* or just plain Tehuacán). Even if you are not an enthusiast of soft drinks you might like to try some of the Mexican ones. Apple-flavored *Sidral* and *sangria*, a mixed-fruit drink, are both interesting and refreshing. Fruit juices, whether ordered in restaurants, in markets or from street vendors, are often freshly squeezed for you. *Jugo* is the word for juice. *Agua fresca* is a fruit juice mixed with a lot of water. It is much cheaper but more risky. *Licuados* are fruit milkshakes, often with eggs added. Try one. Order a *licuado de coco*, coconut shake, from a street vendor.

When you are in the mood for authenticity, try *atole* – cornmeal mixed with water or milk, sugar, and some flavoring to taste (chocolate, vanilla) – or *horchata*, made from ground rice and water. Another pre-Columbian drink is chocolate. Try it instead of coffee one morning. If you stick with coffee, you will find that Nescafé (instant) is most often served. Coffee which is brewed is specified as *café de olla*. *Café con leche* is mostly milk with a little coffee in it: you may have trouble getting coffee with milk served separately, except in tourist areas.

377

ATTRACTIONS

MUSEUMS

MEXICO CITY

In Mexico City the biggest concentration of museums is in Chapultepec Park. They are:

National Museum of Anthropology, tel: 553-6386. Open Tuesday–Sunday 9am–7pm.

Museum of Natural History, tel: 515-2222. Open Tuesday–Sunday 10am–5pm.

Museum of Modern Art, tel: 553-6233. Open Tuesday–Sunday 10am–6pm.

Technological Museum, tel: 516-0964. Open Tuesday–Sunday 9am–7pm.

Rufino Tamayo Museum, tel: 286-5889. Open Tuesday–Sunday 9am–6pm.

Other museums are:

National Postal Museum, Hidalgo 39, tel: 521-2244. Open Tuesday–Sunday 10am–3pm, 4–6pm. Stamp collections since 1856.

Museo del Mural Diego Rivera, Balderas & Colon, tel: 510-2329. Open Tuesday–Sunday 10am–6pm. Enormous mural of Mexican notables of half a century ago.

Museo Nacional de las Culturas, Moneda 13, tel: 512-7452. Open Tuesday–Saturday 9.30am–6pm. Art from around the world.

Museo José Luis Cuevas, Academia 13, tel: 542-6198. Open Tuesday–Sunday 10am–6pm. One of Mexico's most celebrated painters.

Bellas Artes Museum, Alameda, tel: 510-1388. Open Tuesday–Sunday 10am–6pm. Major muralists and changing exhibits.

Museo Nacional de la Revolución, Plaza de la República, tel: 566-1902. Open Tuesday–Saturday 9am–5pm, Sunday 9–3pm. Interesting historical panorama since 1920.

Museo del Templo Mayor, Seminario 8, tel: 542-0606. Open Tuesday–Sunday 9am–5pm. Aztec gods.

Pinacoteca Virreynal, Doctor Mora 7, tel: 510-2793. Open Tuesday–Sunday 9am–5pm. Religious works from the 16th century.

Carranza Home Museum, Lerma 35, tel: 535-2960. Open Monday–Friday 9am–6pm. Artefacts from the life of the former president, assassinated in 1917.

San Carlos Museum, Puente de Alvarado 50. Open Wednesday–Monday 10am–2pm, 4pm–6pm. European art from the 14th to 19th century.

Most of the capital's art galleries are found in the **Zona Rosa**, within a few blocks of Insurgentes and Chapultepec avenues, with two other groups **downtown** around the Alameda and north and east of the Zócalo. There is also a handful of art galleries in the suburbs of **Coyoacán** and **San Angel**.

DANCE

Details below highlight some of the attractions available in Mexico City. Ask at your hotel for current information about dance companies outside the city center.

The **Ballet Folklórico** presents a range of Mexican dances at polished performances on Wednesday and Sunday evenings at the Palacio de Bellas Artes, Eje Central Lázaro Cárdenas, at the eastern end of the Alameda. Tickets can be purchased at the box office (you will have to go in person to reserve seats in advance).

Another, newer Mexican dance company which is worth seeing is the **Ballet Folklórico Nacional Aztlán**, which performs at the refurbished historic Teatro de la Ciudad, Donceles 36, tel: 510-2197.

To see flamenco dancers in *de rigueur* nightclub settings, you should visit **Gitanerías**, Oaxaca, tel: 208-2264 or **El Corral de la Morería**, Londres 161, Zona Rosa, tel: 525-1762.

MUSIC

Mexicans love music and will entertain you with a variety of sounds including classical and opera, jazz, Latin American rhythms, *mariachis* bands, and *peñas*. Ask at your hotel for details of local performances.

PEOPLE-WATCHING

Your best bet for this popular Mexican pastime is to stroll around and then settle down at any sidewalk cafe for a drink and supper.

MOVIES

The Mexican film industry is one of the world's most prolific, and Mexico has provided sites for the shooting of innumerable Hollywood Westerns (the Durango area has specialized in this).

Few Mexican films have attained international prominence. Perhaps the most admired by cinema buffs are Luis Buñuel's *Los Olvidados* and *Nazarín*, and Sergei Eisenstein's *Que Viva México* – a classic film focusing on the visual beauty of life in Mexican Indian villages. Other fine films such as *María Candelaria* and *Animas Trujano* have followed Eisenstein's lead in their Indian settings.

A recent film that has been widely acclaimed internationally is *Como Agua para Chocolate* ("Like Water for Chocolate"), based on the 1990 number-one bestselling novel of the same name by Laura

Esquivel, and set in turn-of-the-century Mexico (see *Further Reading*).

Vintage Mexican films always experience a nostalgic revival in Mexico – pictures such as *Allá en el Rancho Grande*, *Los Tres García*, *Historia de un Gran Amor*, featuring stars such as Jorge Negrete, Pedro Infante, Pedro Armendáriz, Joaquín Pardave, Fernando Soler, María Félix, Marga López and the enduring Dolores del Río.

Cantinflas, once Mexico's best-known comedian, has many movies to his credit. These can also be rated among nostalgia-inducing films. Cinema buffs might perhaps also enjoy the films that feature the bizarre character *Tin-Tán*, who popularized *pachucos*, those snazzy zoot-suiters of yesteryear.

In the cities more and more multiplex cinemas are being built, although they are mostly found wherever there are shopping malls. In Mexico City, the state-sponsored Cineteca Nacional (Metro Coyoacan station) is often worth a visit. Mexico City's English-language *Daily News* for some unfathomable reason does not list current movie showings; you'll have to refer to one of the Spanish dailies although the concierge at most larger hotels usually has a list. There are cinemas showing English-language movies (usually with Spanish subtitles) along Reforma between the Cuauhtemoc and Angel statues and also along Hamburgo in the Zona Rosa.

DIARY OF EVENTS

FIESTAS & FAIRS

(almost all dates are approximate and vary from year to year)

January 6	*Dia de Santos Reyes*: the traditional day for giving Christmas gifts.
January 17	*Dia de San Antonio Abad*: day for blessing animals.
January 18	Taxco, Guerrero: *Fiesta de Santa Prisca*.
January 20	Chiapa de Corzo, Chiapas: *Fiesta de San Sebastián*. Also at León and Guanajuato.
February 2	*Candelaria* feast. *Carnaval* during the week before Lent, notably in Acapulco, Guerrero; Mazatlan, Sinaloa; Merida, Yucatan; Huejotzingo, Puebla; Tepotztlan, Morelos; Veracruz.
February 5	Zitacuaro, Michoacan: fair.
March 1	Durango fair.
March 10	Huachinango, Puebla: dance of the flying men.
March 21	Chichén-Itzá: folk dances celebrate spring festival.
Easter	*Semana Santa* (Holy Week).
April	Xochimilco: festival queen elections.
April 5	Ticul, Yucatán: fair.
April 20	Tuxtla Gutierrez, Chiapas: fair.
April 23	Aztec Day of Tezcatlipoca.
April 29	Puebla: fair.
April–May	Aguascalientes stages San Marcos national fair. Acapulco stages World Table Tennis Championship.
May 1	Morelia, Michoacan: fair.
May 2	Cuernavaca, Morelos: fair.
May 3	Valle de Bravo: fair. *Corpus Christi* Day. Papantla, Veracruz: dance of the flying men.
May 20	Tecoh, Yucatán: festival of the Hammocks.
May 31	Tehuantepec, Oaxaca: crafts fair.
June 13	Uruapan, Michoacan: fair.
June 29	Tlaquepaque, Guadalajara: street fiesta.
July 1	Huamantla, Tlaxcala: fair.
July 7	Comitán, Chiapas: fair (usually the last two Mondays in July). Oaxaca: *Lunes del Cerro* (Indian festival).
August	Puerto Escondido, Oaxaca: International Surfing Competition.
August 1	Saltillo, Coahuila: fair.
August 8	Mérida, Yucatán: fair.
August 15	Many towns have fiestas.
August	Guadalupe Valley Wine Festival. Todos Santos (south of Ensenada): annual regatta.
September 1	Tepotztlan, Morelos: fair.
September 4	Santa Rosalia and Mulege: fiesta.
September 6	Zacatecas: fair.
September 8	La Virgen de Loreto: procession through the streets.
September 10	Chihuahua: fair.
September 12	Ensenada: seafood fair.
September 14	*Charro* Day.
September 15	Independence Day celebrated nationally.
September 19	Caliente: annual Tijuana fair at racetrack.
September 22	Chichén-Itzá: autumnal equinox celebrated.
September	Rosarito-Ensenada: 50 Mile Fun Bicycle Ride.
late September	San Miguel de Allende: fiesta on the Saturday following *Dia de San Miguel*.

October 4	*Dia de San Francisco*: many towns have fiestas; Cuetzalan, Puebla: coffee growers' fair.
October 4	Pachuca, Hidalgo: fair.
October 12	Guadalajara: fair.
October	Rosarito: annual Lobster and Wine Festival.
October	Guanajuato Cervantine Festival.
November 1–2	Day of the Dead celebrated nationally. Janitzio, Michoacan: graveside vigils.
November 20	National holiday celebrates 1910 Revolution.
December 1	Compostela, Nayarit: fair.
December 8	*Dia de Nuestra Señora de la Salud*: Patzcuaro, Michoacan: fair.
December 7	Taxco: silver fair.
December 12	*Dia de Nuestra Señora de Guadalupe:* Many pilgrimages to *La Villa*, the shrine of Our Lady of Guadalupe in Mexico City.
December 18	*Dia de Nuestra Señora de la Soledad*. Oaxaca: fair.

NIGHTLIFE

MEXICO CITY

As early as possible during your visit to the capital, book seats for the **Ballet Folklorico de México** which performs Wednesday and Sunday at the Palacio de Bellas Artes at the eastern end of the Alameda. Advance reservations must be made here in person.

A few blocks north on San Juan de Letrán, behind the Palace of Fine Arts, is the **Teatro Blanquita** which stages variety performances most nights each week (with occasional rock concerts interspersed). Although performances are in Spanish the bill of fare – music, dancing, comedy – is so varied that language is only a minor handicap to enjoyment of the show. Before or after the performance, it's a good plan to visit the lively **Plaza Garibaldi** (almost across the street) where you can audition musicians for impromptu performances and or attend one or another of the *mariachi* nightclubs.

Among the night spots with dance floors are: **Stellaris**, in the Hotel Fiesta America Reforma, Columbus Circle, tel: 706-1516. **Las Galerias,** inside the Hotel Romano, Lerma 237, tel: 211-0109. Resembles an old Spanish galleon. **Grillo's Bar**, Reforma & Niza, (tel: 633-0908). **El Corsario,** in the Mauna Loa restaurant at Av. San Jeronimo 240 in San Angel, tel: 616-2902.

The **Zona Rosa**, with its plethora of bars and sidewalk cafés, is the area which probably has the most to offer after dark.

SHOPPING

What to Buy

Few travelers can resist shopping in Mexico. And for some, shopping may even be the primary purpose of their visit. The price-range is nearly as wide as the range of craft items available, so take your time and choose wisely. Serious shoppers should plan to travel extensively in the countryside, because everything is cheaper at the place where it's made. You may also be lucky enough to watch and photograph the *artesano* at work.

For those limited to one or more cities, the range of possible purchases is still wide. Items from all over Mexico can be bought at the large markets, especially San Juan de Dios in Guadalajara. Prices are well above those paid the artisan at the source, but you can bargain the prices down – even where there are signs saying *precios fijos* (fixed prices). Simply ask for a "discount." You'll have to exercise your Spanish, especially numbers. Begin by asking "¿*Cuánto cuesta*?" (How much?) There's no need to bargain if the asking price is ridiculously low. If it's not, make an offer. Half the asking price is usual in a tourist area; perhaps two-thirds elsewhere. Take your time and work down to a mutually-agreeable figure. Once the vendor has come down substantially to meet your price, do not change your mind and walk away. That is bad manners.

Handicrafts from all over the country are also sold at government-run stores in many cities (see the list *What to Buy*). These are not particularly inexpensive stores, and prices are generally not negotiable, but quality is high. The same is true of many shops and boutiques in stylish areas of town, such as Mexico City's Zona Rosa.

As elsewhere, *caveat emptor*. Always buy jewelry from a reputable store, never from a street vendor. And buy it because you like the design, not because of its silver content. Iron items may be sprayed with paint to imitate copperware. Hand-made clothing may shrink, so buy a larger size if in any doubt. Cotton (*algodón*) is pure cotton, but wool (*lana*) is often a blend of fibers. Machine-made embroidery can be beautiful, but not after you've paid a hand-made price for it, so check first by looking at the reverse side. Hammocks should be pure cotton, of thin thread, and tightly woven. Bees-wax on the thread will make it mildew-resistant. Mexico's beautiful green-glazed pottery cannot be trusted to be lead-free, so use it for decoration or for dry items, not for wet or acidic foods.

Remember, too, when buying ceramics, that you should avoid drinking or eating from pottery containing lead. Oaxacan black ware always contains lead. If the empty article rings like a bell when flicked with the fingernail, it is safe; if it sounds as if you've tapped on wood, it probably contains lead. The glaze on typical traditional pottery is usually brown, at times with green decoration, which is particularly dangerous, since it allows rapid release of lead from the glaze. Highly-colored, lightweight articles are usually glazed with lead. Paint in Mexico contains lead, so painted items will have lead.

Most large stores will pack your purchases carefully and mail them to your home, for a reasonable charge. Items mailed are not counted as part of the US$400-worth of duty-exempt purchases allowed US travellers (see *Customs*).

If you are shopping for gifts, you can have them mailed directly to the recipient in the US. Again, they will not be counted as part of your duty-exempt purchases. Write GIFT clearly on the outside of the package, and indicate the retail value of the contents. You cannot send perfume, tobacco or alcohol. There is a limit: no one can receive more than US$10-worth in one day.

Don't pay high prices for genuine pre-Columbian artifacts. Most will be fakes, though possibly well-made fakes. Very fine ceramic figures are made using original types of clay and authentic firing procedures. Should the artifact be indeed genuine, you will not be permitted to take it out of Mexico (nor to import it into many other countries, including the United States).

The markets of Mexico City are fascinating. The best (and cheapest) for handicrafts and souvenirs is **Artesianas de la Ciudadela** (Ayuntamiento at Balderas) displaying a range of Mexican souvenirs and crafts (blankets, blouses, napkins, silver, *papier-mâché* fruits, toys, leather) and harboring a neat little café in its sunny, central plaza. The **San Juan** market (on Ayuntamiento at Dolores; walk three blocks south on San Juan de Letrán and turn right) boasts 176 stores selling handicrafts but all of it is familiar stuff and there is little variety. The biggest market is probably the immense **Merced** (Metro station), where there is most as much going on outside as under cover – chickens frying; radios blaring; girls rolling, heating and filling *tortillas* from an array of brightly colored plastic bowls. Itinerant peddlers, arms heavy with garments on hangers, sell razors or cosmetics from carrier-bags. A few blocks away, the **Sonora** market on Fray Servando Teresa de Mier at Rosario, is famous for its herbs and cures.

Almost as large as the Merced is the **Lagunilla** market, three blocks along Rayón, about three blocks north of the Plaza Garibaldi. Divided by the main street, it offers chickens, fruit, meat and other types of food on one side and clothes from ballgowns to ranch wear on the other.

SHOPPING AREAS

Ceramics
Tlaquepaque, Jalisco
   A variety of pottery, including replicas of pre-Columbian pieces.

Tonalá, Jalisco
   New innovations as well as traditional styles.

Puebla, Puebla
   Household crockery, tiles, and Talavera ceramics.

Acatlán and Izucar de Matamoros, Puebla; and Metepec, Mexico
   "tree of life" ceramics.

Guanajuato and San Miguel de Allende, Guanajuato
   A variety of pottery styles.

Tzintzuntzan, and San Miguel de Allende, Guanajuato
   Burnished ceramics.

Patamban, Michocán
   Green-glazed pottery.

Guerrero state
   A variety of traditional ceramics.

San Bartolo Coyotepec, Oaxaca
   Burnished black pottery.

Santa María Atzompa, Oaxaca
   Ceramic animals.

Amatenango, Chiapas
   Traditional pottery fired without kilns.

Woodworking and lacquerware
Bahía de Kino, Sonora
   Seri Indians' ironwood animals.

Uruapan, Michoacán
   Masks, lacquerware.

Quiroga, Michoacán
   Painted wooden bowls, household items.

Ixtapán de la Sal, Mexico
   Household items and carved animals.

Cuernavaca, Morelos
   Colonial-style furniture, wooden bowls.

Olinalá, Guerrero
   Jaguar masks, gourd bowls, wooden trays, fine lacquerware.

Ixmiquilpan, Hidalgo
   Bird cages.

Tequisquiapan, Querétaro
   Knockdown wooden stools.

Cuilampan, Oaxaca
   Painted wooden animals.

Chiapa de Corzo, Chiapas
   Masks and other lacquerware.

Mérida, Yucatán; Valladolid, Tabasco; and Campeche
  Mahogany and cedar furniture.

Paracho, Michoacán
  Guitars.

San Juan Chamula, Chiapas
  Guitars and harps.

Basketry and fiber items
Tequisquiapan, Querétaro
  Basketry.

Lerma, Mexico
  Basketry.

Xalitla, Tolima and San Agustín de las Flores, Guerrero
  Huapanec Indians' bark paintings.

San Miguel de Allende and Guanajuato, Guanajuato; Puebla, Puebla; and Otomi Indian villages in the Mezquital valley, Hidalgo
  Cane and reed containers.

San Miguel de Allende
  Paper and papier maché – *piñatas* and masks.

Veracruz coastal area
  Palm-leaf mats and other items.

Ihuatzio, Michoacán
  Reed mats and basketry.

Mixtec area of Oaxaca
  Net carrying bags.

Puebla, Veracruz and San Luis Potosí
  Huastecan Indian cactus fiber bags and wool items.

Mérida, Yucatán
  Hammocks.

Bekal, Campeche
  Panama hats.

Woven wool
Tlaxcala; Cuernavaca and Huejapan, Morelos; Tequisquiapan, Querétaro; San Miguel de Allende, Guanajuato; Teotitlán del Valle, near Oaxaca City; Saltillo, Coahuila; and Zacatecas
  Sarapes.

Otomi Indians of Mezquital Valley, Hildago; Tara-humara Indians of the Barranca del Cobre, Chihuahua; Cora and Huichol Indians of Tepic, Nayarit; Tzotzil Indians of San Juan Chamula, Chiapas
  Handwoven belts and clothing.

Embroidered clothing
Amuzgo Indians near Ometepec, Guerrero, and in Oaxaca
  Cotton *huipiles* (women's blouses).

Yalalag, Oaxaca
  Indian blouses and wrap-around skirts, made with natural dyes.

San Pablito Pahuatlán, Puebla
  Beaded blouses.

Cuetzalan, Puebla
  Embroidered blouses.

San Luis Potosí
  Silk *rebozos* (shawls).

Aguascalientes
  Clothing.

Mérida, Yucatán
  Guayaberas (embroidered shirts for men).

Puebla, Veracruz and San Luis Potosí
  Haustecan Indian's *quechquemetl*, a cross-stitch decorated women's cloak.

Jewelry
Mexico City
  Modern jewelry.

Taxco, Guerrero; Toluca, Mexico; Yalalag, Oaxaca; Querétaro; Veracruz; Yucatán
  Silver jewelry.

Veracruz
  Coral jewelry.

Querétaro
  Semi-precious stones.

Oaxaca, Oaxaca
  Replicas of gold jewelry found at Monte Albán.

Other items
Santa Clara del Cobre (now called Villa Escalante), Michoacán
  Copperware.

Tehuacán, Puebla
  Onyx.

Toluca, Mexico
  Chess games and dominos.

Government Craft Stores
Fonart, a government-sponsored fund for promoting handicrafts, is a good source of arts and crafts. They have outlets in Mexico City on Juárez, downtown, in the Zona Rosa, a warehouse on

Patriotismo, and many locations throughout the country. Their many retail shops around the country control the quality of everything they buy and sell.

MEXICO CITY

Fonart, Avenida Insurgentes Sur 1630, tel: 534-4335.

Fonart, Londres 136 Altos "A", (Zona Rosa), tel: 525-2026.

Juarez, 89, Av. Juárez No. 89, tel: 521-0171.

Fonart, Patriotismo 691, Col. Mixcoac, tel: 563-4060.

Fonart, Presidente Carranza 115, Col. Coyoacán, tel: 554-6270.

Fonart, San Ildefonso 32, Col. Centro, San Ildefonso.

OTHER CITIES

Fonart, Anillo Envolvente Lincoln y Mejía, Ciudad Juárez, Chihuahua, tel: (161) 3-6143.

Fonart, Manuel M. Bravo No. 116, Oaxaca, Oaxaca, tel: (951) 6-5764.

Fonart, Jardín Guerrero 6, San Luis Potosí, San Luis Potosí, tel: (481) 2-7521.

Casa del Conde de la Valena, SA de CV, Km 5 Valenciana, Carretera Guanajuato-Dolores, Hidalgo, tel: 2-2550.

Aeroplazas de México, SA, Aeropuerto Internacional de Puerto Vallarta, Locales Planta Alta y Baja, Puerto Vallarta, tel: (322) 1-1073.

SPORTS

Fishing

Fishing is permitted in Mexico's lakes, rivers and dams, and along its 5,000-odd miles (8,047-odd km) of coastline. Annual fishing tournaments are based in La Paz, Guaymas, Mazatlán, Puerto Vallarta, Barra de Navidad, Manzanillo and Acapulco on the Pacific Coast; in Tampico, Veracruz and Cd. del Carmen on the Gulf of Mexico; and in Cancún and Cozumel on the Caribbean. Most tournaments are in May and June.

Fishing seasons and regulations vary from one area to another, and from one season to another. For information, write to : Departamento de Pesca, Oficina de Permisos de Pesca Deportiva, Avenida Alvaro Obregón No. 269, Planta Baja, Mexico 7, DF. Send a large, stamped, self-addressed envelope and they will send you (in English) information and regulations. If you are already in Mexico, tel: 211-0804, 211-0679. There are also some 150 branch offices of the Departamento de Pesca.

One license will cover you for fresh-water or salt-water fishing anywhere in Mexico. Licenses are issued for periods of three days, one month, three months or one year. You can purchase a license at any Departamento de Pesca office, from any local fish or game warden, or from the captain of any port or fishing facility. You may import your fishing gear without any problem, except for harpoons or spearfishing equipment – these are illegal in Mexico.

Hunting

Mexico abounds with game, both large and small; but there are numerous restrictions on what you may hunt, on hunting zones and seasons, and on what you may export after you have killed it. Your home country will also have restrictions on what you may bring in. Anyone serious about hunting in Mexico should begin planning their trip well in advance. Write to the Dirección General de la Flora y Fauna Silvestre, Río Elba, 8th Floor, Col. Cuauhtémoc, 06500 México, DF. Send a large, stamped, self-addressed envelope, and request a hunting calendar and information on hunting regulations. You can also get information from the Mexican Consulate or National Council of Tourism office nearest you.

You may apply for a hunting license at the same time, from the same office. Include two passport-sized photographs of yourself. Specify in your letter where you want to hunt, what game you are seeking, and when you plan to come. The basic license fee varies according to whether you want to hunt in one or more states. There are special licenses that you have to get if you want to hunt certain species (fox, ocelot, panther, black bear, antelope or wild lamb).

You will also need a license to carry a firearm. Write to or inquire at your nearest Mexican Consulate. Handguns are not permitted. US residents planning to hunt in Mexico and hoping to bring home their trophies should write (in advance, enclosing a stamped self-addressed envelope) to the US Customs Service, PO Box 7118, Washington, DC 20044. Ask for the pamphlet called "Pets and Wildlife." You can also obtain it from your nearest Customs office.

Jai Alai

One of the fastest sports alive is the Basque game of Jai Alai. It is played nightly in Mexico City except Mondays and Wednesday in the Fronton Mexico (tel: 546-1469), opposite the Monument to the Revolution. Games have been played continuously here since 1929. Betting is heavy and fun. Games start at 7pm.

In Cancún you can bet on the games, have a drink and enjoy supper in the Club House restaurant, tel: 83-3900.

Water Sports

Water sports abound around the Mexican coastlines. You will find everything from boat tours, windsurfing, snorkeling, fishing and scuba diving.

Snorkeling and Scuba diving

The generally calms waters of the hotel beaches are great for beginners and children to learn basic snorkel techniques and most have lifeguards. Equipment can be rented from local marinas and some hotels provide it free of charge.

For the more advanced diver, the Belize barrier reef, among the longest in the world, begins (or ends) its 250-km (155-mile) length near the Club

Med at Punta Nizuc, Yucatán. As all beaches are open to the public in Cancún, you could head there to enjoy the sights in the clear shallow water. Cancún is not the most scenic diving spot on the peninsula – Cozumel has that honor – but you can still enjoy yourself. Isla Mujeres is also a popular destination.

Pick up a copy of the magazine *Dive Mexico* for an overview of diving sites.

Bullfighting

Bullfighting is popular throughout Mexico and can be experienced at the Plaza de Toros in various cities. Check with your hotel to see if *corridas* are in season at the time of your trip and obtain information on acquiring tickets.

An afternoon's event usually includes three *toreros* – each fighting and killing two bulls in a highly stylized manner. Two types of seats are available: *sol* (sun), which are cheapest but the least comfortable, and *sombra* (shade).

Horse racing

Watch the races in Mexico City at the Hipódromo de las Américas. Races are held Saturday and Sunday, as well as Thursday, most of the year, starting around 2pm.

Football

The site of two world cup championships, Mexico is a soccer-playing country, with the huge Aztec Stadium (in Mexico City) its largest venue. Enquire at your hotel about the *fútbol* game on Sunday morning.

LANGUAGE

Although many Mexicans speak some English, it is good to have basic Spanish phrases at your disposal; in remote areas, it is essential. In general, Mexicans are delighted with foreigners who try to speak the language, and they'll be patient – if amused. Pronunciation is not difficult. The following is a simplified mini-lesson:

Vowels:
a as in father
e as in bed
i as in police
o as in hole
u as in rude

Consonants are approximately like those in English, the main exceptions being:
c is hard before **a, o,** or **u** (as in English), and is soft before **e** or **i,** when it sounds like **s** (as opposed to the Castilian pronunciation of **th** as in think). Thus, *cen*so (census) sounds like senso.
g is hard before **a, o,** or **u** (as in English), but where English g sounds like **j** – before **e** or **i** – Spanish **g** sounds like a guttural **h**. **G** before **ua** is often soft or silent, so that agua sounds more like awa, and Guadalajara like Wadalajara.
h is silent.
j sounds like the English h.
ll sounds like y.
ñ sounds like ny, as in the familiar Spanish word *señor*.
q is followed by **u** as in English, but the combination sounds like **k** instead of like **kw**. *¿Qué quiere Usted?* is pronounced: Keh kee-ehr-eh oostehd?
r is often rolled.
x between vowels sounds like a guttural **h,** e.g. in México or Oaxaca.
y alone, as the word meaning and, is pronounced **ee**.

Note that **ch** is a separate letter of the Spanish alphabet; if looking in a phone book or dictionary for a word beginning with **ch**, you will find it after the final **c** entry.

Insurgent Mexico, by John Reed. International Publishing, 1969. Exciting account of the 1910 revolution by the reporter famous for his coverage of the Russian Revolution (and the subject of the 1981 film, *Reds*).

The Maya, by Michael Coe. Thames & Hudson, 1980. A good one-volume summary.

Maya History and Religion, by J. Eric Thompson. University of Oklahoma Press, 1976. Also by the same author, *The Rise and Fall of Maya Civilization*. University of Oklahoma Press, 1977. His explanations are based on decades of excavating Mayan temple complexes.

The Mexican War, by Otis Singletary. University of Chicago Press, 1960.

Missionaries, Miners & Indians, by Evelyn Hu-DeHart. Tucson: University of Arizona Press, 1981.

Los Olmecas (The Olmecs), by Jacques Soustelle. For those who can read Spanish or French, a scholarly yet highly readable account of Mexico's "mother culture".

The People of the Sun, by Alfonso Caso. University of Oklahoma Press, 1978. Authoritative source on the Aztecs.

Voyage to the New World: Fact and Fantasy, by Nigel Davies. Morrow, 1979. If you are tempted to subscribe to any of the fashionable theories about the Chinese, Middle Eastern or extra-terrestrial origins of Mexican civilization, read this first.

The Wind that Swept Mexico, by Anita Brenner and George R. Leighton. University of Texas Press, 1971. Brief account of the revolution, with excellent historical photographs.

Yucatán Before and After the Conquest, by Bishop Diego De Landa. Kraus reprint of 1941 Harvard University Peabody Museum Publication. Written by the same man who burned nearly all the Mayan pictographic accounts. This book is the starting-point for all serious research on the Maya.

Zapata and the Mexican Revolution, by John Womack. Knopf, 1968. Readable and well-researched.

MEXICAN WRITERS ON MEXICO

American Extremes, by Daniel Cosio Villages. University of Texas Press, 1964. Cosio Villegas, also the author of a 10-volume history of Mexico, provides in these essays an intelligent perspective on Mexico's problems and its relations with its northern neighbor.

La Democracia en México, by Pablo González Casanova. Democracy in Mexico. A very good book, unfortunately not available in English. Analyzes Mexico's social, political and economic institutions and its overall power structure, and assesses the potential for a more active democratic process.

The Labyrinth of Solitude, by Octavio Paz. Grove, 1962. Paz is perhaps the best-known (outside Mexico) of all Mexico's intellectuals. This book is not easy to read, but is a must for anyone who wants to go beyond a superficial understanding of the psychology and culture of contemporary Mexicans.

Mexican Traditions, by Sebastián Verti. Editorial Diana, 1993. One of Mexico's strongest cultural advocates writes on religious celebrations, regional festivities, dances and traditions, history and legend, the origins of *mariachi* and the charrería and the Mexican culinary legacy. Well-llustrated with color photographs, it includes traditional recipes.

Mexico, Profile of a Nation. Mexico, DF: INEGI, Fomento Cultural Banamex, 1989.

Profile of Man and Culture in Mexico, by Samuel Ramos. University of Texas Press, 1962. A companion piece to Paz's *Labyrinth of Solitude*. Provides particular insight into the psychology of Mexican Indians and their relations with the dominant *mestizo* culture.

FOREIGN WRITERS ON MEXICO

American and British Writers in Mexico, 1556–1973, by Drewey Wayne Gunn. University of Texas Press, 1974.

Barbarous Mexico, by John Kenneth Turner. University of Texas Press, 1969; first published 1908. Turner's reporting of the abject misery and death among the slaves working Mexico's tobacco and henequen plantations led many Americans to question Porfirio Díaz's reputation as a benevolent dictator.

Beyond the Mexique Bay, by Aldous Huxley. Vintage, 1960. Erudite observations on the Mayan cultural remains. Mostly concerned with Guatemala, but worth reading if you'll spend a lot of time in Oaxaca.

Five Families, by Oscar Lewis. Basic Books, 1959. *The Children of Sanchez* (Random House, 1961); *Pedro Martinez* (Random House, 1964); and *A Death in the Sanchez Family* (Random House, 1969). Oscar Lewis spent many years studying Mexico's "culture of poverty" and interviewing its victims.

The Forgotten Peninsula, by Joseph Wood Krutch. William Sloan, 1961. Perhaps the best book about Baja.

Hovering Over Baja, by Erle Stanley Gardner. Morrow, 1961 and *Whispering Sands*. Morrow, 1981. Gardner was a passionate outdoorsman who knew Baja thoroughly from visitng the area when he was not writing detective stories.

Incidents of Travel in Central America, Chiapas and Yucatán, by John L. Stephens. Dover, 1969; first published 1841. Stephens and illustrator Frederick Catherwood had many adventures and made remarkable discoveries. Their book was instrumental in arousing scientific interest in the lost Mayan civilization.

Last Call, by Mauricio González de la Garza. (No English edition). A scathing critique of Mexico's political institutions. The book has been quite controversial and enormously successful in Mexico (over 200,000 copies in print).

The Lawless Roads, by Graham Greene. Heinemann, 1950; published in the US as *Another Mexico*. Viking, 1939. Greene tells entertainingly of his travels, though his views of Catholicism in Mexico are debatable.

Life in Mexico: The Letters of Fanny Calderón de la Barca, with New Material from the Author's Private Journals, by Fanny Calderón de la Barca, edited by H.T. and M.H. Fisher. Doubleday, 1966; first published 1913. The author was a Scotswoman living in Spain, whose husband became Spain's first ambassador to independent Mexico. Madame Calderón de la Barca, intelligent and curious, loved to travel and spoke Spanish fluently.

Like Water for Chocolate, by Laura Esquivel. *Como Agua para Chocolate*; first published 1989; English version, Doubleday, 1992. The 1990 number-one bestseller novel about family life in turn-of-the-century Mexico. Wit, humor, irony and more blend into an easy-to-read, difficult-to-put-down book. The film based on the novel won 11 awards.

The Log from the Sea of Cortés, by John Steinbeck. Viking, 1951. Steinbeck tells of an expedition to gather biological specimens from the Sea of Cortés off Baja California. Recommended for those who will boat or fish in these waters.

Many Mexicos, by Lesley Byrd Simpson. University of California Press, 1966. A good historical analysis.

Mexico's Agricultural Dilemma, by P. Lamartine Yates. University of Arizona Press, 1981. A good source for those interested in Mexico's land problems.

Mexico and its Heritage, by Ernest Gruening. Appleton-Century Crofts, 1928. A dated but insightful historical analysis.

Mexico in its Novel, by John S. Brushwood. University of Texas Press, 1966. A useful guide to Mexican fiction.

Mexico, Terra India, by Jacques Soustelle. (No English edition). Soustelle is an anthropologist who writes with humor and humanism. Recommended most highly for those who read Spanish or French.

Mornings in Mexico, by D.H. Lawrence. Knopf, 1927. Includes several descriptive essays which beautifully express Lawrence's feeling for the country.

Peyote Hunt: The Sacred Journey of the Huichol Indians, by Barbara Myerhoff. Cornell University Press, 1974. An analysis of Huichol religious symbolism and religious use of hallucinogens.

Political Essay on the Kingdom of New Spain, by Alexander Von Humboldt. AMS Press, reprint of 1811 edition. Unusual in that it's not the work of a British or American writer. Von Humboldt traveled through Mexico in 1803–04, studying the country's economic resources and pre-Columbian antiquities. His book, the first systematic study of the country, alerted European powers to the mineral wealth of Mexico.

The Running Indians, by Dick and Mary Lutz. 3280 Oak Hollow Ln, SE, Salem, OR 97302, 1989.

In the Shadow of Tlaloc: Life in a Mexican Village, by Gregory C. Reck. Penguin, 1978. Full of interesting information, like most anthropological studies, but also unusually expressive of the feelings of village life.

The Tall Candle: The Personal Chronicle of a Yaqui Indian, by J. Kelley and William Holden, R. Moises. Lincoln: University of Nebraska Press, 1971.

The Teachings of Don Juan: A Yaqui Way of Knowledge, by Carlos Castañeda. University of California Press, 1968. Also: *A Separate Reality* (Simon & Schuster, 1971); *Journey to Ixtlan* (Simon & Schuster, 1973); *Tales of Power* (Simon & Schuster, 1975); *The Second Ring of Power* (1980); *The Eagle's Gift* (Simon & Schuster, 1981). Read these books for their imaginative insights into spiritual experience – but don't believe every word.

Tortillas for the Gods: A Symbolic Analysis of Zinacanteco Ritual, by Evon Z. Vogt. Harvard University Press, 1976. Good source for those interested in the contemporary Mayan Indians of Chiapas.

Travels in the New World, by Thomas Gage. University of Oklahoma Press, 1969; first published 1648. One of the few accounts of colonial Mexico still worth reading. Gage, a Dominican friar from England, traveled widely in Mexico.

Unknown Mexico: Indians of Mexico, by Carl Lumholtz. Rio Grande Press. Lumoltz was one of the last of the great explorer-anthropologists. Contains an immense amount of information on the Indians of northern Mexico.

Viva México, by Charles Macomb Flandrau. University of Illinois Press, 1964; first published 1908. In the same vein as the writings of Madame Calderón de la Barca, but more limited in scope. The style is charming and unhurried, and some of Flandrau's insights into Mexican character are absolute gems.

FICTION BY MEIXCAN AUTHORS

The Burning Plain, by Juan Rulfo. University of Texas Press, 1967. In spare, suggestive prose, Rulfo gives the reader a deep understanding of the *mestizo* culture that was formed during the colonial era and then left behind by the nation's progress. Also by the same author, *Pedro Paramo* (Grove Press, 1959).

Casi el Paraíso, by Luis Spota. Almost Paradise. A Mexican best-seller, available only in Spanish, in Mexico.

Confabulario, by Juan José Arreola. University of Texas Press, 1964. Highly polished short stories.

The Edge of the Storm, by Agustín Yáñez. University of Texas Press, 1963. A great novel, set in a small town in Jalisco just before the revolution. The atmosphere is heavy, the characters complex. Also, *Lean Lands* (University of Texas Press, 1968).

Memoirs of Pancho Villa, by Martín Luis Guzmán. University of Texas Press, 1965 and *The Eagle and the Serpent* (Peter Smith). Both books are based on the author's personal experiences with Pancho Villa and other revolutionary leaders.

The Underdogs, by Mariano Azuela. New American Library. An excellent novel (based on the author's own life) with insights into the experiences, ideals and frustrations of ordinary men fighting the Mexican revolution.

Where the Air Is Clear, by Carlos Fuentes. Farrar, Straus & Giroux, 1971. Considered by some to be the best novel of modern Mexico. The narrator is a rather mysterious man who spends his life listening to and watching fellow inhabitants of Mexico City, of every social stratum, as they attempt to cope with the various conditions of their lives. Also by the same author, *The Death of Artemio Cruz* (Farrar, Straus & Giroux, 1964), in which the protagonist recalls the revolution and the following years, when he gradually became a cynical opportunist, manipulating old revolutionary contacts to build his fortune.

FICTION BY FOREIGN AUTHORS

The Autobiography of Carlos Williams, by Carlos Williams. New Directions, 1951.

Conquistador, by Archibald MacLeish. Houghton Mifflin, 1932.

The Collected Stories, by Katherine Anne Porter. Harcourt, Brace, 1965; and *The Collected Essays* (Delacorte, 1970). Porter understood the oppressive role the Church had played in Mexican history. She also understood the new Constitution and Mexico's intricate political machinery. Further, Porter was one of the first to appreciate and document the difference between pre-Columbian and contemporary Indian arts.

El Despertar del Tiempo, by Carlos Villa Roiz and Ivonne Carro. Time's Awakening; Plaza y Valdés Editores. A sort of Quantum Leap involving a Mexica warrior frozen for 500 years on the slopes of one of the volcanoes and two Mexican boys of the 90s. Compulsive reading, it describes the Indian-Mestizo "encounter", underscoring the gap between Mexicans separated by a 500-year transition in culture.

The Forgotten Village, by John Steinbeck. Viking, 1941; and *The Pearl* (Viking, 1947).

The General from the Jungle, B. Traven. Robert Hale, 1945; *The Rebellion of the Hanged* (Knopf, 1952); *March to Caobaland* (Robert Hale, 1961); *The Bridge in the Jungle* (Hill & Wang, 1967); *The Treasure of the Sierra Madre* (Hill & Wang, 1967); *The Carreta* (Hill & Wang, 1970); and others. No other author has written so much and so well about Mexico as the mysterious B. Traven (his identity is still a matter of controversy), best-known for *The Treasure of the Sierra Madre*. Most of Traven's books are set in southern Mexico, and his knowledge of that area is astounding.

I Wonder as I Wander, by Langston Hughes. Rinehart, 1956.

Kesey's Garage Sale, by Ken Kesey. Viking, 1973.

Love Among the Cannibals, by Wright Morris. Harcourt, Brace, 1957; and *One Day* (Atheneum, 1965).

Memoirs, by Sherwood Anderson. Harcourt Brace, 1942 and *Letters* (Little, Brown, 1953).

Mexico: An Object Lesson, by Evelyn Waugh. (Little, Brown, 1939); also published under the title *Robbery Under Law*.

The Mexican Night: Travel Journal, by Lawrence Ferlinghetti. New Directions, 1970.

Mosby's Memoirs and Other Stories, by Saul Bellow. Viking, 1968.

The Night of the Iguana, by Tennessee Williams. New Directions, 1962.

The October Country, by Ray Bradbury (Ballantine Books, 1955); *The Machineries of Joy, especially "El Día de la Muerte"* (Simon & Schuster, 1964); and *The Golden Apples* of the Sun (Doubleday, 1966). Among the short stories contained in these four collections are some very good ones set in Mexico.

On the Road, by Jack Kerouac. Viking, 1957; *The Dharma Bums* (Viking, 1958); *Mexico City Blues* (Grove, 1959); and others.

The Plumed Serpent, by D.H. Lawrence. Knopf, 1951. Lawrence takes on profound problems – the meaning of life and death, the relations of man to man and woman to man – and argues for a profound change in Mexico. One of the best novels ever written about Mexico.

The Power and the Glory, by Graham Greene. Viking, 1962. Considered Greene's finest novel by many critics, it takes place in Tabasco during the persecution of the Catholic clergy. Its hero is a priest faced with choosing marriage, exile or the firing squad.

Tales of Southern Rivers, by Zane Grey. Harpers, 1924.

Two Years Before the Mast, by Richard Henry Dana. Ward Ritchie, 1964.

Under the Volcano, by Malcolm Lowry. Lippincott, 1965. Without making any explicit attempt to clarify them, Lowry reveals the hidden forces which move Mexico. In this, his only major work, he tells the deceptively simple story of a British Consul who drinks himself to death during the crisis year when President Cárdenas nationalized the oil industry.

Ushant, by Conrad Aiken. Little, Brown, 1952.

ARTS & CRAFTS OF MEXICO

The Churches of Mexico, by Joseph Baird. University of California Press, 1962. An excellent reference on Mexican colonial art, almost all of which is in churches.

Crafts of Mexico, by Chloe Sayer. Doubleday, 1977. Step-by-step instructions for making traditional Mexican craft items. Excellent photographs.

Ethnic and Tourist Arts, by Nelson H.H. Graburn, editor. University of California Press, 1976. Includes articles by anthropologists on three Mexican art forms popular with foreign travelers: the ironwood carvings of the Seri Indians, the bark paintings of Xalitla, and Teotihuacan-area pottery. These articles explain the cutltural and economic contexts of these so-called "tourist arts."

Guide to Mexican Art, by Justino Fernández. University of Chicago Press, 1969. An excellent introduction; rather dry but certainly informative.

Indian Art of Mexico and Central America, by Miguel Covarrubias. Knop, 1957; and *Mezcala: Ancient Mexican Sculpture* (Andre Emmerich Gallery, 1956). Covarrubias is a respected authority on Mexican art.

Indian Art in Middle America, by Frederick Dockstader and Carmelo Guadagno. New York Graphic Society, 1964.

Made in Mexico: The Story of a Country's Arts and Crafts, by Patricia Fent Ross. Knopf, 1960. This is a classic work on the history of Mexico's popular arts, written by an American who lived for many years in Mexico before the large-scale commercialization of the country's craft traditions.

Mexican Colonial Art, by Manuel Toussaint. University of Texas. The best textbook on the subject, covering everything worth knowing about colonial art in Mexico. Toussaint's newspaper columns in the 1930s and 1940s brought new attention to Mexican colonial art.

Mexican Indian Costumes, by Donald and Dorothy Cordry. University of Texas Press, 1968.

The National Museum of Anthropology, Mexico: Art, Architecture, Archeology, Anthropology, by Pedro Ramírez Vázquez and others. Abrams, 1968. The story of the creation of the National Museum, written by the men responsible and illustrated with excellent photographs of museum exhibits enriching short essays about Mexico's pre-Columbian cultures.

Painted Walls of Mexico, by Emily Edward and Bravo Alvarez. University of Texas Press, 1966. Treats Mexican murals from pre-Columbian examples onward, with special emphasis on the post-revolutionary masters.

Popular Art of Mexico, by Tonatiuh Gutiérrez and Electra. Reprint of a 1960 special issue of the magazine *Artes de México*. Illustrates the crafts of every area of the country. Available in three languages, English, French or Spanish, in FONART stores, Sanborn's bookstores, and museum shops in Mexico.

Popular Arts of Mexico, by Porfirio Martínez Penaloza. Editorial Panorama, 1981. A compact and inexpensive book by one of the outstanding authorities on Mexican art.

Pre-Columbian Art of Mexico and Central America, by Hasso Von Winning. Abrams, 1968. Among coffee-table art books, this one stands out; informative as well as beautiful.

The Sculpture of Ancient Mexico, by Paul Westheim. Doubleday, 1963. Westheim's writings on the aesthetics of pre-Columbian art are hard to surpass for insight and clarity.

A Treasury of Mexican Folkways, by Frances Toor. Crown, 1947. Covers folk art, fiestas, music and dance. A classic in its field.

OTHER INSIGHT GUIDES

Nearly 200 *Insight Guides* and more than 100 *Insight Pocket Guides* cover every major travel destination in the world. Other titles which highlight destinations in this region are:

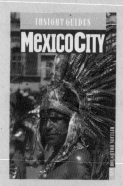

The companion to the present book, *Insight Guide: Mexico City*, provides in-depth coverage of the capital, with revealing features and stunning photography.

Insight Pocket Guide: Mexico City is designed for the visitor with limited time to spare and includes a selection of carefully timed itineraries and personal recommendations.

ART/PHOTO CREDITS

INDEX

A
B
C
D
F
G
H
I
J
a
b
c
d
e
f
g
h
i
j
k